WITHDRAWN

SEVEN VOICES

SEVEN VOICES

Pablo Neruda

Jorge Luis Borges

Miguel Angel Asturias

Octavio Paz

Julio Cortázar

Gabriel García Márquez

Guillermo Cabrera Infante

Seven Latin American Writers Talk to RITA GUIBERT

Translated from the Spanish by Frances Partridge

Introduction by Emir Rodríguez Monegal

 Alfred A. Knopf   New York   1973

Assistance for the translation of this volume was given by the Center for Inter-American Relations.

THIS IS A BORZOI BOOK
PUBLISHED BY ALFRED A. KNOPF, INC.

Interview with Jorge Luis Borges originally appeared in Spanish in *Life En Español*, March 1968. Interview with Julio Cortázar originally appeared in Spanish in *Life En Español*, April 1969.

Library of Congress Cataloging in Publication Data

Guibert, Rita.
  Seven voices.

  CONTENTS: Pablo Neruda.—Jorge Louis Borges.—Miguel Angel Asturias. [etc.]
  1. Authors, Spanish American—Interviews. I. Title.
PQ7081.3.G8 1972   860'.9'98   72–2251
ISBN 0–394–46888–0

Manufactured in the United States of America

FIRST EDITION

To Lidia and Daniel

CONTENTS

ACKNOWLEDGMENTS

While this book simply could not exist without the "seven voices," I particularly would like to express my appreciation to Matilde Urrutia Neruda, Blanca Mora y Araujo Asturias, Marie-José Tramini Paz, and Miriam Gómez Cabrera Infante. I would also like to express my gratitude to Emir Rodríguez Monegal, who gave me moral and intellectual support from the very conception of the book; to Ronald Christ, who "collaborated" in so many and valuable ways too countless to enumerate; to Dick Lurie, who judiciously pruned my Latin loquaciousness; to my editor, Jane Garrett, whose understanding and endurance equal her efficiency; to Frances Partridge, whose English translation of the interviews conveys so well the writers' voices; to Norman Thomas de Giovanni, who assisted in the revision of Jorge Luis Borges's interview in its English translation; to Casa Hispánica of Columbia University for letting me use the library files; and to Enrique Loutsch, who strengthened my belief; to all those who believed; to all those who did not believe; to Luisa Herzberg, who listened; and mainly to my late parents, from whom I learned to listen.

INTRODUCTION

Jacques Vaché was right: "Nothing kills a man more than having to represent a country." With Latin American writers, the burden is even greater. It matters little in what part of the vast continent they were born. Their readers (foreign as well as national) expect them to represent Latin America. As they read their works they ask: Are they Latin American enough? Is it possible to detect in their works the pulse of the earth, the murmur of the plains, the creeping of ferocious tropical insects, or other similar clichés? Why must they always talk about Paris, London, or New York (or Moscow and Peking) instead of talking about their quaint hamlets, their endemic dictators, their guerrillas?

The Latin American writer has had to prove he is Latin American before proving he is a writer. Who would think of asking Pound to be more North American or less Provençal? Who would complain that Nabokov has left out the silence of the vast Russian steppes in his novels? Why doesn't anyone attack Lawrence for having dared to write a novel called Kangaroo? But Latin American writers are always invited to prove their origin before they are asked to show their skills. In dealing with them, criticism seems more preoccupied with geographical and historical than with literary matters. Needless to say, the whole problem is a false one. A Latin American writer must be, above all, a writer. If he has been born and lived in Latin America, the vast continent (and the dictators, jungles, plains, mountains, and guerrillas) will appear in or between the lines of what he writes.

The confusion is resilient, nevertheless. As Marxist criticism took decades to realize that Kafka had anticipated the horrors of the concentration camps in some of his novels and tales, Latin

American Marxists have been late in seeing that Borges's "The Lottery in Babylon" is an accurate description of his chaotic Argentina. They've also been slow in recognizing the surrealistic personae of Vallejo's and Neruda's poetry as valid metaphors for Latin America's alienated man: a man who until quite recently could not find roots in his own land nor discover as an exile a place he could truly call his own. Too sophisticated for many of the developing Latin American countries, he used to feel too provincial in Europe or the United States. Things have changed now in many countries, but writers still feel the burden of alienation in a large part of the continent. And Vallejo's and Neruda's anguish are very relevant today.

But folklore, literary geography, anthropology, and sociology continue to lure many critics. Some years ago, Lionel Trilling said that Latin American literature had only an anthropological value (Borges's best stories were already published). Even today many believe that One Hundred Years of Solitude is the best Latin American novel because it confirms, apparently, the folkloric prejudice—even though García Márquez's novel is mythical in a sense that only a reader of James Joyce or Joseph Campbell can understand.

Seven Voices makes it plain that Latin American writers want to be read, first, as writers, and judged on literary terms. Armed with patience, a tape recorder, and some notebooks, Rita Guibert has hunted down, on three continents, seven of the most important writers of Latin America. Unlike many of her colleagues, she has not attempted to extract programmed answers to equally programmed questions. Her questions are meant to unleash the flow of conversation. Her secret is knowing how to listen. The voice of each of the writers is fully revealed in these pages. A common pursuit—the craft of fiction, the art of poetry—links them beyond idiosyncrasies of age and points of view.

But their seven voices could not be more different. And the differences are not only of temperament and ideology; they go deeper. While Pablo Neruda speaks without reserve and lets the words flow conversationally, Octavio Paz takes notes before speaking, answers with the most extreme caution, and then phrases and rephrases his words until they have the bite of his critical essays. But that difference in their way of talking is also a difference in their way of writing poetry, and even in their way of life. Again,

it is easy to contrast the slow, rhetorical tone of Miguel Angel
Asturias with Gabriel García Márquez's quick and playful delivery.
The public hostility between the two (which is revealed in the
couple of digs they give each other) is more than casual: Asturias
belongs to that generation which believes literature to be something sacred; García Márquez represents that wishing to be free of
all solemnity. Even in two writers who have so much in common,
like Borges and Cortázar, opposing styles are apparent. Borges
answers all questions orally and never drops the conversational
tone. Cortázar carefully edits his answers to a written questionnaire
and turns the interview into a pretext for an essay in which each
word has been painstakingly premeditated.

In the most unusual interview of all, Guillermo Cabrera Infante
puts together a written-spoken text with a palimpsest technique
that recalls his novel Three Trapped Tigers. The swift rhythm is
oral; the writing, however, organizes that spontaneity into a literary
and polemical mosaic. The final effect is dazzling.

Although each of these seven voices is highly individual, it is
possible to recognize in all of them a common preoccupation.
They all are extremely aware of the fact that their readers expect
them to "represent" their native countries. And in a sense they do.

While Asturias, Neruda, and Paz can speak as native Americans (although some of their ancestors were Spaniards), Borges
and Cortázar reflect that part of Latin America in which pre-
hispanic cultures were brutally destroyed, as in the United States,
and successive waves of immigrants have created hybrid nations,
half European, half American. (Borges was educated by an English
grandmother and learned to read in English before he could read
in Spanish; Cortázar was born in Brussels, learned French before
Spanish, and to this day has the French r.) García Márquez and
Cabrera Infante represent a different case: their international background is visible in their work, as is the influence of North American writers, but, on the other hand, it is obvious that they have
not lost contact with the highly mixed substratum of the Colombian and Cuban cultures from which they come.

Those differences of origin and destiny (national as well as individual) do not obliterate a common pursuit. The final paradox
of these very individual writers is that they sometimes cannot
avoid being spokesmen for the whole continent. Even when (like
Borges) they explicitly refuse to do it, their denial is a way of re-

vealing the tension between their individual and their representative personae. The common link of language, a Hispanic tradition
that encompasses and absorbs local traditions, and very obvious
geopolitical ties are always present in their works. Somehow, the
seven have struggled to be themselves and have wonderfully succeeded, but in their work a whole continent is also alive and
visible. Vaché perhaps was wrong.

EMIR RODRÍGUEZ MONEGAL

Yale University

PREFACE

A Latin American is a being who has lived in the suburbs of the West, in the outskirts of history.

OCTAVIO PAZ

This book grew out of a frustration—mine and a continent's. Mine is simply a matter of recognition. For example, when at a New York party someone notices my accent I'm usually asked, "Are you French?" "No, I'm from Argentina," I say, watching the charm of foreign glamour fade from their eyes as my social stock takes a plunge. Americans frequently ask me if Argentines speak Portuguese, or—as I was asked by the principal of one of the largest high schools in Westchester—"How big is Rio de Janeiro, the capital of your country?"

Insignificant as these person-to-person gaffes may be, they are the result of poor intercultural relations; a cultural gap that exists between continents as well. If for many Latin Americans the United States is only an imperialistic land of dollar-makers, gadgets, Marines, and Hollywood stereotypes, for a great many norteamericanos the lands south of the border form a group of indistinguishable countries characterized by countless revolutions, underdevelopment, and bananas, and inhabited by untrustworthy, irresponsible, talkative, sensual men, adept only at guitar playing and lovemaking (though very unreliable in the last pursuit). These images have assumed mythical proportions, obscuring the realities on which they are based.

But there is the other side of the coin. Names like Faulkner and Hemingway, of course, were known in Latin America before they were known in France, but in New York, not long ago, I was discussing a project with the president of a large company dealing in educational tape recording, and I suggested some material about Jorge Luis Borges. "Borges? Who is Borges? You will have to sell

Borges to me." I tried to "sell" Borges, without success, to the president and three editorial advisers, none of whom could identify this world-famous author. And even more recently, when the name of Pablo Neruda—an author who has been discussed throughout the world for the last forty years—made international headlines as a Nobel Laureate, one American writer–editor admitted to me he had never heard of Neruda before, while another New York editor, interrupting my enthusiastic comments about the news, asked, "And who is he?" I was shocked, not surprised. I knew that in spite of the increasing interest in Latin American literature, names like Borges and Neruda, writers of world renown, were known only to a minority of Americans.

One reason for this lack of recognition on the part of Americans is that while much data is available to specialists in Latin American studies, the information about the continent that reaches the general public comes, for the most part, from travel literature or daily news reports on economic and political convulsions or natural disasters. This book, on the other hand, is an attempt to give the American people a broader and deeper view of what's going on in Latin America through the voices of seven outstanding Latin American men of letters from three generations.

Recalling what the Nobel Prize-winning Guatemalan writer Miguel Angel Asturias had been saying for years to his French colleagues—"Now, you sit down, and we are the ones who are going to tell you a few things"—I thought that a presentation of Latin American writers by way of in-depth interviews could convey a broad spectrum of Latin America and its intellectuals.

Since my attempts to involve the most popular media of communication in my project failed, and since "I couldn't dance it, spit it out, shout it, or project it," except in a book, as Julio Cortázar said of Hopscotch, I turned to Alfred A. Knopf, which has a long history of publishing Latin American literature. Hence this book of personal, tape-recorded interviews which took me from the United States to Chile, England, France, and Spain.

For each interview, the mise en scène was different, the personalities distinct, but the spirit of cooperation and the energetic responsiveness to my project were identical. I spent an average of a week with each writer and during that time we passed days and evenings speaking casually and at length about literature and life, current events and trivia. Together, we enjoyed meals and parties at their homes, at their favorite restaurants, and at their friends' houses. In the actual tape-recorded interviews I was more of a catalyst than an interrogator. I tried to evoke a maximum response with a minimum of questioning. My object was, after all, to have these men express themselves, not to speak for myself.

RITA GUIBERT
New York, 1972

PABLO
NERUDA

PABLO NERUDA

Isla Negra, Chile   January 15–31, 1970

After a few days in Stockholm where the sixty-seven-year-old Chilean poet Pablo Neruda received the Nobel Prize for literature in 1971, I traveled with him and his wife, Matilde Urrutia, to Warsaw to attend the Polish premiere of his play Splendor and Death of Joaquín Murieta.

As the charismatic Chilean ambassador to France and second Chilean Nobel Laureate (the first was the poet Gabriela Mistral), he was being toasted, both in Warsaw and in Stockholm, by intellectuals, TV crews, reporters, and photographers. But Neruda, a poet for whom "life is a gift," has always been a magnet for people. As Margarita Aguirre wrote in Las vidas de Pablo Neruda (The Lives of Pablo Neruda), "You don't see that man in vain: his strength and human warmth are overpowering. It is as if something magic, a mysterious attraction, ties us to his presence."

When I first met Neruda in New York in 1966 he had become the star of the PEN Club Congress, and wherever he read his poetry—either at the crowded Poetry Center of New York, or at a small gathering of friends—there was affectionate rapport between him and his poetry and the audience. Yet, of all the Nerudas I met, the one I know best is the Neruda I interviewed in his house at Isla Negra where I was his guest during the last weeks of his political campaign when, because of a divided left, Neruda withdrew as a Communist Party candidate for the presidency in order to support Salvador Allende.

Isla Negra (Black Island) is neither black nor an island. It is an elegant beach resort forty kilometers south of Valparaiso and a two-hour drive from Santiago. No one knows where the name comes from, but Neruda speculates about some black rocks vaguely shaped like an island which he can see from his terrace. Thirty years ago, long before Isla Negra became fashionable, Neruda bought—with the royalties from his books—6,000 square meters of beach front, including a tiny stone house at the top of a steep slope; "Then the house started growing, like the people, like the trees . . ."

Neruda has other houses—one in San Cristobal Hill in Santiago and the other in Valparaiso. To decorate his houses he scours the antique shops and junkyards for all kinds of objects—from windows and doors to figureheads, anchors, lanterns, sextants, and bells. Each object reminds him of an anecdote. "Doesn't he look like Stalin?" he asks, pointing to a bust of the English adventurer Morgan in the dining room at Isla Negra. "The antique dealer in Paris didn't want to sell it to me, but when he heard I was Chilean, he asked me if I knew Pablo Neruda. That's how I persuaded him to sell it."

It is at Isla Negra, on the sea (a constantly recurring theme in his poetry), that Pablo Neruda, the "terrestrial navigator," and Matilde, his third wife ("Patoja," as he affectionately calls her, the "muse" to whom he has written many love poems), have established their most permanent residence.

Tall, stocky, balding, of olive complexion, Neruda's outstanding features are a prominent nose and large hooded brown eyes. His movements are slow but firm. He speaks deliberately, without pomposity, and has a great sense of humor. When he goes for a walk—usually accompanied by his two chows—he wears a long Argentine poncho and carries a rustic cane.

At Isla Negra Neruda entertains a constant stream of visitors, and there is always room at the table for last-minute guests. He does most of his entertaining in the bar, which one enters through a small corridor from a terrace facing the beach. On the corridor floor is a Victorian bidet and an old hand-organ. On the window's shelves there is a collection of bottles. The bar is decorated as a ship's salon, with furniture bolted to the floor and nautical lamps and paintings. The room has glass panel walls facing the sea. On the ceiling and on each of the wood crossbeams a carpenter has carved, in Neruda's handwriting, names of his dead friends: Federico (García Lorca), Paul Eluard, Alberti, Miguel Hernández, Ortiz de Zárate . . .

Behind the bar, on the liquor shelf, is a sign that says "No se fía" (No credit here). Neruda takes his role as bartender very seriously and likes to make elaborate drinks for his guests; he drinks only Scotch and wine. He says he became used to Scotch during his years as consul in India, where it was the cheapest drink. On a wall are two anti-Neruda posters—one which he brought back from his last trip to Caracas. It shows his profile with the legend: "Neruda, go home." The other is a cover from an Argentine magazine with his picture and the legend "Neruda, why doesn't he kill himself?" A huge poster of Twiggy stretches from the ceiling to the floor.

Meals at Isla Negra are typically Chilean. Neruda has mentioned some of them in his poetry: a conger eel soup, a fish with a delicate sauce of tomatoes and baby shrimp, a meat pie. The wine is always Chilean. One of the porcelain wine pitchers, shaped like a bird, sings when the wine is poured. In the summer, lunch is served on a porch facing a garden which has an antique railroad engine. "So powerful, such a cornpicker, such a procreator and whistler and roarer and thunderer . . . I love it because it looks like Walt Whitman."

Neruda likes to read his poems to his guests. One noon in the bar he read "Meditación sobre la sierra maestra" from Canción de gesta. "This autobiographical and political poem," he explained, "is supposed to be written in 2000 A.D., when the American Revolution has been completed. The poem starts then and works its way back to our era." After reading, Neruda proposed a "happening." We all had to sit in the boat, Marval of Isla Negra, that is in the terrace garden. To celebrate the occasion he prepared a special drink made of sparkling white wine and strawberries. We were joined by the Solimanos, old friends who hid Neruda in 1948 when the police were looking for him because, in his famous political speech "I accuse," Neruda sharply criticized the then president of Chile, Gabriel González Videla, in the Senate.

For Neruda there is no dividing line between his poetry and politics. As he said in his acceptance speech for the candidacy for president: "I have never thought of my life as divided between poetry and politics. I am a Chilean who . . . has known the misfortunes and difficulties of our national existence and who has taken part in each sorrow and joy of the people. I am not a stranger to them, I come from them, I am part of the people. I come from a working class family. . . . I have never been in with those in power and have always felt that my vocation and my duty was to serve the Chilean people in my actions and with my poetry. I have lived singing and defending them."

Conversations for the interview were held in short sessions. In the morning—after Neruda had his breakfast in his room—we met in the library, which is a new wing of the house. I would wait while he answered his mail, composed poems for his new book, or corrected the galleys of a new Chilean edition of Veinte poemas de amor y una canción desesperada (*Twenty Love Poems and One Song of Despair*), which was first published in 1924 and has sold almost two million copies. Composing poetry, he writes with green ink in an ordinary composition book. He can write a fairly long poem in a very short time, after which he makes only a few corrections. The poems are then typed by his secretary and close friend for more than fifty years, Homero Arce.

We worked in a small room at the back of the library which he calls la covacha (small cave). Sometimes he linked several of my questions together and answered them slowly as if he were talking to himself. The only time he became impatient was when his niece Alicia Urrutia broke in because of an urgent telephone call while he was talking very passionately about Chile's history. (The only telephone in Isla Negra is at the inn, a five-minute walk from Neruda's house.)

In the afternoon, after his daily nap, we sat on a stone bench on the terrace facing the sea, and Neruda would talk holding the microphone of the tape recorder, which picked up the sound of "the whole vast sea . . . moving wave upon wave" as background for his voice.

Why did you change your name, and why did you choose Pablo Neruda?

I can't really remember. I was thirteen or fourteen years old at the time. I remember that my father, out of the best possible motives, objected to my becoming a writer, because he thought it would ruin the family and me personally, and in particular that I should end by doing nothing at all. He had his domestic reasons for objecting, reasons that carried very little weight with me in my chosen career. And one of the first defensive measures I adopted was changing my name.

Did you choose Neruda after the Czech poet, Jan Neruda?

I'm not sure that I had heard the Czech poet's name. But I did read one of his short stories at about that time. I've never read his poetry. One of his books, *Stories of Mala Strana,* contains stories about the poor people living in that district of Prague. Perhaps that's where my new name came from. As I say, it's so long ago now that I can't remember. However, the Czechs consider me as one of themselves, as belonging to their nation. Ever since that time I've been on very friendly terms with the Czechs.

Do you know that Pablo in Hebrew means someone who says beautiful things?

Are you sure? That must have been the other Pablo, Christ's apostle.

Is this your first presidential campaign?

I've toured the country with left-wing candidates for the presidency before. I accompanied Don Pedro Aguirre Cerda in 1938. It was a triumph for the Popular Front, the first left-wing government there had ever been in this country's history. It was a coalition of communists, radicals, socialists, etc. Since then I've traveled around with other candidates. The present candidate for the Socialist Party, Salvador Allende, has already fought three campaigns without success. I went with him on those presidential campaigns across the whole country, from Arica to beyond Magellan's Strait.

Is this your first presidential campaign for Pablo Neruda?

The first and the last.

What political poets have aspired to the presidency and been successful?

We live in an epoch of poet rulers, such as Mao Tse-tung and Ho Chi Minh. Obviously Mao Tse-tung has other qualities; as you know he's a fine swimmer, something I can't claim to be. There's also a very good poet who is president of the African republic of Senegal, Léopold Senghor, and there's another who writes in French, a surrealist poet who is mayor of Fort de France in Martinique—Aimé Césaire. In my country poets have always been involved in politics. We've never had a poet who was president of the republic, but there have been Latin American writers who were presidents. A great Venezuelan writer, Rómulo Gallegos, was president of the Republic of Venezuela.

How are the presidential campaigns run?

Our activities usually begin in the urban districts of Santiago, especially in the large working-class quarters with hundreds of thousands of inhabitants. A platform is set up, and one climbs onto it. First comes a performance of folk songs, then one of our group explains the strictly political significance of our campaign. When I talk to the working people, I adopt a much broader, much less formal style, a more poetical tone. I nearly always end by reading some poetry. If I didn't read poetry, people would go away disappointed. Of course, they also want to hear what I think about politics, but I don't overdo the politics and economics because I think people also need a different sort of language.

This happened in the United States with Norman Mailer and Eugene McCarthy.

I didn't know. I've always admired the old troubadours, and among North American poets Carl Sandburg, who used to play the guitar and read his poems aloud. I enjoyed that very much. I wish I could have done the same, but I have such a bad ear for music that I can't sing the simplest melody in tune. That gift has been denied me, but I should have liked to possess it more than anything.

How do people respond when you read your poems?

I always have great confidence in the people, and the Chilean people know me well, and I must say I find their love for me very moving. I can't give you details because there are so many. They're amazingly responsive, so much so that I can hardly get in or out of some places. I have to have a special escort to protect me from the embraces of the crowd, because they rush to meet me. This happens to me everywhere.

Don't you have to have a bodyguard?

No, it's not a question of protecting me from attack, quite the opposite. For instance, it's very difficult for Matilde and me to get into the car because the crowd pushes us from one side to the other, and their enthusiasm prevents us from moving.

Is there any danger of physical attack?

No, there's no fear of such a thing, either for candidates or presidents. Our presidents go about the streets unescorted every day.

Is there a possibility of a union of the left?

Yes, we shall have one within a week.

Do you think you will be elected?

I don't think so, but I can't be sure. We're not very individualistic, politically speaking, and we're ready to withdraw my candidacy for the sake of unity. The important thing is popular unity, because there's no other possible way to victory. If the left-wing parties are disunited at this election, they can't confront the traditional right, whose candidate has strong financial support. And the other candidate, the Christian Democrat, is the official government candidate. Such things carry weight. First there's money, and then an official candidate directly supported by the government. Only a great movement uniting all sectors of the left can defeat those two.

What would be your first measures if you were elected president?

This has all been explained in a program subscribed to by all the left-wing candidates. It would take too long to go into all the details, but of course nationalization of the country's natural resources is among them. This country possesses the largest copper mine in the world, Chuquicamata, and it is North American property. The telephone company is North American, the electricity company is North American. When we Chileans turn on the light every evening we are putting money in the pockets of some shareholders living in New York or Detroit who don't even know that Chileans exist. I'm not saying this tragically, because it is comic rather than tragic. That such a colonial system should persist in 1970, when we are approaching the year 2000, is incredible. Nationalization is a common-sense measure, and I think North Americans expect it to come.

But is the country ready to take charge of these companies?

There's always risk in such matters, and problems have already arisen. But they'll pass. What's the use of arranging things so that we are always fighting? Everything should be stated, talked over, discussed, but one shouldn't give in. Many companies in this country have been paying for conversions and technicians for a long time. For instance, there are very few North Americans left working in our great copper mines. In some, less than five men.

Are they technicians?

Some of their technicians still remain, but all the rest are Chileans, because these industries are very old, and Chileans are expert technicians. If there's talk of economic reprisals, we are no longer in an age of such things. The imperialist countries must realize that the age of empires is past, and that neither political nor economic repression makes sense in our epoch. We must aim for a mutual understanding, however painful these measures are. In other words, we don't want to break with the North American government or with the United States just because we're going to nationalize the mines. No. We must go on trying to understand each other better, economically and in every other way, on a basis of mutual respect, both political and economic.

If you become president, will there be freedom of the press?

Of course, we have agreed on that; the popular government's program guarantees freedom for the press. Our popular government would be formed from a coalition of parties, that is to say, it would be a multipartite government, asserting the diversity and richness of experience of every current of popular feeling. Our program guarantees a free press and free opinion.

Do you feel ready—economically, politically, and socially—to take on the responsibility of the presidency?

As I've said before, that responsibility and our program are both anti-personalist. We shall form a collective government. There'll be no shortage of technicians and specialists in every sort of subject. It won't matter whether the president knows a lot or a little. Obviously he mustn't be an ignoramus or a fool. But neither must he be a monarch who arranges everything that is done. No, in this modern age a president must have advisers, he must have specialists, and these are plentiful in our country, and all this is set down in our program. The same popular forces will take care that the promised program is carried out. So I have no fears on that score. In the unlikely event of my being elected, I should have no personal problem of that sort. I don't see why, because I'm a poet, I should be doomed never to be president of the republic. I don't imagine that it's very pleasant being president of the republic, but poets have just as much right to govern as engineers, or businessmen, or lawyers, or politicians, in fact, or soldiers, who have so often seized power by hook or by crook. In fact I think a poet has as much right as anyone to believe that he can do his duty to his people, with those feelings of love and justice that all poets, at least, ought to have.

In 1933, in one of your letters to the Argentine short-story writer, Héctor Eandi, you wrote: "Politically, one has to be either a communist or an anti-communist nowadays. All other doctrines are falling into decay." What doctrines did you mean?

I don't remember the letter, but I suppose I was thinking of the anarchist doctrines which were so important in my life.

Does this idea apply to the present time?

To some extent; I can't say it as dogmatically as I did in my youth, but it's more or less true. Anti-communism always implies a reactionary outlook even when wearing an apolitical or left-wing disguise.

Has the Communist Party many supporters among the young?

A great many. The greatest boom in the history of our party. There are more than 25,000 members in Santiago alone.

And MAPU? (Movement of United Popular Action)

MAPU is a fraction of the Christian Democrats. It represents the Catholic left, a small party that only began to take an active part in politics very recently. They are very interesting politically. So are the militant leftist groups.

Are they the most revolutionary?

They tend toward terrorism and direct action. They are survivors of the old anarchists, and they also have some connection with the world youth movements of the present day.

What do you think of those movements?

It seems to me that their basis is a physically healthy one. It is important that the young should feel rebellious. But if that youthful rebelliousness is channeled into individual, personal, direct action, divorced from any organization, divorced from the people, and above all divorced from the working class, then it won't turn out well. If, after rebelling, these young people begin to understand the workers' movement and the great organizations of the left, then that's a good thing. What do I think about it? Many of these youngsters—and there aren't a lot of them, at least in this country—are university undergraduates, nearly always from well-to-do families, the bourgeoisie, the more prosperous petite bourgeoisie. These young people, and there aren't many of them, as I've said, will eventually succeed in integrating themselves in other popular forces. Or they will move away from the extreme left to become champions of the right, champions of conservatism, of the bourgeoisie. Because this pendulumlike oscillation has always existed among the young. My generation were all anarchists. I was translating anarchist books when I was sixteen. I translated Kropotkin and Jean Graves from the French, as well as other anarchist writers. I read nothing but the great Russian anarchist authors like Andreyev and others. In those days we young anarchists were beginning to find out for ourselves that it was vital for us to join the people's movement, which was also tending toward anarchism at that time. That was the period of the IWW (Industrial Workers of the World) and almost all the syndicates belonged to it; I think Harry Bridges was one of the last representatives in the United States. This group of anarchists, which included martyrs like Sacco and Vanzetti in the United States, was also enormously important in Latin America. But what happened to the young people of that time who were already taking part in terrorist activities, and preaching as I did myself, sabotage, boycott of elections, and opposition to organized movements? What happened? Some of us realized that we must advance by means of organization and cooperation with the workers' movement, others changed sides and began working for the interests of the upper middle classes, capitalism and imperialism. In due course, all these phenomena may repeat themselves. The young must either join the popular movement or join the enemies of the popular movement.

Couldn't they form a new independent front?

Independent of what? The proletariat? I don't think so. At any rate it would be a divided front, without any influence, because the other movements are too large for one or more small groups to carry any weight.

How is it that the Chilean Communist Party is the most important in Latin America?

We had a great organizer; he was called Luis Emilio Recabarren. He was a giant of a man and he founded the working-class press in Chile some forty-five years ago—that's to say, a number of small papers expressing the dissatisfaction of the Chilean people. He founded the first syndicates, the great trade unions, and the Communist Party as well. He was an extraordinary man. He is venerated by the Chilean people, who think of him as the father of their country. By his impassioned efforts, this man laid the foundations of an organic party, an indefatigable party which hasn't deviated either to the right or the left, which has always tried to find a way to confront the enemies of the people and concentrate its strength and efforts on supporting the workers and peasants, a party which has gone on growing in size and importance.

I think this is the first time the communists have campaigned for about thirty-eight years?

Yes, we've refrained from putting up a candidate for a long time. But now we had to do it. Before this we supported a candidate from the popular parties. This time we're entering one of our own.

Do you think you've got a better chance today?

We are the majority left-wing party in Chile, so we've just as good a chance as the rest.

Would you support violence?

There's violence and violence. In countries dominated by fear and fascist violence, I would justify any means to get out of that situation. What can one do when delinquents are in power, as in the case of Papa Doc in Haiti? The prisons there have been full of political prisoners for a long time, as they have in Paraguay. Each nation must choose its own course. One can't say "I don't believe in violence," as if it were a universal political axiom. Violence—that is, the union of a country's revolutionary elements to change the established order—could be preceded by a conjunction of forces that will support a movement of this kind. But individual, solitary acts of violence generally fail, and may lead to repression of the people. Not to mention that much terrorist activity has for centuries been organized by the police.

Will violence be necessary in Chile?

We mustn't even think of such a thing while we are still free to say what we like. It would be insane to advocate violence as a solution.

You have been through some very difficult times in Chile.

There have been few such times in Chilean history, and we Chileans are well versed in our own history. We know that such constraints as I suffered (I took the risk and was persecuted) are transitory, and that it's always the man who has been repressive or violent who pays. So that any violence perpetrated by Chilean governments has weakened them profoundly instead of strengthening them.

Do you believe socialism could save Latin America from colonialism and underdevelopment? If so, why?

Of course the only system that can free Latin America from its appalling backwardness is socialism. We must overcome all attempts at interference—attempts nearly always aimed at preserving colonial exploitation and bleeding our people for the benefit of capitalism. Socialism has creative strength, it represents a revolution of a type entirely suited to Latin American problems. And besides, our continent has no great traditions, and therefore the fertilizing creativity of socialism will take new forms here, and develop in extraordinary ways.

You mean it will take its own line, instead of the Russian, the Maoist, or the Castrist one?

Marxism teaches us that a society's development must be adapted to its history, to its resources, to the whole life of its people; there's no reason for it to follow any model. But it does depend on the experience of the makers of its revolution. In Latin America we have the Cuban Revolution, but we can't say that it must be the archetype for any other. We Chileans live in a very different sort of country from Cuba, we have developed differently, both culturally and economically. And a revolution in Chile would take place in a much more advanced country than Cuba was before its revolution. The people of Chile are outstandingly creative and outstandingly capable of tackling technological problems. Our specialist workers and technicians are accepted all over the Latin American continent, often as experts or advisers. Cuba is a country with sugar and tobacco; but Cuban governments before the revolution neglected industry so shockingly that the revolution found Cuba with a high percentage of people who couldn't do the work in the factories, which Chilean workers and technicians can do, for example. The very fact that Cuba then undertook an internal transformation in this respect, opening other possibilities and awakening interest in industry, has been one of the great successes of her revolution.

You have said the United States continues to be a threat to Latin America.

Unfortunately I'm a peace-loving man, and I find all these notions disagreeable though true. The history of industrial and economic development in the United States has for a long time shown expansionist tendencies. And we haven't suffered only from threats, but often from acts of aggression. The history of Latin America is full of such acts, and they've naturally made a very deep impression on our people. In the last few years we have seen the emphatically imperialist doctrines of the United States reinforced by theories that have gone so far as to justify such an atrocious enterprise as the Vietnam war. It may be strange, but I see no significant theoretical reason why, if North American imperialism has gone so far afield as Vietnam and Korea to spread its theories and implant its rule, it shouldn't do the same in our Latin America, which is so much closer and has always been considered by the North American imperialists as their own territory, their rearguard defense. Their military pacts with Latin American countries have not been made with the assent of our people, and are obviously destined to introduce an aggressive policy and involve us in the aggressive and threatening activities of North American politicians and soldiers. Besides which, we have the experiences of the Dominican Republic and Cuba. Before that there were Nicaragua, Mexico, Central America, Panama— in fact a very long history. But recently these events have been put in perspective by Nelson Rockefeller's famous report. At one time Nelson Rockefeller passed for a man with an intellectual outlook and artistic interests, and I remember that during the great war against fascism he seemed very friendly toward Latin America. In the following years he joined Johnson's bandwagon. And recently he has served President Nixon in a colonialistic capacity. Rockefeller's report to President Nixon, which we've read, was widely published, it's a prodigy of political toughness and total misunderstanding of our moral, historical, and emotional reactions. Now he's advocating open American help to military governments and claiming that these governments could help establish a form of social justice acceptable to North American imperialists of today. That is to say that Nelson Rockefeller, although a man of 1970, and well aware that he has lost his old prestige, is backsliding into the policy started by Theodore Roosevelt, known as the "big stick" policy, which involves stirring up the military castes and all that is implied for Latin America in the way of *caudillismo* and unconstitutional coups. He has also fomented discord and an aggressive militarist spirit among the Latin American countries. This shows that we Latin Americans have very little to hope for from North American policy, unless it undergoes a complete and rational change. In other words, when the United States considers current events, what is happening among its young people, its intellectuals, and in its universities, and sees how its aggressive behavior is condemned in its own country, and when it therefore tries to formulate a new policy to unite our continent, then we shall be able to begin to collaborate with it in many ways. At present the general policy of the United States is aggressive not only toward us but also toward most of the nations of the world. It has set itself up as a super-power determined to establish influence without definite limits, far beyond its own territory. That is the really serious thing. It is a long chapter and we shall have to return

to it often. Talking about imperialism may seem a demagogue's
trick, particularly to a European or a nonpolitical observer, but
we Latin Americans know what we are talking about; nearly all
our countries have suffered the consequences of North American
interference. Even here in Chile—and I'm not speaking for myself alone—Senator Renán Fuentealba, of the Democratic Christian Party (that's to say, representing the Chilean government),
who has close links with the North American politicians and
government, has just declared in public that the CIA is trying
to provoke a military coup in Chile. This is not what I say, it's not
what the communists say—the accusation was made by one of
the senators of a government that has no trace of anti-North
American feeling. This accusation has not been fully investigated.
Yet it was made by a senator of the Democratic Christian Party,
the most important party in the government. He, and his party,
and the Chilean government, must have pretty clear evidence for
such a charge to be made. Of course the harmful influence of
North American politics in our countries is also shown by the
very fact that all investigation of this accusation has now stopped.
A spirit of independence and self-respect should have prompted
the government to investigate it and show the nation how much
truth there might be in the Democratic Christian senator's assertions.

*Do you think some reconciliation between the powers could be
arrived at?*

        I'm on the side of mutual understanding, I'm on the
side of peace. A reconciliation between capitalism and socialism is another matter, that's quite another thing. They are two
organisms fighting to prove the effectiveness of their systems.
Capitalism is in retreat. We're witnessing its decline. Socialism
is a new force and has visibly more strength than capitalism because it is based on a more intelligent understanding of human
relationships and of the means of producing and distributing
wealth among mankind. I don't think it's a question of reconciliation but of having the mutual respect necessary for coexistence.
My old friend Ehrenburg once told me that when he was in New
York he decided to have a conversation with a North American

millionaire. They got hold of the richest millionaire available to talk to a Soviet citizen, and in conversation with Ehrenburg this millionaire said: "Don't kid yourself that we're afraid of your bombs, what we're afraid of is your saucepans—the saucepans of the Soviet Union." I think that's quite understandable. While the saucepans are full, while there are stews in the kitchens of the socialist countries, it proves that the new world economic system is working, is successful, is going ahead. And the supermillionaire was talking a lot of sense. His frankness delighted Ehrenburg.

Do you think there'll be a revolution in the United States?

It's not imminent, but a definite state of rebellion does exist in the United States. I don't know where it will end, but it seems to me that this awakening of the intellectual conscience of the young and the universities must someday have an effect on the direction of the state and the conditions under which life is historically developing in the United States. It's the first stage, the first step of the first stage. I don't know when the second will come, nor yet the third—that depends on the North Americans. It can't be fixed by formula. In my opinion capitalism is heading for a crisis in many other places as well as the United States. One can see at a glance that there's a portentous moral crisis in the North American way of life. It has not exactly introduced happiness with material prosperity, and in many cases it has brought despair to the North American people.

To what do you attribute that?

It seems to me that it's a crisis of the capitalist system. They have decided on a goal of prosperity based on an outburst of savage legislation. I think that this crisis in the general organization is happening all over the world. The Vietnam war has confronted humanity with a truly monstrous event. For all the energies and riches of a great country like the United States to be dedicated to exterminating a distant race unknown to the young Americans who are sent there to kill and be killed is a fact that has illuminated the sleeping conscience of most of the human race with the brightness of spilled blood. The tragedy of Vietnam has aroused a sense of guilt in the United States, or in a certain part of the United States, which has spread and had many results. In some places it provoked rebellion among the young, in others despair. I believe the Vietnam war has had such a catalytic power. For one thing, so unjust a war had never before been seen—men had never before been responsible for such unheard-of and collective excesses of cruelty. And at the same time it must have caused instinctive self-questioning among intellectuals as to how a country that produced such remarkable thinkers as Thoreau and Whitman, and many others, and that had developed man's dimensions in practical ways, a country that had led the industrial revolution and been responsible for so many amazing achievements in the realm of knowledge and culture before the war, could actually outdo Hitler in barbarity and inhumanity. The United States created that huge dream capital, Hollywood, and gave a forward impulse to the art of the cinema which otherwise might have taken another century to develop. In fact such wonderful achievements have been expected of the North Americans, and sometimes fulfilled, as when they explored the moon, that one asks oneself how such a country can devote its strength to extermination and terror. Well, it seems to me that as soon as anyone asks himself that question, he is driven also to doubt the system, the establishment, to doubt the truth of what he is told, and that is the beginning of the bitterness, skepticism, and frequent despair that are to be seen in North American life. Besides the endless wave of terrorism, of such criminal outrages as the deaths of Luther King, President Kennedy, and Senator Kennedy, and the massacres carried out by mere boys, a new type of unbelievable, impersonal, diabolical crime, like the one Truman Capote wrote about in *In Cold Blood*, or that of Charles Manson, are none of them completely isolated cases, but are linked together by some thread connected with the moral crisis in the system and the rising tide of perversity, which was already present in a society hurling itself to destruction and perversion. So that this question and the disjointed thoughts it has aroused connect with your other question: Will there be a revolution? And who will make this revolution? Unless the mass of the workers takes part in this new awareness, the revolution will not come for some time. A revolution cannot be achieved by students in any country. They may realize that the world is in a bad way, but the organizing strength of the movement must come from the people themselves. And I don't see that happening yet in the United States. We have seen a great awakening among the colored population, and it's possible that there will soon be extremely interesting and important revolutionary developments, but further than that I don't know; I'm not informed.

What do you think about the present state of affairs in Cuba?

The Cuban Revolution is such a large and important event that the sole obligation of writers of my generation is to defend it. The Cuban affair is enormously significant for Latin American life. It is perhaps the most decisive happening in our history since the independence movements of 1810. Naturally the course of the Cuban Revolution has been disturbed by a series of factors that have gravely endangered it, and it has needed all its vitality to survive them, especially the extension of the boycott imposed by Latin American governments under orders from the Department of State. That was a tragedy. The first thing we ought to have done was to increase our contacts with Cuba and find out how this great new experiment in our continent was progressing. We should have preserved the relations necessary to an understanding of the revolutionary process. Now such grotesque things are happening as the following: to get to Cuba, the niece of ex-president Jorge Alessandri (now once more presidential candidate for the right) had to go from here to Madrid, from Madrid to Prague, from Prague to Cuba, where she spent one week. To return from Havana she had to fly to Madrid or London, thence to Prague, from Prague to Buenos Aires, and from Buenos Aires to Chile. In fact, a return flight that should have taken about ten hours took four or five days. These are the absurd results of isolating Cuba, blockading her and refusing to let people go in or out. And the very same people who applaud these measures complain of the Iron Curtain and the difficulties it creates for writers; meanwhile an intolerable medieval form of blockade is being imposed on Cuba, disregarding the progress she has made and trying to starve her out. This is completely grotesque as well as unjust. The fact that we cannot visit or carry on trade or diplomatic relations with a Latin American country whose people are so close to our own, our kindred, as it were, who speak our language and share our history, seems to me outrageous. And all because the political system of the country in question doesn't please administrators like Johnson or Nixon or the capitalist creoles. It's utterly grotesque. They are entitled to have whatever regime they want. We Chileans are following the events of the Cuban Revolution with great interest and watching its development with immense sympathy.

And Che Guevara?

Che Guevara has become a myth. He was a very brave man and a very interesting one. There's nothing much left to say, because it's all been said. He has become a myth to the whole world and an active and creative influence on the twentieth century. His fate was very tragic. He was assassinated in a country that soon afterwards was to set up monuments in his honor.

To come back to Cuba, can its blockade be compared to what is happening in East and West Germany?

Ah, that's different. One country is a socialist state and the other a capitalist one. And West Germany was engaged in an intense campaign to destroy the German Democratic Republic. The wall is repugnant, but I believe it was necessary. Meanwhile democratic Germany, East Germany, has risen up and become one of the greatest economic powers in the world. I think it stands ninth among the productive countries of the world. It's marvelous that in spite of being next door to Federal Germany, with its great driving power and the enormous help given by the United States and monopolies, this country should have escaped destruction, arisen from the ruins, and been so successful in constructing a new society. As a general rule, all frontiers between races should be abolished. But some are more distressing than others. I suppose that what has happened in Germany must have caused terrible practical human problems, but it seems to me that because they were so close geographically, there was no other choice but this separation. While East Germany is not recognized, and while there is no mutual respect, things must unfortunately go on as they are. That's why what we Latin Americans want is diplomatic relations with Cuba, recognition of her revolution and of the Cuban state, the actual state that exists in Cuba and the nation as it is, with its revolution and its republic.

Has technology produced a crisis in humanistic cultural values?

Well, some people believe that man is going to be swallowed up by technology. I don't think anything of the sort. I remember how English farmers fought against the first railway, and so did North American farmers. Technology is absolutely necessary to the advance of the human race. There's no need for the development of technology to devour man. This fear of technological progress and its possible offshoots is a cosmic fear—it's as deeply superstitious as the fears of prehistoric tribes. Now we've reached a point at which we are afraid of man himself; we have a cosmic fear of what man might discover. Of course I don't personally feel any panic of this sort. On the contrary, I think men must advance by way of discovery, I think that God abdicated and since then God is man.

People are also afraid that technological progress will be used for purposes of destruction.

The curse of humanity is that once a technological discovery is perfected, it is directed toward the destruction of human life. Well, that is the basis on which the humanism of our epoch must be founded, to strive against war and thermonuclear atomic explosions. But that's a different battle. We mustn't close the door to technological progress just because these things result from it. It's truly horrifying that such means of destruction should exist. In Chile today we have Señor Linus Pauling, a much respected man who has spoken frankly and uttered extraordinary ideas about the atomic destruction that we must guard against. Of course these last years have seen an impressive movement against the atomic threat, and perhaps an agreement will be reached to destroy our stockpiles of bombs or not to use them. At least the great powers are coming closer to an agreement to stop manufacturing them. I don't really know how these negotiations are getting on, but they seem to be serious on both sides.

What do you predict for the next decade?

I'm not sure if they aren't really hopes rather than pre-dictions. I think the problem of Vietnam can be solved, North American troops withdrawn, and the Vietnamese nation allowed to decide its own fate. This is the most serious conflict the hu-man race has to deal with. I also think we are on the way to respecting the two German states as separate republics, of the same race but with different governments; I think this will bring great tranquility to Europe. But I seem to be talking like a clairvoyant.

Well, what do you foresee or hope for from the next ten years?

I really think we shall see the end of that trouble. Then there is also the very serious situation in the Middle East; I see no solution to that problem in the near future. In Latin America I think there will be a general tendency toward greater independ-ence from imperialism. The struggle against imperialism will be intensified, and I think the most important developments will take place in our own country, Chile. I think the popular front will win the election and that we shall see some considerable changes. I don't know what will happen in the other Latin American countries, but conditions are intolerable in many of them.

If you are elected president, will you go on writing?

Writing is like breathing to me. I couldn't live without breathing, nor could I live without writing.

Would you be able to write as much as you have hitherto?

I think so.

I've seen you writing in your car.

I write where I can and when I can, but I'm always writing.

Do you always write in longhand?

After breaking one of my fingers in an accident I couldn't use the typewriter for several months. I went back to the habits of my tender youth and began writing by hand. Afterwards, when my finger got better and I could type again, I discovered that my poetry when written by hand was more sensitive; its plastic forms could change more easily. So I realized that my hand was somehow involved in it. I've just read what Robert Graves said to a journalist who was questioning him: "Haven't you noticed something about this house, about this room? Everything in it is handmade. A writer should only live among handmade things," said Robert Graves. But it seems to me that Robert Graves forgot that poetry too should be handwritten. I feel that the typewriter used to remove me from close intimacy with my poetry, and that my hand has brought that intimacy back again.

What are your working hours?

I don't keep to a timetable, but I prefer the mornings. That's to say, if Rita wasn't making me waste my time and wasting her own as well, I should be writing now.

About how many hours a day do you write?

I don't read or write a lot every day. I would really like to write all day long, but often the full development of a thought, of a phrase, of something that emerges chaotically from my own inspiration, to use a word that is out of fashion, leaves me either exhausted or fulfilled or empty. So that I can't go on. And besides, I enjoy life too much to spend the whole day sitting in my study. That's a thing that doesn't suit me at all, and I like to be involved with the goings-on of life, of my house, of politics, of nature. I'm always going in and out. So I can't say I devote the whole day to my writing. But I write with intense concentration, when I can and wherever I am. I'm not bothered by there being a lot of people around. I can write and develop my thoughts while a lot of people are talking and conversing and arguing or quarreling.

Do you detach yourself completely from your surroundings?

I do detach myself, and it even happens that if everyone falls silent, it immediately disturbs me.

. . . Have you finished your last book?

Yes, I've finished it. It is called *La espada encendida* (The Flaming Sword).

Prose or poetry?

Poetry always. It's about the myth of Adam and Eve, and punishment and guilt, in fact it's a new Adam and Eve. The world has come to an end and Adam is the only man left on earth. The bomb and war have destroyed the world, and he meets another human being, who is Eve. Human life begins again with the two of them. It is a book of great intensity. So, that's the book, you see. I don't really know it well. I've finished writing it, but I haven't read it yet. I don't like correcting a book the very minute I've finished it, because I feel a desire to get away from it. So I'm waiting for a few days until I can look at it again more calmly.

When will it be published?

In March or April of 1971.

Who is the publisher?

Losada of Buenos Aires. He is my publisher and I'm on the best of terms with him. This hasn't always been my fate. I've quarreled with a great many publishers, and the relations between writers and publishers are often difficult, but I've been lucky enough to find a publisher who understands me and we've never had any problems.

Why don't you have a publisher in Chile?

I do, but it's rather a small concern to distribute my books as they should be. My first publishers were Chilean, and from time to time I give them my books—every two or three years. I'm often eager for a book of mine to come out first in a Chilean edition. This has happened with my most recent works. We published a limited edition here and Losada has never raised any objections to it.

Have you another book in mind?

I've only just finished *La espada encendida*. Of course I shall write another, but I can't decide what it will be about. I've not yet planned it. I'm still in the process of correcting this new book. Last year my book *Fin de mundo* (End of the World) was published; it took me more than a year to write.

How long do you generally take to write a book?

About a year. The last book has gone more quickly, although I've had less time.

You haven't given too much consideration to your prose . . .

Prose . . . all my life I've felt the need to write in verse and I'm not interested in expressing myself in prose. I use prose to express certain kinds of transitory feelings or events arising from the narrative. And I've written in prose all my life without paying much attention to it. The truth is that I could easily stop writing prose altogether. I only do it occasionally.

You have been a candidate several times for the Nobel Prize. Could the presidency affect in any way the decision of the Swedish Academy?

That question should be put to the Academy, not to me, and needless to say the Academy wouldn't answer.

If you had to choose between the presidency and the prize, which would you choose?

There's no question of deciding between such illusions.

But supposing the presidency and the prize were put on the table in front of you?

If they were put on the table in front of me I should go and sit at another table.

What do you think of Sartre's attitude when he was awarded the Nobel Prize?

It was a very honorable but personal reaction of his forceful personality. I don't think it's a question one can argue about; I think it was a response entirely worthy of a man as militant and consistent as Sartre.

Do you think it was right to give the prize to Beckett?

Yes, I think so. Beckett has written briefly but exquisitely. And I think that wherever the Nobel Prize falls, it always honors literature, poetry, the novel, or the drama. I'm not one of those who are always discussing whether the prize is bestowed well or badly. The importance of the prize, if it has any, is that it confers a mark of respect on the profession of literature on behalf of the masses, the people, the rest. That's the most important thing.

You have often been very much criticized for your way of life and your economic solvency.

That's mostly a myth. In a sense we Latin Americans have received a rather bad inheritance from Spain. She could never bear her nationals to be outstanding in any way, to distinguish themselves. As you know, Christopher Columbus was put in chains when he returned to Spain. And I think that we got from Spain the reaction of an envious petite bourgeoisie which spends its time brooding over what others possess and it doesn't have itself. I have dedicated my life to the vindication of the people, and what I have in my house, and my books, are the result of my own work. I have never exploited anyone. But this reproach is never directed against people who inherit large fortunes. It's never made against writers who come from rich families. They are thought to have a right to greater prosperity than others. On the other hand, when a writer like me has been writing for fifty years, they keep saying: "Look! Just look at the way he lives. He's got a house by the sea, he drinks good wine!" It's very difficult to drink bad wine in Chile because almost all Chilean wine is good. The fact is, I couldn't care less about this chorus of present-day cretins. It's a situation that in a way reflects the backwardness of our country, the mediocrity of our society, in fact. You told me yourself that Norman Mailer was paid about $90,000 for three articles in a North American magazine. Here, if a Latin American writer were to receive such a reward for his work it would arouse a torrent of protests from other writers, saying, "What an outrage! How shocking! Where will it stop?" instead of everyone being delighted that a writer should be so well paid. Oh well, as I've said, these are the drawbacks of so-called cultural underdevelopment.

Doesn't this accusation gain weight from your belonging to the Communist Party?

That's exactly the strength of a position like mine. A man who has nothing—it is often said—has nothing to lose but his chains. Whereas I am at every moment risking my life, my person, my possessions, my books, my house—I throw all these into the balance to defend the future and justice. My house has been set fire to, I have been persecuted, I have been imprisoned more than once, I've been exiled, declared incommunicado, and hounded everywhere by thousands of police. Very well then. I am not just feathering my own nest. I have put all I possess at the disposal of the people's struggle, and the house you are now in has belonged for the last twenty years to the Communist Party of Chile, to whom I have given it publicly. I live in this house simply as a result of my party's decision and the generosity of my party. I am enjoying the use of something that doesn't belong to me, because I gave it away, along with all my collections and all my books, and everything this house contains. All right, let those who reproach me do the same, or at least leave their shoes somewhere so they can be passed to somebody else!

You've donated several libraries, and at this moment you're planning the writers' city at Isla Negra.

Other opportunities came my way earlier, and I presented more than one entire library to the university of my country. The house in which some of the leaders of my party are living now was also a present from me. I live on the earnings of my books. I haven't saved money, I have nothing to dispose of, except for what my books pay me every month. That's all there is to it. Then, quite recently, I succeeded in buying on installment a large piece of land close to the sea, where future writers can spend the summer and do their creative work in such extraordinarily beautiful surroundings as those of the Fundación Cantalao will be. It will be run by people from the Catholic University, the University of Chile, and the Society of Authors. It will be a foundation where those writers who qualify can live for a year on my royalties as an author, and enjoy a communal center for meetings and performances, and private cabins to work in.

There is said to be some antagonism between you and Borges.

The supposed antagonism between me and Borges is not a fundamental one; perhaps there is an intellectual and cultural difference in our orientation. Surely we can quarrel in peace. But I have other enemies, who are not writers. My enemies are the gorillas, for me the enemy is imperialism, and the capitalists, and the people who drop napalm on Vietnam. But Borges is not my enemy.

What do you think of Borges's writing?

He's a great writer, and good heavens! All Spanish-speaking races are very proud that Borges exists. And Latin Americans in particular, because before Borges we had very few writers to compare with European authors. We have had great writers, but a universal one, such as Borges, is a rarity in our countries. He was one of the first. I can't say that he is the *greatest*, and I only hope there may be a hundred others to surpass him, but at all events he made the breakthrough, and attracted the attention and intellectual curiosity of Europe toward our countries. That's all I can say. But to quarrel with Borges, just because everyone wants to make me quarrel with Borges—that I'll never do. If he thinks like a dinosaur, that has nothing to do with my thinking. He doesn't understand a thing about what's happening in the modern world, and he thinks that I don't either. Therefore, we are in agreement.

On Sunday some young Argentines came to visit you and sang a milonga * by Borges, accompanying themselves on their guitars. I think you liked it very much.

I liked Borges's *milonga* immensely, and especially because it was an instance of such a hermetic poet, such a sophisticated and intellectual writer, so to speak, returning to a popular theme in so confident and genuine a manner. I liked Borges's *milonga* very much, and I think many Latin American poets ought to follow his example, now that almost all of us have the same interest in what is popular and traditional.

Will you write the words of the milonga they asked you for?

I don't think so. It's not a form belonging to my country, it comes from the Río de la Plata, and so I'm not familiar enough with it. To do such things one must master the popular style, one has to be in tune with the people, with the roots of nationality and life.

Have you written anything for Chilean folk music?

I have done a few, and they are very well known in this country.

What are your most vivid memories of your personal, political, and literary life?

I don't know; perhaps the most vivid memories I have are of my life in Spain. A great brotherhood of poets, warm friendship with many of them, a fraternal welcome of a quality I had never met with in this American world of ours, full of malicious gossips—*alacraneos* as they call them in Buenos Aires. Then, afterwards, it was terrible to me to see that republic of comrades and friends, that whole state, that world, destroyed by the civil war, which showed me the dreadful reality of oppression and fascism. My friends were scattered by the war; some were exterminated on the spot, like García Lorca, like Miguel Hernández;

* An Argentine popular dance, resembling the tango; or words written to its music.

others died in exile, and others are still living as exiles. This whole aspect of my life was rich in incidents, in deep emotions, and in decisive changes in my own history and the development of my life.

Then would you say that Spain is the country that is most fundamental to you, both as a human being and a poet?

The most fundamental country to me is my own country. But perhaps, next to my own, Spain is the one that has been most important to me. I don't know what it is like now, with the end of Franco still uncertain. I have never really been able to go back there. I have only passed through its ports.

Do they let you in?

They don't officially forbid me. On the contrary, I was once invited to give readings by the embassy of my country. Everything seemed to be made easy as to visas. It's very likely they would let me in. I don't want to argue the point because it might even be convenient to the Spanish government to show its democratic feelings by allowing entry to people who have opposed it so vigorously. I don't know. I've been prevented from entering so many countries and expelled from so many others that it's a matter that no longer irritates me as it did at first. And with the passage of time these things have become easier. Many of the measures adopted against me to make me leave a country have been changed or abolished, and in any case I have stopped feeling any great resentment about being let in or not, in one place or another.

In your "Ode to Federico García Lorca," written before his death, you in a sense foretold his tragic end.

Yes, it's strange about that poem; it does seem as if I had been somehow predicting his death . . . strange since Federico was such a happy man, such a cheerful creature. I've known very few people like him. He was the incarnation . . . I won't say of success, but of the love of life. He enjoyed every moment of his existence. He was a great spendthrift of happiness.

For that reason his execution was one of the most unforgivable sins of fascism.

You often mention him in your poems, and Miguel Hernández too.

Hernández was like a son to me, he was to some extent my disciple as a poet and practically lived in my house, eating there almost every day. He disproved the lie put out to explain the death of Federico García Lorca, the official lie that attributed the crime to the first moments of confusion caused by the civil war, and of course there was confusion. But if that was so, why then did the fascist government of Spain keep Miguel Hernández, the most remarkable of the poets of the younger generation, in prison for so long after Federico García Lorca had been assassinated? Why did they keep him in prison till he died? Why did they even refuse to move him to a hospital, as suggested by the Chilean Embassy? The death of Miguel Hernández was still another assassination.

What made the most impression on you during your stay in the Far East?

My stay in the Far East was an experience I was not altogether prepared for. I was overwhelmed by the splendor of that hitherto unknown continent, and at the same time being there for so long a time and quite alone filled me with desperation. And I often felt as if I was enclosed inside an endless, marvelous film in Technicolor, but that I should never be allowed out of it and it would go on for eternity. I never experienced the mystical feelings that led many South Americans, and many others too, to go to India. I suppose the people who go to India in search of a religious answer to their problems must see things otherwise. I was deeply moved by that great country, that vast, defenseless, helpless nation subjected to the yoke of empire. English culture itself, for which I have always had a special predilection, at times seemed to me infamous because it was the instrument of the intellectual submission of many Hindus at that time. I also mingled with the rebellious youth, and in spite of my position as consul, I frequented all the revolutionaries. I was in contact with the great movement that later led to India's independence. This brought me into contact with Nehru (with whom I only exchanged a few words and a salute, however) in 1928, and with his father, Pandit Motilal Nehru, and Subhas Chandra Bose—one of the most interesting men of the revolutionary period in India, whose intense patriotism led him to fight on the side of the Japanese in the last war. He was the inspiration of many of those working for the independence of India and other colonies in Asia. For them one master was much like another, and they believed that if they could change colonists, power could be divided. I can't judge Subhas Chandra Bose, although Japan was Hitler's ally at that time. At all events, his memory is still greatly respected in India. I also got to know anonymous students, teachers, and writers—not without some difficulty, because they mistrusted me. They mistrusted everyone, and they were quite right. In such a great struggle, everyone must keep his eyes open.

It was in India that you wrote Residence on Earth.

Yes, but India has had no intellectual influence on my poetry.

Wasn't it from there that you also wrote those very moving letters to the Argentine writer, Héctor Eandi?

Yes, those letters were an important episode in my life. Because, although I didn't know him personally, he played the Good Samaritan and took upon himself the task of keeping me in touch with the news, he sent me the papers at times when I was very much alone. I was even afraid of forgetting my own language, because I was surrounded by people who spoke other languages, and for months and months, years even, I didn't meet anyone to talk Spanish to. I remember writing to Rafael Alberti to ask him to send me a Spanish dictionary. A dictionary that couldn't be got in India. And I may say that there were weeks on end when I didn't see a single human being.

Did you go to India of your own accord?

No, I went as consul, but it was an unimportant post. I was one of those consuls who draw no salary. I lived in great poverty and also in great solitude.

*It was there you had your great romance with Josie Bliss, whom
you mention in many of your poems.*

Yes, Josie Bliss was a woman who left a rather deep
imprint on my poetry. I have always remembered her, even in my
latest books.

Your work, then, is closely linked to your personal life?

Of course. A poet's life must naturally be reflected in
his poetry. That is the law of his trade, and one of the laws of life.

*You are one of the most frequently translated poets—into about
thirty languages, I think.*

I've never counted them, but my poems have been translated in several countries.

In which language do the best translations exist?

I would say in Italian, because there's a similarity of
values between the two languages. English and French, the only
languages I know besides Italian, are languages which do not
correspond to Spanish—neither in vocalization, nor in the place-
ment, nor the color, nor the weight of the words. This means
that the equilibrium of a Spanish poem, which may be written
with verbal lavishness or economy, but has its own order and
way of placing each word, can find no equivalent in French or
English. It's not a question of interpretive equivalents, no; the
sense may be correct, indeed the accuracy of the translation
itself, of the meaning, may be what destroys the poem. That's
why I think that Italian comes closest, because by keeping the
values of the words, the sound helps reflect the sense. In many
of the French translations, I don't say in all, my poetry seems
to me to vanish, nothing is left, yet one can't complain because
they express what one has written. But obviously if I had written
in French, if I had been a French poet, I wouldn't have said
what is said in that poem, because the value of the words, their
color, their smell, their weight is different. I would therefore
have written something else.

And in English?

It seems to me that the English language, so different from Spanish and so much more direct, often expresses the meaning of my poetry but does not convey its atmosphere. The same may well happen when an English poet is translated into Spanish.

You have done translations from English and French into Spanish . . .

I've done many translations from English. I've translated William Blake, Whitman, Shakespeare. I think I did them well. My translations from Blake were made a long time ago. I've reread them because they are sometimes reprinted, and I was quite pleased with them.

Your translation of Romeo and Juliet, *staged in Chile and New York, was very successful wasn't it?*

Yes, it was rather an interesting experience. There's a Shakespeare myth and a Dante myth in Latin American countries, you see. Practically no one who can't read English has read Shakespeare, and practically no one who can't read Italian has read Dante. Translations of Shakespeare, for instance, have cost a lot of hard work and yet have failed to render the radiant complexity of Shakespeare's poetry. This is especially true for tragedies like *Romeo and Juliet,* which is written entirely in verse. We are given hispanicized Shakespeare, translated into the rigid rhetorical poetry of the beginning of the century. I can boast of making a humanized translation of Shakespeare, one that completely respects his meaning. But such a stream of human feeling flows through this version of mine that in all the hundreds of performances that have been given, there has not been a soul in the audience who has not been moved or even wept.

I think the first translations you made were from Rainer Maria Rilke?

In my youth, in the far-off years of my youth, I translated Rilke from the French. I also translated some of Baudelaire.

Your work falls into different phases, doesn't it?

My thoughts on this subject are rather confused. I don't have phases—they are discovered by the critics. One doesn't live in phases. Nobody knows when a phase begins or ends. If my poetry has any virtue it's that it's an organism, it's organic and emanates from my own body. When I was a child, my poetry was childish, it was youthful when I was young, despairing when I was suffering, aggressive when I had to take part in the social struggle, and there is still a mixture of all these different tendencies in the poetry I write now, which may perhaps be at the same time childish, aggressive, and despairing. In fact, I have nothing much more to say on this point. I have always written from some inner necessity, and I suppose this happens to all writers, and especially to all poets. I'm afraid I'm not remarkable in this respect. I'm an anti-intellectual, I don't much care for analysis or for examining literary currents, and I'm not a writer who subsists on books, although books are necessary to my life.

You said of the poems in Residence on Earth, "They don't help one to live. They help one to die."

My book *Residence on Earth* represents an obscure and dangerous moment of my life. It's poetry with no way out. I almost had to be reborn to find the way out of it. In that sense the Spanish war saved me from a fit of despair whose depths I cannot judge today. It coincided with the time of great solitude when I was living in India, which we have already spoken about, when I wrote the greater part of *Residence on Earth*. A great deal has happened to me since then, some of it rather serious, serious enough to give me pause for thought. For example, I said once that if I ever possessed the necessary authority I should ban my own book and make sure that it was never reprinted. Of course I realize that's a rather shocking statement, a rather harsh thing to hear. That book of mine exaggerates, or rather, carries to such lengths, the notion that life is a painful and oppressive burden that it ends by having a rarefied air. Yet I also know that it's one of my best books, because it has a depth derived from the time I was living its poetry. But when one is writing—I don't know if this happens to other writers—one has to think where one's verses will end up. Robert Frost says in one of his prose essays that poetry should be oriented toward pain: "Leave sorrow alone with poetry." He didn't mean to express any civic emotion in this thought; it seemed to him that it would take him from his own center, from his essence. But I don't know what Robert Frost would have thought if some young man committed suicide and left one of his books, covered in blood from a bullet hole, beside his head. That has happened to me here in this country. A boy who was full of life killed himself beside my book. I don't really hold myself responsible for his death. I think a great many problems I know nothing about led that boy to commit suicide. But that page of my poetry stained with a young man's blood ought to give not only one but all poets something to think about. Afterwards, as with everything one says or does, my opponents took political advantage of the censure I gave my own book. Those who criticized me so dogmatically, charging me with party dogmatism and with wanting to write optimistic poetry, an exclusive poetry of happiness, didn't know about this incident. Well, they know now. But I have not at heart renounced expressing my feelings of loneliness, anxiety, or melancholy. What I like is to change tones, seek out all possible sounds, pursue every color, and look for the life forces wherever they may be —in creation or in destruction. It is thus I have tried to carry out my duties as a poet. I hold to no other doctrine, no other truth; my poetry became clear and happy when it branched off toward humbler subjects and things.

As in the Elemental Odes.

Chiefly in the *Elemental Odes*. But I don't put this forward as a precept or recipe. Least of all for young poets. It seems to me they can't reach the elevated realms of the poetry of social feeling, and of protest and combat, unless they've been through the necessary stages, the stages of delirious love and infinite unhappiness. It's natural that everyone's own experience should point the way he must take, and if there's no light shining on that way, the poet's sincerity should express the very darkness that obliterates it. To ask anything else of him would be to drag him out of his world, whereas he ought to emerge from it by his own strength and by following the directions given him by what we call his soul. Afterwards he will write poetry that colors the world anew. Meanwhile we must observe the most absolute of our duties—which is sincerity.

Your last published book, Fin de mundo, *is also rather despairing.*

Yes, it is rather despairing, but in a different way. Its despair is not cosmic, but for all the death and slaughter in the world, in the world I have lived in since the Spanish civil war, the Nazi invasion, Hitler's massacre of the Jews, the hellish bombings, the atom bomb, and so many other terrible things we have had to live with. *Fin de mundo* is so named because I want such a world to end, and yet in spite of my dark picture of that world I think there is a certain gleam of hope. I say in this book that even if in the course of any discovery of space we succeed in reaching another planet, we shall always come back to this corrupt but splendid planet we call the earth, where we shall go on living and where human beings will continue to live.

When you say: "Why do so many things happen, and why do others not happen?" what things that don't happen are you referring to?

Man always believes he is finding salvation, and yet social salvation is so difficult to come by! I don't believe in the salvation of the soul or in all that mystical stuff I find so alien, but only in the salvation that aims at preserving the most important thing that exists—life, the lives of human beings. And as we live under the constant threat of war and annihilation, I asked myself: Why didn't other things happen? Why, for instance, didn't the Spanish war come to a more just conclusion? The truth is that there are reasons for despair and for hope. That's what I wanted to say.

In the chapter called "Siglo" (Century) you say:

> Let us have no illusions,
> the calendar advises us,

everything will go on in the same way,
the earth contains no remedy:
we must seek a lodging
in other heavenly regions.

Of course that reflects a momentary mood. A few pages later on I say exactly the opposite. None of the things I say can stand as permanent statements. As long as I live, I shall be ready to contradict myself.

Would you like to read one of your poems?

WE ARE MANY *

Of all the men that I am, that we are,
I can not find a single one.
They slip away from me beneath the clothes,
they've gone off to another city.

When everything is ready
to show me off as intelligent
the fool that is hidden inside me
speaks up in my mouth.

At other times I fall asleep in the midst
of distinguished company
and when I look for the brave man in me
a coward whom I do not know
runs to take a thousand delightful
precautions with my skeleton.

When a treasured house is on fire
instead of the fireman that I call for
the firebug rushes up
and I am the firebug. I'm a mess.
What must I do to choose myself?
How can I rehabilitate myself?

All the books that I read
sing the praises of shining heroes
always sure of themselves:

* From Pablo Neruda's *Estravagario*. Translated from the Spanish by Donald D. Walsh.

I'd die to be like them,
and in the movies with storms and bullets
I always envy the rider,
I always admire the horse.

But when I ask for the intrepid me,
the old lazy me comes out,
and so I don't know who I am,
I don't know how many I am or how many we may be.
I'd like to ring a bell
and ask for the real me
because if I need myself
I mustn't disappear on myself.

While I write I am absent
and when I return I've already left:
I'm going to see if the same thing
happens to other people as happens to me,
if there are as many of them as of me,
if they look like themselves
and when I've found it out
I'm going to learn things so well
that to explain my problems
I'll talk to them of geography.

In Estravagario a humorous vein is more apparent than in your other books . . .

The mood of my book *Estravagario* hovers between mockery of the intelligence and a gayer approach than is usual in my writing. This has been apparent in my work since *Crepusculario*. It is a vein of self-mockery also. Of course I don't try to achieve what is called humor, nor should I have the smallest success if I did. But humor has always seemed to me an essential ingredient in prose, in novels and drama. Mark Twain is a humorist, but so are Dostoevski and Shakespeare. This essential humor is very far removed from the realm of poetry. In my book *Estravagario*, and in others too, especially in *Fin de mundo*, I admit a more definitive participation of a divided view of the universe. By "divided view" I mean to suggest that a persona, an autobiographer, a poet, contains separate compartments, which express themselves one by one.

One of your first books, Veinte poemas de amor y una canción desesperada (Twenty Love Poems and One Song of Despair), has been and continues to be read by thousands of admirers.

It's a complete enigma; I'm not sure whether literary or human. I said in the foreword to the edition printed to celebrate the millionth copy that now there would soon be two million. I don't really understand what this means, why this book, which is a book full of love–sadness, love–pain, goes on indefinitely being read by so many, by so many young people. Truly, I don't understand it at all. Perhaps this book expresses the many questions that perplex the young, or perhaps it expresses the answers to these questions. It's basically a sad book, yet its attraction hasn't faded.

Cien Sonetos de Amor (One Hundred Love Sonnets), published in 1960, is very different.

That's another sort of love, more mature, more complete love. But on the whole my books represent a change of situation and a change of skin, to borrow the name of one of Carlos Fuentes's books.

Are they very autobiographical?

I don't know. I believe the human organism is constantly changing, as the scientists say. All the cells are renewed and changed, so that nobody is the same after a certain time. Therefore any poet's poetry must undergo fundamental changes and at the same time remain part of his identity. I've often said that I don't care for analysis, nor is my concept of poetry an analytic one. There's very little I can add to what I've already said.

Some symbols keep recurring in your poetry, for instance, the sea, fish, birds . . .

I don't believe in symbols. Those are material things. The sea, fish, and birds have material existence for me. I depend on them just as I depend on daylight. The word "symbol" doesn't express my thought exactly. Some themes persist in my poetry, are constantly reappearing, but they are material entities.

Like flames, wine, or fire.

We live with flames, wine, and fire also. Fire is part of our life in this world.

Doves, guitars—what do they mean?

A dove means a dove and a guitar is a musical instrument called a guitar.

You mean that people who have tried to analyze these images in Freudian terms or otherwise are not falling in with your way of thought?

I have no way of thought. I write because I have to write, and when I see a dove I call it a dove. Whether it's present to me or not at that moment, it has a form for me, it may be subjective or objective, but it is nothing else beyond being a dove.

It has been said of you that you are a poet of books, not poems.

As a matter of fact, if you think about it, they are right that I'm a poet of books not of poems, or perhaps of both. But I think in terms of books. That's why I don't much like publishing my work in magazines. Magazines are the delight of literary adolescents. We are all crazy to write for magazines, publish something in a magazine. But this impatience passes with time. At any rate I feel less and less eager to have my poetry published among other poems in the literary pages of newspapers and magazines. Every day I like magazines less, and every day I like books more. You see, the point of magazines is to be bright, to glitter, everyone wants to please his own epoch, and go with the contemporary trend, as you might say. That doesn't interest me. I've just been reading an excellent interview with Cortázar. After another writer had criticized one of his books, he explained with that lucidity so typical of his controversial spirit that his books formed a spiral; that some writers might be content with a circle and with permanence, but that he saw his work as a spiral forming a pyramidal structure. I don't know what the structure of my books is, whether horizontal or spiral, but I too see my work as a sort of construction. Perhaps I'm less given to definitions than Cortázar, but I do need change and always to be responding to new perspectives. I like to think of my work as an extension and a construction, I don't know exactly of what, it might be a building, it might be a pergola, it might be a balustrade or a square, or a jetty where boats were moored, or it might well be a few stones set up here or there. But the fact is I don't see things in isolation, and if I have felt the desire to create a cyclic work it is in the sense that I always want to extract the last drop from periods of time—to experience them fully, experience every moment, and experience my themes both in depth and extension. Ever since my youth I have been obsessed by extension, distance, space, and the possibilities of man. One of my earliest books is called *Tentativa del hombre infinito* (Attempt of Infinite Man) —well, today I would call it "Of Unfinished Man." Man is an unfinished being, and that lack of a beginning and an end, those two hollows in human life, must be the foundation on which a poet's work is built.

You have always considered that book a very important one, although the critics didn't value it so highly.

I like that book very much, rather as I do *The Inhabitant and His Hope,* which is almost my only prose work. They're the lost fruit among my work, yet they are still germinating. And I'm very glad that they are hidden under the leaves, that people go by without noticing them; I'm very fond of them.

If you had to save your works from a fire, which would you save?

Possibly none of them. What am I going to need them for? I would rather like to save a girl . . . or a good collection of detective stories . . . which would entertain me much more than my own poetry.

Which of your critics has understood your work best?

Oh, my critics! My critics almost shredded me to pieces. They have analyzed me and chopped me into little bits, with the utmost love or dislike. In life, as in work, one can't possibly please everyone; it's always the same thing. And one receives kisses or blows, caresses or kicks—that's a poet's life. It has changed very little since earliest times. What bothers me is the distortion or ill-will with which one's poetry and behavior are interpreted. For instance, as a journalist, you saw for yourself that during my stay in New York for the PEN Club Congress, which brought together so many people from different countries, my statements for the Spanish edition of *Life* * which you reported, were afterwards mutilated or eliminated by the editors or the directors of that magazine. But, as you know, my statement on many of the points we discussed on that occasion expressed anti-imperialist, not anti-American, views. I did, it's true, protest strongly against all the escapades the North American war machine was involving us in: the crimes of Vietnam, the invasion of Cuba, the Dominican Republic. Well, that part of your report and mine never saw the light. And you know too that I gave some readings of my socialist poetry in New York, and more in California, where I read in particular my poems dedicated to Cuba, my poems in support of the Cuban

* Some of the unpublished questions and answers for the *Life en Español* interview, which took place in July 1966. The article appeared on August 1, 1966.

You said that there were more dissidents among writers in capitalist countries than among those in the socialist countries.

Writers tend to be discontented wherever they are. It's part of our profession. You must forgive me for feeling good everywhere. It's my duty to be happy. If that's anti-literary, I'm sorry.

In what way can an author's work be influenced by the knowledge that if he expresses his ideas freely reprisals will be taken?

That story about reprisals seems to me a trifle out of date. Writers are not immune from the common law affecting every citizen. I'm a supporter of the view that in no country should writers be legally prosecuted for anything derived from their books, from their creative activity. However, a single napalm bomb dropped on a hut in Vietnam may burn alive more than one writer—among other people—and many children will never have the freedom to express themselves because the napalm has burned their throats.

Revolution. Who would have thought that millions of copies would be published of a letter, signed by Cuban writers, casting doubt on my opinions, and pointing me out as someone under North American protection, and even stating as a fact that I had gained entry to the United States as a sort of reward? That is completely idiotic, if not libelous, because I went there among a great many other writers from socialist countries; Cuban writers were expected, and at that time entry visas were being accepted from anti-imperialist writers. We didn't cease being anti-imperialists just because we went to New York to speak the truth as we saw it. However, that was what happened, because of haste or bad faith on the part of those writers. I have never undertaken to clarify such a position, nor do I propose to now. The very fact that until a few days ago I was my party's candidate for the presidency of the republic shows that my history is that of a true revolutionary, and it would be very difficult to find among the writers who signed that letter any with a comparable history of dedication to the life and work of organization, to revolutionary work for the masses, or any who could lay claim to even a hundredth part of what I have achieved and fought for. One has to be prepared to accept both critical and personal injustice in this life. Fortunately there are some critics with creative intellects, who respond to the true germ of creation in others. And there are also people of good faith, and people who believe in human beings, and it is to those—who make up the vast majority, and who are called the "people"—I am speaking. That's to say, I am speaking to some on an intellectual level, through their intellectual integrity, and I'm also speaking to those of my own and other nations who have been my companions in a struggle that is not ending now, and never will.

What were your literary influences?

That's an interesting subject. It seems to me that I have been influenced by all the poetry I've ever read, and it's naturally difficult to enumerate so many influences. The truth is that literature is constantly subjected to an influence that may be at times destructive or creative. It is fundamentally an evolutionary process. Just as the action of natural elements pulverizes our deepest feelings and transforms them into an intimate reflective substance, whether emotional or factual, which we call literature, so also it is the writer's duty to contribute his own work to the development of the cultural heritage, by pulverizing, purifying, and constantly transforming it. It is the same effect that nutrition has on the blood, on the circulation. Culture has its roots in culture, but also in life and nature. All these formulas come and go in the mind of the writer, the poet. Walt Whitman has been my constant companion. I haven't been much of a Whitmanian in my style of writing, but I am profoundly Whitmanian as regards his vital message, his acceptance, his way of embracing the world, life, human beings, nature. Walt Whitman was a magnificent machine tirelessly at work on the noblest material that exists on earth. It's very difficult to find any other poet whose attitude is so important. I was also influenced in my time by the whole luminous range of the French symbolists from Rimbaud to the least-known and least-esteemed. At fourteen or fifteen I was an omnivorous reader, and naturally it has all left its trace on my poetry. There's some sort of interchange going on all the time with others; just as the air we breathe doesn't belong to one region, but to the whole atmosphere, we are interchanging experiences, knowledge, and progress. A writer is always moving house; he must change his furniture but not his soul. I've known some writers who feel impoverished by this fact. I remember that Federico García Lorca, who was also a humorist, a great and original humorist, used always to ask me to read him my poems, but when I was halfway through he used to say: "Stop, stop, don't go on, you're influencing me!"

What are your tastes in literature?

Many people find my taste in literature very controversial. But to begin with the most famous people whose writing I admire, I would like to mention briefly, but separately, Ramón Gómez de la Serna. Ramón Gómez de la Serna seems to me a considerable literary phenomenon, rather like Picasso in painting, and having the same virility. He had a fundamentally

creative influence on our language. I think he was better understood in his own country, Spain, and was beginning to be
known all over Europe when the civil war brought him to our
shores, where he stayed until his death. Ramón was a great
river of inspiration and of fabulous inventiveness. That fantastic
world he left us as a legacy has not yet been evaluated. He is
a great transformer of the language; his verbal imagination, his
fantastic associations of ideas are unequaled in the whole history
of the Spanish language. He is both the Quevedo and the
Picasso of modern times. Of course, as happens with many
creative artists, he is too prolific for his work to be recommended
in its entirety, just as Marcel Proust seems interminable and
indigestible to a youthful appetite. In Ramón's case, possibly
the virtuosity of his writing and his tremendous associative power
weary his readers in the long run. But the reader's fatigue in no
way reflects on this giant, who gives off sparks and flashes and
is at the same time full of that humor characteristic of the
great works of great masters. Ramón and I were friends, but
both of us were always so busy that we seldom met. On the
other hand, when I traveled in Europe some years ago, I formed
a very warm and extremely fraternal friendship with Picasso.
He has helped me with my practical and political difficulties
in the most unassuming way, and I have visited his house
many times. I had the privilege, granted to very few, of being
given the key to his studio. Several times I found him painting.
He used to look up in surprise, having quite forgotten that he
had lent me the key.

*About Norman Mailer. You were one of the first writers to call
attention to him.*

I came across Norman Mailer's book *The Naked and
the Dead* in a bookshop in Mexico, soon after it was published.
That was many years ago, and no one had heard of it; even
the bookseller didn't know what it was about. I bought it
because I had to go on a journey and wanted an American
novel. I believed that the novel was dead, after a series of
colossal figures beginning with Dreiser and apparently ending
with Hemingway, Steinbeck, and Faulkner; but I found myself

confronted by a mature, direct man, possessed of amazing ability and verbal force along with great subtlety and marvelous powers of description. I very much admire Pasternak's poetry, but compared with *The Naked and the Dead, Doctor Zhivago* seems to me a boring novel, partly saved by its descriptions of nature, in other words by Pasternak's real poetic sense. Whereas *The Naked and the Dead* struck me as one of the finest novels written in the last fifty years. I haven't followed Mailer closely. I remember that many years ago—I've a very bad memory for dates—I wrote the poem "Let the Rail Splitter Awake," which was amazingly widely read and translated; it was a poem dedicated to world peace, and invoked the figure of Lincoln. Writing about the war, I mentioned Okinawa and the war in Japan, and named Norman Mailer. About this time my poem arrived in Europe and was being translated, and I remember Aragon saying to me: "We've had a devil of a time finding out who Norman Mailer was." In fact no one knew about him, and I feel a certain pride at having been one of the first writers to mention him. It's not much to say, especially now that everybody knows Norman Mailer, but I discovered him in my own way, at any rate I discovered him for myself.

You are a great reader of detective stories. Who are your favorite authors?

The book in this category that has most moved me as good literature in the last few years is Eric Ambler's *A Coffin for Dimitrios*. Since then I've sought out all Ambler's novels and read practically every one of them, but none has the fundamental perfection, the extraordinary intrigue, and the mysterious atmosphere of *A Coffin for Dimitrios*. To me it's one of the best examples of what is now known as the literature of suspense. Among writers devoted almost entirely to this genre, I think James Hadley Chase is the greatest and most influential. Simenon is also very important, but in some of his books James Hadley Chase surpasses everything written for terror, horror, and the spirit of destruction. For instance *No Orchids for Miss Blandish* is now an old book, but it is still a milestone in the history of the detective story. To me there is a curious similarity between

No Orchids for Miss Blandish and *Sanctuary*, William Faulkner's
very disagreeable but at the same time important book. But
I've never been able to determine which was the first of the
two—Faulkner or James Hadley Chase. Of course, when one
talks about detective novels, I always think of Dashiell Hammett,
that great writer who transformed a whole branch of the detective story. It's fair to say that he was the one who dragged it
out of the ghostly subliterary world and gave it a skeleton,
a hard, bony structure. He was the great creator of the genre
in the United States, and hundreds of others have followed,
John D. McDonald among the most brilliant. They are all
prolific writers and work extremely hard. And nearly all North
American novelists belonging to the detective school provide
perhaps the harshest criticism of the collapse of North American
society in the age of capitalism. There is no more forceful
arraignment than that found in the recent detective story, the
really first-rate detective story, of the fatigue and corruption
among politicians and police, the influence money has in great
cities, the corruption appearing everywhere in the North American system, in the "American way of life." Perhaps it is the
most dramatic testimony concerning a period, and the least
permanent, as detective stories are not treated seriously by
literary critics, but its transitoriness in no way detracts from the
profundity of this denunciation of the decadence of the North
American empire.

What other books do you read?

I'm a reader of history, especially the enthralling history
of my country. My country, as is known or can be found out,
has an extraordinary history; a more profound history than most
other countries. Not because of its monuments and ancient sculptures—they don't exist here—but because this country, Chile, was
invented by a poet, Don Alonso de Ercilla y Zúñiga, page of
Carlos V, an aristocrat from the Basque country who arrived in
Chile among the conquistadors. A *rara avis*, as most of those sent
to Chile were men out of prisons and dungeons. It was the
toughest place to come to. The war here went on for centuries,

the war between Araucanians and Spaniards. That was the long-
est patriotic war in human history. The semi-savage tribes of
Araucania fought for three hundred years on end against the
Spanish invaders, for their independence, for their liberty. The
young humanist, Don Alonso de Ercilla y Zúñiga, came with
cruel soldiers and conquistadors who wanted to dominate all
America, and *did* dominate it, with the exception of the
shaggy, wild region called Chile. Don Alonso wrote his poem
"The Araucaniad" in which he set out to create the greatest
poem in Castillian epic literature honoring the unknown tribes
of Araucania—the anonymous heroes he had been the first to
name—rather than his compatriots, the soldiers from Castile.
Published in the sixteenth century, "The Araucaniad" was translated and spread all over Europe, and that was how the name
of Chile was born into the world. A great poem by a great
poet. So the history of Chile derives its epic greatness from
the birth of a nation, and from the blood shed by the indomitable
Araucanians and by heterogeneous Spanish soldiery. But curiously
enough, instead of the cross-breeding that took place in other
parts of Spanish and Indian America, we are not the descendants
of Spanish soldiers and Araucanian women violated or taken as
concubines by them. We Chileans come from the voluntary
or enforced marriages of Araucanian men with Spanish women
taken captive throughout the long years of that tremendous
struggle. We are a curious exception. But later on, after 1810,
came the bloody history of Chile's independence, full of tragedies,
struggle, and disagreement, in which the names of San Martín
and Bolívar, of José Miguel Carrera and O'Higgins figure alter-
nately in an interminable page of successes and misfortunes.
All this made me a reader of books, which I unearth and dust
off and which entertain me enormously as I search for the
significance of this strip of country—so remote from everybody,
so cold in its latitudes, so deserted . . . its saltpeter pampas in
the north, its immense patagonias, so snowy in the Andes, so
florid by the sea. And this is my country, Chile. I am one of
those Chileans in perpetuity, one who, however well treated
everywhere, must always return to his own country. Although
I very much like the large cities of Europe, although I adore

the valley of the Arno and some of the streets of Copenhagen
and Stockholm, and of course Paris, Paris, Paris, I am always
drawn back to Chile with much honor and by much love.

*Another great Chilean poet was Gabriela Mistral, an old friend of
yours. Wasn't she the one who put you on to reading the Russians?*

       Yes, she lent me some books by nineteenth-century Rus-
sians, among others. Gabriela Mistral was a passionate reader . . .
and she was intensely creative. On the whole she's not understood
by literary people of our day. She is one of the most important
Latin American writers, an uneven poet who reaches great heights
and great depths, but in vitality and verbal violence she surpasses
all her contemporary writers in the Spanish language. Above all,
her early poems, those of the period of the "Sonnets of Death,"
and the poems in her book *Desolation*, have few equals in
Spanish poetry, unless perhaps the sonnets of Quevedo, whom
she sometimes resembles in her extraordinary volcanic power,
her emotional scope and depth. I have a great respect for
Gabriela Mistral, and I think that the reason why literary people
of today hardly mention her is partly that she is out of fashion
and chiefly that they haven't read her. She was also a humanist
in her own way. A person of strong and primitive emotions.
She was an autodidact, but an autodidact who had overcome
all difficulties and succeeded in elaborating and creating her
own language. Gabriela Mistral's language in poetry or prose is
extraordinary, and of incalculable worth. Above all, it teaches an
important lesson, because she has developed her style from her
own faults, insisting on her own difficulties in self-expression.
The difficulties she encountered in expressing herself have given
her style an incredible nobility.

What ought to be the function of poetry and literature?

       That's a question that is often asked and always receives
a very vague reply, but it's really the question that is vague.
The position of poetry differs according to period, to epoch.
There may be a need for poetry that is intimate and subjective,
just as it may be necessary for it to be in tune with human
activity, with the convulsions, controversies, and rebellions of

human society. I believe that it is the duty of poetry to embrace everything, from the most secret to the most public, from the most confused and mysterious to the simplest things within reach of one's hand. The poet's heart must be large enough for his poetry to embrace them all. I think it should be concerned with every subject of interest. The greatest human masterpieces, such as Dante's *The Divine Comedy*, contain a considerable element of political pamphleteering. Many works of literature have been almost entirely dedicated to a vigorous struggle against the existing state of things; this was the case with Victor Hugo, Milton himself, or Rimbaud. The controversy between pure and impure poetry is a futile one. There will always be pure poetry and there will always be impure poetry. I stand by them both. I am both pure and impure. That's to say, I want my poetry to express the secrets of my soul and also the simplicity of the essential things that are closest to a human being and even play a part in the relaxation of soldiers and in war itself. War against cruelty, against injustice, for the liberation of man.

Robert Graves has said that poets do not have a public, but are speaking to one person. The trouble with poets like Yevtushenko, he says, is that they are speaking to thousands of people, yet to no one.

I think that's a delightful remark of Robert Graves. I respect Graves very much and love his poetry. But I especially like poetry that speaks to thousands of people, and he's wrong when he says it speaks to no one. If he knew what evidence we have received from people who have been touched by our poetry for the masses, then he would understand that a poet can have another dimension, and I will defend that dimension just as I defend Robert Graves's dimension of speaking to one person. Poetry should very often speak to one person, but it should also very often speak to thousands.

What's your opinion of realism in poetry?

Realism and creative literature are subjects much discussed lately by responsible writers. I share the belief, or attitude, that reality plays a splendid and definitive part in the writer's vision. Just as I do not believe in literary realism, I also believe that symbols have never lost their importance since the French school, or much earlier. A symbol is one of the instruments of poetic creation, yet the symbolist school is a vast cemetery of symbols. I believe that schools and the systems proclaimed by human groups are pernicious. Realism is a basic element of the creative vision and necessary for its successful expression. But as a formula, realism has only produced strange deformations of reality, just as symbolism has cheapened dreams. Reality and symbolism will always be part of the fruitful development of literature. On a certain level they mix and become confused, but as schools they can be deadly. Besides, the very fact of fighting with a label the phantasms set up by other literary epochs shows a certain mistrust of the creative process itself. I think literary, musical, and plastic movements have a life of their own— their own roots, height, foliage, fruits, decay, and funeral. There is no need to fight against any cultural movement. Every new movement carries within it the seeds of maturity and death. I believe that realism, conceived as a vast school formally con- nected with the exterior of humanity, in painting as well as in literature, is a stage that has ended, after ripening, flowering, and producing some splendid fruits. But it has also plunged us into formal ugliness and a characteristic sordidness. It is not that I want art to be sublime, because hermetic vagueness or oneiric, verbalist, and algebraic theorizing may also reduce po- etry to a form of petrified dreaming. It is rather that I believe that schools are unnecessary. Literature must be a profoundly personal experience, in which time, reality, and dreams all play parts. And these formidable ingredients must be arranged and displaced with relation not only to the inner life of the writer but also to the epoch in which he lives.

You have often said that you don't believe in originality.

I don't like treating originality as a fetish. The search for originality at all costs is a contemporary obsession. Minstrels and popular poets of every epoch, like primitive architecture and ancient sculpture, were to some extent anonymous, the products of an epoch. Their achievements were great nonetheless. In our own time, writers want to distinguish themselves in some vital manner, and this concern with superficials ends by becoming a fetish. Each one tries to find a way to be singled out, not for his profundity or his discoveries, but because he has imposed some special method or dissimilarity. I think everyone should solve the problem of originality by expressing his own existence, his own experience, in the most authentic form, in his own language. This need for expression will develop naturally. And even the most original artist will change phases to suit the times, the epoch, and his subjects. The most impressive instance is Picasso, who, although nourishing himself on great cultural movements such as African painting and sculpture or primitive art, sometimes shows such powers of transformation that his works seem like stages in the cultural geology of the world.

Octavio Paz has said in a recent interview that literature, since Cervantes, has had a critical quality which can be seen in our contemporary literature and poetry. Do you agree with this?

This is one of my points of disagreement with his brilliant intellect. I don't believe literature can be treated in such a global, generalized way. It seems to me that the novel has always had critical significance, especially since the Golden Age, especially from the picaresque period to our own day, just as I observed just now about the North American detective story. Great books have been great denunciations, but the critical sense, the desire for examination and self-examination, can sometimes be a weakness and wear away the creative impulse. Wherever the critical spirit enters, it destroys creative spontaneity; above all, it destroys the original impulse and the direct relation that ought to exist between nature, between feelings and their translation into language—into poetical language. For my part, in spite of my political poems—not a large proportion of my work—I feel that all poetry that is critical or self-critical, not in a personal sense but in that of surrendering the poetry to the critical significance, is transitory and perishable. I also think that nothing written about literature does more than present a fugitive aspect of literary creations. I mean that I am in favor of confrontation; I believe poetry should be directly concerned with contemplation, with music, vital energy, and elemental things, but not with reflected emotions adapted to every contemporary phase. It seems to me that poetry should above all fulfill the role of an element; that poetry is another element, just like fire, earth, water, and air. And I cannot allow this spatial function of poetry, its geological, natural, and phenomenal function, to be interrupted by inquiries prompted by a momentary need to analyze these same phenomena of creation. I'm an enemy of manifestos, of all literary discussions. Much more important, as I have often said, is the passionate, desperate struggle by which the poet involves himself with nature or the depths of his own soul. That seems to me the natural and supernatural role of poetry above everything else. Of course in the case of political poetry, to which I concede validity, it is a fact that at certain moments of history, man, the race, and human progress require the poet's help. The poet cannot refuse that appeal . . . if he refuses, he is a coward.

Which of the Russian poets do you like most?

The dominant figure in Russian poetry is still Mayakovsky. He is the celebrator of the Russian Revolution, just as Walt Whitman was of the industrial revolution and the growth of North America. Mayakovsky impregnated poetry in such a way that almost all of it has become Mayakovskian. Besides him, the most important poets were Aleksandr Blok, a marvelous poet, and Yesenin, another extraordinary writer. In the present generation there are many, and of course younger ones. Among the not so young are Kirsanov, Lukonin, Yevtushenko, Voznesensky, and a poetess who besides being a very good poetess is very beautiful—Akhmadulina. There are, in fact, many others and many of them are great friends of mine, but these poets— Yevtushenko, Voznesensky, and Akhmadulina—have broken the ice, and their poetry has once more begun to interest a wide public. I am a wandering poet in the sense that I have traveled all over my own country and most American countries like a troubadour, reading my verses to large crowds, yet I have not met my counterpart, or a similar poet, doing the same anywhere. Neither in capitalist nor in socialist countries. The only one I remember was Carl Sandburg, the great North American poet, who used very often to travel and give recitals to the accompaniment of a guitar. I envy him deeply. He was a great poet, and so were Edgar Lee Masters and Robert Frost. They are the best poets of the post-Whitman period in the United States, with a long line of descendants.

In Russia, poets are again showing their multiple interests as citizens and they have again begun holding public poetry readings. They are almost always held at the base of the statues of Pushkin or Mayakovsky—Pushkin's statue is a fine, romantic monument. Mayakovsky had a face like a pugilist, and his statue is even more like a pugilist—well, I have seen poets recite their poems for hours and hours on end, until two or three o'clock in the morning.

Yevtushenko's readings have become very popular in the United States.

Yevtushenko is a very talented poet, and I like his character as well as his poetry, his argumentativeness, his eccentric and high-spirited attitude, his defiance of established conventions; and perhaps what I admire most of all in him is that in spite of the frankness with which he criticizes both worlds, he remains a great Soviet patriot, proud of the revolution and the socialist structure. The same is true of Voznesensky and Akhmadulina, I'm sure.

Yevtushenko is also a charming man, childishly vain and very gay. He allows himself to do things I have never been able to do because of lack of independence and personality. For example, I put up with a journalist interviewing me for several days on end. Yevtushenko would never have put up with that, but that's the way it is, you see!

What's your opinion of Russian writers who have left Russia?

On the whole I think that if people want to leave a place they ought to leave. These are purely personal problems. The political problems arising from them can be interpreted in many ways. Many Soviet writers may feel dissatisfied with their relation to the literary organizations in their own country. This situation, this special attitude of writers, is found almost all over the world. There may be disagreement. But I have never seen less disagreement between the state and writers than in the socialist countries. I've always found most Russian writers proud of the socialist structure, proud of the Soviet Union's great war of liberation against the Nazis. Proud of the part their people played in the revolution and the Great War. Proud of everything socialism has built up. If there are exceptions, it is a personal concern, and each case must be looked at individually.

But neither writers nor painters can be free in their creative work. It must always reflect the state's point of view.

That's an exaggeration. I've spoken to and known writers and painters who don't hold with this, nor do they think of praising everything to do with the state. They are subjective writers, and I have known a good many. Of course there's a sort of conspiracy to believe that this is imposed in a dogmatic, universal, almost military fashion. It's not basically true. But there's also a problem that could be understood. Every revolution must mobilize its deep-rooted strength. A revolution cannot persist without construction and development; the commotion caused by such a great change as that from capitalism to socialism cannot continue to exist unless that revolution exerts all its strength to claim the support of every stratum of society, among which writers, intellectuals, and artists are of the greatest importance. Think of the North American revolution, the war of independence against England, or our own war of independence against Spanish rule. What would have happened if fifty or sixty years later writers had supported the monarchy or the restitution of English rights over the United States, or of the Spanish kings over the old colonies from which the independent republics of Latin America were born. If in the first ten, twenty, thirty, forty, or fifty years, some writer or painter had exalted colonialism, he would have been acting unpatriotically. He would have been persecuted. There's even greater excuse for a revolution that is trying to construct a society from zero, because the transition from capitalism and private property to socialism and communism had never been attempted before. Therefore these new societies, because of their own specific strength, must speak to and mobilize their people, and ask help from thinkers, and even from those with the creative impulse. Conflicts may arise on the way—it is only human and political for that to happen. But I hope that in time, when socialist societies are completely stabilized, they will feel less need for their writers always to be concerned with social problems—although humanism and the love of justice and truth will never be out of fashion—then writers and artists can really follow their most intimate desires.

What work did you do on the International Committee of the Lenin Prize "For the strengthening of peace among nations"?

The Lenin Prize is a distinction given, not for artistic merit, but for the work done by an individual for the cause of world peace. The list is very long, and I couldn't quote the whole of it, but my vote contributed to the prize being given to such eminent personalities as Pablo Picasso, Paul Robeson, Pastor Martin Niemoeller, the Mexican General Lázaro Cárdenas, the Spanish poet Rafael Alberti, the great Brazilian architect Oscar Niemeyer, the French poet Aragon—in fact a great many champions of world peace. In the present struggle, which is not yet over, against nuclear weapons, against the possible destruction of mankind, all these men have shown character and determination. One of the most important works of the contemporary era is Picasso's *Guernica*, a picture with a terrifying antimilitarist, antiwar content. In it one sees the horror of human beings and animals confronted by the destruction and murder that war implies. Picasso was therefore one of those honored by the Lenin Prize. At every moment in recent years when it has seemed that the sparks of another world war were being ignited, the peace movement has carried decisive weight, nor has it stopped playing its part. In this connection the Lenin Prize has outstanding importance. Fourteen or fifteen of us are members of the committee of the prize, many apolitical, others politically oriented. There are religious people, Buddhists, people from India, Poland, Italy, and France, and for a long time I have been the only member of this committee from America. There's no great difficulty in coming to an agreement, as the candidates have been put forward during the previous year, and deliberations are simple. The awards have always been given unanimously. The prizes are not of enormous monetary value—they can't compare with the Nobel Prize—but they carry prestige and have almost always fallen to extremely deserving people.

What are your preferences in the cinema?

First of all I must tell you that there's no cinema and no theater in Isla Negra. The nearest is twenty-five kilometers away, and it always shows very old films, with lots of breaks, and usually Mexican or cowboy films. I've written a short poem on the subject called "To a Village Cinema." Now and again we go to the cinema in Valparaiso or Santiago. Now we've just seen a Vistavision film about the Far West, called *Custer of the West*. It's one of the few films I've seen in the last six months. Sometimes we go three, four, or five months without going to the cinema. The interesting thing about this film is the drastic way it exposes the motives for the move to the West, the move to take over land from the North American Indian tribes. For the first time, it deals with things as they really were; they say let's go and steal from the Indians, let's go and kill the Indians; we won't spare one because we must take the land from them—in fact, more or less what was done everywhere, in Chile too. But I was surprised, because although it romanticized an aggressively military character, it revealed the hidden truth in a truly extraordinary manner. As for the film's general character, it is a super-production with a great many disasters, natural forces unleashed, battles involving an enormous number of people, and so on. There's nothing inventive or new about it, but there is an underlying pulse of action and violence which interested me. What can I say about other films? I met Buñuel in Spain, and I know his early films and some of the latest. Buñuel is a great figure in the cinema, and so is the Swede Bergman; however, my favorite films are still *Miracle in Milan* by Vittorio de Sica in collaboration with Zavattini, and Chaplin's *Gold Rush*. Those are the films I like best and remember best. I was also moved by the recent revival of Laurel and Hardy; they seemed to me to have amazing quality and greatness as actors. When we were young and saw "the fat and the thin" at the cinema we only appreciated them as comic actors, as clowns. But today, having seen so many of their films, even since they died, I feel they have exceptional importance in the development of cinema. They have a special philosophy, a sort of nihilism with a Kafkaesque or Dostoevskian flavor. Truly, they seem to me astonishing.

Weren't you on the jury of some cinema festivals?

No, not on the jury. I was president of a few cinema festivals. I've never been on a cinema jury, nor would I care to be.

You once had occasion to criticize Hollywood films as products of capitalism.

Well, yes. There are large and horrible and horrific defects to be found in the Hollywood cinema, as well as inventions of genius, and, as I've already said, I think that without Hollywood's contribution, the cinema would not have developed with such fantastic speed and to such a colossal size. My personal view is that developments in the cinema confirm the materialistic theory. A period of renaissance and great prosperity has enabled a new class to surround itself with works of art, and a whole stage of human development has been incredibly speeded up. Perhaps the early European cinema would have attained the same magnitude, but much later and more slowly. It was the impulse of North American capitalism that stimulated the cinema's startling progress and gave it the enormous material support that has brought it to its present splendor. Of course the decadence of North American capitalism is also reflected in the poverty of present-day Hollywood and in its gradual demolition as a factory of dreams.

Would you like to comment on the literary media in Latin America?

Two or three points will show my lack of conformity with the reviews or the judgments of living Latin American writers. For I disagree with these reviews and writers, although I often think well of them. To begin with, if one reads periodicals published in Honduras, or in New York in Spanish, or in Montevideo or Guayaquil, one finds that all or almost all of them present the same fashionable literary catalogue. Formerly one would also find Eliot and Kafka, not exactly as literary models, but among the catalogue of accepted writers. They belong to the establishment today. I wouldn't call this sort of thing snobbishness, but I'm very much afraid that this continuous cataloguing has something to do with our cultural colonialization. And it often happens that interest in our own basic Spanish literature, whether from Spain or Latin America, is livelier when our own roots are planted in the soil of the new criticism and new expressions, and when curiosity is reinforced by a recommendation from Europe. We are all seeking Europe's endorsement. For instance, here in Chile—to move momentarily to another sphere, that of domestic life—when the mistress of the house shows you something, like china plates perhaps, she says with a little smile of satisfaction, "It's imported." Certainly some of the horrible china to be seen in thousands of Chilean houses is imported, and it's of the worst kind produced in the factories of Germany and France. Our housewives think these absurd things are objects of the highest quality just because they are imported. That's what is known as being dissatisfied, frustrated, lacking in self-confidence, or mentally lazy, and perhaps all of it comes under the heading of colonialism. Cultural colonialism, the derivation of our values from Europe, our determination to show that we are on a par with the latest model, with what is fashionable, is typical of us and of our sad cultural situation.

Although we are at present experiencing a very interesting and far-reaching literary renaissance, other problems with a political cast have appeared in the last few years. For instance, years ago when I first embarked on literature and also on politics, that's to say forty years ago, everyone was terribly afraid of being taken for a member of the militant left, everyone was terribly afraid of seeming to entertain any revolutionary ideas. I remember the great Chilean writer Joaquín Edwards Bello telling me how a certain writer had been swallowed up by our great capitalist and conservative paper *El Mercurio*, a paper one hundred and fifty years old, whose ideas are three hundred years behind the times. Well, Joaquín Edwards told me that a well-known writer, whose name he gave (but I naturally won't repeat as he's still alive), was taken on as editor of *El Mercurio*; and "Do you know the first thing he did?" Edwards asked me. "This man who had been vaguely revolutionary bought some pomade to make his hair fall out." He was terrified of looking too young and seeming to have new or youthful ideas. Well, in our own decade and especially since the Cuban Revolution, fashions have changed. Writers live in terror of not being taken for members of the militant left. Every one of them pretends to be on the side of the guerrillas, whatever he writes. Many haven't written a line except to say that they are in the front rank of the war against imperialism. Those of us who really have made war against imperialism and have supported the huge efforts of the masses, putting ourselves in the very heart of the people, and contributed our poetry and our pain, our convictions and our doubts for so long a time, are delighted to see that literature is ranging itself on the side of the people; all the same, we feel that if it is a question of fashion, and if it is a question of fear—fear of not being taken for left wing—we shan't get very far with such revolutionaries as they are. Well, within the literary jungle, all sorts of animals are to be found. On one occasion, after I had been offended during a great many years by one, two, three pertinacious persecutors whose aim was to attack my poetry and my way of life, I said: "Let them alone; there's room for everyone in that jungle, and if there's room for such huge animals as elephants in the jungles of Africa and Ceylon, why shouldn't there be room for all the poets in this jungle, which is sometimes less pleasant and less green than the African one?"

What names of contemporary Latin American writers would you mention?

Several new phenomena have appeared, which are talked of everywhere. But there is no harm in underlining them. The great impulse that Cortázar gave Latin American prose has moved like a shooting star through our literature. I've read your interview with Cortázar in *Life en Español*, where he says so many true things and also speaks of his origins as a writer. I've read his list of what had probably influenced him. Of course things may not happen spontaneously, there may be no spontaneous generation in literature (except for Rimbaud, who was a volcano), but it seems to me that considering all his cultural ingredients Cortázar's work is outstanding. Another phenomenon of our recent literature is the Colombian García Márquez. He's a great writer of a different type. He's like a river brimming with water, and what I like best in him is his gift of easy narrative, of telling us stories until we fall asleep. Of course it's difficult to fall asleep with García Márquez because the chain of events is as marvelous as it is inexhaustible. Carlos Fuentes made his entry into literature with a vigorous Mexican step, and it must of course be admitted that Mexico has been a country of great novelists. Peru has also contributed much, from the Inca Garcilaso to Vargas Llosa, who has rediscovered that country. We musn't forget the Mexican Juan Rulfo who, in spite of his silences and small work, is one of the most important writers of our continent. I may be overlooking many others, but generally speaking the novel has made great strides in Latin America. Nor must we forget the previous generation; it would be unfair not to mention Manuel Rojas or the work of José Eustasio Rivera and Rómulo Gallegos, or of men of my own generation such as Miguel Otero Silva, and Fernando Alegría, Jorge Edwards, and José Miguel Varas of Chile, or such profound writers as Sábato and Onetti of Argentina and Uruguay. In fact, the panorama presented by the novel of today and of the recent past has not been equaled for variety and richness for many generations.

What Latin American painting do you like best?

I am an enthusiast for the kinetic arts, or whatever they are called, of painting, sculpture, movement, electricity, and light, which have proliferated in the last few years, and have ardent practitioners among our Latin Americans. The truth is I never really enjoyed painting, or art for art's sake. I wouldn't have known what to do with a Rembrandt in my house, whereas a Le Parc would give me great satisfaction. I admire Le Parc enormously. I'm only sorry there can't be more of his works. When I think about great artists or great objects, I wish they could be spread through the whole of Latin America, my country I mean, my American country. I would like there to be a Le Parc House, a Le Parc Museum, and a Le Parc Gallery. One should be opened in Buenos Aires, another in Chile, others in Caracas, in Guayaquil, in Mexico—in fact everywhere. Other painters, or sculptors or whatever they are called—high priests of modern painting—are Soto and Alejandro Otero from Venezuela. Otero's colossal mobile constructions, using electricity, lighting, and even running water, are truly enchanting monuments that ought to be in every square and park in our America. I have always liked primitive art, from African and Polynesian to contemporary primitive art, which I take as beginning with the greatest of all, the *douanier* Rousseau, but also including an immense number of humble people in Latin America, who do marvelous instinctive paintings. So that I shall skip almost the whole period of abstract painting, which has on rare, very rare occasions interested me deeply, and move straight on to primitive painting, work that reveals the manual ability of the people, a certain natural and communicable imagination, an innocence and richness that fascinate me. Perhaps the truth is that I'm not enough of an artist, and I can ignore great periods of painting without feeling the lack of them. It's not so with the novel and literature of today.

I think you have been a great admirer of Mexican mural painters?

Mexican mural painters were responsible for an astonishing phase in the history of Latin American painting. I admire them greatly. Recent developments in painting, or perhaps the

dominance of kinetic and abstract art, seem to have led to their
being forgotten, but these great Mexican artists not only made
a fabulous contribution to the evolution of Latin American
painting but also created a splendid school with noble themes
and great originality, amounting to a sort of Mexican renaissance. The fact that other schools of painting are attracting
attention today and enriching the horizons of the plastic arts
is evidence for the eternal search for new methods, and it
seems to me that recent Mexican painting has fallen behind
that of other Latin American countries in which painting and
the plastic arts have been developing more vigorously, rather
as if the stage of mural painting had exhausted a certain creative
period in Mexico. At the present time the most vigorous pictorial
—aesthetic—plastic experiments are probably taking place in
Venezuela and Brazil.

*Is there much animosity between intellectuals, and also against
them, in Latin America?*

Intellectual and material underdevelopment have produced maddening animosities. I believe this to be the reason
why many of our writers prefer to live in peace in Europe.
I will never do that, and I've had to face being under constant
attack on that account. I've had professionals—professional de-
tractors—working against me. There's still a troublemaker from
Uruguay who amuses himself after this fashion and the sole
object of whose existence is to figure among my enemies. I have
been pursued by other enmities for about forty years. Sometimes
these came to a conclusion too tragic to be recorded. But on
the whole I have found the intellectual climate of Europe
healthier and its literary atmosphere purer. Perhaps their great
cities stifle all passions and ambitions, and therefore extra-literary
intrigue as well. Because of my status as a man completely
committed to the people's struggle, I cannot abandon my country.
It would be like abandoning myself. I am essentially a patriot
in the organic sense that my country, its land and its people,
form part of me, and these are not empty words. This is how
I feel, and this is how I live. For this reason I have had to
drag about with me an endless train of professional ill-wishers.

I have hardly even answered their attacks, or at most have answered very briefly, as though to encourage the adverse current a little. A reporter once asked me what was my relationship with my enemies and I replied: "Please don't think I egg them on as a form of propaganda." But it would almost seem so, to judge by the persistence of some of them. They have gone to incredible lengths. They have accused me of all the crimes in the calendar. They've accused me of being poor and being rich, of outrageous originality and plagiarism, of contumaciousness, of being a thief, a swindler, insincere, and a bigamist; in fact, I won't go on, as I can't remember all the crimes I've been accused of. Any writer so persecuted, quite apart from political persecution, would really have no time left for writing if he undertook the enormous task of defending himself. Luckily I haven't defended myself, and so perhaps I've had more time to attend to my own affairs.

Do you think there is an ideological unity among Latin American intellectuals?

I think there is a certain ideological unity. Few writers in Latin America are openly on the side of the old order. Most of our writers have a revolutionary outlook on society. That speaks well for our continent and also for the wisdom of our people, for writers all over this continent are in one way or another involved with the development of our nations, the exploitation and sufferings of our peoples. In this respect Chile has led the way for many years. We have never had an important writer who was a reactionary, who belonged to the right.

What do you feel about the "exiled" Latin American writers?

This is a problem that has been much discussed because some of our more important writers—great and good and young writers of the new generation—live in Europe, though their hearts are in Latin America and their work reflects the life of our countries. It's a serious question, because Latin American writers used formerly to go into exile, as you say. That is to say, they transplanted themselves, with the sole purpose of forgetting their country, their origins, their race, and their conflicts—consigning them to oblivion. Some of our most distinguished writers went so far as to write their names in French, like the poet Vicente Huidobro, who signed some of his books Vincent Huidobro and wrote them in French. There are other writers in Latin America who have spent a lot of time in France and used also to write in French. Of course a writer can write in another language than his own, and we have some extraordinary instances, such as Joseph Conrad, an exiled Pole who took English as his literary language and wrote great and original books in it. But this transplantation of men who took their work and their lives to Europe has been painful to us Latin Americans; their desertion hurt us, because it was not only a question of language—they were ashamed of our poor downtrodden America. For the generation of writers who are now living far from America, such as the Peruvian Vargas Llosa, the Argentine Julio Cortázar, or the Colombian García Márquez, a change of planet, of country, of continent, seems to have made them more national in outlook, given them more subjects from the land and life of our people. How, then, can one condemn their attitude? It would be completely irrational. Naturally it lends itself to discussion—long, almost interminable discussion. The reason for their ostrichlike behavior may be a desire to work in peace. In our own continent, when work becomes important it creates antibodies produced by incredible meanness, spite, and envy. People who devote themselves entirely to persecuting us, who go from country to country making trouble for us, harming us, creating dark legends about us, are to be found among the small-minded petit bourgeois writers of Latin America. This is the reason, or unreason, explaining why some writers say: "All right, I'm bored with this, I'm tired and I'm off. I'm going where I shall be allowed to work in peace."

However there is another side to the coin. It is our duty to work actively and in unity with our people, with our nation, in order to achieve that transformation of society we aspire to. That is the state of affairs, but if there are many who have no vocation for such active strife, I can understand it. My own life has been different. I have been in the thick of a great many contests, yet I have been able to work. Very few writers have been as savagely attacked as I have, but I have been able to go on with my work. I don't repine, and with every day that passes I feel that my life has been an honorable one, and that if I had to choose my own life over again I should choose the one I have had.

In an article called "My Contemporaries," Ernesto Montenegro writes: "It is frankly absurd, the dream of the Uruguayan critic Rodríguez Monegal when he expresses the vain hope that present-day European and North American writers study the work of their colleagues in Latin America if they want to achieve the renovation of their own literature. The ant says to the elephant: 'Climb on my shoulders.' " Then he quotes from Borges's introduction to his Personal Anthology: "*Unlike the barbarous United States, this country (this continent) has not produced a single writer of world importance—an Emerson or Whitman or a Poe—nor yet a great esoteric writer, a Henry James or a Melville.*"

This sort of thing seems to me quite unimportant. One of the signs of the provincialism of our Latin American continent is that we devote ourselves more eagerly to making a name than to working and creating modestly and humbly. What does it matter whether or not we possess names such as Whitman, Baudelaire, or Kafka in our America? The history of literature is as long as the history of humanity and as broad as the whole world. We can't affix labels, one here, one there. The United States, with its prosperous and literate population, and Europe, with a tradition thousands of years old and an enormous population, can't be compared with the millions deprived of books and means of expression of our Latin America. What proportion of our people is capable of producing writers? Of the 250 to 350 million inhabitants of Latin America, the number producing work in the realm of the arts and literature is so small that I daren't mention it. While a vast literate population with a cultural inheritance from many lands was working in the United States or in Europe, the uncultured millions of Latin America (many of them quite illiterate) have produced the same enormous inequality of education among us as might be found in a small town. To throw stones at each other, or spend one's life hoping to outdo this or that other continent seems to me a provincial attitude. Besides, these opinions may be entirely personal. There are many Latin American books that I prefer to European and North American ones, just as there are many North American novelists and European writers I prefer to many South Americans. I don't like this business of parceling out culture and cutting it into chunks; it seems to me a provincial failing. I also think that it is completely futile to hope that Latin America will produce a philosopher or a great essayist. Only countries that have achieved cultural maturity or inherited an ancient civilization can indulge in the luxury of establishing a new and profound examination of ideas. People here are eager to write essays or philosophy, but there is no room for these in a continent of pioneers which has only recently begun to develop. We have also had to bear the weight of the Spanish colonization, a weight of ignorance and reaction, with the entry of books prohibited until 1810. Later, we inherited from the colony a large population without books, schools, or any hope of obtaining them. All this is going to change. The landscape of these countries will change, and I feel sure that the spread of culture will develop normally and calmly, as it does everywhere. And besides, you can say of a great many countries that they possess no Emerson or Whitman. I don't know where you'll find the Emersons and Whitmans in a great many countries I don't wish to name. I don't like these microbiotic examinations under the microscope—they seem to me essentially lacking in subtlety, in true foundation. All this is irrelevant. Instead I would like to trace the contribution writers are making to cultural development in Latin America, the struggle to educate the masses, the struggle for knowledge and for culture to be made available to all. That's what I would like. That's something we can agree about. Of course it is a very long process, and neither the Spanish colonists nor the Creole oligarchies were interested in speeding it up, because they wanted to have plenty of farm laborers and slaves. Now we are in a revolutionary period, in which the people's parties have undertaken to accelerate the spread of culture in this continent, and that is something really important.

But do you think that Europe could look to Latin American literature for its own revival?

They are doing so, according to what I learn from the literary reviews and European cultural circles. They are looking, after a fashion. I don't know—but my books have been published everywhere in Europe. In some countries, like Italy, twenty of my books have been published. But how important is that? Isn't "being" more important than "seeming"? What matters to our countries is work, creation, production. All these arguments get us nowhere. Perhaps they might do for after-dinner conversation, but they lack fundamental interest for me.

Does the fact that the Catholic University has made you a Doctor of Science and Honoris Causa show that there is a new influence at work within the Catholic Church in Chile?

The Cardinal of Chile, Raúl Silva Henríquez, certainly expressed himself very plainly on this subject, probably in reply to some objection. I will read what he said: "My personal opinion is that the poet deserves this honor without any doubt whatever. I think that in granting it the University is making a gesture which may be misunderstood by the foolish, but will be respected by the rest. Our attitude in this matter reflects values of the utmost importance, values that the Church of today ardently desires to express in its behavior and its way of life. The first value is that it has been shown and will be believed, once and for all, that the Church appreciates truth, goodness, and beauty, even when they are to be found in those who do not share her religious convictions. In other words, the Catholic Church and Christianity cannot by their very nature be sectarian: we abjure sectarianism in the deepest core of our being. Here a sane pluralism takes root . . . And what does that signify? Is it possible to have a chair of atheism or Marxism in a Catholic university? I say yes, it is possible, because we Christians are convinced that there is not one of these sciences and doctrines which does not express a part of the truth, and sometimes confront us with criticisms which are most useful for us to know . . . I also think it indispensable for us to recognize the attitudes and worth of those who, out of sincere conviction, have devoted themselves to defending the rights of humble people; and for our recognition to be so clearly expressed as to be beyond all misconception."

Cardinal Silva Henríquez's words seem to me decisive. I think they show so great a change, such progress in the application or revision of the doctrines of the Church, that they must have a profound effect on the ideological climate and the impact between ideas, in my country at least. We have a large Catholic party here, from which a sizable group of militant Catholics recently has separated because they found that the influence of capitalism and imperialism was increasing in the Democratic Christian Party, and that there was a tendency to be allied with these systems instead of fighting them. I think the Church has had an influence on such decisions, the influence initiated some time earlier by Pope John XXIII, so that we can clearly see that in the future the best Christian and Catholic forces in Chile will form an alliance with the great political Marxist forces to bring about a true revolution.

What advice would you give young poets?

Oh! I have no advice to give young poets. They must make their own way. They will find difficulties in expressing themselves, and they must fight against them. But I would never advise them to begin with political poetry. Political poetry should emanate from profound emotion and convictions. Political poetry is more deeply emotional than any other except love poetry, and it cannot be forced without becoming vulgar and unacceptable. You must have traversed the whole of poetry before you become a political poet. And a political poet must be ready to take all the blame heaped on him for betraying poetry and literature by serving a definite cause. Therefore political poetry must arm itself internally with enough substance and content and emotional and intellectual richness to defy anything of the sort. It seldom succeeds.

You are intensely responsive to nature . . .

I think that when writers are separated from nature by being absorbed into great cities, it kills something in their lives. I

said of the novel *Doctor Zhivago* that the only thing I valued in
it was Pasternak's marvelous power of communicating with nature.
If a poet doesn't hold such a communication, he loses a great
deal. Of course, life in the towns and the life of human beings are
also necessary material for a modern writer.

*Have you always been interested in birds, shells, plants, and nature
in general?*

Since my earliest childhood I have loved birds, shells,
woods, and plants. I have been all over the place looking for sea-
shells, as far as the Gulf of California, the coasts of Venezuela,
the southern seas of Chile. I was able to get a fine collection.
Nothing could have been more mysterious, nothing more fascinating to me, while I collected and hunted, than the infinite
diversity of these marine creatures. Their colors, their astonishing,
incredible shapes, their stylistic kinship with the countries they
came from. My collection of shells actually began when a famous
malacologist, Don Carlos de la Torre, an old Cuban scholar who
is now dead, made me a present of the nucleus of his own private
collection; he had already founded the collection in the Havana
Museum. Don Carlos also presented me with a collection of
polymites, those Cuban mollusks which live in the moss on trees.
Polymites are of the most fiery colors, from lemon yellow to
blazing red. Some seem as if they were sprinkled with salt, others
with pepper. I've also studied the life of birds; I followed them
in woods and the jungle. I wrote a book called *Arte de pájaros*
(The Art of Birds). I hunted for plants as well as animals, I
wrote my *Bestiario* (*Bestiary*), my "Maremoto" (Seaquake) and
my *La rosa del herbolario* (The Herbalist's Rose), dedicated to
flowers and fronds and vegetable growth. This whole world,
palpitating with life and shape, has always had an immense appeal
to me, to my feelings, the direction taken by my poetry, my life
itself. I couldn't live apart from nature. I enjoy hotels for a few
days, I like airplanes for an hour, but I am only really happy in
woods, or on the beach, or sailing. I'm happy when I'm in direct
contact with fire, earth, water, and air.

These days at Isla Negra have shown me a Pablo Neruda who is known to very few people, I believe; someone gay, with a great sense of humor and an enjoyment of life which you communicate to everyone around you.

My poetry has passed through the same stages as my life, and after a very lonely childhood and an isolated adolescence in far-off countries, I emerged and became part of the great crowd of humanity. My life matured, that's all there is to it. I think it was the fashion of the last century for poets to be tortured by melancholy, and many of them used to die of tuberculosis, or at least very young. Well, I've done my best to contradict those nineteenth-century ideals. This is an age of realist and vital poets who belong to no school. Of poets who have known life, who have known problems, and who have to live by crossing every stream. And they have to make their way through sadness to maturity.

JORGE LUIS BORGES

JORGE LUIS BORGES

Cambridge, Mass.   January 15-20, 1968

When Borges was a guest lecturer at Harvard I called him asking for an interview. A week later I met him in his Cambridge apartment where he was living with his wife. He had married—at sixty-nine for the first time, a marriage that ended in divorce shortly thereafter.

Borges comes from an intellectual, upper middle class Argentine family and he looks the part, dressing in a conservative fashion, behaving with old-fashioned politesse. While he looks pale and fragile, his voice is deep and vibrant like a much younger man's. In spite of his busy schedule he used to take long walks through the Cambridge streets he loves so much; the cold and snow didn't stop him from walking every day to his office and returning to his apartment for lunch. When I accompanied him on some of these daily strolls he would reminisce about his daily walks through the streets of Buenos Aires, or comment on the old brick houses in Boston, or recite old English sagas in the original Anglo-Saxon.

Near-blind, he has an excellent memory and an acute sense of direction. Sometimes he insisted on walking me to my hotel, a block away from his apartment, never hesitating to return by himself; he could point out the exact spot in the bookcase where one of his books could be located, or would swiftly cross the room to answer the phone or a knock at the door. He was invited to appear on a Boston TV show, and when he was leaving his apartment the taxi driver who was waiting for him at the door said, "I'm here to pick up a blind man." Borges, undisturbed, responded, "I'm the blind man. One moment, please."

He can be as warm and charming as he can be elusive and ironic. When a visitor told him, "Poetry is my hobby," he replied, "It's mine too, but in a South American way." During my week-long interview his moods changed from serenity to anxiety to cheerfulness to an extreme childlike impatience. When the Life photographer didn't arrive the day he was expected, Borges became very restless; when we met a year later it was the first thing he joked about. He listened to my tapes with a boyish enjoyment after I had recorded his casual poetry readings.

At a dinner with his Harvard and Radcliffe students he was cheerful and friendly. According to them, Borges got them so interested in Latin America that they didn't care if they could not discuss contemporary politics with him. As one student summarized his feeling: "He is a present-day figure, much more avantgarde than many of his contemporaries. Because he is not faddish, he continues to be fresh and new."

Borges's writing does reflect his lack of interest in the contemporary world, for he lives in another world, a world of fantasies, mirrors, daggers, labyrinths, imaginary things. But he did speak to me in his beautiful Spanish, with ease and nostalgia, about his life, his work, his dearest friends. To highlight his comments he recited coplas and milongas or asked me to read some of his long poems that he had not memorized.

Reticent about his private life, he alludes to "two Borges"— one the man, the other the writer—and he describes them in his essay "Borges and I." ("The other one, the one called Borges, is the one things happen to.") But the two, the person and "the other one," sometimes become fused. Borges, the man, was moved to tears when in 1971 Columbia University gave him an honorary degree. And, as he confessed in "Borges and I": "It should be an exaggeration to say that ours is a hostile relationship; I live, let myself go on living, so that Borges may contrive his literature, and this literature justifies me."

What effect has the loss of your sight had on your life and work?

On my father's side I belong to the fifth, or possibly sixth generation that included many who lost their sight. I watched my father and my grandmother go blind. My own sight was never good, and I knew what fate had in store for me. I was also able to admire the combination of submissiveness and irony with which my father endured his blindness for more than a year. Perhaps this forbearance is as typical of the blind as irritability is typical of the deaf; maybe a blind man senses the friendliness of the people around him. One proof of this is that there are lots of comic stories about deaf people and none about the blind. It would be too cruel to joke about the blind. I've quite lost count of the operations they have performed on me, and by 1955, when the revolutionary government appointed me director of the National Library, I was no longer able to read. That was when I wrote my "Poem of Gifts," in which I said that God "with magnificent irony, gave me books and darkness at the same time." The books were the 800,000 volumes of the National Library, and I have been getting closer to total darkness ever since that time. But it has hardly been a painful process, because dusk came so very slowly. There was a moment when I could only read books with large print, and then another when I could only read the title page or the words on the spine, and then another when I could read nothing at all. A slow dusk, which wasn't especially painful to me. And now I can still see, but very little; I can't see your face at this moment, but there is an immeasurable difference between seeing very little and not seeing at all. A person who can't see at all is like a prisoner, whereas I can see enough to go about the town—whether it's Cambridge or Buenos Aires—with a certain illusion of liberty. Of course, I can't cross a street without help, and as people are very polite in New England and in Buenos Aires, they generally offer to help of their own accord when they see me hesitating on the edge of the sidewalk.

My blindness has certainly had an effect on my "work," in quotes. I've never written a novel because I think that as a novel has a consecutive existence for the reader it may also have a purely consecutive existence for the writer. On the other hand, a story is something that you take in at a single reading. As Poe used to say: "There's no such thing as a long poem." Poe wrote a number of short poems. The fact that I like to take great trouble over my writing has made me abandon story writing and return to classical poetic forms, because rhyme has mnemonic value. If I know the first line it gives me the fourth where the rhyme recurs. So I've returned to regular verse forms, because a sonnet is a portable thing, as it were. I can go on walking all over the town while I carry a sonnet in my head, polishing and altering as I go. You can't do that with a long piece of prose. I also write verses for *milongas* and other short compositions—such as fables and parables—taking up about a page or a page and a half; these too can be carried in the head, and dictated and corrected later.

There's another thing I would like to mention, and that is that time passes differently when one has lost one's sight. Formerly, if I took a train journey of half an hour or so it used to seem interminable, and I had to read or do something to pass the time. Whereas now that there are inevitable hours of solitude in my life, I've got used to being alone and thinking about something, or else I simply don't think and am merely content to exist. I let time flow past me, and it seems to pass differently. I'm not sure whether it goes faster, but it certainly contains a sort of serenity and much more concentration. Also I have a better memory than I did before; that may be because I used to read superficially, knowing that I could always come back to the book. But if I ask someone to read to me nowadays, I can't keep on pestering him. When someone reads aloud to me I listen more attentively than before. My memory was naturally visual, but now I've had to learn the art of auditory memory. When I could see a little, I used to open a book and know instinctively that what I had read was, let us say, at the bottom of one of the odd pages, and its general whereabouts in the book. Now I have to manage differently. I've got quite a good memory and I began learning Old English in 1955, when I could no longer read. Since then I've held a seminar in Old English for a small group of students. Once I got them to draw on the blackboard in the National Library the two runic letters representing the sound *th* in Anglo-Saxon. I know hundreds of lines of Anglo-Saxon verse by heart, but I couldn't clearly imagine the page they were written on. The students drew them very large, in chalk, and now I have some idea what those unseen pages look like.

From some of your poems, such as "Another Poem of Gifts," and "New England 1967," in which you say "And America is waiting for me at every corner," I gather that you feel affection for the United States.

Ever since the days of my childhood, when I read Mark Twain, Bret Harte, Hawthorne, Jack London, and Edgar Allan Poe, I've been very much attached to the United States. I still am. Perhaps I'm influenced by the fact that I had an English grandmother, and English and Spanish were spoken indiscriminately in our house when I was a boy, so much so that I wasn't even aware that they were separate languages. When I was talking to my paternal grandmother I had to speak in a manner that I afterwards discovered was called English, and when I was talking to my mother or her parents I had to talk a language that afterwards turned out to be Spanish. My affection for the United States makes me deplore the fact that many Latin Americans, and very likely many North Americans as well, admire the United States for the wrong things. For instance, when I think of the United States I visualize those New England houses, houses built of red brick, or else the sort of wooden Parthenons one sees in the South; I think of a way of life, and also of writers who have meant a lot to me. First of all I think of Whitman, Thoreau, Melville, Henry James, and Emerson. But I notice that most people admire this country for its gadgets, its supermarkets and things like paper bags—even garbage bags—and plastics. All these things are perishable, however, and are made for use, not for worship. It seems to me that we should praise or condemn the United States for quite different things. You live here, and I don't suppose you spend all your time thinking about gadgets. And perhaps the streets of New England are more typically American than the skyscrapers, or anyhow people love them more. What I'm trying to say is that it's important to see this side of America too. Although I prefer New England, when I was in New York I felt enormously proud of it, and thought to myself: "Good Lord, how well the city has turned out," just as if I'd built it myself. In my poem "Another Poem of Gifts," I praise God for many things, and among others:

For the hard riders who, on the plains,
Drive on the cattle and the dawn,
For mornings in Montevideo . . .
For the high towers of San Francisco and Manhattan Island . . .

And also for mornings in Texas, for Emerson's poetry, for the events of my life, for music, for English poetry; for my grand- mother, my English grandmother, who when she was dying called us all to her side and said: "Nothing in particular is happening. I'm only an old woman who is dying very, very slowly; there's no reason for the whole house to worry about it. I have to apologize to you all." What a beautiful thing!

> *For Frances Haslam, who begged her children's pardon*
> *For dying so slowly,*
> *For the minutes that precede sleep,*
> *For sleep and death,*
> *Those two hidden treasures,*
> *For the intimate gifts I do not mention,*
> *For music, that mysterious form of time.**

My grandmother was the wife of Colonel Borges, who was killed in action in the revolution of 1874. She had seen life on the frontier among the Indians, and had talked to their chief, Pincén. That was at Junín.

Why do you think the American way of life is being copied every- where?

I think it's part of a general trend. When I was born— in 1899—the world, or Argentina and Buenos Aires at least, looked toward France. That is to say, although we were Argentines we were Frenchmen at heart, or playing at being French. But now the trend is to look toward the United States. This is re- flected in everything: in sports, in people's way of life, in the fact that they used to get drunk on absinthe and now prefer to do it on whiskey, and even when the whiskey is Scotch they think of it as American. It makes no difference. Politics has become so important that at present two countries stand out from the rest, quite apart from our preferences or dislikes. Those two countries are the United States and the Soviet Union. Of course, I per- sonally love England very much and I would like it if people also looked toward England, but I realize that's not happening. In

---

* From *Jorge Luis Borges: Selected Poems 1923–1967*, ed. by Norman Thomas di Giovanni (New York: Delacorte, 1972). Reprinted by per- mission.

the world of today, those two countries stand for history, and are in conflict. We have reached a state of war between the two trends and one or the other will prevail—democracy or communism, or rather what is called democracy and what is called communism.

With which country do you feel most identified—with France, where your talent was first recognized, or with the United States?

With the United States. I am not against France. How could I suggest that we forget the country that produced Voltaire, Verlaine, and Hugo? Without French culture we should not have had the literary renewal called Modernism, we should have had no Rubén Darío, no Lugones. I can never disown the culture of any country. I was educated in Switzerland, and got my baccalaureate in Geneva during the First World War. Although I am very fond of Switzerland, I don't feel identified with that country. Nor, of course, do I want to say a single word against France, yet I wouldn't care to live there either . . . oh well, the fact is I wouldn't like to live anywhere except the Argentine Republic. If I couldn't live in Buenos Aires, my second choice would be Montevideo, which is much the same. Here in the States, I feel homesick for Buenos Aires—that's only too obvious in everything I've written recently. This doesn't mean that Buenos Aires seems to me a particularly beautiful town; on the contrary, I think it's really rather drab. That has nothing to do with it; one doesn't love a town for its architecture.

When did you first come to the United States?

Six years ago. I came with my mother; we spent five months in Texas and I taught Argentine literature there. But I was a student as well as a professor, and attended Dr. Willard's classes in Old English. After that we went to New Mexico, Arizona, and San Francisco—one of the most beautiful cities in the world—and Los Angeles, which is one of the most horrible.

Is this your first visit to Harvard?

I gave a lecture at Harvard a few years ago, but I can't remember much about it; it was just something that turned up.

This is my first official visit. I am the Charles Eliot Norton Professor of Poetry, and some of my distinguished forerunners have been e. e. cummings and the great Spanish poet Jorge Guillén. I was invited to lecture on poetry. I've taken a line from Yeats as my theme and the title of my lectures—"This Craft of Verse." I also gave a course on Argentine poetry here at Harvard.

What can you tell me about your months at Harvard?

I've met with a hospitality, a warmth here that has really amazed me; it has almost frightened me. I've heard applause such as I've never before heard in my life. I have been cheered in Buenos Aires, but partly out of amiability. Here the applause has been so warm-hearted that it has astonished me. I don't know what the reason for this is and I've been trying to think of an explanation. To a certain extent, my being blind may have helped me, although I'm not really entitled to the description because I can still see your face, even if only as a hazy shape. Then there's the fact that I'm a foreigner. Perhaps a foreigner always gets a warmer reception, because he can't be anyone's rival, he's someone who appears and will disappear again. Then I think there may be another reason. Usually when a Latin American or a Spaniard comes here he keeps on emphasizing the exceptional merit of what is being done in his own country, whereas when I give lectures on poetry I take my examples from English poets, Scandinavian poets, Latin, Spanish, and American poets, so they don't feel that I'm "selling anything" as you say here, but am someone who is genuinely interested in poetry. All this may have helped me.

Is there much interest in Argentine literature?

Yes, a great deal. However, I've discovered that very little is known about it, because the teachers are generally Spaniards, who are naturally more inclined to tell about what is being written on the other side of the Atlantic. Or else, if they are Cubans or Mexicans, of course they teach what is nearer at hand and what they themselves like best. Whereas we Argentines are such a long way off that naturally very little is known about us. So very little that when I mention a name like Lugones, for instance, I notice that the students stare at me rather strangely. They have never heard of him.

Which writers did you teach?

I thought that what always interested foreigners most was local color. So, as we have a quite striking literature of this type, I began by talking about the gauchesco poets. I talked about Bartolomé Hidalgo, Hilario Ascasubi, Estanislao del Campo, and José Hernández. I devoted more than one class to *Martín Fierro*, and another to the gaucho novels of Eduardo Gutiérrez; I also talked about *Don Segundo Sombra*, whose author, Ricardo Güiraldes, was a great friend of mine. Then I told them about Sarmiento, Almafuerte, Lugones, Martínez Estrada, Enrique Banchs, and something about Bioy Casares, Carlos Mastronardi, and Manuel Peyrou. You will think that I was unfair to many people, but I preferred the study of a few writers to the listing of many after the manner of a telephone directory. It would be pointless to say that there was a famous poet called Rafael Obligado, give his dates, say that he wrote *Santos Vega*, and pass on to the next. That's no use to anyone. Instead, we read the first part of *Martín Fierro*, many things by Ascasubi, and as for Lugones, I succeeded in interesting my students a great deal in him. I reminded them that in 1907 Lugones had published a book of tales, called *Las fuerzas extrañas* (Strange Forces), and that two of these stories, written under the influence of Wells and Poe, approached what is called science fiction today and, what's more, were very good. One striking story, *Yzur*, is about a monkey, who learns to speak and goes mad in the process. It's a very tragic tale. This sort of science fiction was not being written in Spanish in the year 1907. I've also been delighted to find that my students take an interest in writers who are Argentines but not professionally so. This morning a girl told me she was working on a thesis on Enrique Banchs. He's a great Argentine poet who doesn't try to be particularly Argentine. He writes admirable sonnets with an unconscious Argentine flavor. Other students have brought me theses about the *Lunario sentimental* by Leopoldo Lugones and Banchs's *La urna*. It's clear that these students don't read Argentine books as documents about a far-off and picturesque country; they are in search of literature.

This morning, in the coffee shop, you were very pleased when one of your students told you about the work he was doing on Carlos Mastronardi.

Carlos Mastronardi means a lot to me, and I was very much moved to think that this great poet and friend should be the subject of a New England student's thoughts. He was going to write about the poem "Luz de provincia" (Light of the Province), dedicated to the province of Entre Rios, and almost the only work by Mastronardi. It's a poem I've read with love all through the years, and a line occurs in it which I always remember with pleasure: "the beloved, the gentle, the beloved province"; the word "beloved" returns as if the poet felt it to be the last word, as if he was tired of searching for adjectives and returned to his own love for his province.

In what language did you teach Argentine literature?

In Spanish, and I would say the students' Spanish was good. Of course, my own is less Mexican, less Cuban, and less Spanish than theirs. That's only to be expected, isn't it? But they can follow the classes, and what is more important still, they can tell if a poem is good or bad. I don't think a professor ought to praise everything he teaches, or his students may begin to be a little suspicious. When we were reading the poems of Lugones and I came across a line I didn't like, I either said so or left it to them to find out. I think I succeeded in creating an atmosphere of give-and-take between us, and not just telling them that So-and-So was a great poet and that they must accept him as such. I also achieved my main object: I got them to enjoy Almafuerte, to enjoy Hernández, Lugones, and Banchs. I think this is more important than anything else. When one of my students enjoys these writers, I feel I have achieved something.

Is there a good understanding between you and your students?

I've found the atmosphere very welcoming. Something very strange happens. When I'm talking to the students here at Harvard I forget that I'm speaking English and that I'm at Harvard, and I feel just as if I were talking to my friends in Buenos Aires. They seem to me so alike! I have the same impression of conversation, of discussion, that I remember so well in Buenos Aires. When I'm talking to my students I refuse to be so pedantic as to think of them as students and myself as their professor; we begin to discuss some literary topic and then we become two human beings talking about what interests us. I don't even feel tempted to talk didactically, or give them advice; it's a conversation in which we are both really collaborating. I very much enjoy talking to young people. And I realize from their questions that I am in very intelligent company, and that the students here seem less interested in examinations and degrees than in what they are studying. That's terrific. I've met some people who know my work much better than I do myself, because I only wrote the words once and they have read them several times and tried to analyze them, whereas when I write something I publish it in order to forget about it. They have asked me quite difficult questions showing their interest in the subject, though sometimes I find them puzzling. Often it's because I've forgotten the details of what I've written, and when I'm asked "Why did So-and-So remain silent for a while and then begin to talk?" I say: "Who?" I don't remember the character, and I don't remember why he was doing what he did at that moment. I've also been asked some very intelligent questions. Students found hidden affinities in texts that I thought were very far removed from one another. For instance, they made me see that a story I wrote about the labyrinth had links with a certain detective story, something I hadn't realized myself.

Do you find great differences between American and Argentine students?

On the whole I think that one of the diseases of our time consists in exaggerating the differences between one country and another. I believe young people are much the same everywhere. Possibly Argentine students are more timid than Americans. Here a student can interrupt one and ask a question, but that may be because it's understood here that a student who questions his professor is not doing it out of impertinence but because the subject interests him. In Buenos Aires maybe they think a student asks questions so as to make a nuisance of himself.

Isn't this the result of the attitude of professors in Argentina?

Perhaps. Although I've maintained that it wasn't so, I have found it very difficult to get a classroom discussion going back home. Of course, I prefer discussing with my students rather than laying down the law. I have the impression that they work harder here. At home, as a result of university reform, there were some very idle people who only worked for their examinations. For instance, I was present at an examination when the professor asked one of the students what subject he had chosen. What sort of way is that to conduct an examination? And I remember one girl taking an essay she had brought with her out of her case, and reading it. I interrupted her and said: "Young lady, this is the Faculty of Philosophy and Letters; there's no need for you to prove to us that you can read and write. You chose your subject yourself, why don't you speak about it?" And some of the professors said: "Oh well, we shouldn't expect so much."

What do you think about the hippies and drug-taking?

I don't think either hippies or drugs deserve any encouragement. They seem to me to represent something typical of the United States. In spite of all his good qualities, an American has a tendency to solitude, or rather he's a victim of solitude. I'm reminded of a book by David Riesman, called *The Lonely Crowd*. One of the advantages we Latin Americans have over North Americans is that we can communicate more easily, whereas I've noticed that North Americans experience a difficulty in communication which they try to conceal by means of all their celebrations, like Christmas, and by forming a lot of societies and holding congresses where people wear a little label with their name written on it. All this seems to me a rather pathetic pretense of friendship, or of being among other people, perhaps every one of whom is really very lonely. You notice the same thing in the English, except that an Englishman doesn't mind being alone; he's comfortable when he's alone. I've known of intimate friends in England who have never once confided in each other, yet feel they are friends. Anything I say about hippies, however, is quite valueless, because I've never talked to one in my life. People have drawn my attention to a rather exotically dressed young man in the street, and told me, "That's a hippie"; I pretend to see him but I don't, and afterwards they tell me he has long hair and a beard, and takes drugs. I don't think any of that is much good, nor that it will lead them very far. It's always the same: if someone is against a convention his only way of attacking it is by creating another convention, so that when most people are clean-shaven he grows a beard, and when beards are worn he shaves his off. He's merely changing from one convention to another. I remember that the first night I went out after my arrival, I was told that there were groups of young people dressed with careful extravagance, and that they were hippies. Generalizing as usual, I wondered how I was going to teach Argentine literature to these young people who had resolved to disagree with everything; but when I held my first class I realized that this wasn't so, that not a single one was a hippie.

They disagree with the establishment and the consumers' society.

Yes, and they want to connect this with Thoreau, don't they? I've read Veblen's book, *The Theory of the Leisure Class*, in which he says that one of the characteristics of modern society is that people have to spend money conspicuously, and thus impose a number of obligations on themselves. They have to live in a certain part of town, they must spend their holidays at a certain beach. Veblen says that a tailor in London or Paris receives an exaggerated sum because what people want of him is precisely that his goods should be very expensive. Or, for instance, a painter may paint a contemptible picture, but as he's a famous artist he sells it for an enormously high figure, because the purpose of buying it is that the buyer can say, "I've got a Picasso." Naturally I believe this sort of thing should be opposed, and if the hippies think they can fight it, more power to them. Meanwhile I myself don't hold any of these superstitions. I don't believe one must live in a certain district or dress in a certain fashion.

The hippies also rebel against violence. Do you agree with them about that?

That seems to me an excellent thing. It's rather the same as what Lanza del Vasto used to preach. He gave a lecture in the National Library and spoke in favor of passive resistance. I was foolish enough to ask him: "Tell me, do you believe passive resistance is infallible?" The reply he made was very reasonable. "No," he said, "passive resistance is just as fallible as active resistance. I believe one should attempt it, but it's not a panacea." "Do you believe that passive resistance would have had any effect against the Soviet dictatorship, or Hitler, or Perón?" "Probably not; all the same you take the risk." It's a means to an end which can't be guaranteed, and the hippies seem to think likewise.

Toynbee has said that hippies are the product of technology and science. Do you agree?

It's easier to say that they are the product of technology and science after they've appeared on the scene. The interesting thing would have been to say so before.

Would you say that an Argentine has a distinct identity, just as a modern Frenchman, a Mexican, or American has, for instance?

People often confuse the difficulty of definition with the difficulty of the problems themselves. In this case it would be very hard to define an Argentine, just as it is hard to define the color red, the taste of coffee, or the quality of epic poetry. All the same, we Argentines know, or rather feel, what it means to be Argentines, and that's much more important than any definition. We feel without needing to define it that an Argentine is different from a Spaniard, a Colombian, or a Chilean, and that he differs very little from a Uruguayan. I think that ought to satisfy us, because one doesn't generally conduct one's life by means of definitions so much as by direct intuitions. Although it's hard to define the Argentine way of talking, no sooner does a person start speaking than one knows if he's an Argentine or not, and which region he comes from. I believe we recognize the Argentine flavor, not only in gaucho poetry or the novels of Gutiérrez or Güiraldes, which have deliberately aimed at it, but also in poets who don't set out to be Argentine, who are not professionally and incessantly Argentine. Everyone feels that a poem by Fernández Moreno is an Argentine poem, and I hope that my own pages give a feeling that I'm an Argentine, especially those pages devoid of local color. If I write an article on some abstract problem, or if I discuss some metaphysical theme, my way of doing it is different from what a Spaniard's would be, my syntax is different—one might almost say my tone of voice is different. This is why I believe that although there is such a thing as being Argentine, there's no point in trying to define it. If we did, we should afterwards be pinned to the definition, and no longer be spontaneous Argentines. It's just the same with the language. When I began writing I wanted to write classical seventeenth-century Spanish; afterwards I bought a dictionary of Argentine expressions and became studiously Argentine. Later on I wrote a story like "Hombre de la esquina rosada." (Streetcorner Man), in which I tried to be picturesque and exaggerated the local color. Now I think I've caught the Argentine accent; there's no need to search for it when writing or speaking, because I've got it.

Would you call yourself a typical Argentine?

The fact is that I don't know whether a *typical* Argentine exists; I don't know if there is an Argentine archetype. To say I identify myself with a country is a bit of a fraud; in Buenos Aires I identify myself with six or seven people whom I see all the time. Above all with certain habits: mornings walking down Calle Florida, afternoons walking to the Southside to the National Library.

Have you ever thought of leaving Buenos Aires?

I couldn't live anywhere but Buenos Aires. I'm used to it, just as I'm used to my own voice, to my body, to being Borges, to that series of habits that's known as Borges—and one part of these habits is Buenos Aires. My real life is in Buenos Aires; and besides I'm nearly seventy, it would be absurd for me to want to start a new life elsewhere. Nor have I any reason to do so. My mother lives in Buenos Aires; my sister, my nephews, my friends are all in Buenos Aires, and my life is there. I'm a director of the National Library, occupy the chair of English and American literature at the University, and I also hold a seminar in Old English. A proof that there's still some of the right spirit left in Argentina is that this seminar is attended by a small group, nearly all girls, some of whom have office jobs. They are studying something which will be of no practical use to them.

If an intellectual shuts himself up in an ivory tower, and sometimes even ignores reality, can he contribute to solving the problems of his society?

Possibly shutting oneself in an ivory tower and thinking about other things may be one way of modifying reality. I live in an ivory tower—as you call it—creating a poem, or a book, and that can be just as real as anything else. People are generally wrong when they take reality as meaning daily life, and think of the rest as unreal. In the long run, emotions, ideas, and speculations are just as real as everyday events, and can also cause everyday events. I believe that all the dreamers and philosophers in the world are having an influence on our present-day life.

You've written several milongas lately. Why milongas rather than tangos?

Unlike most Argentines, I believe the tango began to decline with Gardel and the sentimental tangos of the type of "*La comparsita*." The earlier ones were far better, those we call the tangos of the old guard: I'm thinking of "*El cuzquito*," "*El pollito*," "*La morocha*," "*Rodríguez Peña*," "*El choclo*," "*Una noche de garufa*," and "*El apache argentino*." All these tangos had the same spirit of dash and bravery as the *milonga*, which was a much older form. The tango dates from the 1880's, and had its origins in bawdyhouses. The *milonga* was already there. When I was asked to write the lyrics for a tango, I thought to myself: "No, I'd rather write words for *milongas*," and I wrote them all about real persons, using the names of actual hoodlums I had known personally, or whose story or legend I had heard as a boy. My best is one of the first I wrote, the "Milonga of Jacinto Chiclana," which refers to a man who was stabbed to death in a crowd near the Plaza del Once in Buenos Aires.

You've also written about the city of Buenos Aires.

Yes, quite a lot. When I returned from Europe in 1921 I wanted to write a book of memories of the Palermo district. I knew the caudillo Nicolás Paredes at that time. Later I dedicated a *milonga* to him, but in it I called him Nicanor, because relations of his were still living and I didn't know whether they would like what I said about his having killed two men. I made this slight alteration in his name, firstly for reasons of personal security and also because it made for easier rhyming. No one who has lived in Palermo could be unaware that I was really referring to Nicolás Paredes, nor fail to recognize him under my very thin disguise.

When you returned to Buenos Aires in the twenties, why were you so attracted by the compadrito, *or hoodlum?*

Well, that actually came a little later. I felt the attraction because there was something about the old-time hoodlum that struck me as new—the idea of disinterested courage for its own sake. He wasn't defending a position, say, or ready to fight for the money; he fought disinterestedly. I remember a friend of mine, Ernesto Poncio, author of one of the earliest and best tangos, *"Don Juan,"* saying to me: "I've been in prison lots of times, Borges, but always for manslaughter." What he meant by this boast was that he hadn't been a thief or a pimp, but that he'd simply killed a man. He'd gained a reputation as a brave man and he had to live up to it. To me there's something pathetic about such poor men as these hoodlums were—wagon drivers or slaughterhouse workers—clinging to one luxury: that of being brave and quick to kill or be killed at any moment, maybe by someone they didn't know. It's what I tried to convey in my poem "El Tango."

I've talked to lots of people about the early days of the tango, and they all tell me the same thing—that it did not come from the people. It began in brothels, in about 1880, so I was told by one of my uncles, who had been a bit of a rake in his day. I think the proof is that if the tango had been popular its instrument would have been the guitar, as in the case of the *milonga*. Instead, it was played by piano, flute, and violin—instruments belonging to a higher economic level. Where could people living in tenement houses get money to buy pianos? This is confirmed by what contemporaries say, and also by a poem by Marcelo del Mazo, describing a dance at the beginning of the century.

And the bandoneón?

That came much later. And even if it had been earlier, it was never a popular instrument. The guitar is the instrument of the people of Buenos Aires; the *bandoneón* may possibly have been played by the Genoese in the Boca.

Are there any of these old-time hoodlums left today?

I don't think so, nor does the word have the same meaning. In the old days a hoodlum only used to kill once in a blue moon. Today we have gangsters, and now murderous attacks and crimes are frequent in Buenos Aires. It's like your gangsters here; what they do is a matter of economics.

Is there a cult of gauchos and the pampa?

The cult of the gaucho is even more vigorous in Uruguay than among us Argentines. I know this from the experience of an uncle of mine, the Uruguayan writer Luis Melián Lafinur, who went so far as declaring that there was nothing special about the gaucho except, of course, for incest.

The cult of the pampa is perhaps less in evidence. The word is little used in the country; it belongs to literary circles in Buenos Aires. I think one of the false notes in *Don Segundo Sombra* is that the characters talk about the pampa. They say, "We were men of the pampa," for instance. Ascasubi and Hernández used the word, but in a different sense, referring to the territory occupied by Indians. That's why I've done my best to avoid it. On the other hand, "plains," although it's not used in the country, is a less pretentious word. Bioy Casares told me that when he was a boy one very rarely saw a proper gaucho complete with poncho, baggy trousers, and blanket; some wore a poncho, others baggy trousers and blanket, but only today do you see people rigged up from head to foot as gauchos. Strangely enough—so he says— country people don't dress like people of the province of Buenos Aires any more, but like gauchos from Salta. This is because a lot of films have been made about them, and also because gauchos buy whatever they find in the shops. He told me that in the province of Buenos Aires you see gauchos with wide-brimmed hats—a thing that would have amazed any gaucho fifty years ago. The country is full of gauchos nowadays, something that never happened before when the country was more creole.

And what about the cult of mate?

Yes, it is still an Argentine habit. I think they see it as a way of passing time, like cards. It's a form of idleness, not of nourishment. I've not tasted mate for forty years. At one time I used to drink it and was proud of my addiction, but I was very bad at it. There were always a lot of dismal little bits floating in it. After the death of my grandfather, who was a mate drinker, we gave it up.

To return to your work: which writers have inspired you?

I've been inspired by all the books I've ever read and those I've not read as well—all literature before my time. I owe a lot to people whose names I don't know. You see, I write in one language, Spanish, and am influenced by English literature; that means that thousands of persons are influencing me. A language is in itself a literary tradition.

I've spent many years of my life studying Chinese philosophy, for instance, especially Taoism, which interests me very much, but I've also studied Buddhism and am interested in Sufism. Therefore, all this has influenced me, but I don't know to what extent. I'm not sure whether I've studied these religions and Oriental philosophies because of their effect on my thoughts and actions, or from an imaginative point of view, for literary reasons. But I think this may happen with every philosophy. Except for Schopenhauer or Berkeley, no philosopher has ever given me the sensation that I was reading a true or even probable description of the world. I've looked at metaphysics rather more as a branch of fantastic literature. For instance, I'm not sure whether I'm a Christian, but I've read a great many books on theology for the sake of their theological problems—free will, punishment, and eternal happiness. All these problems have interested me as food for my imagination.

Of course, if I may mention some names, it gives me pleasure to acknowledge my gratitude to Whitman, Chesterton, Shaw, and others to whom I often return, like Emerson. I would include some who may not be very famous as writers. For instance, of all the people I've known, the one who impressed me most as a person was Macedonio Fernández, an Argentine writer whose conversation was far above anything he wrote. He was a man who had read little, but thought for himself. He impressed me enormously. I've talked with famous people from other countries, like Waldo Frank and Ortega y Gasset, and I hardly recall those conversations. On the other hand, if I was told it was possible to talk with Macedonio Fernández, quite apart from the miracle of talking to someone who is dead, I'd be so greatly interested in what he said that I'd forget I was conversing with a ghost. A writer called Rafael Cansinos-Assens, an Andalusian Jew, also had a great influence on me; he seemed to belong to every century. I met him in Spain. Of the people I've mentioned, apart from my father, whom I can't judge because I was too close to him, those who have impressed me most were Macedonio Fernández and Cansinos-Assens. I've got very pleasant memories of Lugones, but perhaps I should omit them. What Lugones wrote is more important than my conversations with him. It would seem to me both unjust and illogical not to mention here someone of essential importance to me, one of the few people who have been essential to me, and that is my mother—my mother who is now living in Buenos Aires, who was honorably imprisoned at the time of Perón's dictatorship along with my sister and one of my nephews, my mother, who in spite of having just had her ninety-first birthday is far younger than I am or than most of the women I know. I feel that she has in a sense collaborated in what I have written. And I repeat, it would be absurd to talk about myself and not mention Leonor Acevedo de Borges.

Would you like to say something about the work of the writers you admire so much: Whitman, Chesterton, and Shaw?

Whitman is one of the poets who has most impressed me in the whole of my life. I think there's a tendency to confuse Mr. Walter Whitman, the author of *Leaves of Grass* with Walt Whitman, the protagonist of *Leaves of Grass*, and that Walt Whitman does not provide us with an image so much as a sort of magnification of the poet. In *Leaves of Grass*, Walter Whitman wrote a species of epic whose protagonist was Walt Whitman— not the Whitman who was writing but the man he would like to have been. Of course, I'm not saying this in criticism of Whitman; his work should not be read as the confessions of a man of the nineteenth century, but rather as an epic about an imaginary figure, a utopian figure, who is to some extent a magnification and projection of the writer as well as of the reader. You will remember that in *Leaves of Grass* the author often merges himself with the reader, and of course this expresses his theory of democracy, the idea that a single unique protagonist can represent a whole epoch. The importance of Whitman cannot be overstated. Even taking into account the versicles of the Bible or of Blake, Whitman can be said to be the inventor of free verse. He can be looked at in two ways: there is his civic side—the fact that one is aware of crowds, great cities, and America—and there is also an intimate element, though we can't be sure whether it is genuine or not. The character Whitman has created is one of the most lovable and memorable in all literature. He is a character like Don Quixote or Hamlet, but someone no less complex and possibly more lovable than either of them.

Bernard Shaw is an author to whom I keep returning. I think he too is a writer who is often only read in part. One tends to think particularly of his early work, books in which he fought against the social order of his day. But beyond this, Shaw has epic significance, and is the only writer of our time who has imagined and presented heroes to his readers. On the whole, modern writers tend to reveal men's weaknesses, and seem to delight in their un-

happiness; in Shaw's case, however, we have characters like Major
Barbara or Caesar, who are heroic and whom one can admire.
Contemporary literature since Dostoevski—and even earlier, since
Byron—seems to delight in man's guilt and weaknesses. In Shaw's
work the greatest human virtues are extolled. For example, that a
man can forget his own fate, that a man may not value his own
happiness, that he may say like our Almafuerte: "I'm not interested in my own life," because he is interested in something
beyond personal circumstances. If one had to point out the best
English prose, one would look for it in Shaw's prefaces and in
many speeches of his characters. He is one of the writers I love
best.

I also have a great affection for Chesterton. Chesterton's imagination was of a different sort from Shaw's, but I think Shaw will
last longer than Chesterton. Chesterton's works are full of surprises, and I have come to the conclusion that the element that
wears least well in a book is surprise. Shaw has a classical inspiration that we don't find in Chesterton. It's a pity that Chesterton's
flavor should fade, but I think it likely that in a hundred or two
hundred years' time Chesterton will only figure in histories of
literature, and Shaw in literature itself.

When did you publish your first book?

         In 1923. My father had told me that when I wrote a
book I thought worth printing, he would give me the money to
publish it. I had written two books before this, and had the good
sense to destroy them. One called *Los ritmos rojos* (Red
Rhythms) was as bad as its title, and consisted of poems on the
Russian Revolution. At that time, communism stood for an idea
of universal brotherhood. Next, I wrote a book called *Los naipes
del tahur* (The Sharper's Cards), in which I tried to write like
Pío Baroja. I realized these two books were bad, and I have
expunged them from my memory; I remember their titles but
nothing more. I did publish my third book, *Fervor de Buenos
Aires*, because I was going to Europe for a year and wouldn't
be present when the book came out, giving me a certain im-
punity. Alfredo Bianchi and Roberto Giusti were joint editors
of the magazine *Nosotros*. I had the book printed, and went to

the office of *Nosotros* taking fifty some copies. Bianchi stared at me in horror and said: "But do you want me to sell this book?" "No; I'm not mad," I replied. "What I want is something that the book's format makes possible—for you to slip a copy into the pocket of every overcoat that passes through your office." And in fact, when I returned after a year, not a single copy was left, and laudatory articles had been published about that book. I met young men who had read it and found something in it. That delighted me.

In *Fervor de Buenos Aires*, I wanted to write in a somewhat Latinized Spanish; afterwards, under the influence of Macedonio Fernández, I tried to discover a metaphysical form of poetry, dealing with those perplexities we call philosophy, and later still I wanted to write about Buenos Aires—about my rediscovery of Buenos Aires after so many years in Europe. All this was present in *Fervor de Buenos Aires* in a somewhat incoherent and therefore awkward form. But I think I am in that book, and that everything I have done since is to be found between its lines. I recognize myself in it more than I do in my other books, although I don't suppose the reader would recognize me. It seems to me that in it I was on the point of writing what I was to write thirty or forty years later.

If you read my collected poems you'll see that I have very few themes. I've written three or four poems, I'm not sure which, about the death of my grandfather, Colonel Borges, who was killed in action in 1874; there's a poem about my grandfather in *Fervor de Buenos Aires*, and I see that I've returned to the subject in other books. I think I gave final expression to it in a poem to Junín in my last book. It's as if I had spent my whole life writing seven or eight poems and trying out different variations, as if each book expunged the one before. But I'm not ashamed of this; it's proof that I write sincerely, since it wouldn't be very difficult to find other themes. If I return to the same ones it is because I feel them to be essential, and also because I feel I've not done with them, that I still owe them something. In other cases, I have also written the same poem twice over—for example, "Odyssey, Book 23" and "Alexander Selkirk." When I wrote "Alexander Selkirk" I had no idea that I had already written the same poem about a different character.

Will there be a change of style in your future works?

I began writing in a very self-conscious, baroque style. It was probably due to youthful timidity. The young often suspect that their plots and poems aren't very interesting, so they try to conceal them or elaborate on them by other means. When I began to write I tried to adopt the style of classical Spanish seventeenth-century writers, such as Quevedo or Saavedra Fajardo. Then I reflected that it was my duty as an Argentine to write like an Argentine. I bought a dictionary of Argentinisms, and managed to become so Argentine in my style and vocabulary that people couldn't understand me and I couldn't even remember very well myself what the words meant. Words passed directly from the dictionary to my manuscript without corresponding to any experience. Now, after a great many years, I believe that it's best to write with a very simple vocabulary, and concentrate on the person whom certain modern poets are apt to forget entirely: the reader. Faulkner was a writer of genius, yet he had a perverse, a dreadfully bad influence on other writers. His idea of telling a story by juggling with time, and sometimes having recourse to two characters both with the same name amounts to a way of creating and perfecting chaos. We shouldn't aim at confusion, however easy it is to slip into it. So I try to limit my vocabulary; I don't try to be Argentine, any more than I fatally and necessarily am, and I always try to smooth over the reader's difficulties, which doesn't mean that I always write lucidly. A writer often gives way to clumsiness, either because he is tired, or because he assumes that what he understands will be comprehensible to everyone else.

Don't you think words and quotations in a foreign language may sometimes confuse the reader?

Certainly, but I'm used to thinking in English, and I also believe some English words are untranslatable, so I occasionally use them for the sake of precision. I'm not "showing off." Since I've done most of my reading in English, it's natural that the first word that comes to mind is often an English one. I usually try to reject it in case it might bewilder the reader. Stevenson used to say that on a well-written page the words should all look in the same direction, and perhaps a word in another language looks the other way and may confuse the reader; but there are some words one can't resign oneself to doing without because they express exactly what one wants to say.

Will you go on writing about imaginary things or about real things?

I want to write about real things, but I believe that realism is difficult, particularly if one wants to make it contemporary. If I write a story about some actual street or district of Buenos Aires, someone will immediately point out that people there don't talk like that. Therefore, I think it is more suitable for a writer to look for a subject that is rather further off either in time or space. I'm thinking of setting my stories in a somewhat remote period, say about fifty years ago, and perhaps in somewhat unknown or forgotten quarters of Buenos Aires, so that no one will know exactly how people used to talk and behave there. It seems to me this gives the author's imagination more freedom. I believe the reader is happier when he's reading about something that happened some time ago, because he's not confronted by reality, he's not having to carry out a sort of comparison or inspection of what the author is saying. I think the mistake made in *Don Segundo Sombra* was to aim at very faithful realism in a book which, after all, was an elegy of pastoral life.

Why did you use the pseudonym H. Bustos Domecq in your book Seis problemas para Don Isidro Parodi (Six Problems for Don Isidro Parodi)?

That's quite simple. I wrote the book in collaboration with Adolfo Bioy Casares. We knew that books written in collaboration are read as puzzles, with the reader trying to figure out who wrote this and who wrote that. So, as the book was written more or less as a joke, we decided to create a third man: "H.," because it seemed quite likely that he would have a name no one knew; "Bustos" because that was my great-grandfather's name, and "Domecq" from a great-grandfather of Bioy's. The odd thing is that this third person really exists, because what we write isn't like Bioy's work nor like mine. It has a different style, different idiosyncrasies, even the syntax is different. But in order that this third person should exist we had to forget that there were two of us. As we write, we become Bustos Domecq. If anyone asked me whether the plot was Bioy's or mine, who had invented some metaphor, and if this or that joke came from his side of the table or mine, I wouldn't know. The first time we began writing together, we immediately forgot there were two of us, and sometimes one of us would anticipate what the other was going to say. Actually, we allowed ourselves every possible freedom; we were as free as a single person alone with his thoughts. We got a lot of amusement out of writing. It's very difficult to write in collaboration; I've tried to do it with other friends but we got nowhere. My collaborator either wanted all his suggestions to be adopted or else was so polite that he approved of anything I said. One of the pleasures I promise myself when I return to Argentina is to go on collaborating with Bioy Casares.

Always as Bustos Domecq?

We have another name, Suárez Lynch—"Suárez" was one of my great-grandfathers and "Lynch" one of Bioy's—used when Bustos Domecq was recognized as our joint pen name. Last year we published the *Chronicles of Bustos Domecq,* a series of accounts of imaginary painters, sculptors, architects, cooks, and others. It is a sort of satire. We've got another book in reserve for future publication under the name of Suárez Lynch.

And as Jorge Luis Borges what are you writing at present?

I'm writing a story which will apparently deal with the dictatorship and the 1955 revolution. But that won't be its only subject. There will be another, a very Argentine one—friendship. I think it has a quite good plot, but the importance of it lies behind the events. I began dictating this story to my mother two or three years ago in Buenos Aires, but after two pages I realized that I was making a mistake, and that I had begun in a way that couldn't turn out well. Now, here in New England, I've suddenly seen how I must begin it. Sometimes it's a good thing to be far away from one's manuscript, because if I had been in Buenos Aires I might well have got onto the wrong track again. Now I have the advantage of having forgotten it and of starting from scratch. I think it may be one of my successful stories.

Does it have a title yet?

I think it will be called "Los amigos" (The Friends), but I'm not sure yet. It sounds like the name of a bar.

Have you any other work on hand?

At the moment, I'm working on some sonnets, which come to me slowly. I'm also thinking of writing a book on medieval Anglo-Saxon and Scandinavian literature. I've already done some work on it, but I shall go on with it in Buenos Aires, where I have my library. Later, I want to publish a book of psychological tales. I shall try to do without magic, labyrinths, mirrors, daggers, and all my other manias; there won't be any deaths, and the important thing will be the characters themselves. I want plots too, of course, for the reader's sake. And I continue to add to my collected poems. Every edition gives me a chance to cut out a few poems and add others. Every edition is a little larger than the last. And now the writer Norman Thomas di Giovanni, who has already published an anthology of Jorge Guillén, is working with me on an edition of my poems in English, which will be published in 1972, and contain some hundred poems translated by outstanding American and English poets.

You've also written some film scripts, haven't you?

Hugo Santiago, Adolfo Bioy Casares, and I have written the script of a film called *Invasion*. The setting is Buenos Aires, but a Buenos Aires of dreams or nightmare. The plot is Santiago's, and he will direct it.

Another story of mine, "El muerto" (The Dead Man) may possibly be screened in the United States. The story takes place on the frontier between Brazil and Uruguay, but I think they'll shoot it in the United States; the important thing is the plot rather than local color, and I suggested that they should change the location to the Far West. I think they're already working on the script.

I have written two other film scripts with Adolfo Bioy Casares,

but they were turned down by Argentine producers and have
appeared only in book form. They are called *Los orilleros* (River
Bank Dwellers) and *El paraíso de los creyentes* (The Paradise of
Believers).

What sort of films do you like?

I have to look for films where the dialogue is important,
like *A Man for All Seasons*, or else musicals like *West Side Story*
or *My Fair Lady*. But Italian and Swedish films are forbidden me,
because I understand neither of these languages and cannot see
them. I like westerns very much, and also Hitchcock's films. One
of the films that has impressed me most was *High Noon*. It's a
classic western, one of the best that has been made. Everyone
likes westerns, because they stand for the epic in an age whose
writers have forgotten that it's the oldest form of poetry, or indeed
of literature, since poetry came before prose. Hollywood, with its
westerns, has salvaged the epic for the world. What humanity is
looking for in westerns is the zest and spirit of the epic, enjoyment of courage and adventure. On the whole I prefer American
films to any other. French films seem to me a glorification of
boredom. When I was in Paris talking to French writers, I told
them, with the innocent aim of shocking them but also without
departing from the truth, that I liked American films best. They
all agreed with me that if one went to the cinema in search of
sheer enjoyment, one would find it in American pictures. They
said that films like *Last Year in Marienbad* and *Hiroshima Mon
Amour* were seen out of a sense of duty, and very few people
really enjoyed them.

What about the Argentine cinema?

René Mujica made a film of "*Hombre de la esquina
rosada*"; he did a good job with the possibilities provided by the
plot. I liked it. But on the whole Argentine films aren't popular
in Buenos Aires; people go to them out of a sense of duty, because
they think of them as experimental. There are no directors, and
their plots are very simple. In a country as economically restricted
as ours one should aim at films where the dialogue is important.
For instance, there's no reason why one shouldn't make a film like

The Collector, in which there were only three characters, a lot of dialogue, and no need for great financial outlay.

And the Argentine theater?

There's considerable interest in the theater in Buenos Aires, particularly in the companies of amateur actors who now go by the name of "vocational"; they may well be saving our theater. I've seen performances by them of Shakespeare, Ibsen, and O'Neill. I think the public enjoys good things, and if you give them good films and plays they appreciate them.

Are you interested in detective stories?

Yes. Bioy Casares and I suggested to an Argentine firm that they publish a series of detective stories. At first they said that such novels suited the United States and England, but that no one in the Argentine Republic was going to buy them. In the end we convinced them, but only after a year's persuasion, and now the series called *El séptimo círculo* (The Seventh Circle), edited by Bioy Casares and myself, has published about two hundred titles, and some have gone into three or four editions. I also tried to persuade the same publishers to do a science fiction series and they said that no one would buy them. Another firm is publishing them and I approved the first, Bradbury's *Martian Chronicles.*

In your literary career, what do you remember with most pleasure?

People have been very good to me, and my work has gained a recognition that has been the creation of my admirers rather than the result of its own merit. The strange thing is that all this has been a very slow process; for many years I was the most obscure writer in Buenos Aires. I published a book called *Historia de la eternidad,* (A History of Eternity) and at the end of a year I discovered to my amazement and gratitude that I had sold forty-seven copies. I wanted to seek out each of the purchasers and thank him personally, and ask him to forgive me for all the mistakes in the book. On the other hand, if one sells 470 copies, or 4,700, the number is too great for the buyers to have faces, houses, or relations.

Nowadays, when I see that some book of mine has gone into several editions I'm not surprised; I see it all as an abstract process. Suddenly I've found friends all over the world, and my books have been translated into many languages. Of all the prizes I have been awarded, the one that pleased me most was the Second Municipal Prize of Buenos Aires for a rather poor book called *El idioma de los argentinos* (The Language of Argentines). That prize gave me more pleasure than the Formentor, or the one awarded by the Society of Argentine Writers. Of all my publications, none pleased me more than that of a really *dreadfully* bad poem called "Himno al mar" (Hymn to the Sea), which appeared in a Sevillian magazine around 1918 or 1919.

Three Latin American writers—Borges, Asturias, and Neruda— were mentioned for the 1967 Nobel Prize. How do you feel about being nominated?

When I think of names like Bertrand Russell, Bernard Shaw, or Faulkner, to mention a few that occur to me, I think it would be absurd to give the prize to me.

How do you feel about Asturias winning the prize?

I don't know whether I would have chosen Asturias, but I would have preferred Neruda to Borges, because I consider him a better poet, although we disagree politically. I've only talked to Pablo Neruda once in my life and that was many years ago. We were both young and we came to the conclusion that nothing could be done with the Spanish language, and that we should rather attempt English. Perhaps each of us wanted to startle the other a little, and so we exaggerated our true opinions. I really know Neruda's work very little, but I think he's a worthy follower of Walt Whitman, or perhaps Carl Sandburg.

In a review of your Personal Anthology, Time magazine for March 24, 1967, wrote that Argentina had produced a personality in Borges, but that she had no national literature. What is your view?

I don't think people should make sweeping statements. I ought to feel flattered because it leads to the conclusion that

Argentine literature started with me, but as that is obviously absurd I don't see why I should be grateful for such an inconvenient and outside present—a gigantic present.

Then can we speak of a national literature?

I believe so. We can be prouder of our literature than of some of our other activities. For instance, in the nineteenth century we produced *Facundo* and the gauchesco poets, and later on there was a great revival of literature in the Spanish language on our side of the Atlantic. Then came modernism, beginning with Darío, Lugones, and others. I think we've achieved something. But when I began to write my tales of imagination I was quite unaware of an Argentine tradition, a tradition started by Lugones.

What do you think of literary criticism in Latin America?

Well, I don't want to offend any critics, but those who write in the daily papers are very cautious. Their watchword seems to be neither to blame nor praise excessively. The newspapers do their utmost not to commit themselves. It's different here in the United States, but there are probably economic interests involved as well.

Do you think this economic factor has a great influence on critics?

Maybe. It can also influence writers. Perhaps a writer feels freer when he knows that his work won't earn him much. I remember a time, about 1920 or 1925, when books brought in very little or nothing. This gave a writer great freedom. He couldn't pander to the mob because there was nothing to pander himself for.

Would you say there's greater interest in Latin American literature today?

Yes. For instance, writers like Eduardo Mallea, Bioy Casares, Manuel Mujica Láinez, Julio Cortázar, and myself are pretty well known in Europe, and this has never happened before. When I was in Spain in 1920, talking to Spanish writers,

I thought I would casually mention the name of Lugones, and I came to the conclusion that it meant very little to them, or else they thought of him merely as a follower of Herrera y Reissig. On the other hand, when I went to Spain about three years ago and again talked to Spanish writers, they often introduced quotations from Lugones into their conversation, not out of condescension or politeness but quite spontaneously. The fact that an important writer like Lugones used to be unknown in Europe, whereas nowadays between six and a dozen South American writers are well known there, is evidence of this increased interest.

For instance, five volumes of my stories and poems have been published here in the United States in paperback, and their sales seem to be going up. This never happened to Lugones. Many of my books have been translated in European countries and published in London as well as New York. Such a thing never happened to an Argentine writer thirty years ago. A book like *Don Segundo Sombra* was translated into French, and I think into English as well, but hardly any notice was taken of it at the time. Today people are not merely interested in reading books with local color or social significance; they also want to find out what Latin Americans are thinking or dreaming about.

Would you like to say something about contemporary Latin American literature?

I can't speak about contemporary Latin American literature. For instance, I don't know Cortázar's work at all well, but the little I do know, a few stories, seems to be admirable. I'm proud of the fact that I was the first to publish any work by him. When I was editing a magazine called *Los anales de Buenos Aires*, I remember a tall young man presenting himself in the office and handing me a manuscript. I said I would read it and he came back after a week. The story was called "La casa tomada" (The Occupied House). I told him it was excellent; my sister Norah illustrated it. When I was in Paris we met once or twice, but I've not read his most recent work.

I ought to speak about writers of another generation. In my opinion the best writer of Spanish prose on either side of the Atlantic is still the Mexican Alfonso Reyes. I have very pleasant memories of his friendship and his good nature, but I'm not sure if my memories are accurate. Reyes's works are important for America as well as for Mexico, and they should be for Spain as well. His prose is elegant, economical, and at the same time full of subtlety, irony, and feeling. There is a sort of understatement in Reyes's emotional response. One may read a page which seems cold, and suddenly one becomes aware that there is an underlying current of great sensitivity, that the author feels and perhaps suffers, but doesn't want to show it. It's a sort of modesty. I don't know what is thought of him. Maybe it has been held against him that he doesn't concern himself exclusively and continuously with Mexican themes, although he has written a lot on Mexico. Some people refuse to forgive him for translating the *Iliad* and the *Odyssey*. One thing is certain, and that is that ever since Reyes the Spanish language has had to be written differently. He was a very cosmopolitan writer who had explored many cultures.

Do you think that the spread of works by Latin American writers inside Latin America could have the effect of creating a more unified continental culture?

That's a hard question. We Argentines have a lot in common with Uruguayans, a little with Chileans, and not much I think with Peruvians, Venezuelans, or Mexicans. I therefore don't feel sure to what extent this Latin American awareness may not be a sham, or a generalization in the course of which much could be lost. Take Mexico, for example. There can't be a great similarity between a country of secondary importance like ours and one with a very different history, a very different past. In any case, perhaps the diffusion you mention may lead to the conclusion that we resemble each other very little, that we are different.

What is your view of Spanish literature?

I think that from the beginning of the nineteenth century the Spanish literature of South America has been more important than what Spain herself has produced. Of course, this doesn't mean that I don't admire Unamuno, whom I have read and reread. Though it is years since I opened his pages, I still retain a very vivid impression of him today. Probably his most im-

portant achievement was to leave us an impression of his personality, quite apart from his opinions, with which one may disagree—as with all opinions. I would say that when one thinks of
English literature one generally thinks of individuals, just as one
thinks of the characters of Shakespeare and Dickens. One tends
to think of other literatures in terms of books. This is why one is
very grateful that other literatures possess writers who do not make
one think of a series of books, but whom we are aware of as men,
and one of those men—from his conversation, he must have
known it—is Miguel de Unamuno. Ortega y Gasset was a man
who thought intelligently, a man who never stopped thinking,
but as a writer he doesn't strike me as irreproachable. He ought
to have found a man of letters to put his ideas into words. I admire
him as a thinker, however. García Lorca seems to me quite a
minor poet. His tragic death has favored his reputation. Of course,
I like Lorca's poems, but they don't seem to me very important.
His poetry is visual, decorative, not entirely serious; it's a sort of
baroque entertainment.

I think Spanish literature has been in decline almost since the
seventeenth century; the nineteenth century was extremely un-
productive and there is nothing much better today, certainly
nothing more important than what we have on this side of the
Atlantic.

There are several names of Spanish poets that it would be unforgivable not to mention. Manuel and Antonio Machado, for
instance. (Manuel was an Andalusian who remained one; Antonio
was an Andalusian who made himself into a Castilian.) I would
like to add the name of Jorge Guillén, who is here in Cambridge
and has honored me with his friendship. It's a very pleasant
experience, and not without some small surprises, to meet someone whom one already seems to know intimately through his
writing. As a result of personal contact, one discovers that his
character harmonizes with everything he has written, but not at
all with the image one had formed of him.

What advice would you give a young writer?

I would give him a very simple piece of advice: not to
think about publication but about his work. Not to be in a hurry

to rush into print, and not to forget the reader, and also—if he attempts fiction—to try and describe nothing that he can't honestly imagine. Not to write about events merely because they seem to him surprising, but about those which give his imagination creative scope. As for style, I should advise poverty of vocabulary rather than too much richness. If there's one moral defect that's usually obvious in a work, it is vanity. One of the reasons why I don't altogether like Lugones, although of course I don't deny his talent or even genius, is that I notice a certain vanity in his manner of writing. When all the adjectives and all the metaphors on a single page are new ones, it usually indicates vanity, and a desire to astonish the reader. The reader ought never to feel that the writer is skillful. A writer ought to be skillful, but in an unobtrusive way. When things are extremely well done they seem inevitable as well as easy. If you are aware of a sense of effort, it means failure on the writer's part. Nor do I want to imply that a writer must be spontaneous, because that would mean he hit on the right word straightaway, which is very unlikely. When a piece of work is finished it ought to seem spontaneous, even though it may really be full of secret artifices and modest (not conceited) ingenuity.

You mentioned a project of yours for bilingual education, and the need for teaching English and Spanish in both Americas.

Three years ago I had occasion to travel in the Scandinavian countries—countries I am very fond of. In Sweden and Denmark, I discovered that every one spoke English. English is taught in the primary schools there, so that every Scandinavian is bilingual. It would be extraordinarily useful if English were taught in the primary schools of our republics, and Spanish in the United States and Canada. Then we should have a bilingual continent, since Portuguese is a sort of variation on Spanish or vice versa. If every American possessed two languages, a much wider world would be opened to him; he would have access to two cultures. Perhaps that would be the best means of exorcising the worst enemy in the world—nationalism. I believe it would be of the utmost importance for the history of the world if every man born in America had access to two cultures, the English and

the Spanish. For me, knowledge of two languages doesn't mean
the possession of a repertory of synonyms; it doesn't mean knowing that in Spanish you say *"ancho"* and in English "wide" or
"broad." What is important is to learn to think in two different
ways, and to have access to two literatures. If a man grows up
within a single culture, if he gets used to seeing other languages
as hostile or arbitrary dialects, his mental development will be
constricted. If, however, he gets used to thinking in two languages
and to the idea that his mind has developed from two great
literatures, that must surely benefit him. To teach English in the
primary schools of Latin America, and eventually of Spain, and to
teach Spanish in the primary schools of the United States, Canada, and eventually of Great Britain, would be a simple matter
involving no difficulty. You will say that it's easier for a Dane to
study English than for a Spanish-speaking person to learn English
or an Englishman Spanish; but I don't think this is true, because
English is a Latin language as well as a Germanic one. At least
half the English vocabulary is Latin. Remember that in English
there are two words for every idea: one Saxon and one Latin. You
can say "Holy Ghost" or "Holy Spirit," "sacred" or "holy."
There's always a slight difference, but one that's very important
for poetry, the difference between "dark" and "obscure" for
instance, or "regal" and "kingly," or "fraternal" and "brotherly."
In the English language almost all words representing abstract
ideas come from Latin, and those for concrete ideas from Saxon,
but there aren't so very many concrete ideas. This experiment
ought to be carried out at once. I suggested it to the Argentine
Academy of Letters in Buenos Aires, and now that I'm in the
United States I shall not lose the opportunity of suggesting it
again. I believe it would be one means of achieving world peace.

What's your political position?

        I belong to the Conservative Party and I'll explain why. I
joined the Conservative Party a few days before the presidential
elections. I've always been a radical, but by family tradition. My
maternal grandfather, Acevedo, was a great friend of Alem's, so
that it was a case of loyalty rather than conviction or judgment.
Later on, I got the impression that the radicals wanted to come to

terms with the communists. Four or five days before the elections
I went to see Hardoy and told him I wanted to join the con-
servatives. He looked at me in horror and said: "But we haven't
a chance of winning." My answer was: "A gentleman is only
interested in lost causes." "Well, if you're out for lost causes," he
said, "don't go a step farther, you've got one right here." We both
laughed, and I joined—to the obvious advantage of the radicals.
I've had to explain to lots of people, especially here, that to be
a conservative in Argentina is not to belong to the right but the
center. I detest the nationalists and fascists just as much as I do
the communists, so that I think I'm still in the position I've always
held. I more or less believe in democracy, and of course I've
always been against Peronism. Perón's government never had any
doubts about that. They attacked me by throwing me out of a
small post I held, and my mother, sister, and one of my nephews
were imprisoned.

Who are the communists in Argentina?

All the communists are intellectuals, not working class.
The communists of today are also nationalists, so of course they
are against the United States.

What do you think is the reason for this anti-Yankee feeling?

I would say that in the Argentine Republic this feeling
is artificial. Formerly it didn't exist; I think it's due to communist
influence. In our country there used to be no hostility to America,
but now, through Cuban influence perhaps, and of course through
Russian influence, it does exist. But at the same time the very
people who hate the United States want them to help us economically; they are the ones who spend their lives trying to be
like Americans. It's very strange, but I think this feeling is mostly
artificial. It's like anti-Semitism in our country.

Is there much anti-Semitism?

Only among small groups of nationalists. If there's one
thing that interests nobody in our country, it's what race a person
belongs to. During the war in the Middle East we all felt great

sympathy for Israel. I remember that on the day war was declared I signed a declaration in favor of Israel; next day I was walking along Corrientes and I suddenly felt that something was about to happen. What actually happened was a sonnet about Israel. As soon as I had it worked out in my head, I went to the offices of *Davar*, asked for the director and said to him: "Have you a typewriter in the house?" "Certainly, we have seventy or eighty," he told me. "I need one." "What for?" "Because I've just produced a poem on Israel." "What's it like?" "I don't know if it's good or bad, but as it came to me spontaneously it shouldn't be too bad." I dictated it and *Davar* published it.

Do you believe in the literature of commitment?

My only commitment is to literature and my own sincerity. As for my political attitude, I've always made it perfectly clear: I've been anti-communist, anti-Hitler, anti-Peronist, and anti-nationalist, but I've done my best to prevent these opinions of mine (which are merely opinions, and may well be superficial) from intruding into what may be called my aesthetic output. A writer can satisfy his conscience and act as he believes is right, but I do not think literature should consist in fables or tracts. A writer should preserve the freedom of the imagination, the freedom of dreams. I have tried never to let my opinions intrude into my work; I would almost prefer people to be unaware of what these opinions are. If a story or a poem of mine is successful, its success springs from a deeper source than my political views, which may be erroneous and are dictated by circumstances. In my case, my knowledge of what is called political reality is very incomplete. My life is really spent among books, many of them from a past age, so that I may well be mistaken.

Are you religious?

No.

You said in the course of our conversation that you weren't sure whether you were a Christian? Why is that?

There are moments when I feel I am a Christian, and then when I reflect that to admit it involves accepting a whole theological system, I see that I'm not really one. I feel attracted to Protestantism, or to certain forms of it, and what attracts me is its absence of hierarchy. Many people are drawn to the Catholic Church by its pageantry, its ritual, its ecclesiastic hierarchy and splendid architecture. These things are precisely what repel me. As I've said, I don't know whether I am a Christian, but if I am I'm closer to Methodism than to the Catholic Church. I say this with all respect. I'm expressing what I feel, a spiritual tendency.

I've also done all I could to become a Jew. I've never stopped searching for Jewish ancestors. My mother's family is called Acevedo, and they may have been Portuguese Jews. I've given a great many lectures to the Argentine Jewish Society; I'm deeply interested in the Cabala and in Spinoza's philosophy, and I have sometimes thought of writing a book about him. I have written a poem about Spinoza.

Apart from the accidents of blood, we are all both Greeks and Hebrews. We are Greeks because Rome was merely an extension of Greece. One can't conceive of the *Aeneid* without the *Iliad*, the poetry of Lucretius without Epicurean philosophy, or Seneca without the Stoics. All Latin literature and philosophy is based on Greek literature and philosophy. On the other hand, whether we believe in Christianity or not, we cannot deny that it was derived from Judaism.

Do you believe that the current liberal movement in the Catholic Church is important?

I think it's a sign of weakness. When the Church was strong it was intolerant; it went in for burning and persecution. It seems to me that the Church's present tolerance largely derives from weakness; it's not that it has become more broad-minded, because that's impossible. No church—whether Catholic or Protestant—has ever been tolerant, nor is there any reason for them to be tolerant. If I believe I am in possession of the truth there is no reason for me to be tolerant of those who are risking their own salvation by holding erroneous beliefs. On the contrary, it's my duty to persecute them. I can't say: "It doesn't matter that you are a Protestant because we're all brothers of Christ in the end." No, that would be a proof of skepticism.

I believe you travel a lot. Do you enjoy it?

I don't enjoy traveling one bit, but I very much like having traveled. One travels for the sake of one's memories, but of course for something to exist in the past it must once have been the present.

Which of the countries that you don't know would you like to visit?

I would like to imitate William Morris, who made a pilgrimage to Iceland in the last century. The word "pilgrimage" is not an overstatement here, or a pointless exaggeration. I've begun studying Icelandic, and I believe that the literature produced during the Middle Ages in that remote island close to the Arctic Circle is one of the most important in the world. I would like to get to know Norway and Israel too, and to return to the countries I love most, Scotland and England. These are my geographical ambitions.

Have you been to Russia?

No. I've been invited by some of the countries on the other side of the Iron Curtain, but I thought that as I should go with a bias against them my visit might not be pleasant either for my hosts or for me. I preferred to abstain, because I think one should travel in a cordial frame of mind, and in the case of Russia I don't know to what extent I should be capable of it. If I make an experiment, I'd rather make one that is likely to succeed.

Your life must be full of interesting anecdotes. Can you remember any?

I can't remember anecdotes. One thing that has always amazed me has been the extraordinary patience and kindness people have shown and still show me. I try to think about my enemies and I can hardly think of any—in fact, I can't think of one. Some of the articles written about me have been considered too savage, but I've thought to myself: "Good Lord, if I'd written that article I would have made it a lot more savage!" When I think about my contemporaries, it's with a feeling of gratitude, a somewhat amazed gratitude. People have, on the whole, treated me better than I deserve.

I remember the case of Ricardo Güiraldes. He and I edited the magazine *Proa* together for a year. I was writing some undoubtedly mediocre poems at the time, which were afterwards published in a book called *Luna de enfrente* (Moon Across the Way). I showed Güiraldes these poems; he read them and divined what I had wanted to say, not what my clumsiness had prevented me from saying. Afterwards, Güiraldes discussed my poems with other people, but instead of talking about the poem I had written, he talked about the one I had wanted to write and which he had perceived in the very awkward draft I had shown him. The people he talked to became enthusiastic about my poem, looked for it in the book I had published, and of course failed to find it. It was as if Güiraldes had given me a gift, and I think that was what he was unconsciously doing. I may say that I have the warmest recollections of Güiraldes, of his generous friendship and his strange destiny; though all destinies are strange.

Have you a message for the younger generation?

No, I don't think I can give advice to other people. I've hardly been able to manage my own life. I've drifted somewhat.

MIGUEL ANGEL ASTURIAS

MIGUEL ANGEL ASTURIAS

Paris   November 6–10, 1970

Like Neruda, Guatemala's Nobel Laureate Miguel Angel Asturias sings "the praise of good eating in verse and prose." In fact the book Sentimental Journey Around the Hungarian Cuisine was born out of the two writers meeting in Hungary. Asturias, a believer that "the vida viva starts at the table," defends in an essay the habits of good eating. "Life is being besieged in its castle built of fruits, food, fish, meat, and all the delicacies of a plentiful table. The final assault is prepared scientifically by the dietitians or dieteticians, aesthetically by the tailors and dressmakers, religiously by the ascetics and the daily worshippers, economically by the tradesmen, and chronometrically by hours and the observance of time."

And also like Neruda, Asturias, although reserved, leads a gregarious life. Settled in Paris with his attractive and vivacious Argentine wife, Blanca Mora y Araujo, in a five-room co-op apartment in the 17th arrondissement, Asturias—when he is not lecturing at European universities or secluded in Mallorca just writing and swimming—meets with friends from the French government and from intellectual circles. He has been a Parisian for many years, first as a student, then as the Guatemalan ambassador to France, and now as a private citizen.

In his seventies, Asturias, like many Guatemaltecos, bears traces of his Mayan ancestry. He is tall, bulky, with a prominent hawk nose that accentuates his strong features. Yet, at first glance he looks not unlike the late Sydney Greenstreet. He is not talkative, but is an attentive listener. There is in his melancholic reserve and calmness that ceremonial quality typical of the natives of his country.

Asturias doesn't dance or eat as he once did, but he continues to believe in the value of a good nap, so our conversations for the interview were held at five thirty—after he had awakened and we had taken tea—in the apartment's living-dining room. The room is furnished with a mixture of antiques, which Asturias picks out himself, and modern paintings by Latin American artists. Well represented is the Argentine painter Ronaldo de Juan, now living in New York, who illustrated several of Asturias's books and prepared the setting and costumes of the Parisian performance of Asturias's play Torotumbo. There are also two large portraits of Asturias, one by the Argentine painter Juan Castagnino, the other by the Ecuadorian Guayasamin.

The bookshelves of his studio and the apartment's corridor feature the complete works of Valéry, Quevedo, Cervantes, Rafael Alberti, Hemingway, Shakespeare, Dostoevski, and a large collection of books on Mayan and pre-Colombian civilizations as well as his own works. He is particularly proud of the numerous translations of El señor presidente, including those in Vietnamese and Cambodian.

During the one-hour interviews, Asturias, casually dressed in flannel trousers, open-neck shirt, an ascot, a gray cardigan sweater and slippers, talked freely and heartily. His deep, musical voice would change tones according to the subject. When he was remembering his mother and his childhood he closed his eyes, and his measured words sounded as if he were reciting poetry. When describing Guatemala's countryside, his voice became exuberant, then passionate when talking about his country's dictators. When I quoted a García Márquez statement about engagé poetry, he became so angry he lost his temper.

He put so much of himself into the interview that he would tire at the end of an hour and politely say, "Enough for today." Then, turning on the television, Asturias left his Guatemalan memories and the mysterious Mayan world to return to the realities and dreams of the contemporary world.

"A mi madre que me contaba cuentos" (To my mother who used to tell me stories) is the dedication of your first book, Leyendas de Guatemala (Legends of Guatemala), published in Madrid in

1930, described by Valéry *as a "little book which should be drunk rather than read."*

There is filial love in this dedication, a son's gratitude to his mother, the person who not only gave him life but afterwards set him on the spiritual path. In *Leyendas de Guatemala* I was expressing my devotion to my country, to my little native land, to my little corner of volcanoes, lakes, mountains, clouds, birds, and flowers. I felt that this book needed some sort of ornament, something analogous to a jewel on its breast, and I therefore thought of the hendecasyllable: "A *mi madre que me contaba cuentos.*" These stories were in part Guatemalan legends, in part accounts of everyday events, in part what I was told by my mother as I fell asleep, as well as from her silence, which was another form of telling stories and talking. But I would like to say now—and I'm saying it for the first time—that as I wrote that dedication I thought of it not only in Spanish words or as a phrase, but as embracing a wider ambit. So that it was logical that in writing *Leyendas de Guatemala* I should return as a native rather than a Spaniard to the emotions, to the philosophy, and to the tread of barefoot Indians around all that makes up the universe of American man, and in my case of Indo-American man, a universe in which women's powers, and especially their creative powers, are interpreted as a spring and essential cause. It is the woman, it is the mother, it is the matrix within the beliefs of the Mayas, of the Quiché Mayas—the Mayas' descendants now occupying Guatemalan territory, to whom I am linked by my mestizo blood—it is the maternal telluric forces, the strength of the earth, upon which the Mayan world largely depends. The earth is the fundamental element, the earth is the mother, the earth is what conceives us, supports us, and afterwards protects us in her bosom. When I wrote "To my mother who used to tell me stories" at the beginning of my book of Guatemalan legends, I was remembering the vital, substantial, and universal elements of that great cosmic force represented by the mother among the Indians and in Mayan beliefs, and before the mother by the grandmother, by the earth whence all other elements of life spring. Strangely enough, the Quiché Bible, the *Popol Vuh*, describes the mother—the great sorceress, the great healer, the greatest of all the stars—as the one who helps her grandchildren and children in their struggles and conflicts between good and evil. It is she who keeps alive the memory of her offspring when they are first defeated by the forces of evil, and it is she who watches over the objects used in the game of pelota, so that they can find them later and use them in the struggle between good and evil. All this is contained in that hendecasyllable, "*A mi madre que me contaba cuentos,*" but is amplified into a whole mythology, a whole cosmogony, a whole series of beliefs derived from the deepest origins of the Mayan Indians.

You have always been proud of your mixed blood, because—as you've said—the future of America depends on miscegenation. Can you explain that idea?

It seems to me that our great America, the America we carry in our hearts and bear on our shoulders and which has its own problems, the America which Martí called "ours," because it was our poor America, was born on the night when the first Spaniard surprised an Indian woman, drew her into his arms, raped her and made her pregnant. It was at that moment, at that instant, from that sunrise, that a man was to be born, a new element, a being part Spanish and part Indian. I'm thinking of Garcilaso the Inca. Garcilaso the Inca was the son of a Peruvian of royal blood and a Spaniard. This superb Peruvian woman and a Spaniard made love and as a result the first mestizo writer of America was born. So that when they call us mestizos, or when we call ourselves mestizos, we feel linked first of all to that noble spirit Garcilaso the Inca, and to everything he wrote. At the same time we think of another great poet of his period, the Guatemalan poet Rafael Landívar, who was exiled from Guatemala when Carlos III decreed that the Jesuits should leave Spain and her dominions. So Father Landívar left and went to Mexico, and from Mexico he moved on to Italy, arriving at Bologna. After a time, oppressed by homesickness, he wrote his *Rusticatio Mexicana*, more than three thousand Latin hexameters, in which he sang first of Guatemala, then of the fertile Central American mountains, and then of America as a whole, displaying it to Europeans as a continent that lacked none of Europe's beauties.

He wrote that in that far-off America there were splendid herds of horses and cattle, flocks of sheep, volcanoes as fine as Etna and Vesuvius and medicinal springs, and moreover that there was a victimized race there—the Indians—a race of great wisdom, a hard-working race who had been slandered to the Europeans. Father Landívar is not as well known as he should be, but to Don Marcelino Menéndez y Pelayo he was the Vergil of modern Latin. Today we think of those mestizos, we think of the Inca, of Landívar, and of Bello, another exile who sang of the tropics, of the riches of sugar, of cattle, of coffee, of our tropics. These are the mestizos who were to build America, and—with all possible detachment—I am proud to feel that I'm a mestizo. I'm proud to belong to this race of men resulting from the blending of two waters, two oceans, two ways of feeling: the Indian and the European. The European who arrived on our shores tired and oppressed, and the native who was reborn pure, elemental, and with his eyes full of dreams. That is why I believe that our America of mestizos is the America of tomorrow. Luckily, we are not purebred, we needn't complain that our stock is dying out, because it is renewing itself every day, and was afterwards renewed by the African strain added to it at the tragic time when black slaves were brought to our shores. New elements of life and substance were thus added to the mestizo with his European and Indian blood, and a more musical feeling for life perhaps. At that moment our American life entered a new phase, whether from the mingling of Negro with ladino, of Negro with European, or of Negro with mestizo; and from those groups, those elements, and that race, present-day man has emerged, the man who inhabits our countries, who works in our countries. So that when I say that I'm a mestizo and the son of mestizo parents, I am not sad but filled with pride, because it is through this cross-breeding that America is talking a new language and creating a new man.

Who were your first European ancestors?

My father's grandfathers and great-great-grandfathers were Spanish. My first Spanish ancestor arrived here between 1770 and 1780. He was a certain Don Sancho Alvarez de las Asturias, Conde de Nava y Noroño. He came straight from

Oviedo to Guatemala; his brothers followed, soon intermarried
with the Indians and founded the Asturias family. At first they
simply called themselves Alvarez, then Alvarez de las Asturias;
next the Alvarez was suppressed, leaving de las Asturias; and
finally the "de las" was suppressed, leaving Asturias. On my
father's side there is a known connection with the Oviedo branch
of the family; my mother was also of mixed blood, born of Spanish and Indian stock. My parents were morally admirable; they
had studied, made efforts to improve themselves, and were lovers
of liberty, in the cause of which they were terribly persecuted
during the dictatorship of the "Señor presidente."

Did you study in Guatemala City?

Yes, until I finished my training as a lawyer and solicitor.
I began my education about 1903–04 in a place called Salamá
where my parents lived for some years. My father was called to
the bar in 1887 with very high qualifications, and my mother was
a teacher. They set up house, and when José María Barrios became president he gave my father one of the most interesting jobs
a young lawyer could have. My father would have gone far if this
president hadn't died and been followed by Estrada Cabrera, who
was the original of *El señor presidente,* and who had his knife
into everyone who had held office before. This meant that my
parents became poor and had to leave the capital. My maternal
grandfather suggested that they would do better to go with their
two sons to one of his properties in Salamá. My brother Marco
Antonio remained in Guatemala City with my maternal grandmother, and I went off with my parents to this little town, while
still a very small boy. Here my education began, and here too
something began which must have had paramount influence on
my artistic development. In this place there is a river with a very
curious name, the Orotava, as if it were a river whose sands
flowed over some buried seam of gold. I used often to run and
play beside this river, shouting "Orotava!"; it seemed to me a
euphoric word. In the waters of that river, at dusk, and in the
enormous stones, I undoubtedly found a source of legend, en-
chantment, and purity. I went to school to learn the alphabet,
but it was in the river, in those evenings, in those lights and

leaves that I learned to know the magic of my country, the voice of my country.

When I was three or four years old my grandfather began taking me on his journeys through his estates, and while he was engaged in business, or with his herds, he used to leave me on one of the native ranches, so that I shouldn't get sunstroke or become tired out. These ranches were usually like small villages built around a square, and there would be three or four farms all belonging to one family, to the parents and their married children. I would stay there playing with Indian boys of my own age or a little older—four- or five-year-olds. This was my first contact with the Indians, a very direct and immediate contact, and I must have retained something from it in my unconscious mind, although I cannot say exactly what. Sometimes I shut my eyes and vaguely remember some enormous turkeys—or *chompipes* as we used to call them—and troughs full of water and cooked ground maize; people busy shelling coffee beans, and leaves of tobacco hanging up to dry in the sun. There were also some monkeys, small deer, squirrels, all kept as pets by the Indians. All this I see surrounding those houses and in an atmosphere where life was lived rhythmically in the Indian style, where there was never any hurry, where things were done according to the movement of the sun, and where the first stage in my relationship with the Indians began. I listened to them talking their language, I learned a few of their words, and they laughed heartily when they heard me say them. Curiously enough, my grandfather didn't like me to say these Indian words, he wanted me to speak Spanish. Perhaps this is why I cannot now understand the Kechit language they used. We grew up at a period when it was necessary to appear to be European, when it was thought wrong to speak the native language, behave as a native, or show that one was in contact with the Indians. I remember Guatemala City as a place where men wore frock coats and women long dresses, and they bowed to each other deeply as if they had walked out of a copy of the French magazine *Illustration*. Naturally nothing could be more displeasing to such people than for one to be friendly with the Indians. My generation had to wait until the year 1920, when the great Mexican mural paintings began, when the Mexican Revolution was over and the First World War had ended, for our

eyes to be opened by archaeological discoveries, and for us to
begin wondering how we could go on thinking about Europe,
when we had so much that was admirable in our natives. But
the first of our painters to paint Indian subjects, and my own first
stories, were criticized by everyone; it was said that we were
discrediting our country, and that the Europeans would think we
were Indians and unworthy to call ourselves Europeans.

*Is that why you devoted your thesis for your doctorate of law to
the subject of the social problems of the Indian?*

When I look back today, I think it was partly fate. By
then I had completely forgotten my contacts with the natives as
a small boy, but in 1921–23 I got in touch with them again. I was
a student of law and studying sociology—it was beginning to be
taught then—when I went back and chose the native question
for my thesis. I returned once again to the native villages near the
capital and again made contact with their way of life, their marriages, manner of cultivating the land, family relationships, and
everything that contributed to my thesis. So that, almost as if it
were fate, I was thrown among the natives for a second time.
But there was something more. When my parents returned to
the capital in 1911 they bought property and set up a large business for the sale of products from abroad, flour, sugar, and so
on. Goods were sold retail in the store at the front of the house,
but at the back was an enormous patio with a few trees and a big
gate for mules and bullock carts to come through, and here
people came to buy wholesale. At night bonfires were lit, and my
brother and I, then between eleven and fourteen years old, used
to join the people sitting around the bonfires and listen to them
singing and talking. This experience has been very useful to me.
In all my books, most of the dialogues between the characters are
memories of the conversations that went on during those long,
brilliant Guatemalan nights. In my dialogues I almost hear the
voices of the people I knew. When one is young, and especially
when one is a child, this is all fresh material and the important
things are imprinted for life. I think a writer is formed in childhood or youth, because it is then that he has a number of experiences which afterwards reappear in his work. Once adult, one is

more impervious, and must search within oneself for what was stamped on one's feelings and mind in childhood and youth.

Some years later you had to leave Guatemala for political reasons. Can you recall this period which was so decisive for your life and work?

We twenty-year-old students—the "generation of 1920" as we were called, because we became writers and journalists at the end of the European war—had all fought against the dictatorship of Estrada Cabrera, a dictatorship that lasted twenty-two years, and we succeeded in overthrowing it. A democratic government was set up in Guatemala, but it lasted a very short while, because there was soon a military coup d'état, and the old dictatorship continued under a new name. We thereupon withdrew from politics and founded the People's University. We thought that before attempting political propaganda we must educate the people. The aim of the People's University was to teach them to read and write, but although that was very important, the thing that interested us most was to teach them at the same time what were their obligations and rights according to the constitution. We were trying to create a country whose people were not ignorant of their political rights and obligations, because we understood that we had been saddled with a dictatorship after overthrowing Estrada Cabrera not because there were men eager to exercise power, but because the people were too ignorant to defend rights and liberties they didn't even know existed. The university prospered and still exists. We invited lawyers, engineers, and doctors to come and teach and they gave classes for nothing. This in itself was asking them to make a sacrifice, because generally a student's training is paid for by the nation, but once he takes his degree, far from doing something to help his country, he is more likely to exploit it with the help of his degree. What we were asking of these professional men was that in the midst of so much exploitation and privilege they should give up something for the sake of the people. Our plans turned out very well. Academics of all ages, old and young, left their work and arrived on winter evenings to give classes between seven and eleven at night. Our policy was to educate the people, and we had converted ourselves into real teachers. The university became so important that even some women shut up in brothels asked us to go there and teach them to read and write. Some brothel-keepers gave permission, but when our teachers had taught them reading and writing and began to teach them about their rights, many of the procuresses became indignant. This shows how everyone wants those who are exploited to remain in ignorance, so that they can go on being exploited. The People's University was doing magnificently, and I had by now become a lawyer, when something very unfortunate happened. An officer who was going through the streets of Guatemala with his patrol killed a high-up army officer who tried to take his patrol away from him. He was prosecuted and we took up the defense of this young man of twenty-four; we said that he could not be shot according to military regulations, because he was in command of a patrol, and these same military regulations decreed that the patrol could not be handed over except in the barracks whence it had emerged. We did everything possible in his defense, in spite of which he was sentenced to death and shot, to our great distress. At this time we were publishing a weekly called *Tiempos nuevos* (New Times), and we devoted a whole issue to an analysis of the military reasons that had led to this measure, and we mounted a violent attack on the military authorities. When the magazine came out, one of the directors of *Tiempos nuevos*, Dr. Epaminondas Quintana, was beaten up in the Callejón de Jesús, one of the central streets of Guatemala City; his eardrum and nose were broken and he was badly injured. As I was a director of the weekly, with Quintana and others, my parents, who had already suffered very greatly under the dictatorship, kept me indoors and at once made preparations for me to leave Guatemala. It was very brave of them, particularly my mother, to part with their eldest son. But she preferred me to go, rather than see me beaten up in my own country. I believe every man is born to a destiny, and that my destiny was to be an exile. I left Guatemala on the German ship *Teutonia* for Panama, and from there I took an English boat to Liverpool, and thence to London. It was my father's idea that I should study political economy there, but I became much more enamored of the British Museum, where I saw real treasures of

Indian art, important books, and precious Guatemalan objects to be found only in that marvelous museum. Thus it was my fate or luck to return once more among the Indians. But London is a very cold place. I had come from a country of brilliant light and marvelous skies into those terrible foggy days. I wrote home that I would go to Paris on July 14 to see the celebrations, and when I arrived there on that day in 1923 I was immediately fascinated by the city. I went to the Sorbonne and found an announcement of a course on the myths and gods of Central America—in other words Mayan America—by Professor Georges Raynaud. I began studying with Raynaud, who explained the *Popol Vuh*, the sacred book of the Quichés, in which all the elements concerning their origins are brought together. It begins by telling how the gods created the universe, describing the creation of man and woman, the struggle between good and evil, and how good succeeded in vanquishing evil. Then comes a series of stories about animals—the parrot, the macaw—which are in reality moral fables to enrich the spiritual life of the natives. The professor explained and illustrated the mythological and agricultural aspects of this book, very important factors in the development of native culture. After the first two years of studying this and other texts, Raynaud had finished translating, after forty years' work, the *Popol Vuh* from Quiché into French. I then had the idea that under his supervision I might translate it from French into Spanish. Translation of this sort of text is exceptionally difficult; it is like translating the Bible or the Koran. Each word has its special meaning, and a great many synonyms must be examined to find which is the most exact. I had constantly to consult the Quiché original so as not to lose contact with the language the book had been written in. I worked at this translation with a Mexican student, now dead, J. M. González de Mendoza, who signed his work with the name Abate de Mendoza.

It was during those years that you wrote Leyendas de Guatemala. *What relation is there between that book and the work you were doing?*

That book was, as it were, the reaction of my aesthetic feelings to the dry scientific work I was doing with Professor Raynaud. It was research; we had to pore over books,

go to the library and stay there six or seven hours a day reading
and searching for words to clarify native concepts. It was a
very valuable undertaking, but also very exhausting. As I had a
more creative mind I began making a record of the legends, and
writing that book of mine. When Raynaud discovered I had
written it he looked at me with a certain commiseration, because
he was a scientist and this creativity formed no part of his science.

Did you go on taking part in your country's politics?

          I took part in politics when I was young and a student,
until I was twenty-three or twenty-four. After that I took no
further part, because I was living away from Guatemala nearly
the whole time. When I was thirty-three I returned to my country during the dictatorial government of General Jorge Ubico, a
time when politics didn't exist because the president thought, felt,
and spoke for us all. I had nothing more to do with politics until
1944–45, the year when Ubico fell from power and two revolutionary governments followed—those of Dr. Juan José Arévalo
and of Colonel Jacobo Arbenz. I belonged to no party at that
time; I was appointed to diplomatic posts but I never took part
in politics or belonged to any party. It has always been my policy
to defend Latin America against the encroachments of North
American imperialism. Wherever I was living, whether in Paris,
Buenos Aires, or Mexico, I always joined anti-imperialist groups
and I have always expressed this attitude in my works. I'm a
writer, not a politician, and I have never pretended to be one. I
have been pursued by politics. I am political in my books but
politics has never been a way of life for me.

Why did you let sixteen years pass between the publication of
Leyendas de Guatemala *(1930) and* El señor presidente?

          Because we were living for fourteen years under Jorge
Ubico's dictatorship. When I went back to Guatemala I left a
copy of the book I had just finished with a French professor,
Georges Pillement. He afterwards translated it into French, but
didn't send me a copy, as that would have been very dangerous.
In Guatemala I worked at journalism and wrote some son-
nets—"Fantominas," "Rayitos de estrella," "Emulo Lipolidón,"
"Alcasán," and "El rey de la altanería"—which were published

together in a little book, and *El señor presidente* appeared in
Mexico in 1946.

How did you come to write that book?

In 1923 there was a competition for stories in the Guatemalan paper *El imparcial*. I had written a story called "Los
mendigos políticos" (The Political Beggars), which is almost the
same as the first chapter of *El señor presidente*. I hadn't time to
send my story to the paper, and when I returned to Europe I
packed it in my luggage. When I met my Spanish American
friends in Paris, each of them had anecdotes to tell about the
dictators in their countries, and I remembered what I had heard
at home in Estrada Cabrera's time. We used to shut the doors
and make a thorough search, and as soon as it was certain that no
one could hear us, people began to talk. No one mentioned
Cabrera's name, he was called "the man," and they would describe how he had killed, poisoned, or tortured someone at the
police station. One day I began to link these memories together in
"Los mendigos políticos," and this is how the novel began, with
the story of General Canales and the lawyer who was con-
victed of the death of the "*loquito*." Almost all the characters
correspond to real people, combined with mythology and all
the imagination there is in the book. In "Angel Face" I tried to
unite two or three very important figures of the time. I made this
character beautiful because he partly represented a brilliant and
handsome lawyer called Francisco Galves Portocarrero who was
profoundly perverted by Cabrera. He died at the hands of the
people, undeservedly, because he wasn't a criminal but a man
Cabrera had used for his own ends. There is a moment when
Angel Face fails to respond as the dictator wishes, and wants to
escape, to flee from this situation. Here Cabrera's intuition enters in, a sort of sense of smell or power of divination that dictators have, and which means that it's not everyone who can be
one. He begins to mistrust Angel Face, to suspect that though remaining in his company he is no longer on his side, and he eliminates him in the most horrifying way in prison, making him
think his wife has become the dictator's mistress, and leaving her
in doubt whether her husband has gone away and abandoned

her. All this is true. These dictatorships, when the leaders kept themselves hidden, spinning evil from secret corners like spiders, belonged to the days before fascism. Cabrera was a sort of Borgia, entirely capable of poisoning people. Whereas, later on, a dictator like Ubico used to appear in the public places of Guatemala in his splendid uniforms, with his motorbikes and loudspeakers. This was already fascism, nazism, but the other was a muffled and terrifying dictatorship, because modern methods of communication didn't yet exist. Cabrera had complete control over the country's two ports, on the Atlantic and the Pacific; no newspapers were allowed in, only those published by him, nor was there any radio. A dictatorship cannot isolate a country now as it did then, because people can turn on their radios in secret and hear what is going on. During Cabrera's dictatorship isolation became so normal that world celebrities who had never been to see what was happening wrote articles in praise of our festivals of Minerva. As a result of propaganda—photographs of children singing to Minerva—they believed that our country was a paradise and Cabrera a sort of Pericles. My generation could not get papers or books, so we only read Spanish and French writers— Victor Hugo, Dumas, and Zola—and all the dusty old books in our houses. A dictatorship like Cabrera's can never be repeated. Two generations brought it to an end: that of 1907, a generation of doctors and lawyers almost all educated in France, only realized what the dictatorship was like when they returned to Guatemala. They plotted to kill the president with a bomb, which unfortunately killed the coachman and horses while Cabrera remained alive. It was believed at first that the coachman had died saving the president's life, and he was given a fabulous funeral, attended by generals, the members of the assembly, and public officials, his portrait was published in the newspapers, he was made a martyr; but when in all ignorance, his wife showed the chief of police some papers she had found in his house, and it was proved that the coachman had been in the plot, they dug up the corpse and threw it out. Of the five men implicated in the plot, all doctors, one was shot in prison and the brothers Valdés— Blanco, who were planning to escape to Mexico, were discovered in a house where they had taken refuge. In the end it was never known whether one of them killed the others and then committed suicide, or whether they were all murdered. Afterwards there was an attempt by the cadets, but this also failed although the best shot in the military college was chosen to kill the president. When Cabrera arrived at the palace the young man fired at close range, but the bullet hit a flag that was lowered in salute to the president and he was only wounded in the hand. Cabrera fell to the ground, and thinking he was dead, the cadets didn't finish him off. In his frenzy Cabrera disbanded the cadet corps and had the college set on fire, destroying it completely. I remember that in 1919 when some of us students and workers began a nonviolent campaign against him, my mother's hair turned white at the mere thought that we too might be killed. We issued several manifestos declaring: "You can have our lives if necessary, but we are fighting for what we want—the freedom of our country," and these we signed. When I read these manifestos now, I feel afraid, and wonder how we could have written them to that wild beast.

Once talking about Latin American dictators, you said that presidents of this sort could only appear in countries where mythology prevailed.

For a president of that sort to exist there must be myths, and Estrada Cabrera became a myth. He himself was seen by no one; he was a hidden divinity, a truly mythological being.

Did your contacts with surrealism begin when you were a student at the Sorbonne?

That was a little later. I was a student when surrealism first appeared, but my earliest contact with it was in about 1929 or 1930, when I had already left the Sorbonne. I was a great friend of some of the surrealists, especially Robert Desnos, who died in a concentration camp and belonged to the same group as Breton, Eluard, and Aragon. I also often met Tristan Tzara, father of Dada. I went with many other Latin Americans—the great Peruvian poet Vallejo was living in Paris at the time—to the meetings they sometimes held in Montparnasse. Surrealism certainly opened a door for us and thrilled us greatly.

What sort of influence did surrealism have on you?

We felt it gave us freedom to create. Belonging as we did to different races, and pledged to rules of artistic creation governed by intelligence and reason, we felt that surrealism opened a door by which to express the unconscious internal message springing from the depths of our being. Automatic writing and all these new forms of self-expression were like a lash of the whip for us since we already had a primitive and infantile form of surrealism. There's undoubtedly something elemental in surrealism, something psychologically elemental; but this new school enabled us to give life to what we carried within us. Some Indian texts, like the *Popol Vuh* or the *Anales de los Xahil*, are truly surrealist. They possess the same duality between reality and dream; there is a kind of dream, of unreality, which when told in all its detail seems more real than reality itself. From this springs what we call "magic realism." There are events that really happen and afterwards become legends, and there are legends which afterwards become events; there are no boundaries between reality and dreams, between reality and fiction, between what is seen and what is imagined. The magic of our climate and light gives our stories a double aspect—from one side they seem dreams, from the other, they are realities.

There was another group of surrealist writers, including Gertrude Stein, James Joyce, and Léon Paul Fargue, who were preoccupied with words, the meaning of words and plays upon words. We were much more interested in words than in surrealism itself, because the word has special importance to Latin Americans and above all, to primitive races. Not only does the word transmit thought and feeling, it also contains a magical aspect. These new investigators of words found other concepts, according to how the vocables were united, lying behind the forms of speech. We began to try out these formulas in Spanish, formulas able to produce true delirium, but which greatly enriched the language, particularly by euphony and onomatopoeia. The repetition of certain words and certain sounds is an essential factor in primitive literatures, that of the Indians for example. This aspect, developing simultaneously with surrealism, excited us considerably.

You show this preoccupation with language in all your work.

Yes, but it is a somewhat telluric preoccupation, like that of the Indians, who conceive of the word as sacred. According to them the word gives power over the thing one names. I say "house," and I take possession of a house, it is one way of making it my own. Native wisdom says "in the word, everything; outside the word, nothing." This means that when our literature has its roots in native life it is bound to be substantially preoccupied with words.

Since your linguistic creativity springs from the daily talk of Guatemalans, isn't it affected by your living outside your country?

It is both advantageous and harmful to a writer to live outside his country. By going away he loses the pristine inspiration of its auditive, olfactive elements, and even the gustative ones, as every country has its own dishes; on the other hand it's useful to go away, because it is then that one appreciates the landscape better, sees characters and hears sounds more clearly. There is a space separating the writer or artist from what is closest to him. When one returns after a time one finds a new world, though it soon loses its novelty. For instance, in Guatemala we have marvelous sunsets; one arrives and gazes at them in ecstasy, but after a while one ceases to appreciate them because they have become part of the landscape itself. The ideal would be for the artist to live part of the year in his own country, and part of the year abroad.

Although you've spent most of your life abroad, the theme of your books has always been Guatemala.

I'm one of those who believe that one should move from the particular to the universal. There was at one time a great movement toward cosmopolitanism, and extremely important writers whom I knew in Paris—Enrique Gómez Carrillo, the famous essayist of Guatemala, the Peruvian writers Don Ventura and Don Francisco García Calderón, and the great Ecuadorian writer Gonzalo Zaldumbide—didn't concentrate on their own countries, nor take them as their point of departure, but concentrated on the universal. It must be admitted that the work of these writers, important though it was and is, has been lost and is now scarcely remembered. Whereas the work of writers who began by writing about their own countries is not forgotten. Those works are always remembered because they are milestones, they enrich the world's literature. Ever since the First World War, Latin American writers have been devoting their attention to their own countries, have begun to stress what concerns their own world, and in this way our literature has been renewed, enriched, and broadened. It has departed from cosmopolitanism and gone straight to what is individual, characteristic, native, and creole—not that a writer has to confine himself solely to what is native and creole. I believe that the writer's world should continually be expanding, starting from his own country, from the particular. I remember that when I visited Valéry to thank him for his letter to Francis de Miomandre about a French translation of my *Leyendas de Guatemala*—the letter in which Valéry said that the legends were magic in the language of another planet, and that to a European understanding it was an utterly strange book, to be drunk rather than read—he made me promise him that I would leave Paris, because if I stayed I would turn into just another author writing about the Seine, about Nôtre Dame and Versailles, and that—he said—was done much better by the French. Many Hispano-Americans who come here fail for this reason, they forget their essence, their elements. This advice of Valéry's turned out very well for me, because when I returned to my country after ten or twelve years in Europe I took a new and more complete view of it, as if I had absorbed like a sponge all the landscape and life that had gone into my books, especially *Hombres de maíz* (Men of Maize) and *Mulata*. In these works I expressed a different view of my country from that in *Las leyendas*, which I wrote when I was more American, so to speak, more closed to impressions.

The telluric and mythological vein also predominates in your writing.

Nature is my book. On the whole I think that what characterizes Latin American literature is the realization that man is not supreme in nature, whereas in other literatures and other schools of fiction such as the European, nature has always been dominated by man, and indeed figures very little because the novels develop in surroundings of cement and glass. In our American novels nature not only figures as decoration, or stage scenery if you like; it is the chief character in many of them. Take for example *La vorágine* (The Whirlpool) by the famous Colombian novelist Eustasio Rivera: here we see nature, the immense forest, the forest like an ocean, gradually becoming the hero of the novel, and we realize its importance. The characters are two young people who go deep into the forest, and who first show us the tragedy of their love, of a pure, heroic love; they slowly vanish as one reads, advancing into the forest until they have ceased to be essential elements of the novel, leaving only the woods, only the huge trees, only the terrifying snakes, all the animals and the tragic world of skeletons of creatures who have got lost in the forest and died of hunger or their wounds. There are other novels in which the same thing happens. In *Don Segundo Sombra*, the famous Argentine novel, by presenting us with those great herds of horses and the gauchos' journeys on horseback, Güiraldes is making us aware of the immensity of the pampas; the pampas, not the men journeying across it, dominates the book, the pampas is what attracts us, we forget the gauchos themselves and are left with the movement of horses' hooves on the vast and infinite Argentine plain. In none of these Latin American novels has nature been subdued, she figures in the foreground, not as in European fiction. But when the romantic movement began, and Europeans turned their attention to America, we find Chateaubriand, in *Atala* and *Les Natchez*, painting nature as though it were the scenery in a theater. His descriptions of nature can be taken away or left, they neither add to nor diminish the novel, the characters, or the situations. Whereas to take away nature from Hispano-American novels would be like removing the lungs from a human being, because they breathe really through those green lungs which are a part of themselves. They aren't ornament, or theatrical decor, they are in fact a vital and essential part of the novel, its characters, and situations. In my books, the natural aspect of Guatemala occupies a preponderant, central, important place. In Guatemala, as in all Central

America, a phenomenon occurs which Europeans can find only in Greece. The land becomes much narrower, oceans approach one another, and the Central American isthmus is reduced to an exceedingly slender strip. There are also rivers and an infinity of lakes in the interior of Central America, immense lakes at different altitudes such as those of Guatemala, from Lake Atitlán at 2,000 meters to Lake Amatitlán at sea level. The sun beats down on the sea, beats down on the rivers and lakes, and is reflected back from the water into the atmosphere; this is why the Guatemalan light always seems like damp crystal. No objects look near at hand, things never seem close, there is always a distance; it is as if they were reflected in a mirror or through a lens or crystal. When traveling from Guatemala to Mexico one can appreciate this phenomenon. On arrival at Mexico City after two hours in an airplane, one sees a completely different light, because there isn't the same evaporation of water that exists in Guatemala, and things seem to crowd in upon one. This action of the light has undoubtedly influenced Guatemalan literature, its novels, myself, my poems. Our literature is very different from that of the southern countries; it is a literature at water level, on the surface, a literature of greater charm. This is not a modern phenomenon, but centuries old. When we approach the great ceremonial cities of the Mayas of Guatemala, just as in Yucatán, where the light has the same quality, we notice that the great sculptors of those days took the light as an element in their alto- and bas-reliefs. There are palaces and temples—in Palenque for instance— where we notice that the sculptors who worked inside those vast domes didn't dig deeply with their chisels, because these decorations were to be seen by the light of candles or torches. It is different with the great carved masses of Tikal, Copán, Uxmal, Quen Santo, or Quiriguá. There we see that the Mayan sculptors, well understanding the effect of light, made deep incisions with their chisels so that when the masses were illuminated they should have the necessary backing of shadow to give the sculpture its full value and magnificence. I think the light has a very direct effect, I might add a tyrannical effect, on the arts in our countries, particularly in Guatemala where works receive their baptism of clear illumination. In Guatemala, and this is a fact though it seems like a metaphor, there are red twilights, so red, and so blazing with light, that if there is a basin of water in the patio one has to touch it to prove that it is not blood but the reflected redness of the sky. The impact of another phenomenon, undoubtedly to be found in the pages of my books, is the shape of our hills and volcanoes. They are undulating, almost as if waves of the sea had been turned to stone all in a moment; and we see this undulation repeated in Mayan monuments. In all the work of the great artists of those days straight lines and rigidity hardly exist. The Mayans used curved lines in their decorations, they manipulated curves to make them like the curves of the mountains and hills. There are no large plains in Guatemala except on the south coast toward the Pacific. Except for these plains, all the rest is broken ground, it seems a country built like a sky-scraper, because one can climb from the seashore with a temperature of 45 to 50 degrees centigrade, up to 3,000 meters where the climate is colder. All these phenomena are to be found in my works. In the *Leyendas de Guatemala* this quality of our landscape constantly appears, the beauty of the cottony softness of our rosy dawns and warm evenings, and the splendor and truly marvelous coloring of our trees. There are some huge trees that turn rose-red at some seasons and lose all their green leaves; from a distance one sees fields and fields of pink trees as in some Oriental tale. There are all sorts of orchids growing within reach of the traveler, and some regions are always clothed and bathed in roses and carnations. And there are birds with brilliant plumage, gold and emerald plumage.

In the *Leyendas de Guatemala* mountains and rivers are often personified, either through being transformed into people, or by people taking on these natural forms. In *Hombres de maíz*, for example, one of the characters is María Tecún, the *tecuna*, the woman who is always running away. In the west of Guatemala there is a high plateau on which stands a huge stone that is very seldom visible because it is always shrouded in mist; this stone is known as María Tecún. These great rocks are often given names of persons or figures from legends and so develop an almost human quality; there is a relation between nature and humanity. Guatemala is a preeminently green country; this is why the natives are called Quichés, which comes from a native word signifying "country of green trees." Green is our color, and everywhere there are greens of every shade. Over the paths in this green landscape, over this green carpet, over these mountains of every shade of green, the natives make their way, men and women dressed in different bright colors. They too form part of our landscape and give it a special character with their brilliance. Each place has its own local dress. The women of Aticalán, for example, wear a red petticoat wound around them in the Oriental style, an embroidered *güipil* (as we call their sleeveless chemise), and a bright blue sash, and, most remarkable feature of all, their long plaits are interlaced with a broad, bright red ribbon and bound round their heads so that they look like enormous red plates. Our villages also imitate the shapes of the mountains in building their cupolas, and anywhere from the east to the west of the country one can see from afar the interplay of these cupolas with the surrounding mountains. All this gives the landscape unity and makes it unique. It is unique because of its light, because of its greenness, and because of the enormous number of birds and flowers.

All this has influenced my writing, and is the reason why it never becomes excessively bitter, excessively bloodthirsty, or excessively powerful; this would be inconceivable in our natural surroundings. Their natural surroundings are reflected in the way of life of the inhabitants, and if people sometimes find a certain languor in the characters in my books it is because the characters correspond to their environment. If we think of the reflected light we can see why legends, magic, witch doctors, and sorcerers circulate among us—all that world and underworld, both visible and invisible, which helps those poor people to exist. They don't rely on their gods alone, but on everything that surrounds them and holds them open-eyed in a sort of sleepwalkers' amazement before the marvelous Guatemalan landscape.

What is the source of the humor one finds in your writing?

A French critic said of *El señor presidente* that an essential element in it is that whenever all seems lost there will be one character who sees the sky, sees the stars, sees the light, and the reader emerges from gloom. I think the humor in my books is partly derived from what we Guatemalans call *"humor chapin—"*

people born in the capital are called "*chapin.*" It's typical of their way of talking always to make a joke or a witticism, which gives any event a pleasanter color. This quality has been much cultivated, and we have a magnificent poet, one of the great romantic poets of the 1830's, Pepe Batres Montúfar, who in spite of all his bitterness, of all his pain, has the ability to produce in the most painful moments of his poems a charming phrase that makes one smile a little and go on reading.

The Spanish of Hispano-American literature has been losing the purity of Castilian and acquiring characteristics of its own, sometimes local ones. What causes have determined this change? Are you in sympathy with it?

One feature of the Hispano-American novel is the Spanish we write in. Our spoken language, especially in countries like Mexico, Guatemala, Peru, Bolivia, and Ecuador—countries with large native populations, where native languages dating from before the Conquest are still spoken—is a Spanish with a very individual, very special character. Castilian syntax has been forgotten and native forms have been amalgamated into our way of speech. Consciously or unconsciously, Central American writers, and I for one, make use of features of Indian speech, for example the parallelism which consists in repeating the same idea in different words. Our language has also been enriched by a great many names of animals, precious stones, minerals, vegetables, flowers, and substances not to be found in Spanish dictionaries. I think that what characterizes my books is the words I use rather than my sentences. On the whole, Spanish, particularly Castilian, uses long sentences. I don't use those long sentences, because the phrase is not so important in native dialects, but as I have already said the word has sacred significance, "in the word everything, outside the word nothing." In fact it was by means of the word that the gods created all elements of life, and by means of the word that the gods related themselves to them. The creation of the world, the creation of man, everything implied in the theories and cosmogonic formulas of creation among the Mayan Quichés, is all based on the value of words. Words are so important to them that if one arrives at a native village and asks the name of

a woman passing by, they will answer "María," because all
women are María and all men are Juan. They don't tell you the
person's exact name, because knowing it would give one magic
power over them. Besides, they don't believe in death as we do,
they believe in disappearance, therefore they don't say "he died"
but "he disappeared" because the person who leaves life is beginning a journey through an unknown world. The departed must
know—and they do know—each of the words that must be said
at the crossroads they will come to after death. This is much like
the wisdom of the Egyptian Osirians, and like the Osirians they
have to know when they arrive at the white path, the red path,
the green path, and the black path exactly how to reply to the
questions asked them by invisible voices. They all treasure this
wisdom and practice it, particularly the oldest among them, for
their own safety and so as to avoid despair and desolation and
arrive at places where life is pleasant. They believe that heaven
has thirteen levels and only a few will reach the upper levels of
heaven, most of them will go to the lower levels which are
pleasant and contain all the fountains and banquets of the paradise they have constructed for themselves. This is a vital, human,
and transcendent relation of language. In all my books words
acquire essential value, and perhaps therein lies the difficulty I
find in writing. Sometimes I spend whole days and nights trying
to find the exact word to go in a paragraph or phrase already
written. If the word I have written doesn't satisfy me, I search
for the one that most adequately describes the character, event,
or landscape. The word must be as precise as possible, because
the more precise it is the more completely does one take possession of that object or person. Such a use of words takes us very
far away from Castilian; we say that we speak Spanish but that it
is a Spanish "impregnated" with all the native languages. This
effect of the Indian language and world is so natural to Latin
Americans that the first Spaniards who came to America soon
began to write with a different syntax themselves. It happened to
Bernal Díaz del Castillo who came with Hernán Cortés to con-
quer Mexico and afterwards remained in Guatemala. When he
was eighty, this old man with an amazing memory wrote his
Historia verdadera de la conquista de la Nueva España (True
History of the Conquest of New Spain), and when Menéndez y

Pelayo read the book he was astonished to find a Castilian soldier writing a language that bore no relation to Castilian. What had happened was that Díaz del Castillo had gradually, by osmosis, by listening, reading, and living, acquired a different form of speech. The air, the very light of America had transformed his language. An inhabitant of Castile cannot speak the same Spanish as someone living among the mountains of Bolivia or the heights of Mexico. So our language goes on changing, changes constantly, and is enriched in new ways. If we study what has happened in Argentina, and particularly in Buenos Aires, we see how European languages have been combined with Spanish to create an idiom that many people can't understand, but which is a new language, a refreshed language. I'm not against such additions, because I believe that our Hispano-American language is being enriched all the time—in Argentina by what immigrants have introduced, and in Mexico or Peru by what the Indians have left behind. It is rather like what is happening to the English language, which is constantly being enriched, and not at all like the Spanish of Spain which remains unchanged. We have had to use new expressions, new verbs, new ways of arranging words, because we belong to completely different worlds. For instance, in my book *Maladrón*, besides describing the cult of Maladrón as practiced by the Sadducees, I depict the lives of five Spaniards lost in our jungle, who gradually lose their Spanish character and become part of nature herself, of the leaves, of the flowers, of those mysterious trees of our country—the mimosas. I also wanted to bring to that novel the rich language of Alfonso Reyes, Rubén Darío, Huidobro, Neruda and many of our great writers, a language which is being forgotten. In *Maladrón* I tried to write a sumptuous and sonorous Spanish, reminiscent of the sixteenth or seventeenth century, but less archaic—modern and readable today.

What significance has the repetition of syllables and words in your style?

The Indians use repetition of syllables and words to produce superlatives. There are no superlatives in native languages, at least in Guatemala. When they say "white, white, white," it is equivalent to "very white" or "extremely white." They also repeat syllables; for "enchanting" they would say 're-reenchanting," each "re" giving greater emphasis.

It's a style that isn't always accessible to the ordinary reader.

My books aren't easy to read because they have the baroque quality of our language, a thing that some praise and others condemn. But baroque is probably essential to the ladino. When the Spaniards arrived in our countries and began building their cathedrals, they used the decorative forms of Spanish churches and cathedrals on their portals and altars. But the work was carried out by natives—the Spaniards couldn't have built so many temples and palaces as were constructed during the four centuries of their rule without native labor—and they added to the Spanish decorations something of their own style, a little plant or a little stylized eagle, so that we see the decoration becoming over-elaborate, and this elaboration is the same as the baroque style of our literature. I think there's another aspect of my writing which isn't easy, and that's the fact that it's very much connected with the primitive books of the Mayas, the Quichés, the Aztecs, the Nahualans, and that entire literary and artistic world which is now being rediscovered, and is emerging with renewed strength after staying hidden for nearly five centuries. I avoid native words in my books as far as possible, because they exclude the reader from the text, and I try to find some equivalent in Spanish. Nor do I much like using creole expressions or any of the forms that correspond exclusively to each particular country. I try to make my writing universally understandable, although entirely Guatemalan.

Which of your books do you like best yourself?

One loves books as one loves one's children, but the one I like best is *Hombres de maíz*, although I recognize that *El señor presidente* is a book of fundamental literary importance. *Hombres de maíz* is a more obscure book, there are no concessions to a reader who doesn't know too much literature, and it's a book that can be read as a novel but is profound too; each one of its pages can be interpreted. When I return to it myself I find a great many native elements, vegetable elements, so that it's as if, on opening the book, a series of phantoms and myths emerged that had been shut up inside. The lives of the characters form curves, some start as phantoms and become real, and others begin as real and end as phantoms, as invisible beings, imagined beings, illusory beings. There are also some true things, like the German characters who put on their dinner jackets to go and play in the village of Salamá at night; that really happened. In that desolate place where there was nothing but malaria and mosquitos, these shopkeepers, who spent their days in their stores, used to put on evening clothes and embark on another life, the drawing-room life, the life of music, the life of Bach, the composer they most often played. And the Spanish language of *Hombres de maíz* doesn't always seem like Spanish, at times it seems to be the music of another tongue.

*Your trilogy of the banana plantations—*Viento fuerte (*Strong Wind*), El papa verde (*The Green Pope*), *and* Los ojos de los enterrados (*The Eyes of the Buried*) *didn't get very good reviews, and according to some critics these novels are reportage rather than literature.*

That may be so. but I think they are the marrow of my work. With the passage of time I find that the "banana plantation trilogy" contains elements that are really vital to Guatemalan life. Some of the characters in *Strong Wind* are so much alive that if you went to Guatemala you would meet them. The criticisms I make in it of North American society were part of my life, I didn't invent them. *The Green Pope* is a character who interests me very much. Since he's a North American I intended to make him an odious man, but as the novel progressed he became more and more attractive until, by the end, he's a man everyone loves and helps. Of the three, I think *Los ojos de los enterrados* is most truly a novel, because the characters have validity. But the critics may be right when they say these books are to some extent reportage. On my way from Buenos Aires to Guatemala I spent a long time in the fruit-growing country; I already knew it, but I now saw that way of life with new eyes, and perhaps a little as a journalist. Perhaps the novel was written the wrong way round; first I wrote "El huracán" (The Hurricane), and I intended to publish it as a short story, but when the Panamanian poet and writer, Rogelio Sinán, read it on his way through Guatemala, he told me it would make a magnificent beginning for a novel. So I began to think and brood over it, and then the characters came to life. Another reason for these books being partly reportage may be that I was greatly inspired by a book called *The Banana Empire: A Case Study of Economic Imperialism*, written by two North American journalists who had toured the plantations. The allegations I put into the mouth of Mr. Smith, the millionaire who visits the plantations in disguise (his remarks to the shareholders), are taken from that book. I thought no one would read a technical book, a bureaucratic report like *The Banana Empire*, so I put what these journalists said in the mouth of one of my characters.

Do you think the critics have understood your work?

There must be much that is telluric in what one does, a sort of foreknowledge, because after my books have been published I have read theses and studies written about them and found that critics and students are constantly discovering secrets in them that I didn't know about myself. The critical work done on my books has enlightened me about a lot of things I have put into them—unconsciously if you like—and which play an important part in them. I think on the whole the critics have shown understanding of my work, and I ought to mention one in particular, the great Belgian writer and poet Vandercamen, who was the first to reveal many things to me. When he wrote to me about *Weekend en Guatemala* he said, "In the old days the characters in European novels, particularly those of Victor Hugo and Flaubert, moved along the roads, and through the cities and drawing rooms of America, but now it's the other way around, your characters are beginning to move through the cities of Europe, and we are getting to know them, they are becoming familiar to us. I know some of your characters well, like Goya Yic, he comes into my house, I talk to him and greet him."

Where have your books been most read and best understood?

I would say in Europe rather than in Latin America. In France, Holland, Germany, and Italy there are people exclusively occupied in studying my works. In my country the first studies are being produced, two or three books have been published, and in Argentina a very important book has recently come out by Professor Iber Verdugo of the University of Córdoba, called *La obra de Miguel Angel Asturias en relación con la literatura hispano-americana* (The Work of Miguel Angel Asturias in Relation to Hispano-American Literature), analyzing every epoch of twentieth-century Hispano-American literature reflected in my work.

What does the "literature of commitment" mean to you?

A great deal has been spoken and written about the literature of commitment, or literature that is *engagé* or committed, and there will doubtless be still more discussion on the subject. The term *"engagé"* was used a few years ago by the review *L'Esprit,* and afterwards Jean Paul Sartre used it in his study of that type of literature. Many people use the term "committed" in a definite political sense, that is to say, when they call an author committed they are labeling him as communist, pro-communist, left-wing, or leftish. This veiled manner of describing certain authors doesn't help us to see what is meant by committed literature. Many people understand by commitment that the author writes under direction, which is something quite different. Directed literature is written to serve a political cause, a religion or ideology. The directed author obeys certain obligations, definite aims, and so on. On the other hand *committed literature* implies responsibility, and in Latin America we used to speak of "responsible literature." Some writers were responsible and others were not, with regard to themselves, their conduct, their race, and the hardships they suffered. By *committed literature* I understand a literature responsive to the needs of a nation, which acts as the voice of that people and at the same time as a bridge to transmit to other minds and other men the echo of the hardships and sufferings or happiness of their country, so as to create a worldwide repercussion. If by literature of commitment is understood that which has always made itself responsible for the great events of our countries and also for the hardships and difficulties involved in oppression, tyranny, suffering, poverty, hunger, and lack of land, then our Latin American literature has always been *a committed, a responsible literature.* From the earliest times until the present day, the great works of our countries have been written in response to a vital need, a need of the people, and therefore almost all our literature is committed. Only as an exception do some of our writers enclose themselves in golden cages or ivory towers, isolate themselves and become uninterested in what is happening around them; such writers are concerned with psychological or egocentric subjects and the problems of a personality out of contact with surrounding reality. Perhaps it would be better to call our literature "invaded" literature, rather than committed—because it is invaded by life. We may, for instance, be writing a page of a novel when we hear a child crying; so we go out to see what's happpening and see this child, without shoes or clothes, with an enormous stomach, and we realize that it is the image of the poverty and physical misery surrounding us. It would be illogical and show lack of sensibility to go on writing our page and thinking about Versailles or Greece or try to spin words as Shakespeare did when there is something closer at hand, when the vision of something sterner and more real is invading life, something that forces us to take our pen and at once write some protest against the situation of these people translated into a story or a chapter in a novel. Committed literature has given us a number of very important works: I could mention *El hijo de salitre* (The Son of Saltpetre) by Teitelboin, *La sangre y la esperanza* (Blood and Hope) by Nicomedes Guzmán, *El río obscuro* (The Dark River) by Alfredo Varela, *El metal del diablo* (The Devil's Metal) by Augusto Céspedes, *Mamita Yunai* by Carlos Luis Fallas, *Pedro Páramo* by Juan Rulfo, *Prisión verde* (Green Prison) by Amado Amador, *Casas muertas* (Dead Houses), and *Oficina número uno* (Office Number One) by Otero Silva, *Hijo de hombre* (Son of Man) by Roa Bastos, and others. In native literature, which is intensely committed, we could mention *Yanakuna* by

Jesús Lara, or Ciro Alegría, who left two very important novels—
Los perros hambrients (The Hungry Dogs) and *El mundo es
ancho y ajeno* (Broad and Alien Is the World)—*Huasipungo* by
Jorge Icaza, and two other important novels by José María
Arguedas: *Los ríos profundos* (Deep Rivers) and *Todas las sangres*
(All the Bloods). All this South American fiction has made its way
into Europe. All these novels, without paying much attention to
certain forms nor imitating Europeans, have laid our problems before the conscience of the world, and made Europeans notice our
literature. Our literature has entered Europe by virtue of its
aesthetic value, its value as linguistic creativity, but most readers
have been interested in it because it speaks responsibly to Europeans about our problems, about everything human that fills our
pages, about social problems, and about economic problems.
Europeans have been interested to know how laborers die in the
banana plantations of Central America, how many die in the
quebracho forests of Argentina, how others die in the Bolivian
mines; how workers in the oil fields suffer. All this living human
world has been responsible for the breakthrough, and we must
therefore admit that this committed literature, literature invaded
by life, responsible literature, has opened the way for Europeans
to take an interest in what we Latin Americans write. To believe
that we Latin Americans are going to teach Europeans to reflect,
to philosophize, to write egocentric or psychological novels, to
believe that we are already a mature enough society to produce a
Proust or a Goethe—that would be daydreaming and self-decep-
tion. We are living in an epoch of creative literature, but it is a
fighting literature, sowing for tomorrow that sense of responsibility which will make future authors follow in the steps of great
Latin American writers and write responsible works of their own.
The new society being created in our countries, that society of
small or great industry, that society in which we see the wealthy
classes of former days replaced by the new middle classes, who
begin to play their part in commerce and big business, will also
have its writers, but they will be responsible, committed writers.
Some writers are accused of being committed only when they belong to the left, but it is possible to be committed to the right;
they can be committed to imperialism, against their race, against
their countries, against the world and Latin American ideals.

In the socialist countries, on the other hand, they have criticized the mythological vein in your work, arguing that it weakens the social indictment and the image of reality.

I've been called a "committed writer," using the word "committed" to signify that I'm a writer of the left, that I represent left-wing views, while other groups—people who would like me to be in the literary trenches firing off words and more words without any sense of responsibility and creating a rootless literature—say that in my books I fail in my duties as a committed writer by creating a literature of myth, legend, and belief. I have discussed all this a good deal, especially with some students who were preparing a thesis on *Hombres de maíz* for the University of Moscow. They asked me why there were so many references to myths in this book, so much witchcraft and sorcery—things which were false and spoiled the book. I told them that I couldn't write about the native races of Guatemala without mentioning the witch doctors, sorcerers, ghosts, and legends still alive among them, and that for me to ignore all that and write a "social" novel would certainly detract from my work and the image I have formed of my society. It has been said that in *El señor presidente* I provide no answer to dictatorship. I didn't want to give this novel a pleasant ending, firstly because I believe not only that dictatorship in Latin America didn't end with Estrada Cabrera, but that it has gone on and will go on for a long time. Therefore I couldn't end the book by inventing characters who would carry out a glorious revolution and set up a democratic government—that would be false. It would please a lot of people by relieving them of the pain of knowing that dictatorship goes on, but at the same time I would be falsifying reality. Secondly, I think a novelist can give evidence and make protests in his books, but he cannot and should not be asked to provide answers; those should be left for sociologists and historians. It's very difficult to satisfy everyone with one's books. A book is like a letter sent to a great many people; some answer, others don't. I think the basis for my work is the mythological one, its connection with the beliefs and other aspects of the rustic, primitive, and mentally childish life of the Indians, and advancing along this path I deal with the social problems that concern them. In

Hombres de maíz, which is a mythological novel, I show the constant struggle between the dealer in maize and the Indian, and the different sorts of life led by these poor people subjected to corrupt masters and the misfortunes that nearly always pursue them. My readers will therefore find commitment in my books, or else that life has invaded me when I deal with social problems, and they will find profounder explanations of life itself which I cannot keep separate. As I've said, it's impossible for me to stop talking about myths and the beliefs of my race, and set myself to write a novel which might equally well take place in Guatemala as in the Antipodes, in Europe, or in Asia.

What books influenced your development as a writer?

Native texts and my studies of *Popol Vuh,* the *Anales de los Xahil, Rabinal-Achi, Chilam-Balan;* my constant reading of these has influenced me a great deal. At present I prefer to read all sorts of books connected with Mayan culture, many that I didn't know before and that have helped me complete my understanding of that culture. There's a revival of interest in Indian studies, especially in Mexico, Guatemala, and the United States. A great many North Americans come to Guatemala today and carry out very fundamental researches into the life of the natives, their traditions, beliefs, and knowledge of their time. For instance, at the University of Pennsylvania there has been archaeological research into the city of Tikal, one of the great ceremonial centers of Petén in the heart of Guatemala. In time we shall have new information about native literature before the Conquest. It was disastrous that the conquistadors and the priests who came with them were complete barbarians and burned all the important books of our culture, believing that they emanated from the devil. It was only later that other monks arrived, known as "wise monks," and realized the value of these chronicles. They began mixing with the oldest members of every village, talking to them and taking down in Latin what these people told them in their native tongue; as a result we now have immense transcriptions dating from this period. All these have had a great influence on me. In the mornings before I begin to write I like to open one of these native texts and read some paragraphs or poems; this lightens my heart and helps me get on with my own work. I was and am a reader of Quevedo and Cervantes. There is much of Quevedo in my work, as many have pointed out. I have also been influenced by the great Europeans like Victor Hugo, Zola, Proust, and most certainly Flaubert, who is the master of the novel. I advise every novelist to read them, and also Perez Galdós and Eca de Queiros, two masterly writers. Panaït Istrati, and the works of Dostoevski, Tolstoy, and other Russians published in Barcelona before the war also had a great influence on me; they are writers who have much in common with our world and literature. Russian literature touches us closely because the mujik is rather like the peasant. In Anglo-Saxon literature I am an admirer of Lawrence, particularly *The Plumed Serpent*, and of North American novelists I put Faulkner first; he seems to me to resemble our novelists, except that he writes about Negroes instead of Indians. The great North American writers have certainly had a lot of influence on our development, and I would say that the new generation of Latin American writers is more influenced by North American than French literature, and, of course, by Joyce.

What's your opinion of the contemporary European novel?

In Europe everything is rational, everything is Cartesian. The French, like other Europeans, submit everything to rigorous logic, analyze everything. There is no spontaneity, no beliefs, no myths, no room for the world of imagination and dreams, which is a part of literature and which makes literature what it fundamentally is, a dream that we make the reader share. Many myths have come to an end in Europe, but others are now being created, for instance the myth of speed, to which hundreds of lives are sacrificed on the roads every week. Earlier myths, telluric myths, have vanished, although not completely, because we read every so often in the papers published over there about witch doctors and even magicians. Literature has gotten rid of myths, but those myths have remained alive in the minds of many people. In France, besides, the group of the *nouveau roman* there are some novelists as important as Malraux, Aragon, Bosquet, Sabatier, Pierre Gascar. In Spain they are beginning to revive this great current of fiction, which has been quite silent for years. In Italy there are Moravia, Pratolini, and Elio Vittorini, in Germany Günter Grass. But I think that Latin American fiction—not forgetting the great writers of Brazil, such as Jorge Amado and Guimarães Rosa (the latter vanished at the height of his creative powers)—can compare with them all for vigor, strength, and originality, and they certainly have a larger audience than many European and North American novelists.

That reminds me that once you said Borges was "a great writer, but one of the great European writers."

As an American-Indian, when I read Borges I get the impression that he's a European author, deeply versed in European culture, a man whose interests are European, who is constantly analyzing his own personality, his ego. There is plenty of European lucubration in his writing, and I don't find American roots in it, our preferences, nor if you like our defects. This in no way decreases his stature as a great writer, but I question whether he is representative of Latin American literature.

When you talk of representative literature, are you also referring to folklore?

No, quite the reverse. I'm speaking of *Facundo* by Sarmiento, *Amalia* by Mármol, *Doña Bárbara* by Rómulo Gallegos, *La vorágine* by José Eustasio Rivera, and *Huasipungo* by Jorge Icaza; these are not folklore, but they are ours. To me, the literature of folklore, regional literature, is a false literature. We don't possess much folklore. Russia and Spain have folklore; what we possess is a native tradition in some regions, which doesn't belong to folklore. Unfortunately this tradition is now being transformed into folklore for tourists.

Do you think the Indian should be encouraged to stay as he is within his culture and traditions, or should he be incorporated into our civilization?

My ideas on this subject seem to have changed completely. In the thesis I presented in 1923, "The Social Problem of

the Indian," referring to the Guatemalan Indian, I spoke of the
necessity or the urgency of giving the Indian a chance to become
part of Western culture. Now, with the passage of years, I realize
that that was a mistake, and that what we ought to do is to get
the native to develop his own culture, at any rate that of Guatemalan Maya and Quiché Maya. I realized that the Indian may
well be more cultured than we are—using the word "culture" in
the sense of depth of thought, depth of feeling, and a disciplined
way of life—and that it is the cultural elements the Indians have
inherited from their earliest ancestors that they should be developing. The Indian is an artist, as we see from the pots and
cloth he makes. He hardly ever copies the design on a material;
he invents new colors and figures at his loom, he is a constant
creator. When he has clay in his hands he invents the forms he
gives to his pots and jugs, and nearly all his pottery is decorated
with animals, flowers, or a god. At the same time he is economically wiser than we are; for instance when the Indians and
ladinos go down to the coast to work in a torrid climate, the only
ones who return are the Indians, most of the ladinos die on
the coast. The Indian works but doesn't buy perfume or nylon
stockings or alcohol; he returns to his mountains with his small
earnings to buy a little piece of land or a cow. He also leads a very
well-organized life. Guatemalan Indians generally get up at five
in the morning and have a bath every day, their houses have
earth floors but are kept clean, they lead regular sex lives, marry
and have children, adultery is practically nonexistent. Their
chief fault is drunkenness, they get dead drunk on their saint's day
and are left lying in the streets, but they only smoke when they
are all gathered together; otherwise they are without vices. Why,
then, don't we try to develop this world of the Indian, all his
virtues, all the qualities we have tried to ignore, so as to raise him
up within the sphere of his own beliefs and culture without
sacrificing anything; once the level of his culture has been raised
he will transform it himself and make a useful contribution to
our own. The danger at present is that the purity of native life
and culture is threatened by tourism. In the designs on native
textiles we now see airplanes, motor cars, and other technical
products appearing beside the little suns, moons, and symbolical

figures of the past. Yet this very fact shows how adaptable the Indian is to all the forms of life with which he comes in contact; he has improved his craftsmanship through tourism and can also earn his living. He is not a mere cipher, he too is alive to external stimulation. In Guatemala the natives are preferred as workers throughout the electrical industries, because of their manual skill.

How have your working methods been influenced by voluntary and involuntary periods of exile and your numerous different occupations?

They say every artist has his hours of lucidity, when it is easiest for him to write, invent, produce; mine are from five to eight in the morning. When I'm working on a novel, as soon as I'm awake and have drunk a cup of tea I sit down to my typewriter, often without knowing what I'm going to write but remembering the previous chapter or paragraph of the book in hand, and go on automatically as if my brain were unrolling a recording tape. After two or three hours of work I feel a sort of tic in my head; then I stop and busy myself with my correspondence or other activities. This is because the first post I held was as a professor in the University of Guatemala and I had to arrive at nine every morning to give my class; after that I was a journalist and worked in the mornings for an evening paper, and when in '47 I became a diplomat in Buenos Aires it made it easier for me to get up early to write and be at the embassy punctually at ten. I'm completely useless in the afternoon and evening. I never try to write at night, and whenever I have done so I have to correct a lot the next day because I repeat the same word in different paragraphs as if out of fatigue. So it's difficult to give a fixed time for finishing a book and I don't think creative work can be measured by hours, days, months, or even years. I generally make a first draft of what is most important, chapter by chapter. I keep this draft even if it's not finished, for one, two, or three months, and when I have the impression that this first attempt has grown cold I read it again. If I have to correct anything I abstract what seems to me good and make a long second manuscript of the novel which again I keep for two or three

months when once more I read and correct it and make a
"montage," as they say in the cinema. I give this second completely revised copy to the typist for a definitive copy to be made.
I think my writing is auditory rather than visual, thus when I
have written a paragraph or a page or a piece of dialogue I read
it aloud to find out if it's euphonious, and if it isn't I correct it
until it has achieved euphony. I remember that I corrected and
read *El señor presidente* so many times—when one is young
one has time for that sort of thing—that I knew whole chapters
by heart. Lately I've tried using a tape recorder, but I gave it
up because I realized that although it was interesting to do, it
might result in an oratorical literature with the sentences becoming purely verbal and losing weight. Writing a novel is more
difficult than writing a story or a poem, although poetry is an
important form, because the novelist has to become a slave to
his novel; it's a sort of mental bureaucracy. One must sit at
least two hours a day at one's work table, even when there's
nothing to say, because a break would mean reestablishing the
creative rhythm, and some of the atmosphere of the novel would
be lost. The novelist must be exacting with himself, because
nothing is lazier than the mind. A friend calling, a program
on television, shopping, any pretext is good enough to put a
stop to writing; he must therefore force himself not to be carried
away by every external stimulation.

What is the process by which your novel takes shape?

I usually try to find a subject relative to my own life,
and particularly to my life as a Guatemalan. After the subject has
been chosen, and after a lot of thought, muttering, and fitting
things together, the day comes when—sometimes on the typewriter, sometimes in handwriting—I begin to develop the chapters. The first thirty pages are the hardest, from page 30 to
70 the going is easier, but on page 70 or 80 a number of
difficulties begin to arise, I don't know why. I feel a sort of
discouragement and dejection, but then I read part of what
I've written (although I hardly ever read all of it until the end)
and that gives me a fresh impulse to go on. Some novelists plan

their novel beforehand as if it were a game of chess and they were moving the pieces. The opposite happens to me, I begin with one, two, or three characters, but others keep on appearing. What is happening—as an Italian critic pointed out—is that I destroy them as fast as I create them, instead of giving them positive characteristics I give them negative ones; "Asturias assumes," he says, "that the reader has already grasped his character and he tries to destroy it." The end of the novel comes as a surprise, and I don't plan it ahead. I believe that one of the most interesting phenomena in the creation of a poem or a novel is the decisive factor that makes it end at a certain line or paragraph; it could go on, but no, it ends with a full stop. Why? Impossible to say. But although literary creation is one of the most admirable activities, and one is amazed by the possibilities of the brain, I also think there is a great deal of chance and luck in many works. It has happened to me that I have found the suggestion for a name I was looking for on a poster in the street.

When and how do you decide on your title?

The title is one of the hardest problems. Usually my books have been born with a title, for example *Mulata de tal*, *Los ojos de los enterrados*, a native legend according to which the Indians are buried with their eyes open waiting for the day of judgment, and *El papa verde*. *El señor presidente* was at first called *Los mendigos políticos* (The Political Beggars); afterwards, as I was a great reader of Dante, it was for some time called *Malevolge*, the last circle of Dante's inferno, that terrible funnel full of fire and flames; and later still, when I was studying America, I called it *Tohil*, the name of the god who stole fire from the tribes, and exacted human sacrifices for its return—there were no human sacrifices among the Mayas, those came later with the Aztecs. The final title emerged when I told the plot of the novel to a Mexican publisher and he said, "Then it's the story of the señor presidente." I adopted it at once, feeling that this was the novel's true name.

Skira, the Geneva publishers, have invited you, Octavio Paz, and other writers to collaborate on the collection Les Sentiers de la Création (The Paths of Creation). Could you say in advance what will be the title of your book and how you envisage its subject?

In this book I have to explain how I decided to be a writer, and how I set about it, but above all I have to tell the reader how the idea of creation came to me. I went to Mallorca, whose landscape reminds me of Guatemala, to work on the book I called *Trois des quatre soleils* (Three Out of Four Suns). The name was based on a Mayan belief that the world had already passed through four phases. Each of these great phases or cosmic eras, as they are called, corresponds to one sun. The first sun corresponds to the Neolithic age, when the earth was taking shape, the time of the great ice ages, but for all its strength this first sun couldn't free the earth completely from ice, and it was devoured by wild beasts. After the sun had been devoured, the first age ended, and there came an immense cataclysm, like an apocalyptic cataclysm, after which the sun of the wind appeared; it was a motionless sun, but the wind began driving it so that it moved through space—the Mayas believed that it was the sun that moved and not the earth. It was part of their mythology that the sun was the greatest of the gods, the supreme being, and naturally they couldn't and didn't conceive that after arriving in the middle of the sky at noon, in the eye of the grain of maize as they put it, it would descend into the west and die; it was theologically impossible for them to accept the daily death of the God Sun. So they imagined that the horizon in the west was an immense concave mirror, that as the sun returned to its mansion for the night it was reflected in this western mirror, and it was the reflection that disappeared and died, never the sun itself. During the third sun men and the first plants began to appear; the sun helped transform the vegetable kingdom. After that came a fourth sun, and so we on earth have lived through four ages. Now we are in the fifth sun, the sun of movement, and according to Mayan beliefs, at a given moment there will be another huge cataclysm, as there was in the past, and the fifth sun will end with this immense destruction of the universe. Some European writers, particularly writers of the literature of the fantastic, have supposed that the end of the fifth sun as conceived by the Mayas will be an atomic war, in which (as we now know), if all the means to create an atomic explosion possessed by the great powers are used, life on this earth will disappear completely and an upheaval will coincide with the fall of the fifth sun.

What relation have these suns to your creative activity?

My creative activity began as a result of the earthquake that destroyed Guatemala City on December 25, 1917. The tremors began at ten o'clock at night and by dawn the whole capital had been destroyed. We all went out and lived in encampments, in houses made out of sheets and paper, and it was there that I started writing a sort of a diary in a notebook —afterwards it turned into short stories—about what I saw around me in that large camp, one of the central ones. Rafael Alberti, the great Spanish poet, once told me that the worst thing that could happen to a writer was not to have an aunt, and that's quite true because I used to read my first writings to my aunt in the evenings. If I had gone to my parents at that time, who were much preoccupied with the loss of their property, they wouldn't have paid much attention. Therefore I think my creative activity sprang directly from the trauma suffered by the earth, by nature, by my mind, by myself. I must explain too that besides writing I began making figures out of clay. So that besides the written language, a primitive language was expressing itself through my fingers in the creation of those little clay figures. My figures, especially the clay ones, under a subsequent sun are now ceasing to be mere figures, for I have placed them where they are reflected in water, where I find a second subject for creativity, a second literary subject: the image. So that besides their material and plastic values, there is that of the image, corresponding somewhat to dreams, to a comparison with other forms, and all this has gone to form what afterwards became my language.

Are you interested in analysis?

The most important thing to me is imagination—"the

mad woman in the house"—imagery, euphony, but I think there is very little analysis in my works. I haven't an analytic or scientific mind, I have a literary and creative one.

Of all the stages in the growth of a novel, which gives you most satisfaction?

The euphoric moment, the moment when I feel at my best—it's as if I were bathing in delight or drinking some mysterious elixir—is the moment of writing, because there is something childish and primitive in inventing things and linking words together. Whereas the moment that can be most distressing is when one reads the two hundred pages of the book one has been working on and wonders if it will do or not. There are moments of appalling despair, and only the euphoria when something goes right can make up for them.

It's said that the novel form is disappearing. Do you believe that?

The form is said to be disappearing, either because of the cinema or television, because people haven't got time to read, or because the novel has been transformed into a puzzle, a scientific experiment. But I think it will always be a very attractive form, because when reading a novel one becomes absorbed, is removed from time, is removed from reality and enters and inhabits a world apart. On the other hand I think the cinema, particularly that designed for the masses, can be a more contemporary form of expression than the novel, because of the greater immediacy of its images.

Erotic literature in all its forms is flourishing today. Does this sort of literature interest you?

It seems to me that the recent increase in erotic literature is not an isolated event but part of a whole wave of eroticism, sexuality, and sensuality, which is invading almost every country, particularly the Western world. It's curious that it is in countries with austere standards of behavior and a tradition of great reserve, like the Scandinavian countries, Great Britain and the United States—to judge by magazines, books, and films—that one sees this erotic fashion developing, though it is pornographic rather than erotic. For my part I don't feel sympathy for this kind of literature or this type of images, and I always used to wonder what was the cause of my lack of interest, since I attribute no transcendental value to it, in spite of all the research devoted to it. I recently read a book by Aldous Huxley describing a visit he paid years ago to the ruins of the ceremonial cities of Mexico and Guatemala. Huxley explained that in their works of art the Mayas never produced anything pornographic, hermaphroditic, or related to sexual or sensual activity. That's interesting, because it shows how mistaken it is to think that Mayan art, cities, monuments, and hieroglyphics have any close relation to the Orient. If there were such a relation it would be logical for Mayan art to present sensual scenes in the Oriental style, but for one thing, women's bodies do not figure in Mayan monumental art, and for another, when a man does appear he is covered with ornaments, jewels, and feather corselets. So that he is not a figure to arouse the instincts or the imagination. As I read this book, I reflected that it might be my Mayan ancestry that made me unsympathetic to all these spectacles and manifestations. When I was a member of the cinematographic jury at Cannes, besides the official films, some erotic ones produced in Germany and Denmark were shown. I hadn't time to see them, but some young people from different countries told me they were interesting for a short while but after that they were tedious. I think such art forms to some extent express the subversive and antagonistic feelings of the young toward the old inflexible formulas concerning the relations between men and women, or else they respond to the needs of tired, blasé people, who find stimulation in such films as these.

You have written some books of sonnets and poems, the last Clarivigilia primaveral (1965), and works for the theater, Soluna (1955) and La audiencia de los confines (1957). Are you still interested in these forms?

Poetry is like a lighted lamp which goes with one all through life. In the youthful period it burns as ardently as young blood, and in my case I might say that it became subterranean, in the sense that it ran underneath the land of my prose, my novels. Poetry, my poetry, is the respiration of the green world surrounding the characters in my fictional universe. By which, of course, I do not mean to deny that at times I have written poems properly so-called.

As for the theater it seems to me to present a number of problems which the novelist doesn't have to face. A producer, choreographer, and performers must all be found, and there mustn't be too many characters because of the expense of putting it on; in other words there are a number of limitations that don't beset the novelist. I have greater freedom of work and action, for I can use all my characters, even if they only figure on one or two pages. My play, *La audiencia de los confines*, was based on the life of Fray Bartolomé de las Casas—protector of the Indians, who retired as bishop of Chiapas in Central America after Charles V's "Laws of the Indias," and ordained that no absolution should be given to Spaniards who owned slaves. It was acted in Guatemala in 1961 by a group of young students and aroused the same storm of hatred and ill will against Fray Bartolomé and against me as the one aroused by the monk in the year 1700. It seems that all the same problems still exist today, and I think that if the monk's voice was heard now, as it was then, he would be just as bitterly attacked as at that time. Here in Paris a French adaptation of "Torotumbo," the last story in *Weekend en Guatemala*, has been made, and it is also being put on in Italy, by the students of Verona.

Besides your literary output you have made some important translations.

My most important translation was the one I undertook at the Sorbonne (1923–24) in collaboration with the scholarly Mexican, J. M. González de Mendoza, of that monumental work the Mayan bible, the *Popol Vuh*. We also translated the *Anales de los Xahil*, of the Cachiqueles Indians. Then I did some translations with my wife, Blanca, my collaborator when we were living in exile. We translated Claude Simon's novel *L'Herbe*, which I believe to be one of the most successful of the *nouveaux romans*. We found that translation very difficult, because it's a novel without punctuation and there are sentences covering four or five pages, also Simon describes events simultaneously. We had to work nearly a year to reach a satisfactory translation. We also translated some of the plays of Jean Paul Sartre published by Losada, and a play by Anouilh. Translation is a very thankless task and not paid as well as it should be.

Blanca's collaboration must be a great help to you . . .

She's above all a very stern critic; when something doesn't satisfy her we discuss it, and from our conversation and discussion my first attempt emerges improved. She also helps me study certain passages, look up facts in books, and has made an almost complete collection of my literary correspondence, all biographical and bibliographical material and newspaper reviews since 1950.

In which language do you think the translations of your books have been most successful?

They have been very well translated into French. There are two ways of translating—one is to stick to the Spanish text, word by word, without allowing any freedom to the translator, and the other is to do like Francis de Miomandre, a great poet whose mastery over the French language permitted him to make marvelous translations in which he reconstituted sentences, pages, and the book itself. He was my first translator and produced masterly versions of *Leyendas de Guatemala, Hombres de maíz,* and *The Green Pope.* Unfortunately he died before he could translate the banana plantation trilogy as he had intended. But in French I've also had Georges Pillement and now Claude Couffon who have made magnificent translations. I've been lucky too with some of my Italian translators. I can't judge the translations into English and Russian as I don't know those languages; the Russian ones are said to be good. *Weekend en Guatemala* and *El señor presidente* were translated in England, but should be done again in the United States because American English is richer and more popular, and the colloquialisms in my books go into it more easily than into the English of Great Britain. I have heard that Professor Rabassa of the United States has made an excellent translation of *Mulata,* which is exceptionally difficult to translate.

*Do you think the diplomatic posts you held adversely affected your
literary work?*

On the contrary, they have helped me. As I wasn't
a man of means I wouldn't have been able to travel except
for those posts. When Juan José Arévalo, president of Guatemala,
appointed me minister–counsellor in Buenos Aires in 1948, he
told me I should be able to work as a writer there, and find
a response to my literature. During the years of my ministry
I wrote *Hombres de maíz*, *The Green Pope*, a great many
poems published at the time, and *Weekend en Guatemala*, published later. From Buenos Aires they sent me to Paris where
I was able to make new contacts with friends who were writers
and translators. I was also ambassador to Salvador, whence I
could observe the invasion of Guatemala in '54 from near at
hand. From Salvador we returned as exiles to Buenos Aires
where I wrote almost all my books at a farm called Shangri-la
on the Delta of Paraná, where I used to shut myself up for
three or four months to write.

*Because of your post as ambassador in Paris, from which you re-
tired in July 1970, many Latin American writers have accused you
of representing a dictatorship.*

They did in fact blame me a good deal for accepting
the post of ambassador in Paris, but I have always made it
clear why I accepted. While I was in Italy the battle over the
Guatemalan elections began, and there were four military candidates running against a single civilian, Méndez Montenegro.
The government in office, a *de facto* military government, had
prepared a constitution that depended on having a soldier in
power, but the people said "no" to the army and Montenegro
was elected. I had written in the Italian papers about this situation and felt myself somewhat involved with this new civil
government, a government corresponding to some extent with
those of the revolution. When the post in Paris was offered me,
I reflected that I was giving my services to Guatemala, and as I
had lived in France from 1920–30 and had friends on newspapers
and in the ministries (I have been a friend of André Malraux,
minister for cultural affairs, ever since that time) it was my

duty as a Guatemalan to serve my country in a position which would contribute to its fame. I accepted the ambassadorship and realized one of my most important aims, which was to give back to Guatemala its part in Mayan culture. Whenever there is talk of Mayan culture, and Mayan exhibitions are arranged, people speak of Mexico, yet the Mayans were strictly Guatemalan. They were born in Guatemala, spread through Guatemala, and afterwards went to Yucatán and Mexico. I therefore planned an exhibition of Mayan art from Guatemala, in which I received the most generous support from the minister Malraux, who sent teams of underwater swimmers to search the lakes of Guatemala, where they found pottery and other objects. In 1968 the exhibition of 420 archaeological Mayan items was held, occupying an area of 2,000 square meters in the Grand Palais. This was a great event in Paris, and it was a way of giving back to Guatemala that ancient archaeological-artistic treasure for which she was famous. This work, along with other cultural activities—we gained nineteen technical scholarships— was achieved through my being at the embassy. Once this service to my country was over I thought I might conveniently retire. As for criticism I remember that I was very much criticized when I was ambassador under Jacobo Arbenz in Ecuador; then it was the right who called me "the ambassador of the communist government." Now it was the extreme left who criticized me for representing a government that had not carried out and was not carrying out its obligations, but in both cases I fulfilled my duty as a Guatemalan, the only consideration that guided me.

What are your plans?

To devote myself to my writing. My age doesn't allow me the luxury of wasting time, and now that I'm lucky enough to be free to do so, I would like to leave behind two or three more novels, a long poem, and a play. At the end of the year I hope to return to Mallorca and go on with my new novel, which consists of two volumes: *Viernes de dolores* (Friday of Sorrows) and *Dos veces bastardo* (Twice a Bastard). It's a novel on a social theme, which might be complementary to the banana plantation trilogy.

It's partly a biography of my "generation of the twenties": I describe how that brilliant generation, fully aware of the state of things in Guatemala—not only did we found the People's University which I have already spoken about, but we wrote and circulated books and pamphlets intended to enlighten our people about social and sociological subjects—nevertheless separated when we reached the age of thirty or forty, and out came the famous slippers by the fireside. Lawyers, doctors, and engineers were absorbed in their professions and all forgot the obligations they had contracted at the university. In this novel I describe how such a group of professionals or careerists is trained in Latin American universities, which are maintained by the people, and how, far from being of service to them, these careerists became exploiters of the very people who had made their studies possible. When we are at the university we are all revolutionaries, we are all Marxists, we are all anarchists, we want to declare ourselves, we want to finish everything, we want to transform society; yet when it is our turn to play a part in life we forget our past, we think of it as youthful madness, we leave it piously behind us and go on leading the routine existence of our countries. The belief I am defending in this thesis is that when this group of students become professional men they should keep at least 70 percent of their ideas; I'm not saying they should want to hang the Pope as they did as students, but that they should at least retain some of their ideas for developing and revolutionizing their spheres of work, whether it is the judiciary, the hospitals, etc. The downfall of our countries is partly due to the fact that the elite trained in our universities betray them, and when their active life begins, they ally themselves with the great North American trusts, sometimes for the sake of good salaries, thus helping the American domination of Latin America.

The politics of the United States and the great trusts have always received your severest criticism. Would you like to enlarge on that theme?

That seems to me an extraordinarily interesting question, particularly because your book will be published in English

and will give many North Americans an opportunity to discover our position and attitude of mind, or mine at least. We
have read the remark made by the liberator Simón Bolívar in
1811: that the Creator had placed the United States in its
present position so as to prevent progress and the improvement
and freedom of Latin American countries. This might have
seemed a false conclusion to many at the time, but we have
seen it confirmed since then. We can't talk of the relations of
the United States with Latin America as if they constituted
a single episode, a single stage. Many of us only consider what
is closest, and therefore look at what is happening now, particularly among the young, in relation with Cuba and so on,
but I believe we should go back in time and think of the situation
as a whole. We ought to see how the United States developed
and grew more powerful, and then, just when the Latin American countries were in danger of being disputed over and occupied by the European powers, we had the "Monroe doctrine"
—we call it "doctrine" because no treaty was involved—when
President Monroe declared that America was for the Americans
and that no European country could set foot in our countries.
Naturally Monroe's idea was that America belonged to all of
us Americans, but it has often been interpreted to mean that
America is for the North Americans. Throughout the nineteenth century the United States made armed interventions in
our countries: it intervened in Mexico at the time of the
death of the heroic boys, in Nicaragua, in Guatemala, in Venezuela, in Cuba with the Platt Amendment, in Santo Domingo,
Haiti, Costa Rica, and Honduras. The political situation was
evolving, the Pan-American system was beginning to take shape,
and in several Pan-American congresses in Montevideo, Buenos
Aires, and Washington—where the first congress took place—
there emerged what might be called the American claim, the
inter-American claim, to guarantee and defend our lives, our
economy, and our independence. It is curious to remember that
José Martí was present as a journalist at the first Pan-American
Congress in Washington, and in one of his articles in the
Buenos Aires *Nación* he said, "I regret very much that, instead
of discussing problems and ideas, this congress has kept the
delegates visiting nothing but industries, factories, and Wall

Street." We were thenceforth given to understand that Pan-
Americanism signified a form of economic penetration of our
countries, until the politics of the good neighbor was inculcated
by Franklin Roosevelt, whose attitude to Latin American problems was very different from Theodore Roosevelt's. The United
States now began to find solutions at the conference table,
rather than by dollars or the big stick. This was a period of
great mutual understanding. The Latin American countries had
democratic governments, important links were established, and
at one of the conferences, called Inter-American instead of Pan-
American, the delegates voted in favor of a formula of nonintervention. This policy of nonintervention lasted until the
tenth Inter-American conference at Caracas, where Foster Dulles
accused Guatemala of being a "red bridge" and being ready to
launch an attack—so it was said at the conference—on the
Panama Canal in the south, or else on the United States'
oil wells. From that moment Dulles insisted on intervening in
Guatemala, so breaking the important and hitherto successful
nonintervention policy. The United States intervened in Guatemala, disguising the criminality of its mercenary invasion
behind an ex-colonel Castillo Armas, and curiously enough, the
North American ambassador, Peurifoy, always carried a revolver
like a Chicago gangster. The intervention was a brutal one, the
Guatemalan president Jacobo Arbenz had to resign, and a puppet
was installed in his place. The United States abandoned its
policy of nonintervention and went on to intervene in the
most cruel and terrifying manner in Santo Domingo. We who
watched events from Europe were surprised when the Europeans
were so outraged by the Russian interventions in Hungary and
Czechoslovakia yet kept completely silent over the United States'
brutal and bloody intervention in Santo Domingo. I have said
this to show that there has been no coherent policy toward our
republics, and to explain why Latin Americans must oppose
the Department of State. We hope that nonintervention projects
may again be formed with the United States, and that the
United States will not intervene politically, militarily, or economically, nor impose governments on our republics, great and
small, and that by respecting our way of life it may cause us
to respect that of the North Americans. And I also believe that

NERUDA

NERUDA AT HOME, ISLA NEGRA

BORGES

ASTURIAS

Octavio Paz

CORTÁZAR

PHOTOGRAPHS BY SARA FACIO—ALICIA D'AMICO

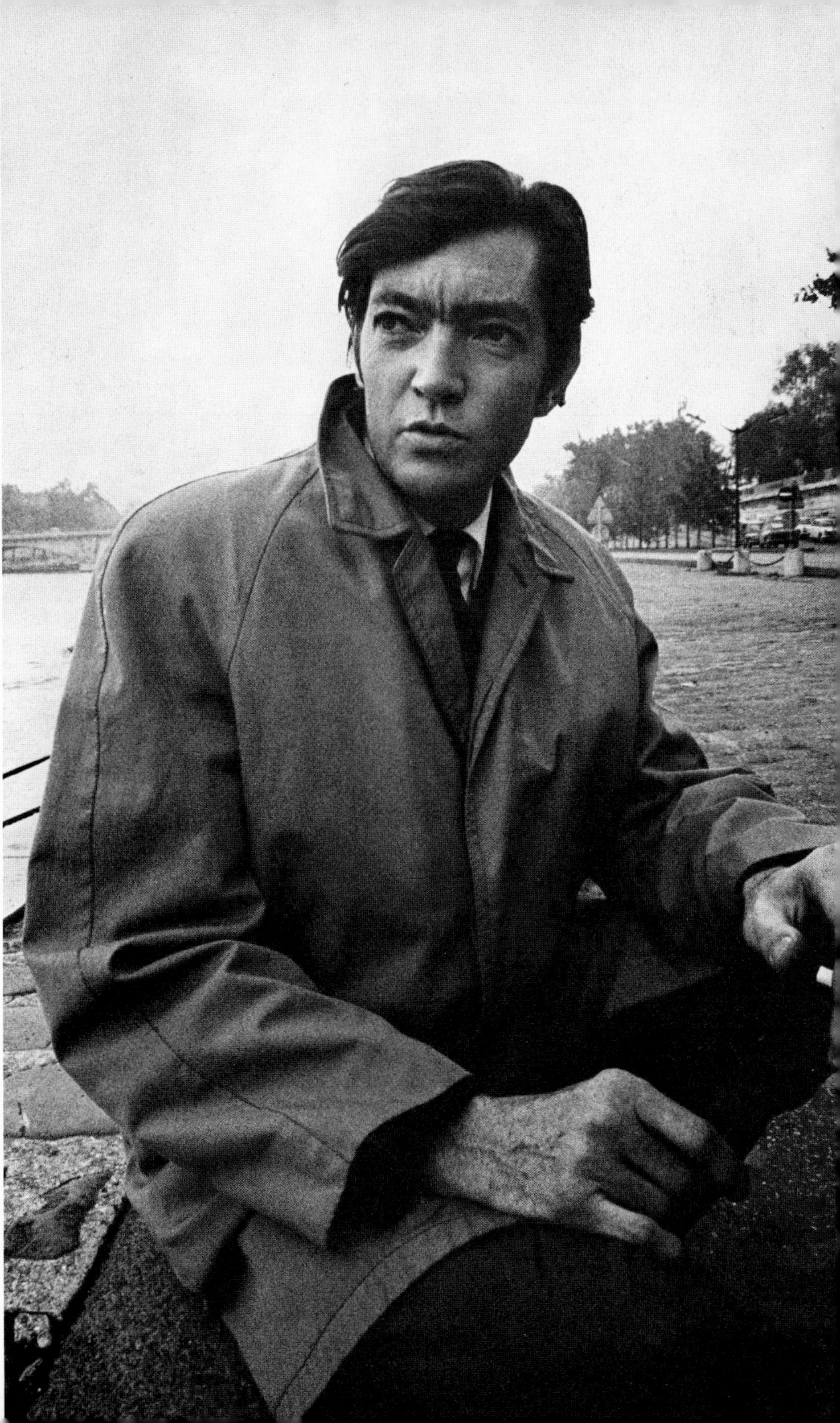

CABRERA INFANTE

RITA GUIBERT WITH NERUDA

we, who have always been anti-imperialists, have made it clear
that we have not been exploited by the people of the United
States but by her great trusts. These trusts, besides being North
American, are huge international capitals—such as the United
Fruit Company in Central America, the Venezuelan petroleum
companies, the copper companies of Chile and Peru, and the
tin companies of Bolivia—and they represent the most terrible
and destructive image of the United States to our eyes. We
are not opposed to the activities of the United Fruit Company
in Central America, as long as it respects the laws of each of
our republics, but in Guatemala, for example, it did not respect
our laws, but made its own. In the territory belonging to the
company in Tiquisate or on the banana plantations, the Guatemalan flag was not displayed, Spanish was not spoken, and
the currency was not in our quetzals. The currency was in
dollars, the United States flag was flying, and English was
spoken. The citizens of the United States ought to know these
facts, because if such a thing happened to them they would
feel the same indignation that we do. The hatred and anger,
which makes us see the United States as our enemy, not our
friend as we could wish, are not gratuitous or false but are
based on daily events, on current events, on our politico-social
and cultural relations.

Do you see any possibility of a better understanding?

What is happening in the universities of the United
States is very important. University students have started traveling
through our countries and making contact with the writers and
students of Latin America, and I think this will open great
possibilities. I also believe that the United States has realized
that it may be possible to create in Latin America some system
allowing the riches at present in the hands of a very few to
be distributed. In this connection homage is due to President
John Kennedy for his projected reforms for Latin America, when,
in his thesis for an Alliance for Progress, he suggested the
possibility of agrarian reforms by which wealth could be better
distributed. He saw, as all of us—except our own ruling classes
who don't see—that a redistribution of wealth is necessary or

else tomorrow will bring famine, no quarter will be given, and the rich will lay the blame on anarchism. There is no anarchism, but there is a hungry people who feel exploited and hopeless, and who will someday rise up against those who might have avoided this bloody revolution by sharing some of their land in a logical manner and giving work to those who have none.

Do you support violence?

Violence must be seen in relation to the different occasions for it. I was present at the so-called students' revolution in Paris in 1968, and I realized that at the beginning of their struggle the students had absolutely coherent and defensible claims connected with the university. One of these was for the public authorities, and particularly those of the university, to elect students to form part of the governing bodies of the universities of Paris and other towns. In Latin America this was already an old story. In 1917, a manifesto from Córdoba in Argentina had as its chief demand that students should be elected by the students themselves to represent them on the governing boards of universities. In theory this is the case in almost all our countries, but in Europe it is still not so; few conceive of such an idea and few accept it. The students' first demand was to take part in the government of their universities. There was a second demand referring to the lack of classroom space—some classrooms large enough to accommodate 500 people were used by from 1,000 to 1,500. In such conditions the students' claims were absolutely justified. There were other claims as well; the students opposed or rejected the idea of being trained like an army—an army that was to form part of big business, big business which was exploiting the workers. They demanded a change in the social structure, above all in the exploitation of the workers. A political aspect was thus added to the purely university one at a given moment. In our day it is very difficult to separate political claims from those concerned with the university, feminism, or the Church. So the students' ambitions grew broader in scope, and violence broke out, violence that becomes much more serious in Latin America. In France only one death took place during the May revolution, but as you know the streets in Latin America are spattered with the blood of our students. Violence takes a more extreme form there, comes into fierce collision with the police and the army, and ends in the greatly lamented death of many of those young people. I believe violence is a weapon which must be used at the right time, like all weapons. Violence should be approached by degrees. The discussion that always takes place with the students and youth of Latin America is as follows: we say that it is necessary to prepare the people, train them politically and make them understand their rights and duties, whereas the students believe that this means waiting a decade or two longer. They prefer the struggle to begin at once, and violence to be used, but then the workers and peasants refuse to take part because they haven't been inoculated with the current social ideologies. I therefore believe that violence should only be used as a last resort, when legal means, democratic weapons, propaganda, and the informative media now in existence have all been exhausted.

These are the means we should use to fight for the transformation of our society without violence. This is what we hope will happen, and what I greatly hope will happen in Chile, where a very important social reform can be realized by constitutional and legal means without recourse to violence. Of all the Latin American countries, I think Chile is best prepared for such a transformation, since it is a profoundly political country and has always allowed great freedom of thought.

What do you wish for during the next few decades?

I hope that many new artists, novelists, and poets may arise in Latin America. . . . I think our literature has arrived at an important juncture, and possesses many great figures, who ought to be followed by others. I hope that Latin American literature will establish itself completely in the world of letters, and that our poets and writers—some of them are in the first rank—will have no cause to envy writers of other lands. My advice to Latin American writers is that they should work hard because, as someone said, "Genius is work." I have a great belief in our youth, particularly if they direct their interests toward our living media, our national characteristics and ambitions. As I am always saying, the young must write about the guerrillas, about the internal struggles and impoverishment of our countries; a new chapter that was closed to us now lies open before them. If writers of my age tried to write a novel about the guerrillas we would falsify everything. I also think that a great many young people should go about the country with tape recorders and hear what our people have to say, and, armed with this material, say to the Europeans: "Listen, my friends, it is now our turn to begin telling stories, and we are going to tell you at interminable length what you have told us in different words."

Gabriel García Márquez gave it as his personal opinion—according to an interview—that "the committed novel condemns the reader to a partial view of the world and life . . . I don't think American readers need to have their own drama of oppression and injustice told over and over because they have more than enough evidence of it in their daily life, and what they expect of a novel is that it reveal something new."

I think García Márquez's statement is really a disguised formula designed to prevent our novels from dealing with our own problems. This declaration of García Márquez makes me indignant, because it is inviting our future writers to conceal our tragedy. If it is true that we are describing our own drama and pain and that Latin America is already tired of hearing about it, let her go on listening all the same, because as long as we listen it may be remedied, but it will never be remedied if, as he suggests, we hide our tragedies and take subjects to write about from what is not ours and does not concern us, and try to create beautiful literature by dishing up plots that are alien to us and are taken directly from European books. Gabriel García Márquez in *One Hundred Years of Solitude*, for example, transferred plots and characters from Balzac's *La recherche de l'absolu* (The Search for the Absolute).

We do not create literature in order to amuse and entertain people, but as part of the struggle for an America which has a right to its proper place among the nations. While we suffer, while the Negro suffers in those countries where there are Negroes, while women suffer, while I see that children do not

go to school and are hungry, while I see that there are dictatorships and big businesses that support those dictators, I will write
and I invite the young to go on writing—our own sort of
novel, novels that are white-hot, strong, and blazing, and not
to accept advice which diverts us from the path of our own
novel, which is the novel of the vital, distressing times in which
our people live.

*To what do you attribute the recognition Latin American litera-
ture is receiving?*

    In the last few months, and particularly in Spain, I've
noticed that the Latin American novel is thought to have appeared by a sort of miracle, with what is called the "boom" of
the new novel. All Spaniards rightly admire our fiction, and
believe that it has just appeared with the new novelists. This
isn't so. The Latin American novel traveled a long way before
it succeeded in imposing itself on Europe, and that long journey
was initiated by the Peruvians Ventura García Calderón and
Francisco García Calderón who lived and died in Paris, and by
Rubén Darío, Amado Nervo, and Enrique Gómez Carrillo. These
writers, who lived in Paris, were writing in the last century and
at the beginning of this. It's true that our literature attracted
very little attention at that time, it's true that it was the work
of writers who were diplomats, who wrote to entertain their
friends, but already when Gabriela Mistral won the Nobel Prize,
and with the Peruvian authoress Clorinda Matto de Turner and
other Mexican writers, some attention was attracted to our fiction,
although it may not have gone beyond diplomatic and cultural
circles. But there was a moment when French translators like
Francis de Miomandre, a great translator of all the Latin Americans, Georges Pillement, and many others were translating Latin
American books and creating a certain interest in our literature,
although still very academic. After the end of the war, publishers
began looking for new books and texts, and translations of
*La vorágine, Don Segundo Sombra, El río obscuro, Los de
abajo, Doña Barbara,* and *Huasipungo* were published. Besides
this, chains of Spanish literature existed in the universities of
France and Italy, to which supplementary teaching in Hispano-
American literature was now added as a part of Spanish literature.

From 1963 onward, students in French universities began writing theses on Latin American texts. I myself am touring all the French and Italian universities—from Naples to Cagliari, from Rome to Genoa—giving a series of five lectures on Hispano-American literature, the themes of which are: general view of its origins; the use of words; how we have used our landscape; conflicts in our fiction, in the sense of its relation to social conflicts and the novel of protest; and the relevance of our texts to sociological studies. To these must be added translations of important works, and the Nobel Prize awarded me in 1967, which is a form of testimony to the universal importance of our literature. In Germany today, thanks to the work of Rafael Gutiérrez Girardot at the University of Bonn, as in almost all European universities, the course in Hispano-American literature is separate from that in Spanish literature. All these contributions help us to say that the "boom" is not a miracle but the logical result of the work of many people for the last twenty years.

Will you accept the invitations you have received from several North American universities?

I refused them for reasons of health, but perhaps after my other books are published I may go to the United States and repeat the work I've done in the universities of Europe. It is very important to make contact and have discussions with students of those universities that are interested in our problems and might help us to solve them. What we want is to solve them, and discuss them with those who are able and willing to do so.

The history of your life is a succession of transcendental moments and phases. Which have had most effect on you?

I could mention some very important moments throughout my life. . . . When I first arrived in Paris that July 14th, I remember how people were dancing in the streets, and how the crazy world of Paris at that time impressed me. I was also deeply moved by the birth of my children, that emotion, that mixture of tenderness, sadness, and many other things is impossible to express. The most absolute impression of my whole life was the destruction of Guatemala City in 1917. That earth-quake helped alter my sensibility, and transformed me from an eighteen-year-old boy, enclosed in certain ways of thought, certain beliefs, and certain habits, to someone ready to go out and battle with the world . . . It seems to me that life is a thankless affair, the good cards are dealt to one at the end of the game, the honors and advantages one obtains would have been of more use before one was fifty; after fifty, all these tributes seem like a preparation for disappearance. It was also a crucially auspicious moment for me when I met my wife, Blanca Mora y Araujo, in Buenos Aires, at the house of the poet Oliverio Girondo and Norah Lange de Girondo, a meeting that was decisive in my life and hers. She was preparing a thesis on *El señor presidente* in the Faculty of Letters of the University of Buenos Aires, and when she saw me she couldn't believe I was a real, live author. From that evening, from that meeting, from that spark, my new life was born. And in one of my sonnets I say, *"She who sang songs in a voice born to bathe this blind man's face, so that he opened his eyes and believed in life."* Through her I began to believe in life again, in other words I was reborn and have become a different person.

What did your Nobel Prize of 1967 mean to you, and if you had received it sooner what effect would it have had?

Receiving it sooner would have been like a lash of the whip to a racehorse, but I never thought I should be awarded the prize, although my name was mentioned year after year. I thought it must have been given to Rómulo Gallegos, who certainly deserved it, and I was one of those who signed a request to the Academy on his behalf. I also believed that certain capitalist influences had a considerable effect on the Stockholm Committee, and that it was logical for them to oppose a writer like myself, who had written as I did in my trilogy. However, paradoxically enough, it was awarded me precisely for my concern for the workers on the banana plantations. From the very first I got the impression that they were giving the prize to me as a representative of Latin America and its im-portant position in world literature. Thirty-five years had passed since they gave the previous one to Gabriela Mistral. At the moment when a speech about my work was read and the prize was presented I experienced a sensation of distress and happiness combined, because I wished my parents had been alive, that those I had loved had been alive, and that my friends could have been present. It is this sensation of being an orphan that one feels in moments of greatest happiness.

I think the Lenin Peace Prize (1966) and the Légion d'Honneur (1970) also meant a lot to you.

When they gave me the Lenin Prize I was at Genoa, and I sent a cable of thanks to the secretary of the prize committee, at the same time begging that the prosecutions against the Russian writers should be reviewed, so that they could defend themselves. As a writer who had suffered persecution, I thought it my duty to make this request for them to be set free. As for the Légion d'Honneur, I knew at the end of my term as ambassador that I should be given it, like other ambassadors, but I never imagined that it would be in the rank of *grand officer*, which is that of a chief of state. In the years when De Gaulle delivered his call to arms from London, I was director of a daily paper in Guatemala, and we contributed our support and a great deal of propaganda to the cause of Free France. The minister Schuman made it clear in his speech that it was for this contribution that I was being given that rank; he was holding in his hands a bulky file containing everything I had written and said in support of that cause. It was an extremely great satisfaction to me, because I esteem France for many reasons and consider her to some extent as my spiritual home.

The Brazilian writer Guimarães Rosa, when interviewed by the German critic Günther Lorenz, said, "I love Asturias because he is so unlike me. That man is a volcano, an exception, he follows his own laws . . . he lives dangerously: he thinks ideologically . . . but his has something of the incorruptible detachment of a high priest: he enunciates the Ten Commandments every time . . . Asturias is the voice of the Last Judgment."

That comment is very characteristic of Guimarães. He used to have that wonderfully ingenious way of saying things.

Whenever we met he used to greet me with salutations of the same sort, they seemed like the famous compliments we used to be in the habit of paying each other at balls. Guimarães Rosa and Juan Rulfo are the writers who have most moved me, who have touched me most nearly. Guimarães and I were united by the fact, according to the critics, that we invented a language, he in Portuguese and I in Spanish. He reinvented *sertão*, the language of the interior, and *Hombres de maíz* is written in a language of my own. I think he should be studied, and that he will become one of the most respected and best-loved writers. As well as being the inventor of a language and of bringing a whole world, the world of the *sertão* to Brazilian fiction, he was a man who, as he himself used to say, didn't write committed literature because he was committed, "I belong to the *sertão*, I belong to the peasants, I belong to the drivers of ox carts, and the only thing I do is translate what those masses of people imprint on my ears and my sensibility." The death of Guimarães Rosa is an enormous loss for Brazilian literature and for our Latin American literature.

"Cabezas cortadas" (Severed Heads) was your suggestion for the title of this book. Why?

Because you have cut off all our heads—they are severed heads placed on a dish, like that of Saint John the Baptist—and carried them off.

OCTAVIO
PAZ

OCTAVIO PAZ

Churchill College, Cambridge
September 30–October 4, 1970.

"In the universe of Latin American writing," wrote
Ronald Christ, "Neruda's poetry is solar: a lavish, Hispanic ful-
mination—like a Tamayo watermelon—and Paz's poetry lunar:
a rarer, Gallic luminosity—like a Magritte moon . . . while
Neruda is directly concerned with the world, its objects and
processes (including poetry), Paz is more frequently concerned
with poetry, its procedures and words (meaning things)." But
Paz, who is often considered the spokesman for the Mexican
writers of his generation, is also an essayist whose work in each
genre is intimately related.

Following a tradition of Latin American writers, Paz, who was
born in 1914, has also been a diplomat, as have Asturias and
Neruda. After serving for six years as Mexico's ambassador to
India, Paz, complying with his belief that a writer should keep
himself independent of ideological or political servitude, resigned
his ambassadorship in 1968 when his government's violent measures to suppress a student demonstration ended with a massacre
in Mexico City.

Since his resignation from the diplomatic service, Paz has remained active in both cultural and political activities. When I
first interviewed him, Paz was holding the Simón Bolívar chair of
Latin America Literature at Cambridge University in England.
With his wife Marie-José—a lively and glamorous French woman
who has translated some of his works—Paz was living in a house
for guest professors at Churchill College where I interviewed him;
at his invitation, I was staying in one of the wings of the college's
modern main building, a five minutes' walk from his house.

The relaxing atmosphere of the British town at the start of

the new school year favored the interview, a product of long conversations in both the morning and evening hours. However, these conversations were not all casual because Paz, who is deeply interested in language itself, loves nothing "more than verbal perfection." He sometimes took brief notes before answering my questions or asked me to erase his recorded answers until they corresponded exactly in meaning and form with his thoughts. Furthermore, in the typed manuscript I sent him for approval, Paz rewrote some of his answers, deleted others, and inserted new ones in an attempt to reconcile his pluralities of voice, of thought, and of ego.

After leaving Cambridge, and before returning to Mexico in 1971, Paz went to Paris, where he was interviewed by the French media on the occasion of the simultaneous publication of three of his books, an event celebrated in two central pages of a Le Monde literary supplement under the general title: "Octavio Paz, the Search for Universal Truth."

Because of Paz's subsequent political activities I interviewed him for the second time on one of his short trips to New York while he was the Charles Eliot Norton Professor of Poetry at Harvard. This time the atmosphere was not so relaxed. After meeting Marie-José and Octavio in their impersonal hotel quarters we finished our conversation in a crowded and noisy bar, reminiscing about their cozy British house and our long walks through that English town that Paz found "aesthetically prodigious."

Now, however, Paz and his wife, both in style of dress and bearing reflecting the essential cosmopolitanism of his works, seemed to be two more of New York's "beautiful people." Clearly, the work of this poet with strong Mexican roots, who is in search of universal truth, merits in all ways the description: universal.

You say in your book Corriente Alterna (Alternating Current) that the students' rebellion and women's rebellion are the two most important movements of recent years, and that the rebellion of women is undoubtedly the more important and permanent.

    Before answering your question, I must make it clear that I wasn't referring to the Women's Liberation Movement, because when I wrote the essays collected in *Corriente Alterna,* between 1958 and 1964, that movement wasn't yet in existence. I was alluding rather to women's appearance in public life— something which dates back nearly a century, and has decisively changed (and will change even more) the physiognomy of modern societies. At the end of the Neolithic period woman suffered an eclipse, and her reappearance at the end of the last century is an event with incalculable consequences, beside which the rebellion of youth and the other disturbances and conflicts of our century grow pale and are seen as mere epiphenomena.

We are living in a revolutionary epoch . . .

Throughout the nineteenth century and what we have seen of the twentieth we have been obsessed by the idea of revolution: the myth of revolution, the myth of change: the violent and sudden substitution of one system for another. However, the great historical events of the second half of the twentieth century do not entirely fit into this scheme. Revolutionary thought had assigned the function of changing the world to the proletariat, but as we all know the working classes have not been the principal agents of the historical changes of the twentieth century. For one thing, in underdeveloped countries we have had revolts, disturbances, and changes in which the protagonists have not been the workers; such changes—including those in Russia and China—do not all correspond to what Marx believed would be the international revolution of the workers. Secondly, in developed countries, where the proletariat is a strong historical reality, instead of the great revolutionary transformation we have had several distinct rebellions: since the middle of the last century, the rebellion of artists, the criticism from intellectuals, and the appearance of woman as a public figure; now there is the rebellion of youth; and lastly a recrudescence of struggles on the part of social, religious, and linguistic minorities. These changes were not foreseen by revolutionary thinkers, and in my opinion form the essence of what we are now experiencing.

What do you think of the Women's Liberation Movement in the United States?

It's difficult to give an opinion. There's an erotic rebellion, both feminine and masculine; and also, and independently, a political rebellion of women. But one mustn't confuse the two. For instance, I've read that the leaders of the feminine movement believe that the essence of copulation is political. Well, that's colossal rubbish. All social behavior, every human act is tinged with politics, everything is contaminated by history, but the sexual act is not determined by relations of domination but by biological ones. Not history but nature: the body.

But woman has been and still is oppressed.

Yes, probably since the end of the Neolithic age. It's a terrible thing, because we probably owe the fundamental arts of all civilizations to women: agriculture, pottery, cooking, and textiles. And all these are peaceful arts. The slavery of woman, if we are to believe some anthropologists, began with urban civilizations: the discovery of metals and the consequent advances in the art of war; the invention of writing and the consequent appearances of the great religious bureaucracies and state monopolies of learning; the first cities and the consequent demand for menial labor. Thus the servitude of women began when the human race came of age. With what is called the state, history . . . But there is a great gulf between this and what some of the leaders of the Women's Liberation Movement say. It's absurd to compare women to the proletariat and blacks: women are neither a class nor a race. Such analogies are false. Women must not make use of historical and political categories, foreign to their situation—that's a new form of alienation. To become effectively free they would have to depart from their own reality . . .

Some feminists adopt an antimasculine attitude.

I'm all for equality, but equality doesn't mean identity, homogeneity. Men are—thank goodness—all different one from another; and—thank goodness again—men are different from women. In a really free society the important thing would be to cultivate those differences: what distinguishes us is what unites us. We ought to conceive of society as an association of complementary opposites, the chief opposition being between masculine and feminine. I'll go further: I think that from the interplay of masculine and feminine a new and hitherto un-dreamed-of culture and creativity might arise. The opposition of feminine and masculine is of a complementary order. And it is reborn within the bosom of every man and every woman, so that every man is partly feminine and every woman partly masculine.

In modern society there's opposition, but not the complementary opposition you describe.

When a society presents the masculine as its sole archetype, violence and distortion result. This is what has hap-pened in the Protestant capitalist society of the United States: their model has been primarily a masculine archetype, and women have had to adapt themselves to this model; by masculinizing herself, woman has become deformed. But man has mutilated himself as well. Man is not only a man, he is also a woman. When North American man thinks that work, thrift, and domina-tion are the fundamentals . . . when he conceives of sport as competition and war . . . when he also sees pleasure as a form of work and the number of orgasms as equivalent to the number of rounds in a boxing match or the number of dollars in his bank account . . . when this happens, man is being mutilated by the masculine archetype. Western civilization should be feminized.

Are there any examples?

Of course there are. I'll give you an example: Indian civilization. Compare Christ and Buddha. Christ is made up of straight lines, there's not a single feminine curve in him. It's hardly strange that Christianity has been the religion of the Crusades, the Inquisition, and capitalism. Islam, the religion of the sword, is also preponderantly masculine. Whereas in the

figures of Buddha and Shiva we find a certain femininity inte-
grated with their masculinity. The Indian goddesses are the
acme of femininity—with broad, rounded hips and immense
breasts—yet they ride on tigers and lions and fight against
monsters: they are warriors, virile. In India there was interpenetration between virility and femininity. Our men should be
more feminine and our women more masculine. The drama of
North American feminism depends on the fact that their archetype is masculine. Yankee women, including feminists, see themselves through masculine eyes. The true revolution would consist
of women imposing masculine and feminine archetypes on
society, and men seeing ourselves in them.

*Masculinization and feminization that have nothing to do with
homosexuality.*

Homosexuality is a deviation. We ought not to pursue
deviations. Nor yet idealize them. But perhaps we should begin
by *not* labeling pederasty, lesbianism, and other erotic eccentricities as deviations and perversions. Those names are one
more sign of the repressive character of our society . . .

Of ours, or of them all?

Of them all . . . although each in a different way.
At any rate, Fourier gave those penchants of the flesh and the
imagination a more human and more realistic name: manias.
Yes, they are notes at the extreme ends of the erotic harmony,
shades in the universal tapestry. That is, parts of that vast system
of attractions and repulsions that is eroticism. But they aren't
the center of the system. The pivot of sexuality, what gives
movement to everything, is the universal and complementary
opposition between masculine and feminine. Hence my interest
in the example of India. In Indian art and religion there are
no homosexual gods or lesbian goddesses; on the other hand in
Greek mythology, where the central archetype is masculine,
relationships of a homosexual type frequently occur. In the
Middle Ages we have a contrary phenomenon, the cult of the
Virgin. It was a prodigious attempt on the part of the Church
to feminize Christianity. And it was what gave the Middle Ages

their extraordinary vitality, as well as producing superb art, as
we know. Provençal poetry invented a feminine archetype and
converted woman into a sort of depository of cosmic health.
Woman was the intermediary between heaven and earth, between the pure world of ideas and man. The Church expropriated,
as one might say, that vision of woman and founded the cult
of the Virgin. Today we need an archetype similar to the Virgin
of the Middle Ages. We ought to return to the source, to
Provençal poetry.

*You mean that the feminine movement could become more
constructive?*

The rebellion of woman is one aspect of the changes
now going on in the West. When one takes a look at contemporary civilization, one becomes pessimistic: it is the reign
of violence and lies. But there are some movements involving
possibilities of reform, like those of racial minorities and youth.
Women are not a minority, however, but half the human race.
But, I repeat, to me the essential thing is not that women
should have identical rights with men—although that may be
necessary, urgent, and indispensable—but that they should be
aware of themselves, especially of their bodies. Only if woman
is aware of her own corporal peculiarity can she create erotic
archetypes of masculine and feminine. Starting from her body
she should construct her image of man and her image of herself.
By freeing herself from the distorted image of herself imposed
on her by man, woman will also liberate man.

How?

When, at the beginning of the industrial revolution,
woman left home to work in factories and offices, she swelled
the armies of wage earners. That was no liberation! From that
point of view the liberation of woman is part of the general
liberation of wage earners. But I'm also speaking of *another
liberation*, one that woman alone can realize: to change Western
eroticism, to feminize our aggressive civilization and give us
erotic archetypes different from those that modern industrial
society—in its two aspects, capitalist and communist—has im-

posed on our whole planet. To put an end to the myths of
work which convert body and soul into mere instruments of
production.

*In Conjunctions and Disjunctions you say that "the character and
future of every society depend to some extent on the relation
between the signs 'body' and 'non-body.' " Would you like to
expand that idea?*

I think that those two signs, "body" and "non-body"
are to be found in all civilizations. Of course the sign "body"
can be called nature or matter, and the term "non-body" can be
called soul, spirit, nirvana, atman, etc. The entity denoted by
the word "soul" and that denoted by the word "atman" can't
be translated into another language. But it is possible to translate
the relation of complementary opposition between one term
and another. There are civilizations in which this relation is
contradictory and disjunctive; there are others in which it is
conjunctive. If the conjunction is excessive, that society becomes
gravely sick; but an excessive disjunction is also dangerous. The
ideal is a certain harmonious disequilibrium. If there is a slight
preeminence of the body, the spirit can answer the body; if
there's a slight preeminence of the spirit, the body can answer
the spirit. Example: Romanesque art of the West and Buddhist
art in India between the second century B.C. and the third A.D.
Buddhist shrines represent the Buddha disembodied, and are
indeed a negation of the body—but those monuments are
surrounded by balustrades with reliefs showing scenes from daily
life, extremely sensual scenes. This continuous dialogue between
eroticism and holiness, between spirit and body, is what gave
life to Buddhism at a certain period, and also to Christianity in
the Middle Ages . . . I think the time we are now living in
is the end of an epoch. The nineteenth century was the century
of the negation of the body; we are now facing a great rebellion
of the body. . . . But it is an equivocal rebellion.

Why is it equivocal?

Because it assumes intellectual forms, more appropriate
to the sign "non-body." I'll explain myself. . . . It's clear that

one of the great moments in this rebellion of the body was the work of the Marquis de Sade. The few who studied Sade's work in the nineteenth century said that he was a great discoverer of sexual deviations and disturbances. That's true, but I don't think Sade's originality lies in his discoveries in sexual pathology. The ancients knew the sexual practices Sade describes and many of them were erotic rites in primitive religions. What was absolutely new was Sade's attitude to those practices: they were no longer abominations or rituals, but had become philosophical opinions. The title of one of his books is revealing: *La Philosophie dans le Boudoir*. Eroticism converted into philosophy, and philosophy converted into criticism: eroticism serving the cause of universal negation. That was something absolutely new. . . . Negation is the function par excellence of the mind, in Christian theology and in Dante or Milton, as well as in modern thought. For Hegel the concept was negation—and it was man who introduced negation into the universe. When eroticism becomes philosophical and critical, it stops being corporal. This is what is happening with the present feminist movement in the United States. Of course those combative and optimistic ladies are a very long way from Sade. They are an optimistic caricature of Sade. In short, the rebellion of the body is equivocal because it's a rebellion in the name of noncorporal, critical, and intellectual principles. A rebellion which makes use of the body to criticize society. Thus, on one hand it denounces our nostalgia for the reality of the body, for the truth of pleasure, which is an instantaneous truth, while at the same time the spirit, the "non-body" *sign*, the *sign* of oppression and repression, the *sign* of the Inquisition, the sadistic *sign* par excellence, disguises itself as *body* and so denies it. Because the body is neither idea nor criticism: it is pleasure, fiesta, imagination.

You also say: "No civilization, with the possible exception of the Aztec, can offer an art that rivals that of the West in sexual ferocity."

We'd better not talk about the Aztecs, because it might annoy a great many of my fellow-countrymen. Let's take some other examples: medieval Christian art or Tibetan art are cruel because they are religious. The cruelty of modern erotic art is not religious but philosophical. Think of the novelistic tradition that goes from Sade to the *Histoire d'O*. In all those works, some of them extraordinary, the body ceases to be body and becomes a sign of the destruction of the world. Not only did Sade want to destroy the world for the sake of the sensation, he also wanted to destroy the sensation itself. Sade's greatest creation is Juliette, a terrible character—and this is admirable in Sade: instead of the prince of evil being a man, it's a woman, that fascinating Juliette. . . . Well, Juliette puts too much passion into her terrible pleasures. And one of her friends, the lesbian Clairwill, says to her: "A true libertine is unmoved. You are too ardent." What the libertine philosopher is seeking through sensations is . . . insensibility. The perfect state of libertinism is a negative state. Sade's model is not a volcano, although he liked volcanoes very much, but cold lava. When I think of Sade's world, I think of an extinct volcano. When I think of libertinism, I think of a landscape of lava. The landscape of destruction.

In your opinion how does eroticism differ from sexuality?

I would say that sexuality embraces a very much wider sphere than eroticism. Sexuality is animal and also vegetable; eroticism is uniquely and exclusively human and social. In eroticism the animal forms of sexuality are transformed. I'll give you an example: the habit couples have of calling each other by animal names: "my dove," "my little turtle," "my tiger," etc. Both verbally and physically, eroticism is a metaphor for animal sexuality. Human beings imitate, verbally or physically, the way lions, tigers, and doves make love. Or the praying mantis or any other sinister insect. Now: we imitate the sexual behavior of the animals, but they don't imitate us. This imitation is eroticism. There is an element of freedom and imagination in eroticism which doesn't figure in sexuality. Eroticism is the representation of sexuality, its metaphor. Sometimes a consecration of sexuality, as in the Provençal courts of love, at other times a profanation, as in Sade. Eroticism is inseparable from language, and it is therefore culture, history. We use language to transform animal sexuality into a practice in which man, on the one hand, sees himself reflected in nature as in a mirror, and on the other hand, denies nature. Eroticism is an affirmation of sexuality and at the same time a negation of it. This is something man has added to nature.

Is eroticism love?

There are three levels: the sexual, biological, and animal level; the erotic and social level; and the personal level, or love. Eroticism belongs to all societies and civilizations; love seems to be an invention of the West. It originated as a poetic creation in Provence, and the Church fought against it from the beginning. From the first, love was a transgression of the social norms, a breaking of bonds, whether of family or class, racial or conjugal. Love has been the secret underground cult of the West. Denis de Rougemont has written a remarkable book on the subject. There's a strange ambivalence in Western consciousness: it exalts love and at the same time condemns it as an antisocial passion. In my view the difference between love and eroticism could be expressed thus: eroticism is social and plural; love is interpersonal. The idea of love implies the choice of a unique body and soul: a person. Thus, in our idea of love for a person there is a Platonic and Christian element (the soul) and a transgression of Christianity and Platonism: thus unique soul is inseparable from an equally unique body.

What is your view of the position of love in the modern world?

The modern decadence of love is the result of the decadence of the notion of personality and the idea of the soul. Modern promiscuity negates the central myth of the West, and this I find disturbing. The last great spiritual movement of this century was surrealism, which always exalted love—and love that was unique, not promiscuous. Surrealism affirmed the most complete erotic liberty and unique love simultaneously. I don't believe we can build a new civilization in the West except on the basis of love. For me, erotic freedom is linked to choice in love, and both are opposed to promiscuity.

What is the significance of the fact that books like The Sensuous Woman *and* Everything You Always Wanted to Know about Sex *have been for months best-sellers in the United States?*

    It is a rebellion of puritanism. But it is a very Yankee naïveté to think that a book can teach us to copulate better. It's an example of North American idealism and optimism—it's blind faith in education. There have been treatises and manuals of erotology ever since ancient times, but love is not merely a technique: it's an art, an invention. The number of positions is limited, yet every time we make love we do it in different ways. Imagination and body; skin and passion, all participate in the erotic act.

Are you in favor of sexual education?

    In a modern context sexual education means sexual hygiene. The important thing is that we should have erotic education, erotic culture. Both spheres of the modern world, the communist and the capitalist, degrade eroticism. One through publicity, the other through politics. Capitalism has degraded eroticism by converting it into a commercial product; revolutionary movements, including the present feminist movement, convert erotic pleasure, which belongs to the domain of the senses and imagination, into a critique of society.

To finish with women . . . what are the differences between North American and Latin American women?

    They are cultural and historical differences. One is the product of Protestant and democratic capitalism; the other of Catholic societies still bearing the marks of the Counter-Reformation, feudalism, and now, colonialism. Latin American women live in hierarchic, authoritarian societies, in which the traditional Catholic family is still a potent reality. Woman is the repository of traditional values, and so, as guardian of the home, her archetype is the mother. But this traditional Catholic concept of the mother has had another superimposed on it: the Moorish. Spain is a European country, but it is also a Moorish one, as Américo Castro clearly saw. These two ideas—woman as mother and woman as man's possession, an object of pleasure—determine the passivity of Latin American women and their servile position. From this point of view the North American woman is much more free. She is an individual, mistress of her own life, and has admirable autonomy.

Then it would be a good thing for Latin American women to follow the example of North American women.

Ah, I'm not sure about that. The situation is altered if instead of talking about woman's relation to society we talk of her relation to her own body. North American woman has been molded by a society whose archetype is exclusively masculine—an archetype which in its turn emphasizes certain virile qualities and rejects others. Protestant capitalist society has been the one which has most radically rejected the body and sexuality, and most passionately exalted the value of work, economy, and competition. North American woman lives in a society based on the ethics of work and competition, on conceiving of the body in terms of health and hygiene but not in terms of pleasure. All this means that the North American woman's relation to her body is as insecure as the North American man's relation to his. Both have been mutilated by Protestant and capitalist ethics. Hence this brutal rebellion of the body in Protestant societies.

You say some of this in Conjunctions and Disjunctions.

Psychoanalysis has shown us that there is a relation between the retention of excrement and capitalist saving, with its sublimation of material gold in the form of abstract symbols— money, stocks. It can also be shown that there is a relationship of inverse symmetry, as Lévi-Strauss would say, between retention of excrement and premature ejaculation. It's also possible to see this same contradictory symmetry between Tantrist Buddhism and Protestant capitalism; in the first, to the retention of semen and its sublimation of the sperm as a "thought of illumination" corresponds an attitude not of horror toward excrement but one of ritual "jouissance" which can go as far as real or symbolical swallowing of it in the Tantrist feast; while in the second case, premature ejaculation corresponds to the retention of excrement and its sublimation as abstract money. Another revealing difference: in Tantrism woman occupies a central place, while Protestantism is a religion of men. Capitalism is a masculine society.

Latin America is a Catholic civilization.

Precisely for that reason the body occupies a different place among us. The body and pleasure. There is, it's true, *machismo* and its violence, but on the whole Latin American woman has a less anxious relation with her body. For one thing, the central idea in Catholicism is not abstract morality but ritual —Catholicism is a corporal, carnal religion . . . it is the religion of the incarnation of divinity, even though it has been adapting itself to the modern world by "protestantizing" itself more and more; for another, the position of Latin American woman—the fact that she is seen as an object of pleasure or purely of reproduction—gives her a very lively awareness of her body. Although Latin American woman has read none of the books now being published in the United States, she possesses an instinctive erotic wisdom derived from the knowledge that her body is an object of pleasure, both for herself and for another. In Latin American woman, sensuality has been numbed by social morality or humiliated by *machismo;* in North American woman there is exasperation and frigidity. Different tyrannies—different mutilations.

Do you think a woman could govern a country?

Since the two Catharines and the two Isabellas; since Mrs. Indira Gandhi, Mrs. Bandaranaike of Ceylon, Mrs. Meir of Israel, and above all since Penthesilea, Queen of the Amazons, that question is superfluous.

How did Queen Penthesilea rule?

We don't know. The Uruguayan poet Herrera y Reissig said, "on a throne of vertigo and tides."

The generation gap is much wider today than in past times. Why do you think this is so?

In the past, the young wanted to oust the old from their positions and take their place. There was a battle between the generations rather than a subversion of values. Something quite different is happening today: the young have stopped believing in the values of the old. It's true that current values were also criticized in the past, but always by dissident minorities. In this respect, the only philosopher who clearly saw what was going to happen in our day was Nietzsche, who spoke of the subversion of values. The rebellion of youth should be seen as part of the great phenomenon of the subversion of values in the West. The tragedy of the youth movement lies in the fact that whenever the young reject the values of the old they are right, but they haven't been able to create new values to take the place of the old. Nor have they been able to live what Nietzsche called total or absolute nihilism. In this, Nietzsche was just as mistaken as Marx, or more: he foretold the appearance of a superman, who would be the complete nihilist, like a god, but all we have is the "superman" of the comics.

I think that the attitude toward death of many of these young people is also different; they don't deny it, as you said of the North American in The Labyrinth of Solitude.

I don't know. But I'll tell you what I think about our views of death, and certain changes I've noticed in them. The contemporary rebellion of the body means that the present appears as a privileged value: the time of the body is the time of the present. It is thus opposed to the civilization of progress which always concealed the image of death. A civilization which makes its supreme values savings, work, and the accumulation of wealth, and whose paradise is framed in terms not of eternity but of the future . . . it's only natural that such a civilization rejects death. Death has meaning for a Christian, it's a passing, it's the leap into eternity; death also has meaning for a Hindu: it is a liberation. But for a civilization which believes in the future and has the religion of progress, death is a reality without meaning, because it negates the future and negates progress. The abstraction we call humanity can progress, but I don't progress: I die. Moreover, I shall never arrive at the future. Thus, the rebellion of the body, which is a rebellion against the future and proclaims the present as the fundamental value, also implies the reappearance of death. If the time of the body is the present, it is both life and death simultaneously. The rebellion of the body, as well as inventing a new eroticism, must give us a new image of death. This will be one of man's great conquests: for man at last to see death, not disguised as eternal life as in the old religions, nor put out of sight as in the modern world. For him to see it and face it. But in order to face it he must see it—and see it as an integral part of life.

It's difficult, don't you think so?

Not as difficult as it seems. In eroticism, which is the time of the body, death appears as aggression or auto-aggression. In love it appears differently: in loving the woman I love, I know I am loving a mortal being. And I know that I too am mortal. Love is always linked to the awareness of death, to the mortality of the beloved and my own.

Are there any civilizations that don't believe in love?

I think the majority of civilizations disbelieve in love. The sole civilization which has exalted love is that of the West, but at the same time it has seen love as a heterodoxy, a transgression. What the West has always affirmed is the sanctity of the family, not of love. On the contrary, love has been a wicked passion. That is why it is still a revolutionary force in the twentieth century. Eroticism is not, any more: it has been expropriated, confiscated by industry and entertainment, by the cinema. It's not possible to use the word "eroticism" any more, it has been soiled by publicity and fashion. Past societies used erotic rites in their religious spectacles, but it fell to industrial capitalist society to forfeit eroticism to the ends of business and publicity. That is why I say that eroticism is all the time becoming less of a revolutionary force. Whereas love, which is a personal and intimate passion, can still be a revolutionary or, at least, a dissenting force. Love is a transgression of contemporary promiscuity.

Don't you think there is also significance in the change in religious beliefs, and the emergence of new myths, such as we see in music festivals, for instance?

It's obvious that since the nineteenth century we have been witnessing a slow erosion of religious beliefs. An erosion which has made a desert of the soul of Western man. Well, religion has been for millions of years men's traditional response to the most extraordinary fact of all, the fact that we are men. That is: to the fact of knowing we are mortal: is there another world? what is the meaning of our being here? Besides answering these and similar questions, religions have sanctified the links between men, and in the same way have made it possible for the living to commune with the dead, with the gods, and with nature. Religion thus carries out two functions: it is a response to the fact of being men, and a form of participation in this world and the next.

Don't other institutions and activities fulfill the same functions?

Yes and no. As to the first, I would say that philosophy also provides answers, although obviously they are much less moving than those of religion. Montaigne said that to philosophize is to learn to die. In some cases, and for some individuals, philosophy fills the void left by religion. At the end of antiquity and in face of the decadence of pagan religions, Stoicism and other schools effectively gave a certain wisdom to men. The modern world needs a *sagesse* like that of the ancient Stoics.

And the other function?

The other consists in opening the doors of communion with men and with the cosmos. I believe that eroticism, and above all, love—"sublime love" as Benjamin Péret called it—can make such communion possible. All lovers suddenly feel separate from society but united with the cosmos and so part of a reality vaster than themselves. Art and poetry also give us the power to commune with others and with ourselves. Lastly there is action, shared adventure. The dream of revolutionary brotherhood has fascinated men of the twentieth century: comradeship, fraternity in the struggle to build something different from sordid contemporary society. But religion provides something more than—and different from—the consoling answers given by philosophy and the exaltation produced by love, poetry, and revolutionary activity. Religion is a permanent social structure; it is ritual, ceremony, fiesta. In ritual, man communes with all ages, time is dissolved in a magic present—a present that is repeated because it is inscribed in the sacred calendar. Well, there are no rituals in the modern world.

There's a good deal of talk about contemporary rituals and myths.

Yes, those of politics, sport, fashion, publicity, television. All these serve to occupy the void left by the authentic myths and rites of the only religion the West has ever had: Christianity. Some of them, like the beatification of propaganda or the deification of fashion, are caricatures of religious devotion; others, such as political idolatries and inquisitions, are perversions of the sacred. All such pseudo-myths are substitutes, and their proliferation reveals the persistence of what we must needs call the "religious instinct." Hence, too, the attempts to create new rituals, music festivals, and nostalgia for orgies. Christianity suppressed the orgiastic character of religion, and the decadence of Christianity is provoking the resurrection of bacchanals and orgies, in the ancient religious sense of those two words. In all these youthful movements one can see a thirst for religion, a nostalgia for rituals. These movements aren't truly religious, but pre-religious. And they are not religious because they lack the essential ingredient of ritual: the repetition of the sacred days. Also they lack revelation, a doctrine, prophets and martyrs. The youth movement betrays our deficiencies, it shows that there is a vacuum at the heart of contemporary society, which neither philosophy, nor politics, nor science, nor art has succeeded in filling. But the youth movement is not the answer we are hoping for; it is an explosion of despair.

Can that answer be found?

I can only reply with a phrase from Novalis: "When we dream that we are dreaming, we are very nearly awake." If we know what we need, perhaps we can discover a way to obtain it. Twenty-five years ago André Breton said that modern man ought to discover a new holiness (not a religious one) which could be the point of convergence of liberty, love, and poetry. It's curious: during the rebellion of the young in Paris in 1968 these ideas reappeared and it was very obvious that the deepest influence, the underground influence in the youth movement, did not come primarily from political theory but from the poets. It seems to me that the youth movement, in its para-religious or pre-religious aspect and also as political rebellion, has its roots buried in our romantic heritage.

Do you think romanticism is a modern phenomenon?

That depends on what you mean by contemporary and also on what you mean by romanticism. Romantic art is part of our heritage, but I'm not referring to that. I'm referring to an underground stream which passed through the whole of the nineteenth century to burst forth in the second half of the twentieth. That stream originated with the great romantics. I'm thinking of prophet-poets like William Blake, of nature poets like Wordsworth, and figures like Hölderlin and Novalis. This stream reappeared in France in the second half of the nineteenth century, with Baudelaire, Lautréamont, Mallarmé, Rimbaud, poets who had an influence on surrealism. In this sense romanticism isn't an artistic school but a spiritual family. So that from this point of view, romanticism is modern, although it would be absurd to try to revive romantic forms.

I thought our age was a scientific and technological age.

One doesn't exclude the other. Romanticism is present not only in the art and movements of our epoch but also in science itself. One example is linguistics. As you know, linguistics became a science at the moment when, thanks to Saussure, it succeeded in making language an object. Well, one of the most brilliant linguists of our day, Chomsky, has reintroduced the subject into linguistics, and in this sense has returned to romanticism. On one hand he has returned to Descartes, and on the other to Humboldt and romantic thought. By introducing the subject into modern linguistics, Chomsky has built a bridge between the concepts of modern linguistics and the ideas of modern poets, from the romantics and symbolists to the surrealists. It's not accidental that Chomsky is also a political thinker with leanings toward anarchism. During the nineteenth century and the first half of the twentieth anarchism represented the romantic aspect of revolution. So that, both in the science of linguistics and in politics, Chomsky reintroduces the subject, which is not the same as the self. The romantic cult of the self is a form of complacency, an idolatry; the reintroduction of the subject is the reinsertion of subjectivity, without violating the objectivity of science, and of liberty into politics.

Talking of linguistics, in a recent article in the Times Literary Supplement *you put in doubt the existence of prose. What did you mean by that?*

The characteristic of poetry is that each poetical phrase contains a plurality of meanings. Whereas prose, ruled by reason, tries to give each word and each sentence a unique meaning. Since this stipulation is ideal and unattainable, prose doesn't really exist.

Pasternak said that it was no longer possible to express the immensity of our experience through lyric poetry. "We have acquired values that can be better expressed in prose."

I suppose Pasternak was thinking principally about the novel. The novel isn't prose. The novel is a very strange and paradoxical literary form. Certainly a novel isn't written in verse. But the language of a novel is not the prose of a scientific or philosophical discourse; it's a language in which the rhythm, play on words, metaphors, and ambiguity of poetry all reappear. The language of the novel oscillates between true prose and poetry. The same happens with the characters in novels: the heroes of the old epics were heroes through and through, models. The heroes of the novel are anti-social or asocial, they aren't typical, they are individual cases, and we could call them anti-heroes. They are the heroes of a critical epic. The novel, as has often been said, is the epic of the bourgeois society, that's to say of a society in which the ruling principle is not revelation of divinity but critical reason. When the bourgeoisie took over the power, they did so in the name of reason, not in the name of God. Their epic is a critical, anti-heroic epic, reflecting and judging the world it depicts. The novel is ambiguous, because its language oscillates between poetry and prose, and because its heroes and the world in which they live belong partly to the epic and partly to criticism. Well, there comes a moment when the criticism of society (as in Balzac or Dickens) becomes also a criticism of language. This is the moment when the novel and poetry coincide.

Novel and poetry are the same?

Modern poetry and the novel spring from the same source and in our time they are reunited again. The point of union was symbolism. The symbolists inherited the visionary and prophetic tradition of the romantic poets, but they also made use of criticism and negation, as a method of creation. Mallarmé questions language, refutes language by language, and nullifies the poem within the poem. Poetry is a verbal creation and Mallarmé introduces negation, silence, and doubt into that creation. Later on, some of the greatest twentieth-century novelists learned this lesson from the poets, and in their turn criticized language within the novel. The creative destruction of language transforms the modern novel into poetry. This is particularly clear in one of the most important writers of our day, James Joyce. In Joyce's work the distinction between poetry and the novel has almost completely disappeared. In his work the central element is language. His characters are, quite literally, puns.

Do you think there's more interest in poetry today?

In the United States and England, yes. Not in France, nor in Italy, Spain, and Latin America. Why? I don't know. Perhaps it's something to do with a Latin or Roman heritage. We often confuse eloquence with poetry . . . Moreover, the new phe-

nomenon consists in the disappearance of literary forms—or rather
in their fusion. Novels tend more and more to become verbal
experiments, not without structural similarity to poems. And some
poets are regaining an epic spirit and thus coinciding with the
novel. Besides this continual interpenetration between the literary
forms, there is the appearance—or more exactly the reappearance
—of the spoken word: radio, TV, poetry festivals. This is particularly noticeable in the Saxon countries. In Latin countries
they don't read poems in public, perhaps from instinctive mistrust of eloquence and declamation. It's a pity because Spanish
is a language rich in rhythms. Our poetry has a marvelous spoken
tradition . . . a poetry that was sung and danced.

*You mentioned the reappearance of the spoken word in radio and
television . . . but although the means of communication are
increasing, less and less communication actually takes place in our
civilization.*

That's quite true. The civilization that has invented the
most perfect instruments of communication is the same one that
is now suffering from lack of communication. Jakobson said once
that language is our only entirely socialized possession. In fact we
are all producers and consumers of language. Linguistic material
is the property of no one. Well, we all have the faculty of speech
but very few of us can use it through the media of communication.
Worse still: besides being given no chance to speak we are forced
to listen to the same slogans, the same lies, the same nonsense.
Private companies or governments have confiscated the linguistic
functions—talking, listening, answering—and converted them into
a monopoly. A business transaction or a form of political domination, with the interlocutor converted into a client or a supporter. For me, socialism begins—or ought to begin—with the
freedom of all and everyone to speak, listen, and reply. Especially
the last: the right to reply—something that is getting more difficult all the time in a technological society. Whereas in primitive
societies this verbal socialism really did exist . . . The new media
of communication have not so far been a means of liberating mankind: on the contrary they have helped to dominate it. Language
is social, but the media of communication are not owned by

society. This is the fundamental contradiction. McLuhan doesn't investigate it, but it seems to me the basis, the essence of what is happening.

Do you agree with Cortázar when he says in Ultimo Round *(Last Round) that there is no erotic language in Spanish literature such as there is in American literature with Henry Miller?*

Yes, Julio is right, especially where modern literature is concerned. But in the Middle Ages our erotic tradition was no less rich than that of the French or English. Few literatures possess a book comparable to the Archpriest of Hita's *Libro del buen amor*, which ought to be called the book of wild love, the book of passionate, sensual love. Later, during the Renaissance, we have two marvelous books: *La Celestina* and *La lozana andaluza* (The Andalusian Whore), a much less well-known work. It's the history of a Spanish courtesan in Rome written by a priest, Francisco Delgado. This book is extremely rich in erotic expressions and to some extent supplies what Cortázar is asking for. But it's true to say that the erotic vein dwindled afterwards. There was a terrible censorship against the body in Spain and the same happened in Latin America. The erotic vein reappears at the end of the century with the "modernist" poets as they are called. One of these is the Mexican poet, Salvador Díaz Mirón. In his poetry the perfection of the language is allied to great erotic violence. Another example of "fin de siécle" eroticism is the Andalusian poet Salvador Rueda, author of a novel whose title is *Cópula* (Copulation). Neither more nor less! Among poets of today there are some in whom one finds an erotic element, apart from the amorous tone noticed by Cortázar. I'm thinking of Pablo Neruda . . .

And in your own poetry.

Well, so you say . . . There's another poet, Luis Cernuda. Cernuda's message is moral as well as poetical. He published his first books between 1925 and 1930, and declared in them that he was a homosexual. Publishing poems of that sort, in those years and in Spain, was proof of great courage. Cernuda ran a risk and I believe that without risk there can be neither great

art nor eroticism. Eroticism always skirts the boundaries of prohibition, and death—and the same happens with art . . . Finally,
I think that what interests Cortázar, as it does me, is not so much
erotic literature—I mean, literature which describes erotic things
—as the erotization of language. In that connection, how badly
has been read 62, *Modelo para armar* (62: *A Model Kit*) which
ought to be called Model to Love, a perfect mixture of eroticism
and oneirism. But there is no erotic thought in our language,
there are no reflections on eroticism. We have had no Bataille,
Blanchot, nor Klossowski.

Why not?

          For a long time thinking has been a defunct activity in
Latin America and Spain.

What about you?

          Since you tempt me, I will say, at the risk of seeming
vain, that yes, I am one of the few who have written on the
subject in our language.

You wrote a poem about Sade.

          Towards Sade . . . I wrote it about a quarter of a
century ago. Later on I published a long essay on him. It may
be the first in our language. If I remember rightly, the first translator of Sade was the Chilean poet Braulio Arenas, but I don't
know if he has written any essays or reflections on those themes.
Nor do I remember the dates of the studies and essays by the Argentine critic, Revol, or of Gaitán Durán, the Colombian poet. I
published my essay in *Sur*, when it was edited by José Bianco (a
key figure in the history of our modern literature). It also appeared in the *Review of the University of Mexico*, edited at the
time by the poet and critic Jaime García Terrés. I've published
other studies on the same subject since then. In 1969 *Conjunctions and Disjunctions* appeared, whose theme is a polemical
dialogue between the genital and the facial organs, the hidden
face and the uncovered face.

In Corriente alterna (Alternating Current) you are much concerned with a comparison between wine and drugs.

I wrote on that subject about fifteen years ago, and now a whole heap of platitudes has been written about it. Briefly, my idea is that wine and drugs represent different attitudes to communication. We are traditionally offered two models for wine-drinking: the Platonic banquet and the Last Supper. In the first case, wine is allied to the highest form of conversation: philosophic dialogue; in the other, it acts as a metaphor for the blood of God, as a symbol for the utmost form of communication with Him: holy communion. The archetype of the East is very different: the Buddha, the hermit, sitting alone under a tree or on top of a mountain, meditates and interiorizes the world until he annihilates it. Negation of language and dialogue, exaltation of solitude and silence. In the East drugs have always been used as aids to meditation and mental concentration. Well, drunkenness is a failed attempt at communication, an exaggeration and caricature of communication: drunkards begin by embracing each other and end up fighting. So that when the young decide to give up alcohol, which is exaggerated communication, in favor of drugs, it means that they are renouncing the dialogue and, in a profound sense, rejecting one of the central archetypes of our civilization. They are either renouncing communication or else looking for a nonverbal form of it. Someone who gets drunk is conforming to Western tradition, if he takes drugs he is a dissident. This is another sign that we are living in a period of change. In the drug habit we again find a criticism of Western tradition, a portent of imminent change. Of course, one doesn't achieve anything with drugs, or eroticism, or festivals. Again, every time the dissidents say *no* to contemporary society I understand them, and sometimes concur in their negation. But insofar as they affirm something, I dissent.

You also mentioned Henri Michaux and his experiments with mescalin.

Yes, I wrote an essay on Michaux's poetry and painting. I also studied his experiences with certain hallucinogens—mushrooms, mescalin. The essential thing seems to me that Michaux has *lived* certain ideas, and ventured into dangerous and little understood psychic territory. A real "spiritual experience," as it used to be called some years ago. So that Michaux is a poet who can answer for almost everything he has written.

Do you agree with the literary critics when they say there is a "boom" in Latin American literature?

I find the word "boom" repulsive. There can be a "boom" in petroleum or wheat, but there can't be a boom in the novel and less still in poetry. One mustn't confuse success, publicity, or sales with literature. Of course I don't deny the existence and excellence of the new Latin American novelists. That would be absurd and small-minded. What I am opposed to is that criticism should be supplanted by propaganda and an attempt made to reduce Latin American literature to the novel alone, for commercial or publishing reasons. A mutilation amputating half its body: poetry. Imagine what North American literature would be like without Pound, Lowell, Zukofsky, Creeley—or French literature without Char, Ponge, Bonnefoy! None of these poets is a best-seller . . . so what?

Would it be correct to say that there is a Mexican literature?

I don't believe in the existence of Mexican literature, any more than I believe in the existence of Argentine, Chilean, or Cuban literature. I believe in Hispano-American literature. Aesthetic styles and trends transcend nationality and have nothing to do with frontiers. Mexican literature is one of the tributaries of Hispano-American literature. But some great writers were born in Mexico, for instance Ramón López Velarde, Alfonso Reyes, Sor Juana Inés de la Cruz . . .

Do you really believe Mexican literature has no special character of its own? Isn't Juan Rulfo very Mexican?

Rulfo is one of the founders of the new Hispano-American literature. The translator of Rulfo into French, who is also a specialist in Persian literature, told me that *Pedro Páramo* reminded him of *The Blind Owl*, the great modern Persian novel so much admired by André Breton. Influence? No: coincidence, confluence. Modern literature is *one*, despite the plurality of languages and traditions. No, there isn't a Mexican style, any more than there is a Spanish, Peruvian, or Chilean style. Styles are historic, they have never been exclusively national, and they leap across walls and frontiers. Although symbolism originated in France it isn't exclusively French; romanticism, realism, fantastic literature—are they German, English, French, or Russian? The "most Mexican" of Mexican poets, López Velarde, reminds one particularly of the Argentine poet Lugones, who resembles a French poet, Laforgue. And, who is "more Hispano-American," the Mexican Reyes, who wrote "Ifigenia cruel" in transparent language without local flavor, or the Galician Valle-Inclán, author of the marvelous *Tirano banderas*, which is the height of verbal Americanism? A writer is always a plurality of voices, every language is a plurality of languages. In Carlos Fuentes, for instance, several voices coexist, and each of these voices, each of these dialects is equally his own: how can one decide which is the Mexican and which is foreign in this plurality? The Mexican voice is the impact and confluence between them all. No, there's no Mexican style: but there is a great tradition, which was born in the sixteenth century and has continued until our day. Something unique in Hispano-America. I don't say this out of nationalism but to balance the scales. There's a lot of talk about Whitman or Darío and very little about Sor Juana.

But Sor Juana wrote in the seventeenth century!

And she still lives. Her work, if not her memory. A great poet and perhaps the most important woman in the history of our continent, as much in the Latin half as in the Saxon. A good subject for the Women's Liberation Movement, although some radical intellectuals might be shocked by Sor Juana's extreme refinement and elegance. A fascinating figure: she was beautiful, she was unhappy, she loved knowledge. The ecclesiastical hierarchy persecuted her because, though a nun, she showed a great aptitude for profane and none for sacred literature. She was a true intellectual, something very rare in the Hispanic tradition. For Spaniards, theology was everything, and now that theology has disappeared, ideology is everything for them, as well as for Hispano-Americans. Ideology, that is: politics. Politics has taken the place of theology. Or rather, Hispano-American politics is theological politics. But Sor Juana is the opposite of a theologian, although one of her writings, her criticism of the Jesuit Vieyra, is theological. I am passionately fond of Sor Juana because as a poet she was also an intellectual. Those two aspects of her work, the baroque poetess and the thinking being, are combined in an extraordinary work, "Primero sueño" (First Dream). It is one of the two great poems of the seventeenth century (the other is Gongora's "Fábula de Polifemo" (Fable of Polyphemus). The subject of Sor Juana's poem is knowledge. The spirit and human reason desire knowledge, but knowledge is a dream: the spirit dashes itself to pieces against the absolute and falls headlong into the relative. A theme which doesn't appear in the literature of that period and which anticipates modern ideas. It is remarkable that a woman should have constructed that baroque but rational edifice called "Primero sueño." If I were an anti-feminist I should say she had a masculine temperament, but it isn't true, she was profoundly intelligent and profoundly feminine.

You have gone back to the first century to explain certain contemporary events . . . could we now move backwards a mere half century, and talk about Octavio Paz, his boyhood, his life and work?

I come from a typical Mexican family. My father's family is a very old one, from Jalisco State. A mestizo family. My paternal grandfather was a Mexican with markedly Indian features. My mother's parents were Andalusians and my mother was born in Mexico. So that my family is European on one side and Indian on the other. My paternal grandfather was a well-known journalist and writer. He campaigned against French intervention and was a supporter of Porfirio Díaz, although at the end of his life he opposed the old dictator. My father took part in the Mexican Revolution and represented Zapata in the United States. He was one of the founders of agrarian reform. I was born in Mexico City, but as a boy I lived in a place called Mixcoac, near the capital. We lived in a large house with a garden. Our family had been impoverished by the revolution and the civil war. Our house, full of antique furniture, books, and other objects, was gradually crumbling to bits. As rooms collapsed we moved the furniture into another. I remember that for a long time I lived in a spacious room with part of one of the walls missing. Some magnificent screens protected me inadequately from wind and rain. A creeper invaded my room . . . A premonition of that surrealist exhibition where there was a bed lying in a swamp.

Your family were Catholic, weren't they?

As in all Mexican houses at that time, at least those of the bourgeoisie and middle classes, the men of my house weren't very good Catholics, but *rather* freethinkers, Masons, or liberals. Whereas the women were devout Catholics. As a boy, because of my aunt and my mother, I went to a French school kept by Marist fathers, and like all boys I went through a crisis of religious enthusiasm. I was very anxious to find out if my grandfather, who wasn't a believer but whom I considered to be one of the best men in the world, would be saved or not. For him to be condemned to hell seemed to me atrocious. An incongruity on God's part: to condemn a good man simply because he didn't believe in Him. And this made me reflect that the pagan philosophers and the heroes we were taught to admire at school had also ended up in hell. I was horrified by all this, but at the same time it fomented my ardor.

Did this conflict make you lose your faith?

No, neither Alexander nor any of the other famous pagans condemned to hell were responsible for that. I went astray out of boredom. It's the devil's most powerful weapon, you know. . . . Going to Mass was compulsory, and Mass was held in a very beautiful chapel—the school was a *hacienda* of the end of the eighteenth or beginning of the nineteenth century. The Mass was long, the sermons tedious, and my faith began to grow cold. I was bored and that was blasphemy because I realized I was bored. Also I was thinking about girls. The Church became a purveyor of ever more indecent erotic daydreams; and those dreams made me more and more doubtful, and my doubts nourished my anger against God. One fine day, as I left the Church, I realized once more that communion had had no effect on me. I was just as much fallen from God's grace after communion as I had been before it. I spat on the ground as if to get rid of the host, I danced on my spittle, uttered two or three curses and defied God. From that day, although I told no one, I was a belligerent atheist.

When did you first go to Europe?

I went to Spain in 1937 for a congress of antifascist writers. After the congress my colleagues went back to Paris and then to their own countries, but I stayed in Spain about a year. After that I returned to Mexico.

Did you fight in the civil war?

I was at the front, but I didn't really fight. I spent some time at the southern front with a Mexican who afterwards died, Juan B. Gómez. He was colonel of a brigade. I was in Madrid before that and afterwards in Valencia, in different jobs.

Did Spain have a great influence on you?

Spain taught me the meaning of the word "fraternity." There are some things I shall never forget. One Sunday I went with two friends, the poets Manuel Altolaguirre and Arturo Serrano Plaja, to a place near Valencia, and we had to return on foot because we missed the last bus. It was already night, we were walking along the road and suddenly the sky was lit up by antiaircraft guns. Enemy planes couldn't penetrate over Valencia because of the fire from Republican batteries, and they started to unload their bombs in the outskirts of the city, exactly where we were. The next village we came to was lit up by the glare of the explosions. We went through it singing the "Internationale" to keep up our own courage and also to encourage the inhabitants, and then we took shelter in a vegetable garden. The peasants came to look at us and were interested to hear I was a Mexican. Mexico was sending help to the Republicans, and some of those peasants were anarchists. They went back to their houses in the middle of the bombardment to look for food, and brought us a little bread, a melon, cheese and wine. Eating with those peasants during a bombardment . . . that's something I can't forget.

I think you first came in contact with surrealist thought at that time. How did it affect you?

From Spain I went to Paris where I met several of the friends I had made at the congress. Alejo Carpentier among others. He took me to see Robert Desnos and that was my first contact with the surrealists, though Desnos wasn't any longer a member of the group. I didn't really know what surrealism was at that time, though I felt a lot of sympathy for them. My experiences in Spain confirmed my revolutionary ardor, but at the same time made me mistrust revolutionary theories. This brought me closer to the political attitude of the surrealists. And the more I saw of them, the more I realized how much we agreed, not only because all my reading of the German romantics and William Blake had prepared me to accept surrealism, but also because its political attitude was fairly close to mine. But that happened later.

When did you return to Mexico?

In 1938. I worked for the Spanish Republicans. Those were the years of my most intense political activity. I was on the editorial board of *El Popular*, the daily paper of a union of Mexican workers. I wrote a daily article commenting on international politics. When I was a journalist I never wrote about literary subjects. Since before my visit to Spain I had had serious differences of opinion with the communist bureaucracy, especially with the supporters of social realism. When the Munich pact was signed a group of the staff of *El Popular* criticized the bourgeois democracies for capitulating to Hitler, adding that this was the result of the policy of the Third International, and resigned from the paper. However I stayed on, and only left it at the time of the German-Soviet pact. I then almost entirely withdrew from political activity, although for a time I went on collaborating with the revolutionary opposition. I had some Trotskyite friends, among others José Ferrer, editor of *Clave*, the magazine of the Fourth International in Mexico.

Had you given up literature?

By no means. In those years, I founded two magazines with other writers: first, *Taller*, and afterwards *El hijo pródigo* (The Prodigal Son). At my suggestion Ferrer translated Rimbaud's *Une saison en enfer*, which was published in *Taller*, and Lautréamont's *Poèsies*, which appeared in *El hijo pródigo*. They were the first translations of these two texts into Spanish. *Taller* also printed the first anthology of T. S. Eliot in Spanish. It was wartime, and many revolutionary intellectuals and artists had taken refuge in Mexico. I soon got to know Victor Serge, one of the founders of the Third International, who had been persecuted by Stalin. Indeed I owe to Victor Serge my first reading of Henri Michaux, a great poet whom I met some years later and to whom I'm now bound by close friendship. Michaux was a discovery of capital importance for me—his work constitutes a vertiginous verbal and spiritual universe. Another of my friends then (and always) was Benjamin Péret, who also was a refugee in Mexico. Through Péret I got to know the other surrealists living in Mexico, like Paalen and Leonora Carrington—an extraordinary woman, a bewitched enchantress.

And Buñuel?

No, I met Buñuel years later in Paris. I showed *Los olvidados* (The Forgotten) at the Cannes film festival, in spite of opposition from many Mexicans in official positions. They thought it was derogatory to Mexico. The film won a prize, and although this enraged them even more, it made them shut up.

Los olvidados marked Buñuel's return to world cinema.

I would say: his return to great art, to his passionate and critical vision. A return to *L'age d'or* (The Golden Age) and *Le chien andalou* (The Andalusian Dog), films which literally opened our eyes to what we really are. All realism is visionary . . . But we were in Mexico during the war years. I had broken with the communists at that time and found myself involved in a great many controversies about what was called "social realism." I got into serious difficulties with a poet I admire—Pablo Neruda.

When I think back to those years I wonder how it was possible for so many remarkable minds to suffer the contagion of that moral leprosy, Stalinism. Aberrations of the religious instinct—an instinct that has been much too little studied.

Where were you during the war?

In Mexico first, and in the United States at the end. In 1944 I got a Guggenheim fellowship. My stay in the United States was a great experience, no less decisive than that in Spain. On one hand there was the amazing and terrible reality of North American civilization; on the other, my reading and discovery of a number of poets: Eliot, Pound, William Carlos Williams, Wallace Stevens, Cummings. Years later I met William Carlos Williams, who translated my poem "Himno entre Ruinas" (Hymn Among Ruins), and also Cummings. I saw more of Cummings, and translated some of his poems. But let's go back to those years . . . When the war ended I was in Paris. There I met Peret. He took me to see Breton and that was how my friendship and collaboration with the surrealists began. I was very fond of André Breton and Peret.

Do you feel closer to French or to North American poetry?

Instead of answering that question, it would be better to tell you where I stand in the tradition of modern poetry. Much of what I've written has been an attempt to insert myself into the history of modern poetry. I think that is a need all poets feel, and in the case of a Latin American poet it is an even deeper need. A Latin American is a being who has lived in the suburbs of the West, in the outskirts of history. At the same time he feels (*and is*) part of a tradition which despised him until a short while ago. Darío and Vallejo passed through Paris without being noticed by anyone. That's why every Latin American poet affirms with the same emphasis—it should be said: with the same desperation and exasperation—his Latin American origins and his part in world tradition. The two great movements in Latin American poetry, the modernists and the avant-garde, were simultaneously cosmopolitan and nativist. Every Latin American work is a prolongation and a transgression of the Western tradition. I have discussed this in several of my books, particularly *El arco y la lira* (The Bow and the Lyre).

Is your work prolongation or transgression?

I would like it to be prolongation *and* transgression. A crossroads. I feel myself to be the result of a tradition that seems to me central to modern Western poetry and which began with certain German and English romantic poets. Romanticism was the beginning of modern poetry in my eyes. A paradoxical beginning, because romanticism is at the same time the expression of the modern age and its negation. The modern age stands for the triumph of reason, the bourgeoisie, science—the end of monarchy and religion, the beginning of the profane history of the West—the beginning of the lineal view of time: the future of progress dethrones Christian eternity. The attitude of the romantics toward the modern revolution is ambiguous, and that ambiguity was to be a persistent note in modern poetry until the surrealists and the Russian futurists. The critical spirit had literally demolished the great religious myths of the West, and the romantics were trying to build the myths (truths) of poetry on that empty space: religious revelation was substituted for poetic revelation. The true religion of humanity is imagination, Blake had said. The romantics conceived of the poet as a seer, and what that seer sees with the eyes of the imagination, not of the face, is universal analogy, the correspondence between the macrocosm and man. All these ideas circulate like a sort of spiritual blood in poets as different as Coleridge and Novalis, Wordsworth and Hölderlin.

A religious attitude . . .

Which is not contained in any religion, in any dogma. An attitude which attempts to combine essentially critical revolutionary activity, which is essentially critical, with poetic vision. And there's a marvelous moment when poetic thought, analogical thought, is combined with revolutionary thought. The name of this moment is Charles Fourier, so-called utopian socialist. Fourier applied the romantic theory of correspondences to society and even to eroticism. . . . French poetry, from Nerval and Baudelaire to Rimbaud and Mallarmé, receives the romantic heritage. All these tendencies appear afresh in the splendid explosion of the first quarter of this century (the Russian futurists, Apollinaire, the great Portuguese poet Pessõa) and reached their maximum concentration and violence in the surrealist movement. Surrealism was not merely an aesthetic, poetic, and political doctrine, although it was all these things; it was a vital attitude. A negation of the contemporary world and at the same time an attempt to substitute other values for those of democratic bourgeois society: eroticism, poetry, imagination, liberty, spiritual adventure, vision. All this is very modern, yet at the same time the voices of the great romantic precursors are heard in it . . . Well, the poetry I have written seems to me to form part of this current, or is trying to form part of it.

You feel yourself a surrealist?

In this sense I do feel a surrealist, although from another point of view I feel myself far removed from surrealist aesthetics. Take automatic writing, for instance . . . I practiced it once for a time. But I believe poetry to be the fruit of a collaboration, or a collision, between the dark and the light halves of man. I wouldn't have been able to write "Blanco," "Wind from All Compass Points" or even "Sun Stone" by automatic writing, although there is some oneirism and automatism in these poems. No, my concept of a poem, especially of a long poem, is rather close to that of the North American poets. And first of all and above all to that of some of my contemporaries and predecessors in my own language: Huidobro, Villaurrutia, Tablada's *haiku*, and simultaneist poetry . . . At the present moment it seems to me it would be absurd to return to the poetic forms of surrealism, but it would be stupid to disown it. Surrealism was a great moment for the human imagination. And it will return, under another name perhaps and in other forms.

What circumstances led you into a diplomatic career?

Chance, and thanks to two friends: Francisco Castillo Nájera and José Gorostiza. The first had been a friend of my father's, and like him had taken part in the Mexican Revolution.

He was appointed minister for foreign affairs, and he gave me the chance to enter the diplomatic service. In those days (1945) I was living in New York under considerable financial difficulties, and naturally I accepted. That admirable poet José Gorostiza was head of the diplomatic service, and he decided to send me to Paris . . . I'll tell you something which makes me laugh now (it's better to laugh at oneself than cry): I accepted with the secret hope that I should witness the European revolution of the proletariat. The fiesta of the century. In 1944 and 1945 Victor Serge and many others thought the same. Marxism or the dialectic of illusions . . .

In Mexico there's a tradition of diplomatic poets, isn't there?

In Mexico and many other Latin American countries: Darío was a minister and Pablo Neruda consul general. In Mexico, until a little while ago, writers and artists also collaborated with the state. It's explicable. Once the violent phase of the Mexican Revolution was over, the revolutionary regime needed technicians and administrators and called on the intellectuals to occupy important posts, some as experts, others as political and economic advisers, others as diplomats. The populist post-revolutionary state also called on artists, and so we see Marxist painters like Rivera and Siqueiros covering kilometers of wall with their paintings. Collaboration between intellectuals and governments is an example that shouldn't be followed.

Why not?

Because it isn't the function of writers to contribute to good administration but to criticize that administration. As Camus said, writers are the witnesses of this world. Witnesses, not functionaries.

What do you remember about those years in the diplomatic service?

My career wasn't brilliant and my advancement was slow. That didn't worry me because what I wanted was to work more or less anonymously and have the opportunity to write.

Above all to write poetry, which was and is my first love. I always wrote somewhat against the current—and against myself. *The Labyrinth of Solitude* cost me a lot of appallingly hard work. While I was writing it I felt a huge weight in my stomach. Pregnant women must feel like that. I was secretary to our embassy in Paris at the time and I could only devote my weekends to my book. On Friday nights I shut myself indoors and worked until Sunday. . . .

Did you have financial difficulties?

A lot. Before entering the diplomatic service I went through some very difficult times. I had no fixed profession, and I jumped from one job to another, all of them temporary. At one time I was employed counting old banknotes. The Central Bank of Mexico issues money and also destroys it. They paid us to count packets of unserviceable notes. Each packet contained three thousand notes. The already counted packets were put into sacks. And every month a large furnace on the roof terrace of the bank was lit and millions were burned. A hellish business. Money is an abstraction, a symbol, but that symbol became a dirty piece of paper and had to be burned. So as not to catch any diseases we wore red rubber gloves. I was bad at counting, I always had too many or too few notes. At first this worried me, but afterwards I decided that the world wouldn't be any poorer or richer because of five or six notes too few or too many. In the end I decided to give up counting, and spent the hours composing poems in my head. I used fixed meters and rhymes so as not to forget them. In this way I wrote a number of pretty mournful sonnets.

And in the United States?

I had some bad times in San Francisco. I was living in a little hotel but I came to the end of my money. I told the manager of the hotel what a fix I was in—he was an excellent person, a Mr. Mendelson—and he offered me a bargain: to live in the basement. An old ladies' club met there every afternoon. There was a small cloakroom, practically a closet, and this was my room for months. The only trouble was that I had to wait for the old ladies to go before I could enter my cellar. But those San Fran-

cisco days were marvelous—a sort of physical and intellectual intoxication, a great mouthful of fresh air. That was where I embarked on my path in poetry—if there are paths in poetry.

When did you first come in contact with the Orient?

In 1951 I was in New Delhi for some months and from
there I went to Tokyo.

As ambassador?

No! No! No!

But you did finally become ambassador in India?

Yes, for six years, until 1968.

Were you interested in Indian religion?

No, I was interested in Indian traditional thought, especially the Buddhist current—Nagarjuna and his commentators.

What influence did those years in India have on you?

Mainly a personal one. In India I met my wife, Marie-
Jo. After being born, that's the most important thing that has
happened to me.

Were you married there?

Yes, under a big tree. A very leafy *nim*. That tree was
full of squirrels, and eaglets would sometimes perch on the highest
branches and a lot of ravens as well. Close to our house there
were some Moslem mausoleums. Every morning we used to see
flocks of parakeets coming from the farther end of the city to the
tombs; and at dusk we saw the same flocks of birds flying above
our house. More than once, while we were having breakfast in the
garden, suddenly we saw descending over us, in a straight line,
a dark shadow that clashed against the table and disappeared. It
was a sparrow hawk, a thief of food. At dusk, the garden's sky
was covered by birds flying in lazy circles. Then I discovered that
they weren't birds but bats. No, they aren't disgusting creatures.

. . . On winter afternoons, that garden was flooded by a smooth light—beyond time, I would say, an impartial, reflective light. I remember saying to Marie-Jo: "It will be difficult to forget the metaphysical lessons of this garden." Today I would put it differently. Why metaphysical? "It will be difficult to forget the lessons of this garden."

What lessons were they?

I don't know—friendship, a feeling of brotherhood for plants and animals. We are all part of the same unity. For Westerners, nature is a part of reality to be dominated and used. That belief is the basis, the foundation of our science and our technology. For the Indians nature is still a mother who may be benevolent or terrible. And there are no definite frontiers between the animal and the human world. You know that India not only suffers from an excess of human but also of bovine population. Well, I read a very serious editorial in a Delhi newspaper suggesting—this was before the days of the pill and the loop—that a factory should be set up to produce millions of uterine diaphragms of two types, one for women and the other for cows.

It seems to me you feel a great affection for India.

India taught Marie-Jo and me that a civilization different from our own existed. And we learned to love it, as well as to respect it. Above all we learned to be silent. There's nothing that irritates me more than all those journalists, technicians, and experts who have hardly disembarked at Bombay when they begin giving advice to the Indians. I don't doubt their good intentions as Christians, capitalists, or Marxist-Leninists. Nor do I doubt their ignorance and arrogance. They are no less ethnocentric than the imperialists of the eighteenth and nineteenth centuries.

Did your interest in the Orient date from before your travels, or was it a result of them?

From before. But my discovery of Chinese and Japanese poetry was a result of my first journey to Japan in 1952. My case isn't unique. Think of Claudel and Segalen. Or Paulhan and

Eluard, who practiced *haiku*. And in English, Waley and Pound,
not to mention more recent figures like Donald Keene. Have
you read his translation of Kenko, *Essays on Idleness?* A beautiful
book. And among the new translator-poets, the pair Vincent
McHugh and C. H. Kwoc. Look at what I've just been reading in
Delos. Read it yourself, I can't—my English is an unintelligible
language of my own invention:

> *Dawn*
> > *Leaving Po-ti*
> > > *high up in colored cloud*
> > *back down*
> > > *before dark*
> > > > *to faraway Chiang-ling*
> > *From both cliffs*
> > > *endlessly*
> > > > *gibbons howling*
> > *my light boat*
> > > *passing through a thousand gorges.*

An absolutely visual poem, but it flows, glides and dissolves . . .
In our language, Oriental literature, especially *haiku*, appears in
the work of the Mexican José Juan Tablada. The two initiators
of the avant-garde in the Spanish language were the Chilean
Vicente Huidobro, a fine poet, and the Mexican José Juan
Tablada. Although Tablada was a lesser poet, as to the dimensions
of his poems among other things, some of them are unforgettable and will last. Poetry is concentrated language, and
Tablada knew that better than anyone.

*Rules for writing are a very individual matter. For instance, is
solitude necessary to you?*

One has to write in front of something—noise, the city,
trees. . . Literature is transgression, of language first of all. And
the subversion of language is also revealed in the writer's attitude
toward reality. A writer always writes in front of something, and
often against something. When I say *against* I don't mean with
hatred. *Against* could be love. In any case poetry is a breaking up
of the language.

Does this make actual writing painful?

Sometimes, not always. Sometimes it brings great happiness.

Have you favorite hours for writing?

No, my timetable is irregular. I work in the mornings or in the afternoons. I work a little every day, and I read too. That's one of the things I enjoy most, reading. Reading and talking. The thing I like least is writing.

Before you answer some of my questions—a great many of them, in fact—you make a few brief notes. Why is that?

Lack of confidence in the spoken word. I still belong to the generation of the book, not of the tape recorder. Writing and talking are different and in a way opposite activities. That's a curious thing. In France, today, writers often use the word *"écriture."* Like Derrida, they think that writing came before speech. I don't believe that. But without going into this problem, it's curious that the concept of *"écriture"* should predominate in France, while in the United States and in England the notion of "speech" predominates. They are two different ideas of literature. In France writing comes first, and therefore reading: eyes and silence. In the English-speaking countries poetry is the spoken word: the voice and hearing.

Which do you prefer: writing or speech?

Poetry originated as spoken words. It has continued as such and always will. Fundamentally, poetry is rhythm. To think of poetry solely as writing is an error. But one must not forget another tradition: visual poetry. I distinguish between written and visual poetry. Or rather, I don't think there is such a thing as written poetry. When we read a poem with our eyes, if we read properly, we say it mentally. Therefore there is oral and visual poetry.

Do both traditions exist in our poetry?

Hispanic poetry—that's to say Hispano-American and Castilian, but also Portuguese, Galician, and Catalan—is one of the richest in the world. Basically it's a spoken poetry—remember our marvelous medieval poetry and ballads—but there are also examples of visual poetry in the baroque period which really anticipate calligrams. Well, the great models of visual poetry are not to be found in the West but in the East: in Arab and Persian poetry, Sanskrit, and above all, Chinese. Thanks to ideograms, a page can at the same time have visual, auditory, and semantic value. There is a triple interplay between the form of the ideograms, the sound of the words, and the sense. In Western poetry the interplay has been basically between sound and sense. There is, however, a tradition of visual poetry beginning in Greece and continuing to Mallarmé and Apollinaire. In Latin America, Huidobro anticipated Apollinaire's experiments, and Tablada was producing ideographic poems in 1921. However, it was the Brazilian poets who formulated the theory of concrete poetry in the most radical and intelligent way. Haroldo and Augusto de Campos, as well as Decio Pignatari, are penetrating and lucid theoreticians of the poetic avant-garde, as well as good poets.

Weren't you the first Hispano-American poet to write (or draw?) concrete poetry?

I couldn't tell you, nor does priority interest me . . . I followed the Brazilian's example and made some experiments in concrete poetry. Do you know *Topoemas? Topos + poemas.* I tried to find plastic, semantic, and oral relations among the words. For example, this *Topoema* is a tribute to the Indian philosopher Nagarjuna: negation leads to the abolition of the illusion of the ego: the word NIEGO (I deny) is broken into two: NI EGO.

And your poems in the form of visual disks?

They were a little gimmick of mine. In itself it's not a new process—it's very well known in advertising—but it's not been used in poetry before. The object consists in two superimposed cardboard disks; as the upper disk is rotated, the "windows" in it reveal the text of a short poem written on the lower disk. My purpose was twofold: firstly, to give the text mobility by means of visual rhythm; secondly, to ensure slower reading. It's the fashion today to read quickly, and there are even institutions given over to teaching this. An abomination . . . I think one should learn to read slowly, especially poetry.

Any other formal experiments?

There isn't a form and a content. Or rather: every form emits its meaning, its meanings. The typography of *Topoemas* and the slowly moving texts of the *Discos visuales* (Visual Disks) led to another idea: to make a film from my poem "Blanco." It's an extensive composition, divided into several parts which can be combined in different ways, producing different forms and meanings. "Blanco" is a love poem and at the same time a poem about language—the woman's body is seen and felt as a language, the language is seen as a landscape and the landscape is read like a vanishing text. Analogy between touching a body, walking through a landscape, and reading a page. In the three acts there is the phenomenon of the appearance of the object—feminine body, physical world, letters—which vanish at the very moment when we are united with them. That's why the poem is called "Blanco," in the triple sense of the word: the color white, synthesis of all colors and their nullification; white meaning the center of a target; and white in the sense of blank. Well, the only characters in my film would be the letters and sounds. A "passion" of phonemes and signs. I've had the script ready for three years but in India I hadn't the technical means nor the cash to make the film. Since then I've led a wandering life. Perhaps when I return to Mexico . . .

When you write a poem, do your associations flow freely, or are they the result of elaboration?

I don't usually have a clear idea of what I'm going to do. Many times I feel empty, without ideas—and then suddenly the first sentence appears. Valéry used to say that the first line is a gift. It's true: we write the first line from dictation. Who presents us with that line? I don't know. In the past people believed it was the gods, the muse, God—some power outside ourselves. In the nineteenth century it was thought to be a gift from the poet's genius. But what does *genius* mean? Later on it was the unconscious, just another word. The fact is that a line appears and that line controls the whole poem. The poem is a development of that line: sometimes it is written against it; at others in support of it; sometimes, when the poem is finished that first line disappears. In fact, I write that line and it is also written by someone other than myself.

And the elaboration?

Then a dialogue develops between the person who wrote the first line and the other, who goes on with the writing. There's a splitting-up, a plurality of poets. Of course that doesn't happen only to writers: we are all several people at the same time. And we all have a tendency to destroy that plurality in favor of some supposed unity. In the case of literature, when one of the voices suppresses the others, we say that the writer has found what is called a style of his own. We can also say that the writer has met death as a writer, petrifaction. A writer should live by dialogue, not only with others—his public, his style, fame, eternity, or what have you?—but also with himself. Great writers—yes, the word "great" is repulsive—living writers, even if they have written no more than five lines, those are the ones who preserve their plurality, the dialogue between their egos. Suppression is self-mutilation. The suppressed ego, the corporal ego, the indecent ego, the cynical ego should all speak through the writer's voice. The page comes alive when the suppressed voices appear on it. I've always thought of literature as a language, but by language I mean the plurality of visions of the world. That is: I am talking about the suppressed voices. There's nothing I love more than verbal perfection, but only if that language suddenly opens, and as it does so we see and hear another reality in the abysmal— literally abysmal—breach. A reality that we didn't know and a voice we had hoped never to hear: the voice of death, the voice of the flesh. Great poetry, great literature, doesn't reveal man as an affirmation, as a unity, as something solid, but as a cleft, a fissure. Man fighting with himself. This seems to me the true modern vision of man.

Does this plurality also emerge when you write essays?

There's always someone else collaborating with me. And he generally collaborates by contradicting me. The danger is that the voice refuting what we say may be so strong as to silence us. But it's worthwhile running the risk: it's better for the contradicter to silence us than for us to silence the contradicter. When we silence him our writing becomes pedagogic, moral, and boring. It turns into a declamation, a lesson. If I opposed *"engagé"* art, "social art," and all the rest of what was being written for many years in Latin America, it was because it seemed to me immoral that a writer should assume that reason, justice, and history were on his side. It's horrible for a writer to claim to be right, not only in front of the world, but in front of his other self. . . .

Do you correct your writing a great deal?

Yes, because the other keeps on talking. The other is a pretty perverse and unbearable being who says *no* to everything I say. The result is this continual stammering, this continual indecision, this continual change in all I say.

Doesn't this contradiction destroy spontaneity?

Well, spontaneity is nourished by the dialogue. If there's no "other," there's no spontaneity. The monologue is the enemy of spontaneity.

Do you compose your poems on a typewriter?

No. And that's a pity: the machine provides greater plastic possibilities than writing does. Cummings used to write his poems directly onto the typewriter. Handwriting is too subjective, it's infected with too much that is personal, sentimental.

Do you like to discuss what you're writing at the moment?

I used to formerly, but not now. I used to think what I was writing was important. . . .

Let's ignore that remark . . . have you written much lately?

This year I've written a certain number of poems, some articles, and a little book, *Le singe grammairien* (The Monkey Grammarian). The publisher Skira has started a collection called *Les sentiers de la création* (The Paths of Creation). They are books about poetic and pictorial creation; *Le singe grammairien* will appear in that series. First in French, and afterwards probably in Spanish. . . . As I've written very often about poetic creation, it seemed difficult to return to the subject. It occurred to me to take the phrase "the path of creation" literally. That is: a path had to be invented, created. And what path could it be? Well, the path of the writing. The path is the text itself, a path invented by the writer as he writes, and which dissolves as we read it. The path we make as we write and which dissolves as we read: that could be the paradox of creation, a paradox similar to those of love and contemplation. In a way it's another version of "Blanco." A text that melts ceaselessly, a path which vanishes.

Has this negation something to do with Buddhism?

Yes, certainly, but also with modern philosophy. And specially with the philosopher Wittgenstein, who taught here in Cambridge. It also has something to do with what I have thought and lived, with my personal experience. It has something to do with my idea of love and my idea of language. It's a negation, but it's a negation that by negating itself affirms something. So it's creation. I've always believed that creation is criticism. There's a moment when language turns on itself, denies itself, and thus affirms itself.

What does the title Le singe grammairien *mean?*

It's an allusion to the monkey god, Hanuman. He's a very popular god, one of the heroes of the *Ramayana*, the epic poem describing the exploits of Rama and his love for Sita.

Rama's messenger is Hanuman. An Indian version of the Holy Ghost: he's the wind, the messenger of the gods. He's therefore a poet, and—as master of the language—a grammarian. It's also said that Hanuman wrote a play on the same subject as the *Ramayana*—or rather that he engraved it on rocks and stones. Therefore nature is a form of writing and the author is merely the first reader to decipher the text of the landscape.

How are your views of the creator as a translator and your interest in Buddhism connected with modern poetry?

Do you know what *renga* is?

No.

It's a Japanese poetic form. Do you know what *tanka* is?

No.

Tanka is a poem of five lines which falls easily into two verses, one of three lines and one of two. A dual structure. From the beginning of Japanese poetry a *tanka* could always be divided into two parts. One poet used to write the first part and another the conclusion. Soon a series of *tankas* by different poets began to appear. This new form was called *renga*. Its form is like a road, a flowing river, a melody. *Renga* is a collective poetic form and it's curious that some of the best poems of the Japanese tradition are *rengas*. What interests me is that this poetic form denies the idea of a single author. I find two apparently contradictory elements in the *renga*: it's collective writing and yet it has remarkable unity as a composition.

Negation of the author?

Rather of *our* idea of the author. The myth of the unique author. Because the language—an "author" that includes all authors—passes through the mind and hand of that supposedly unique author. . . . However, don't imagine that I deny the author's existence—someone has got to write the text—I'm only saying that the fundamental literary reality is the work and not that "someone." In 1968 I was in Paris on my way home from

India, and one morning it occurred to me that we ought to try the experiment in the West. I talked about this with a French friend, the poet Jacques Roubaud, and suggested that we write a *renga* in four languages.

Why in four languages?

Every language possesses a different poetic tradition. All the same, without denying the special character of the poetry of each nation, it's also true that there exists a poetic tradition common to the whole of the West. Our *renga* was intended, among other things, to show the common tradition of the West, especially at the present time. Another problem: what poetic form should we choose? We decided that the Western equivalent of the *tanka* is the sonnet. It's a traditional form shared by the whole European tradition. Naturally the sonnet of our *renga* had no rhyme—it's very difficult to preserve rhyme in a poem in several languages—nor yet fixed meter. Once we had decided the form of our *renga*, we invited two other poets we admired to join us, who in a sense represent the two poles in European poetry at this moment: the Italian Eduardo Sanguineti and the Englishman Charles Tomlinson.

How did you settle the economic aspect?

Our friend Claude Roy spoke to Claude Gallimard, who took a very generous interest in our idea and made the journeys of Sanguineti and Tomlinson possible. One day in April 1969 we four met in Paris. We were living in the Hotel Saint Simon, and Marie-Jo discovered a little room in the basement of the hotel, a sort of sumptuous underground crypt. There we spent five days writing our poem. The book was called *Renga* and is dedicated to André Breton.

Why to André Breton?

Surrealism banned the idea of the author. Breton emphasized the intervention of the unconscious in poetic creation, and declared that language made use of the poet, and not the reverse. Besides, our experiment coincides with some ideas about translation. Baudelaire said that the poet is a translator because he deciphers nature, the signs of the cosmos. The poet is the reader of the book of the universe. (The "book of the universe" is an old metaphor inherited by the romantics from the Renaissance!) But in the same way the poet deciphers universal poetic tradition and translates it into his own. In that sense, our *Renga* is a tribute to Ezra Pound and Eliot, who were the first poets of the modern era to incorporate quotations in other languages in their poems. We had incorporated texts in four languages in one poem, so as to demonstrate the unity of our poetic tradition and also the possibility of infinite translation in the form of poetic texts.

Your Renga is a crossroads.

A point of intersection between surrealism, which said that "another voice" spoke through the poet's mouth (a voice that was not the poet's) and the tendency known as *"literature citationelle"* initiated in the modern period by Pound and Eliot. At the same time it is governed by another idea: literary creation presents undoubted affinities with a combinative mechanism ruled at the same time by chance and calculus. A literary text is a combination of signs. Well, now, instead of combining signs, we wanted to combine producers of signs: poets.

Do you think of repeating the experiment?

I talked about *Renga* to a North American friend, the poet Robert Duncan. He thinks a *renga* of the American continent should be written with a Brazilian, a Hispano-American, and a North American poet, and a poet writing in French, either from Haiti or Canada.

What were the first books you read?

My grandfather had collected a fine library and I had completely free access to it in childhood. The first pornographic works I read were some of the classics. I remember being extraordinarily disturbed by *The Golden Ass*. There were also a lot of French literature and the poets and novelists of the end of the last century in our language. The Latin American "modernists" had

a prominent place on the bookshelves. Those years of my childhood and adolescence saw a great explosion of avant-garde poetry
and painting. It was also the time when our great baroque poets
were discovered, especially Góngora. I read a lot of Góngora, and
I go on reading him all the time. Also Quevedo. At school they
made us hate our own classics, but afterwards I went back to
medieval or traditional poetry. I also read and keep reading the
Archpriest of Hita. But that was much later.

Did you also read the modern poets?

I discovered Hispano-American and Spanish poetry at
about that time. I oscillated successively and passionately between
Jiménez and Lorca, Guillén and Alberti, Neruda and Borges,
Pellicer and Villaurrutia. The magazine *Contemporáneos* gave
me an unforgettable jolt: I read in it, and in the same issue, the
first Spanish translations of *The Waste Land* and St. John Perse's
Anabasis. A little later, another jolt: André Breton's *L'amour fou*.
Thanks to Villaurrutia I read Blake. Those were the years too
when I first read Hölderlin and the German romantics.

Only poetry?

No, I read a lot of the publications of the *Revista de
Occidente*, edited by Ortega y Gasset, and it was through it that
my generation became familiar with modern German philosophy,
the phenomenology of Husserl and his followers. We were deeply
impressed by Heidegger's *What Is Philosophy*, in a Spanish translation by Zuburí published in José Bergamín's review, *Cruz y
raya*.

Did you feel very cut off in Mexico?

As you know, unlike Argentina which is an open country,
Mexico is concentrated and closed to outer influences. But the
years before the Second World War were cosmopolitan, even in
Mexico. We were fairly well informed as to what was happening,
because there were some excellent magazines in Spanish at that
time: the *Revista de Occidente* and *Cruz y raya* in Madrid, *Sur*
in Buenos Aires, and *Contemporáneos* in Mexico. There's nothing

of the sort today. And we were interested in politics and read a lot of revolutionary books, particularly those tending toward Marxism. Strange as it may appear I read Nietzsche with equal enthusiasm. For months and months I drank—that's the only word for it—the maxims of *The Gay Science*. A unique form of spiritual intoxication. But we were none of us acquainted with modern English and North American philosophy. Russell we only knew through a collection of his essays, *Marriage and Morals*. Nothing of Wittgenstein . . . I was a great reader of novels. Whereas now I prefer books about anthropology, history, or travel.

In one of our conversations without the tape recorder you mentioned that one of your favorite books was the dictionary.

I read it every day. It's my adviser, my elder brother. It's magic, a fountain of surprises: you look for a word and always find another. The truth about the world ought to be found in the dictionary, since its pages contain all the nouns in the world. But it's not: the dictionary presents us with a list of words, and it's for men, not only writers, to link them together so that one of those precarious associations formulates the truth about the world, a relative truth that dissolves as it is read. My favorite book is Corominas's *Diccionario etimológico de la lengua española* (Etymological Dictionary of the Spanish Language). It is the work of a Catalan. A salutory lesson for Castilians, a further lesson given by great Catalonia to proud Castile. Because in the old dispute between Castile and the other provinces of Spain, I'm not on the side of the centralists but of the rest, the Basques, Galicians, and Catalans. In the introduction to his dictionary Corominas says that no other Western language contains so many phantom words as Castilian. I tremble to think that there are words that have become disembodied, floating words, whose meaning we no longer know.

What other books do you read?

I'm always reading poetry. Like Christians saying their prayers every night, I try always, every day, to read a poem or poetical text. During my last years in India I read Mallarmé passionately and patiently. That led me to translate one of his sonnets, the "Sonnet in Ix," and write a commentary on it. Last year, when I was in Pittsburgh, I read Dante. It was a great experience. I discovered that Dante was the great poet of the West. I hadn't known that . . . I also read Spanish and Latin American poetry. In the last few months I've been rereading the medieval poets. They are a mine of rhythms, a continuous spring of verbal forms. Originally, Spanish poetry was rhythmical, accentual: the scansion of syllables was not as important as tonic accents. Afterwards, at first through Italian influence and later, in the eighteenth century, through that of France, syllabic versification and metrical regularity prevailed. Thus, modern free verse is a return to irregular, rhythmic versification: to the origins of the language.

And what other poets have you read at Cambridge besides the medieval Spaniards?

While I've been here, I've read Wordsworth, another revelation. I didn't know him at all well. Luis Cernuda used to talk to me a lot about Wordsworth, but I've only lately read him properly. He was an undergraduate at St. John's, and in *The Prelude* he describes how he was sometimes unable to sleep because his room was close to Trinity College Chapel: the striking of the clock woke him, and just as he was falling asleep it struck the hour again! The other morning I went with Marie-Jo to Trinity College and we listened to the clock striking eleven twice, as it did in Wordsworth's day. Sometimes reading foreign poets leads to my translating them. This summer I reread William Carlos Williams and translated ten of his poems.

You've made several translations of poetry.

Four of Nerval's *Chimères*, poems by Apollinaire and Cummings, Marvell and Donne, contemporary Swedish poets, Tomlinson . . . I'm working on a book to be called *Versiones y diversiones* (Versions and Diversions). Among the poems I have written and been pleased with are some translations from Fernando Pessõa. Translation is to me a special form of creation. And no distinction should be drawn between original creation and poetic translation. All the poems we write are translations of other poems.

Yet many people think poetry is untranslatable.

Every translation is a metaphor of the poem translated. In this sense the phrase "poetry is untranslatable" is the exact equivalent of the phrase "all poetry is translatable": the only possible translation is poetic transmutation or metaphor. But I would also say that in writing an original poem we are translating the world, transmuting it. Everything we do is translation, and all translations are in a way creations. Only one must be modest and not talk about creation. I'm rather shocked by Huidobro's often-repeated phrase: "the poet is a little god." No, the poet is not a creator, he's not a god: he's the universal translator. But if he were a god, he wouldn't be little.

What has interested you most in Oriental literature?

There isn't one Oriental literature, but many. I told you about my interest in the poetry and thought of China and Japan. In fact I spent my first months at Cambridge correcting my translation of the *Oku-no-Hosomichi* of Basho. I translated that little book in Mexico about fifteen years ago with my friend E. Hayashiya. It was the first translation of this Japanese classic into a Western language. It didn't get a single review, and the edition of a thousand copies took ten years to sell. Now the Spanish poet Carlos Barral has suggested publishing a new edition in Barcelona. I've written a fresh foreword. I only hope it'll have better luck this time. . . .

Can one get to know a literature through translations?

It depends on the translations. And besides, what is "to know"? All literatures are metaphors or metonymies for non-verbal realities which they attempt to reflect. There are no original texts: all are translations, metaphors of another text. Language itself is a translation: each word and each phrase explains (translates) what other words and phrases mean. Speech is continual translation within the same language. . . . Having said which, I will add that there are excellent translations of Chinese and Japanese literature. I'm thinking especially of translations into English: Pound, Waley, Donald Keene . . . On the other hand the literatures of India, whether in Sanskrit, Pali, or modern languages, have not been very fortunate in the West. I'm talking about literary texts, not philosophical or religious ones. The only good translation I can think of is Ingalls's *Sanskrit Court Poems*. What a pity that no poet has translated Sanskrit poetry (Kavya) into Spanish. In the versions of Chinese poetry by Ezra Pound, verbal economy is a fundamental element; but in order to translate Sanskrit poetry what we need is not an Ezra Pound but a modern Góngora. I should have liked to translate a lesser poet, Dharmakirti. He's less famous as a poet than as a Buddhist logician. . . .

Do you feel close to Buddhism?

By no means. But I believe that the philosophical viewpoint of Buddhism is profoundly modern. Buddhism is above all a critical form of thought, and modern thought is critical. There is no more complete and radical criticism of existence: it affirms that the world has neither meaning nor substance. But criticism of the world and existence is, in its turn, converted into criticism of criticism, negation of negation. At that moment negation becomes creative and the world and existence reappear. Criticism of criticism reveals the fact that the words existence/nonexistence, real/unreal are relative, and that the truth (another ambiguous word), *what is* and *what is not*, lies beyond opposition. At the same time this state of suspension of judgment is inexpressible. The Buddhist dialectic puts us in a situation similar to Wittgenstein's when he says that his philosophical speculations are like a ladder, up whose rungs the reader climbs: when he has reached the last rung the reader must throw away the ladder. . . .

Then what interests you in Buddhism is its philosophy?

And what interests me in philosophy is that all philosophies end in a paradox or a tautology. Buddhism interests me because it's a paradox . . . I feel the same about Nietzsche, although in his case affirmation—that great *Yes* of vital energy which excludes nothing, not even death—plays the same part as negation does in Buddhism. My other passion was for Heidegger, a philosopher who is also connected with Buddhism by his attempt to think about nothing. Heidegger was introduced into our language by the Spanish philosopher José Gaos, a man to whom Mexicans owe much . . . and eight years ago in India, just when I was reading certain Buddhist texts, I began to read Wittgenstein. . . .

Why are you so interested in philosophy?

Perhaps because I would like to find such wisdom as the Stoics found in antiquity. Poetry and thought don't live in separate houses. In some poets I find what I do in Wittgenstein, something that can't be reduced to words and that needs to be expressed either by paradox or poetic metaphor.

Do you always read such serious books?

I read history and travel books too. Herodotus, for instance.

Don't you read detective stories?

It amuses me more to find out about the customs of the Egyptians or what happened to the Great King than about the stratagems of the criminal and the astuteness of the detective. I enjoy reading travel books, accounts of explorations, primitive texts. Alexis Leger told me that one of the books that had influenced him most was the *Memoirs* of Babur, conqueror of India. It's a book I like very much myself. Another passion: vanished civilizations. I'm not a Mexican for nothing. From history I went on to archaeology, and from archaeology to anthropology.

You're very much interested in Lévi-Strauss, aren't you?

Yes, I wrote a little book about him. Lévi-Strauss introduced me to linguistics, chiefly to Jakobson, who brought me back to poetry. Because linguistics is another approach to poetry. In *El arco y la lira* (The Bow and the Lyre) I said that the question "What is poetry?" is immediately transformed into the question "What is a poem?" Linguistics can't tell us what a poem is, but it does tell us, in an admirable way, how a poem is, how poems are made. You see how reading is linked to life. I can't myself distinguish between reading, writing, and living. Life is a fabric, almost a text. Or rather, a text is a fabric made of experiences and visions as well as words.

In El arco y la lira you say "the modern poet has no place in society because he is in fact 'no-one' . . . Poetry doesn't exist for the bourgeoisie and proletariat of today." Were you thinking of Latin American poets, or of all poets?

I was thinking of the modern world, not only of Latin America. But it's not enough to say that in our time poetry is marginal. Everything has become marginal and alienation is at present universal. Very well, if alienation is universal, if everyone feels alienated, then poetry resumes its central position as the voice of alienation. I'll explain. . . . The modern world adores numbers and is becoming used to measuring the importance of a work by the number of its readers. That's idiotic. In his day, when he was a truly revolutionary author, Marx was very little read. Nowadays everyone repeats like a parrot that God is dead, but when Nietzsche said it very few listened. On the whole, minority writers are the really important ones. The inventors are left alone, and it's the imitators, those who propagate their poetical inventions, who become best-sellers. Thus when I say that poetry is a central voice in our time because it is the voice of alienation itself, I don't mean that poets are popular. Because they are central, it doesn't follow that everyone listens to them; it means that they are in the heart and center of the world. In that sense some modern poets have been the voice in that deserted square that is the center of contemporary man. In that empty place poetry speaks with an empty voice. The best contemporary poetry is that which has given us the terrible sensation of alienation, of being on the margin—a universal situation common to all modern men.

Another of your interests—the plastic arts.

Yes, and once more I'm not a Mexican for nothing. The air in the Mexican plateau—now full of smog—once used to be extraordinarily transparent, so that objects tended to turn themselves immediately into sculptures or drawings. A landscape whose light was geometry. Perhaps Mexicans are predisposed to be pictorial and architectonic. Nevertheless, Mexican mural painting has provoked my criticism rather than my praise.

It was an expression of the social ideas of the period.

      As you know, the Mexican Revolution revealed their own country to Mexicans. During the nineteenth century the Mexican oligarchy had denied Mexican reality, our characteristics as a mestizo race, our folklore, our poverty, in fact they had invented a nonexistent European country. In Mexico we have the Indian world and the Spanish world—which in its turn is a combination of Moorish and Jewish. The Mexican Revolution was an explosion of that underground Mexico, an explosion which opened artists' eyes. Think of an artist like Diego Rivera, who had spent part of his youth in Europe and taken part in modern movements in painting, especially cubism. . . .

That stage of Rivera's development isn't well known.

      Here in England, in the Tate Gallery, in the room devoted to the cubist painters, there's an excellent painting by Diego Rivera. In Mexico hardly any paintings of Rivera's cubist period have survived, and it's a pity because it was one of his best moments. . . . Diego Rivera, Orozco, and other painters were invited by José Vasconcelos, founder of the new education in Mexico, to paint the walls of public buildings. At first their painting took the form of a powerful explosion of forms and colors; those walls combined the plastic experiments of the times with the discovery of the art and people of Mexico. But also, from the outset a facile expressionism and superficial rhetoric were visible. Declamatory painting, gesticulatory painting, serving the cause of official and bureaucratic nationalism or "social realism," the two great aesthetic frauds of the twentieth century. There was a group of painters who rebelled against this official art. Rufino Tamayo was one of them.

There's said to be a certain affinity between you and Tamayo.

Our paths crossed although only for a short space of time.
It's strange that at the moment when Rufino Tamayo was planning to reveal, in very personal language, the plastic relations between modern painting and Mexico's pre-Hispanic art—it's a
strange fact that I should have been interested in similar ideas at
that moment. That was the stage of poems such as "Himno entre
ruinas" (Hymn Among Ruins) and others which were to be collected later in *La estacion violenta* (The Violent Season). Also of
Aguila o sol? (Eagle or Sun?), a little book in which the pre-Columbian world appears as part of my own psychological subsoil. A
discovery that coincided with my encounter with surrealist poetry
and Henri Michaux. Although that book shared the same fate as
Basho's (it didn't get a single review), it seems to me it has
exercised a certain influence on some Latin American prose
writers as well as poets.

*You wrote an important essay about the work of Marcel
Duchamp. Would you care to say something about it?*

I don't know what more I can say. What interested me in
Duchamp's work was again the creative function of negation. In
Duchamp's work painting becomes a criticism of painting. He
did not postulate a philosophy of painting, nor make philosophical paintings: his painting contains a criticism of itself, it destroys
and recreates itself. Duchamp belongs to the same stock as Mallarmé: the creative method is the critical method. The critical
element—meta-irony as Duchamp called it—is allied with the
erotic element in all his work and particularly in his painting "The
Bride Stripped Naked by Her Bachelors, Even . . ." ("The
Great Glass"), and in the sculpture made during his last years.

No one knew about that work until after his death.

We all believed that Duchamp had stopped painting, but
in the last ten years of his life he was at work on this sculpture.
It represents a naked girl with her legs apart lying on a bed of
branches, and holding an electric torch. Behind her is a silent
cascade and the whole is illumined by an almost abstract light.

The same elements are present as in "The Great Glass": water, electricity, sexuality, "voyeurism." The girl of the cascade can only be seen through the holes in a wooden door which bars the way into the room in which the sculpture stands. Thus Duchamp forces us to participate in the work. Or rather, the work consists in the *act of seeing*. In "The Great Glass" the spectator formed part of the painting, and in this new work Duchamp offers us a variant of the same idea: the act of seeing in some way *creates* the work. Another similarity: in both cases one is trying to see *through something*. . . . In "The Great Glass" the external world is seen through the painting; in the second work the sculpture is seen through the holes in the shut door (that is, in the external world). Third similarity: in the two works the woman is seen as a motor, a source of energy—the cascade and the electric torch. . . .

Do you think this new work by Duchamp in any way modifies what you have written about him?

No. . . . It seems to me to confirm everything he did before. It's the logical conclusion of his life and his work. Or rather: the *meta-ironic* conclusion. It's all very disturbing. I think Duchamp is telling us that a work of art isn't an end but a means. What is interesting is not the work itself but what it allows us to see even if it's only emptiness. People want to possess things: pictures, sculptures, houses, cars. But a work of art isn't a thing. It's not something to be treasured in a bank, a house, or a museum. A work of art is a mechanism which allows anyone able to manipulate it sensitively, the reader or the contemplator, to discover . . . something. At that moment the work of art disappears and what is left is this "something."

Some painters deny the past.

The avant-garde always deny the past and back the future with equal frenzy. But now we are witnessing the negation of the future: the "happening" which only occurs once; conceptual art, which is an idea, not an object; art made of ephemeral substances. All these are variations on the same idea. Well, I would say that we aren't facing new artistic forms but a criticism of art —a criticism, moreover, that had already been made by Duchamp,

Picabia, and the Dadaists. To sum up, these manifestations are
not so much new art as signs indicating a change in contemporary
sensibility. At bottom what we all want is not artistic art, museum
art, but to return to two art forms: to the fiesta and to art as
contemplation, whether religious, intellectual, or sensual. The
fiesta is collective art, and its fullest development is communion;
contemplation is solitary art. Neither of the two eliminates past or
future, but they are made to coincide in the present. Both are
repetition, that's to say, the opposite of the *happening* and other
current manifestations. Repetition is ritual: a returning date.

You've also written a poem about Cage.

I'm fascinated by John Cage. His writings provide another example of a text which destroys the meanings it gives off, a
text that dissolves so that another meaning can appear. . . .

Do you like reading your earliest poems?

Whenever I reread my work I feel embarrassed. And not
only embarrassed, sometimes I feel nausea. But now and again I say
to myself, well, that wasn't too bad.

Which of them "weren't too bad"?

The most recent. It's natural, isn't it? For instance *Conjunctions and Disjunctions*, my essay on the relation between
the *body* and the *non-body*. In poetry, of course, *Ladera este*. It
seems to me my best book. . . . And the one I wrote this summer, *Le singe grammairien*. Everything I'd ever done before in
prose and poetry converges in this little book. It all converges
. . . and then vanishes. There's also that same convergence between thought and poetry in another book of mine: *Eagle or Sun?*
This was an exploration of the mythical subsoil, so to speak, of
Mexico, and at the same time a self-exploration. An attempt to
create a world of images in which modern and ancient sensibility were fused, the images of the buried Mexico and those of the
modern world. A North American friend pointed out that there
was an analogy between my book and one by William Carlos Wil-

liams, published years earlier: *Kora in Hell.* The similarity isn't textual but as to aims. In fact, both books are poems in prose, inspired by French poetry. However, *Kora in Hell* is a deeply American book and could only have been written by a North American. In the same way I think *Eagle or Sun?* could only have been written in Mexico. . . . Another similarity: William Carlos Williams also wrote a very beautiful book called *In the American Grain,* a collection of essays on American themes. Well, *The Labyrinth of Solitude* fulfills a corresponding purpose. I wrote *The Labyrinth* first as a confession or to relieve my feelings, and immediately afterwards I wrote *Eagle or Sun?*

The Labyrinth of Solitude, that started in the United States; is it a search for Mexico's roots?

Not exactly. North Americans are concerned with the problem of their origins, because what previously existed in America, the native world, was completely destroyed. The United States is built on the void left by destroying Indian cultures. The attitude of North Americans to the Indian world is part of their attitude to nature; they don't see it as a reality to be fused with, but to be dominated. The destruction of the native world foreshadowed their assault on nature. North American civilization has set out to dominate, tame, and make use of nature exactly as a race or a people are conquered. In a way they have treated the natural world as an enemy.

To what do you attribute this attitude?

It's a Protestant concept of the world: the condemnation of the body is also applied to nature. If the body is natural, nature is corporal and both are fallen states, forms of original sin. The world is redeemed through work, and the body through repentance. Nature is neither a subject for contemplation nor an erotic symbol, it is neither the great mother nor the great tomb: it is a reality which man must transform and redeem through work. Thus North Americans feel strangers in their own land on two counts: because they are immigrants and because they are Protestants. A twofold rupture with the natural world. North Americans have made their country their own through work, not

by consecration. Hence their painful feelings about their own
countryside, and their search for roots—it is the need they feel
to invent a past.

Isn't that a universal phenomenon?

          No, the United States has no past in a very special
sense . . . exactly in the same sense that the proletariat was an
uprooted class to Marx. Hence the anxiety which made Eliot return to England to recover the past and thus forget the future,
which was the United States. This is why Pound disinterred
Chinese and Greek archetypes from the graveyard of universal
history. Because the United States is a country whose sole tradition is the future: it was founded by, for, and toward the
future. The opposite has happened to us Mexicans: our roots are
choking us. We have too many roots, we have too many pasts. The
history of Mexico can be seen like those pre-Columbian pyramids
on which new races built other pyramids, and afterwards other
races built even more. Mexico is a superimposition of epochs, all
of them alive. It's a country that has still not succeeded in
combining its pasts into *one real past. The Labyrinth* was an attempt to exorcise the phantoms of our pasts and to see clearly
among that profusion of roots.

*You mean that you are anxious to discover what it is to be a
Mexican, just as an American is anxious to discover what it is to
be American?*

          The whole continent is obsessed by the questions: what
is it to be American? What is it to be Mexican? But I don't conceive of history as essence, I conceive of it as transition. What
is "Mexican" is an arrangement of historic features in perpetual
motion, forming and dissolving. What is "Mexican" is a sort of
mask. A mask in motion.

Then the complexity of Mexico . . .

          Her complexity comes from that plurality of pasts, that
profusion of roots I mentioned before. Think of the extraordinary
complexity of the ancient Mexican civilizations—Olmec, Mayan,

Teotihuacan, Zapotec, Mixtec, Aztec—and of the complexity of
the Spanish world—Iberians, Phoenicians, Romans, Visigoths,
Arabs, Jews. . . . Another paradox: the Spain that conquered us
was a Christian country, but the imprint she left is profoundly
Moslem. I saw this very clearly in India.

Why in India?

The Moslem conquest of India was colored by religion,
was inseparable from religion: conquest was a synonym for
conversion. The same thing happened in America. The imperialist
expansion of other European nations was essentially profane. They
were imperialisms in the modern sense of the word, by definition
excluding all religious coloring. After three centuries of English
domination there are only a few million Christians in India. . . .
And the Indian Christians were never looked upon by the English
as brothers in the faith but as "*natives*." A radically opposed attitude to that of the Moslems and Spaniards. The conquest of
America by Spaniards was a religious enterprise, like the conquest
of India by Moslems—although in both cases greed and plunder
were also notable characteristics. But what shocked other Europeans was not the Spaniards' greed for gold but their theological
ferocity. That was the origin of the "black legend."

*Is what you've been saying applicable to Mexico and Peru alone,
or to the whole of Latin America?*

To the whole of Latin America, although of course there
are differences. In Mexico and Peru the Spaniards found very
complex civilizations. In other regions, such as the West Indies,
the Indian population was exterminated by the Spaniards. Or, to
be more exact, by the diseases brought to them by the Spaniards
and the terrible exploitation they were subjected to. In some Latin
American countries, destruction was wreaked by those who
came after the Spaniards. Argentina and Uruguay are both guilty
of the crime of the North Americans. The lack of sensitivity of
many Argentines to this fact is incredible. It doesn't affect them,
nor do they believe it affects the fate of Argentina.

Do you think that has affected the genuineness of Argentines?

The Argentines have won their own originality and are as genuine as the Mexicans. But the extermination of the Indians in Argentina is very far from being a blessing. It's time for Argentines to take a fresh view of men like Sarmiento and Alberti. The extermination of the Indians in Argentina was the result of an absurd imitation of North American policies. Invoking the slogan: "To govern is to colonize," the Indians were exterminated. Thus Argentina lost something very valuable: a sensibility, a special way of viewing the world. She lost the possibility of seeing the world and herself through other eyes. . . . Although perhaps the destruction was not complete. A French anthropologist, Alfred Metraux, commenting on the attitude of some Argentine intellectuals said to me: "Don't believe that lie about Argentina being a country populated by European colonists alone, Octavio. A great deal of miscegenation went on there. But the Argentines don't know, or what's worse, don't want to know about it. The whole northern part of the country is mestizo." Another of Argentina's tragedies was Peronism. A failed revolution, and one which failed in the worst possible way: Perón was a clown, and Evita a third-rate actress. It's sad, because what lay behind Peronism was very important—an authentic social revolt.

The sequel to The Labyrinth of Solitude, The Other Mexico: Critique of the Pyramid, *might be said to explain the reasons why you gave up being ambassador in India. Could you say something about those events?*

I've little to add to *The Other Mexico*. The events of 1968 revealed something which we, some Mexican writers and intellectuals, had been denouncing for a long time. Under the regimes that followed the Mexican Revolution, the country has made great progress, unique in Latin America. At the same time, in the last fifteen years the contradictions and inequalities have become acute. The first great contradiction: Mexico is two countries, one developed and the other desperately poor and underdeveloped. The remarkable economic progress in the first Mexico, the developed one, has not been translated into social progress (I mean that the differences between rich and poor are immense)

and even less into political progress. The events of 1968 showed
that the contradictions in developed Mexico had sharpened, and
violence resulted. To understand the meaning of the crisis, and the
significance of those contradictions, one must reflect that the
progress achieved in the last thirty years has created new social
structures—a new working class, an important middle class, a new
intelligentsia—without modifying archaic political structures. Well,
without some change in political structures it won't be possible
to tackle social reform and suppress not only the more acute
contradictions in the developed half of the country but the gravest
and most decisive disequilibrium of all: the existence of two
Mexicos, one modern and the other traditional and poor.

Of what do these archaic political structures consist?

The Mexican Revolution broke out in 1910. For more
than ten years Mexicans were fighting among themselves. It was
a cruel and terrible civil war with much bloodshed; many Mexicans died, many more emigrated to the United States, where, as
you know, they became victims of unjust treatment. The first
problem confronting the victors, the revolutionary "caudillos,"
was to preserve revolutionary unity, so the Partido Nacional
Revolucionario was formed. The PNR prevented Mexico from
contracting that endemic disease of Latin America which consists in passing from anarchy to dictatorship and vice versa. By
preventing a return to anarchy the PNR also suppressed personal dictatorship. The PNR was a party dictatorship, an insti-
tutional dictatorship, and it eliminated that heritage of the Arab
and Spanish world: caudillism. The caudillos might be a Simón
Bolívar or a Fidel Castro, but also they might be such sinister
individuals as Santa Ana, Dr. Francia, Ubico, and that whole
gallery of crocodiles and tigers in gold braid who have passed
through our countries since independence. Caudillism, whether
the caudillo be good or bad, is an abnormal regime. The caudillo
is an extraordinary being and I want for Latin America the opposite: to be an extraordinary people governed by ordinary leaders!

Who would you describe as an ordinary leader?

One who accepts the existence of other people and
doesn't believe himself to be the incarnation of goodness, or

history, or any other entelechy. A friend I greatly love and admire, carried away by the famous speech in which Castro confessed that the affair of the ten million tons of sugar had been a mistake, said to me: "An extraordinary speech, and only an extraordinary man could have dared to utter it." I reflected that what would have been extraordinary would have been if an ordinary man, any Cuban, had told the extraordinary man he had made a mistake. . . . But let's get back to Mexico, which is neither a model state, nor anything like it. The party passed through three stages. First it was called the Partido Nacional Revolucionario, with the accent on the *nacional*. Created after the civil war, its first objective was to secure peace and the unity of the country. Lázaro Cárdenas, that extraordinary man who had the grace to relinquish power of his own free will and become an ordinary man, modified the party, which now called itself the Partido de la Revolución Mexicana. The emphasis was now on *revolución*. Through the PRM Cárdenas realized decisive changes and laid the foundations of modern Mexico, such as agrarian reform and nationalization of petroleum. Cárdenas's foreign policy was also excellent; support for the Spanish Republic, political asylum for Trotsky, anti-Nazism and anti-imperialism. Yet Cárdenas didn't attempt to change the political structures. Thus, although it's true that the party eliminated caudillism of the Hispano-American brand, it is also true that it transformed itself into the instrument of the sexennial appointment of the president. In Mexico we don't keep our leaders in perpetuity, but every six years (there's no reelection) the almost sacred figure of a new president ascends into the political heaven. He isn't a Hispano-Arab caudillo but a figure who unites in modern political terms the prestige of the Aztec priest-leader and of a colonial viceroy. The caudillo is epic, the president is ritual. In short, the political structures—the party and its ramifications in the organizations of the workers, peasants, and middle classes—became one vast, specialized bureaucracy which controls and manipulates political life. At the same time, since we had to deal with the problem of our industrial and economic backwardness, the question of development emerged as the central task. The need to accelerate economic development favored private interests and put a brake on social and political reform.

Thus it was that in its third stage the party adopted the depressing name of the Partido Revolucionario Institucional. Without the stability the PRI gave the country, perhaps there would have been no economic development. But at the same time, the PRI upset the social program of the revolution and deformed political life. On the other hand economic development stimulated social mobility, and created, as I have already said, a new working class, groups of prosperous peasants in some regions, and above all, for the first time in Mexican history, a middle class. Well, political immobility is incompatible with the existence of a modern society or one on the way to modernization—and this is as true in Russia as in Mexico. For modern society and democracy are complementary terms.

But the events of 1968 in Mexico reflect what was happening in other parts of the world. The rebellion of youth is worldwide.

Yes. And expresses a general crisis in the modern world, a change of values. Nevertheless, this rebellion assumes different characteristics in every country. In Mexico it was (and is) an expression of what I've just been saying. Unlike the French students in May of that same year, Mexican youths didn't want a violent and revolutionary change in society. Nor did the orgiastic and para-religious tone of the hippies appear in the Mexican youth movement. It was a movement for democratic reform, despite the fact that some of the student leaders belonged to the extreme left. Can one attribute the moderation of student demands to a tactical maneuver? I don't think so. The truth is that neither the temper of the Mexican people nor the historical situation of the country is revolutionary. What the majority want is reform: for social conditions in Mexico to be in harmony with the economic progress the country has achieved in the last forty years. But the struggle against social inequalities and contradiction entails political reform and the establishment of a democratic society. It implies an end to the one-party system and therefore to the masquerade of democracy in popular organizations. Workers and peasant unions must regain their autonomy. That is: the Mexican people must regain their power to decide and participate which has been seized and usurped by political and syndical bureaucracies, now acting as accomplices of the Mexican financiers and United States imperialism.

Then the program is solely political?

Firstly it's not a program. Secondly, I think political reform will open the way to social reform. It will also make it possible to discuss Mexico's real problems, which are immense: the population growth, the underdevelopment of Mexico, our relations with the United States. . . . Lastly—and this is decisive in my opinion —only in an atmosphere of freedom can Mexicans ask themselves several questions about development. "Until the present time there were two models of development: the North American and the Soviet models, and both are disastrous. An impartial reading of what is happening in our country as well as in other parts of the world would lead us to take a new view of the problem of development at once and at all costs. Let us for a moment forget the crimes and stupidities committed everywhere in the name of development, from Communist Russia to Nasser's Egypt, and look at what is happening in the United States and Western Europe: the destruction of ecological equilibrium, the contamination of minds, which is as grave as that of the lungs or more so, the over-crowded cities and polluted air, the damage done to the adolescent psyche, the abandonment of the old, the erosion of sensibility, the corruption of the imagination, the degradation of Eros, the accumulation of refuse, the explosion of hate. . . . How can one fail to recoil before a vision, and search for some *other* model of development? This is an urgent task, requiring science and imagination, honesty and sensibility in equal proportions; a task without precedent, because all the models of development we know, whether in the East or West, are heading for disaster. In present circumstances the race for development is a mere rush to damnation. . . ." I've read you this paragraph from *The Other Mexico* because I would like to repeat it to everyone in the Third World . . . But in Mexico we are forbidden to talk about these subjects; meanwhile we haven't achieved even a minimum, in other words: democratic reform of the regime.

Did the students raise these problems?

No, but the student revolt laid the basis for democratic reform in Mexico. Instead of profiting by the student rebellion to rectify and straighten out their policy—that is: to return to the traditions of the Mexican Revolution—the regime responded with violence and force. As you know the student movement coincided with preparations for the world Olympiads which were held in Mexico in 1968. The fact that the Olympic Games were to take place in Mexico showed that the country had developed considerably. In 1920 or 1945 Mexico couldn't have aspired to be the headquarters of the Games. It's safe to say that the student revolt and the celebration of the Olympiads in Mexico were complementary facts: both were signs of the relative development of the country. It was the attitude of the government that was discordant. For one thing, the students were not menacing the regime, nor confronting it with a really revolutionary situation. For another, no act of any government in 1968 was as ferocious—there's no other word for it—as Mexican repression was. You know that on October 2, 1968, probably three hundred people died in the plaza of Tlatelolco.

Do you think there's any remedy for the Mexican situation?

The reaction of the regime revealed its sclerosis, its inability to change. All the same, I'm not entirely pessimistic. Mexicans are confronted by the following dilemma: either political immobility which will sooner or later provoke explosions of violence, or the regime will initiate the democratic reform demanded by the country. When those events took place I decided to dissociate myself from the government and criticize it from outside.

How was your book The Other Mexico *received in Mexico?*

Five editions in a year: about 30,000 copies. It was read by young people, but also by certain sections of the working class. But as for the reviews, they were deplorable. Journalists who supported the regime, or rather were employed by it, insulted me. Some said, as usual, that I was a communist agent; others that I was an agent of the CIA. Nor was the book well received by those who postulate that violent revolution in Mexico is both necessary and possible.

What were the critic's arguments?

Arguments? With a few exceptions, all they produced were hints—attacks, denunciations, suppositions. . . . Two ideas seem to have worried both sides alike. The first was that I described the PRI as a bureaucratic caste, not unlike other twentieth-century political bureaucracies, such as the communist parties in the East.

Could you elaborate on that?

As it concerns a subject that goes beyond the Mexican case, I would prefer to deal with it later. At present I will just say that what I said upset those of the right, the supporters of PRI, as much as it did on the left. . . . The same thing happened with another of my observations: when analyzing the political situation in Mexico, I noticed the presence of modes of thinking and feeling (more of the latter than the former) which seemed to me to have been inherited from the *other* Mexico. *Other* not in the sense of economic and social underdevelopment, but of *another* reality. An underground reality, embedded in modern Mexico, but which now and again bursts out and appears among us. Our image of authority and of a leader has its roots in pre-Columbian and colonial Mexico. I say *image* because it is in fact an image and not a concept. The Aztec archetype of domination, a sacro-political archetype, survived the colonial period and reached the twentieth century, allied to concepts of Spanish absolutism. This idea seemed reactionary to pseudo-Marxists, and anti-Mexican to reactionaries.

It's an idea belonging to social psychology?

Yet without the smallest connection with Jung's archetypes. In reality, as I say in *The Other Mexico*, my idea comes as much from Freud's notion of the (individual) unconscious as from Marx's (social) ideology. An ideology representing what Marx himself called "the absurd consciousness of the world," and which is never conscious at all. But I was also (and above all) inspired by Dumèzil, who has shown the existence in every society of certain complexes, presuppositions, and mental structures which stubbornly resist the erosion of history and its changes. At the end of my little book I say that only critical thinking can dissipate these terrible Mexican phantoms. As I wrote that I was thinking of Marx, who had said: "Criticism of heaven precedes criticism of the earth." For Marx, criticism of heaven meant criticism of religious myths; for us, it means criticism of ideologies—our pseudo-myths. In short, I was talking about criticism and therefore about liberty. However, they accused me of being a fatalist! The saddest thing of all is the low intellectual and moral level of controversy. Like all Latin America, Mexico is suffering from a sort of moral and intellectual degradation: intellectual discussions at once become personal quarrels. When the insults come from the traditional right I shrug my shoulders: it's to be expected. When they come from the left I'm alarmed, because that means that the degeneration of critical thought is practically complete.

Is this crisis in critical intellectual thought characteristic of Latin American countries only?

It's a phenomenon that embraces all Latin America, and also Spain and Portugal. The exercise of criticism is generally connected with the intellectual capacity, but in my opinion the problem is a moral and historical one. For a long time there has been discussion of the subject: why Spain, a country of great poets and novelists, had no great philosophers? Well, Spain has had some great theologians, so that there can be no doubt about her intellectual capacity. What Spaniards did not, and still do not, possess, is the liberty of spirit required by modern philosophy. In Spain there was really no eighteenth century, no great critical reform such as the one that transformed the intellectual and political life of Europe. Nor, later on, did we—the Spaniards and Latin Americans—have a democratic revolution of the bourgeoisie. Our war of independence strengthened our native oligarchies and the regimes based on monopoly of land—the very opposite of a bourgeois revolution. The lack of democratic tradition, the lack of a true eighteenth century and a true nineteenth century, explain our critical incapacity and emphasize our personalism and individualism. Some Hispano-American critics—among them, one who is very distinguished: Emir Rodríguez Monegal—have believed that I was denying that there were any critics in our language. How could I deny a Reyes, a Henríquez Ureña! No, I was referring to that *tradition of critical thought* that began at the end of the seventeenth century and forms the intellectual bloodstream of Europe. That tradition scarcely exists in Spain and her old colonies.

We also lack the tolerant atmosphere that makes it possible to discuss ideas.

Yes, we live between silence and shouting. Latin America is infested with caudillos, great and small. Latin American writers can be divided into three groups. Some are leaders of gangs and bands; others are Robinson Crusoes or hermits; and others are members of a clique. . . . There is no criticism in Latin America for the same reason that there is no democratic life. Critical thought and democracy are complementary. Only in an effectively democratic atmosphere can criticism exist, whether literary and artistic or philosophic and political. Our critical incapacity isn't intellectual incapacity but a moral defect, which in its turn is the result of a historical defect.

Aren't we influenced by what Unamuno called "Hispanic envy"?

Envy isn't the result of excess but of lack of criticism. Resentment is the consequence of the intellectual asphyxia of our societies. A historical defect, not a racial one. . . . In short, we have critics but no criticism. A paradox that isn't really one. In the sense of free confrontation of ideas and hypotheses—that movement which inspired Kant's *Critique of Reason*, Nietzsche's critique of values, and Bertrand Russell's of language—in that sense there is no criticism in our countries. But we have critics and essayists. For instance, in the field that interests me particularly, that of the frontiers between thought and sensibility, Ramón Xirau has done work of real importance, in which rigorous thinking intersects with poetry. In Venezuela there is another writer, Guillermo Sucre, who is one of our best critics and an authentic poet as well. And there are others, others. . . . But all these swallows don't make a summer.

You have said that The Other Mexico is "a preface to an unwritten book." What book?

One on Latin America. I would like to compare the evolution of India, China, and Japan with our own. In those three countries "modernization" has been synonymous with "westernization." To comply with the modern world of science and technology these three ancient countries have had to leap from one civilization to another. We still don't know what will be the results of this impressive operation—in the surgical sense of the word—which has consisted of eradicating one part of its tradition and grafting on a fragment of another, alien one. Nor have they followed the same models: the Japanese took as their model the development of Western capitalism; the Chinese a *sui generis* version of Marxism; and India . . . that's a different case again. Unlike China and Japan it was a Western colony, but also a nation —or a collection of nations, for India isn't a country but a civilization—which hasn't yet succeeded in leaping into modernity. Gandhi wasn't only anti-Mao, he was anti-Meiji. The case of Latin America is very different from that of these three countries. It's enough to reflect that we are Christians, we speak Spanish and Portuguese and gained our independence with the tools of French and English ideas, to realize how much separates us historically from the Orient. Of course we are part of the Third World, if we think in economic and social terms: we are economically dependent, underdeveloped, and have immense social and political problems; however, in historical terms we are part of the civilization of the West. We live on its periphery, as the United States and Russia did until half a century ago. From this point of view, the vision of Latin America as a part of the Third World is oversimple. . . . Of course when I speak of Western civilization I include that of Russia, in spite of its Byzantine origins. Modern Russia is one of the eccentric versions of the West.

Which are the others?

The United States and Latin America. That is, they are the heirs of eccentric England and no less eccentric Spain. I have a profound belief in the realities called civilizations, and, within them, in the persistence of certain structures and attitudes toward reality. I'm convinced that the opposition between Latin America and the United States is not reducible to economic and political differences, such as development and underdevelopment, imperialism and colonialism, capitalist democracy and feudal caudillism, etc. If those differences were to disappear, other more profound ones would persist: two contradictory views of time, work, the body, leisure, death, good, and all things in this and the next world.

This reminds me of the documentary we saw yesterday on television, made by a French producer at the time of the French minister Betancourt's visit to China.

What impressed me most about that documentary was the constant presence of Mao: his face, his book, his thoughts. Magic thoughts: they would do as well for someone swimming across a river as for a surgeon performing a graft or a workman increasing the production of a factory. It's sad that all this is done in the name of revolution and in a country like China. But it's true that Chinese civilization never knew democracy or criticism. The Sinologue Levenson says that the Chinese had no word for the concept "revolution" in the modern and Western sense of the term, so they had to use a traditional expression: Change of Mandate from Heaven—in other words: change of dynasty. Another Sinologue, Etienne Balazs, points out that the Chinese have no word for the idea "liberty" either, and that the circumlocutions they use to express this philosophical and political category are made up of the notions of "relaxation" or "transgression." Liberty as a deficiency or an excess.

Is modern China a continuation of the Old China?

Mao's regime has made a break, but a break reminiscent of another—the break when imperial China began. The figure of Mao to some extent repeats that of the First Emperor, as he was called, the founder of the Ch'in dynasty and the imperial regime. Yes, China is being modernized, but in her own way. For example, in that film, art was talked of as being "for the edification of man?" To edify, edification, are words with a Confucian flavor! I thought art was to liberate, was an instrument of negation, that's to say, of the liberation of man. It is also sad to see that country, heir to an extraordinary artistic tradition, producing an art which makes me think of the worst bourgeois art and the mediocre work produced in Russia under Stalin. What we saw in that film isn't Chinese, but petit bourgeois art. Those operas and songs and the actors' gestures belong to the heroic gesticulation of the bourgeoisie. Another disturbing feature: it seems that the artisans who once used to produce images of personages from Chinese art, religion, or history are now exclusively producing images of the new saints: Stalin, Lenin, Mao, Marx, and Engels. If Marx, Engels, and Lenin were to return to this world they would certainly be ashamed to find themselves beside Mao and Stalin. These two represent something radically different from Marxism in its original form: critical thinking and revolutionary action designed to liberate men from religion, authority, and the state. Here we find the opposite. Once again there is confusion between politics and religion: the leader has been deified, sanctified.

Do you think we are witnessing the end of an epoch?

You have asked me for my ideas on various subjects which appear now and then in my writings, especially in *Corriente alterna* and *Conjunctions and Disjunctions*: the rebellion of youth, the revolt of the countries of the Third World, the rebellion of women, the possibility of founding a new erotism, the reinvention of love, as Rimbaud called it. . . . All these themes are connected to a central theme: the end of lineal time. Yes, I think we are at the end of an epoch. It's an idea I share with a great many others. It has been one of the commonplaces of contemporary thought for some forty to fifty years. . . . I'll explain myself. I begin with this: all civilizations and cultures possess an idea of time and express a vision of time. In general, from primitive man to the Greeks, Chinese, and Aztecs, men believed in cyclical, circular time. Societies that postulate this cyclical concept of time nearly always go to the past for their archetype and model. The past is the repository of values. Other civilizations have thought that perfection and essential values lay outside of time. Time is an illusion, but there is a time outside time in which temporal contradictions disappear. Indian civilization looks upon time as an illusion, and therefore ignores history; nevertheless, there is a point outside of time where the illusion disappears and true reality appears: Brahman, nirvana. Christianity postulated two separate times: historical time with a beginning and an end, and a time outside time, the eternity of heaven and hell.

Christianity was a break with the past.

The great break. And it presented itself as a break with ancient time and as an end of all times for Christian eternity implies an end of time. On the other hand, the historical time of Christianity is completely different from that of antiquity: it isn't cyclical but lineal. It has a beginning and an end. The beginning is the fall of Adam, man expelled from eternity, expelled from paradise; the end is the Last Judgment; between these two come the redemption and incarnation of Christ. Thus Christianity postulated a time that was historical, consecutive, lineal, and finite, while also affirming the existence of timeless time: eternity, the next world. At the end of history, after the Last Judgment, time comes to an end, the future ceases to exist, all is an endless present: eternal bliss or eternal suffering. End of the future. That's a thing neither you nor I can clearly understand because we've lost the religious dimension of existence. For us, fundamental values exist in time. For the modern age illusion is not time; illusion consists in believing that there can be a time out of time. For the Christian, Hindu, or Buddhist the real is what lies beyond time, whether Brahman, nirvana, or heaven. For us everything that is beyond time is illusion and the sole reality is what exists in time. First fundamental change between traditional societies and the modern world: negation of the other world.

Loss of the religious dimension.

Not only that. When a pagan philosopher denies the existence of the next world, he is affirming the value of the past (the Golden Age or some similar archetype), or, like the hedonists, affirming the present. Whereas modern society doesn't exalt either the past or the present but the future. Modern society has inherited the lineal, consecutive, and unrepeatable time of Christianity while profoundly modifying it: in the first place, lineal time is no longer finite but has become infinite; in the second, the protagonist of time is no longer the individual soul which comes here to be saved or lost, but the human race—in other words, the idea of salvation has been replaced by historic evolution; lastly, the archetype of modern time, the repository of values, is the future. To the medieval Christian, history was a trial; for us, history is the fundamental value: history is time and time is progress.

But what does the present crisis involve?

Our idea of time. The idea of time as an infinite progress has two versions or variants: one is evolution, the other is revolution. The idea of historic evolution is an ingenuous application of Darwin's evolutionism to society, an explanation of history in biological terms, I would say. But at the end of the eighteenth century another extraordinary idea appeared: the realization of progress could not merely take the form of gradual, evolutive change, it must be sudden, complete, and radical. Previously the word "revolution" meant the rotation of the heavenly bodies, thus illustrating the old cyclic idea of time; after the eighteenth century "revolution" meant sudden change, the substitution of one system by another. At first the revolutionary agent was a vague entity: the people. After the Utopian socialists, and especially after Marx, the agent was the proletariat. Time which is progress was incarnated in different classes, and the final class chosen to consummate liberation was the working class. You notice that the two versions of the idea of lineal time as progress, the evolutional and the revolutionary, both claim to hold the keys of history and be the owners of the future, and both are attempts to colonize it.

And what has happened?

Why, the opposite. The present is not only failing to confirm these predictions, it is refuting them. As for Marxism, the most remarkable thing has been that the class that should have acted as agent of international revolution, the proletariat, has turned out to be neither revolutionary nor internationalist. Failure of the central dogma of Marxism, failure of the idea of lineal time as a revolutionary, dialectic leap from one stage to the next. But although we have had no proletarian revolutions in the developed countries, we have had revolts—I am intentionally using the word "revolt" instead of "revolution"—in countries that are insufficiently developed. Well, from China to Cuba, the historical agent of those changes has not been the working class.

And in Russia?

Nor was there a really proletarian revolution in Russia. A group of professional revolutionaries, the Bolsheviks, took over, guided and directed the great popular revolt of soldiers, peasants, and workers in 1917. The result was the change from the authoritarian Tsarist regime, with its incipient capitalism, to a bureaucratic regime which we cannot call socialist without corrupting the term. A linguistic corruption which is a political and moral corruption as well. Socialism signifies the collective ownership of the means of production, and this in turn demands authentic democracy among the workers. In the Soviet Union the state is the proprietor of the workers as well as the means of production; and the state has in its turn become the property of a political bureaucracy, the Communist Party.

And in the West?

If forecasts concerning the development of history from the revolutionary viewpoint have proved false, the evolutionist predictions of the bourgeoisie have been no better. Liberals believe that social progress should be endless, and have promised us that, thanks to technical improvements and representative democracy, commercial economy and enlightened capitalism, we shall build a society in which abundance will reign and social conflicts (particularly the central conflict between workers and capitalists) will almost entirely disappear. It's hardly necessary to say that representative democracy is steadily becoming less democratic and representative: the political parties have been transformed into

gigantic bureaucracies. Besides political bureaucracies we have
unions' bureaucracies, and besides economic monopolies we have
monopolies of information.

And of arms.

Exactly. What is called the military–financial complex,
and is merely the form taken in the United States by the disease
of the twentieth century: bureaucracy. In short, capitalist societies
tend in their own way toward uniformity, just as communist
societies do. In about 1950 many sociologists said that our era
was witnessing the end of ideologies, and pointed out that social
contradictions, far from becoming more acute as the Marxists
had predicted, were diminishing and on the point of disappearing
altogether. Now, in 1970, we realize that although it is true that
they don't correspond to the classical schema of Marxism (capital
versus labor), social contradictions have been aggravated and
have led to unparalleled violence. Think of racial problems, the
rebellion of youth, and all the other conflicts. The forecasts of
liberal thought have proved completely false. The evolutionist and
bourgeois version of the lineal and progressive idea of history
promised a prosperous society, a free society, and a society without social conflicts. The truth is that prosperity is Tantalic, it's a
swindle: our society doesn't really own the objects it produces
and consumes—it is their slave. Liberty means the coexistence
of differences and individual characteristics, it means plurality, but
capitalist society tends toward uniformity and homogeneity.
Lastly, invisible and visible pressures are provoking violent explosions: social conflicts have acquired terrible virulence. I conclude: we are neither happier nor freer nor wiser than our ancestors.

Has the West failed then?

The failure of neo-capitalism is no less complete than
that of socialism. But the ideologists of the "end of ideologies"
were right, although not in the sense they thought: the two
variants of the idea of lineal time, the two ideologies that have

dominated the history of the West for the last century, have proved unworkable. Those ideologies have fallen into disuse. And with them the idea of time as endless progress. We are witnessing the end of the idea of the future rather than the end of ideologies.

Do you think Marxism has completely failed?

Yes, insofar as it claims to be a scientific explanation of history; no, insofar as it was, and still to some extent is, critical thought. And besides, my reservations concerning Marxism as a science of history are one thing and my attitude to socialism is quite another: to renounce that idea is to renounce our moral and political tradition. There is one Marxist statement that remains valid in my opinion: capitalist society is a constitutionally sick society. But it seems to me that capitalist and socialist societies are equally affected by the disease. The contemporary crisis of Marxism is the crisis of the idea of time as lineal sequence and infinite progress. And that crisis is also that of the ideas motivating capitalist society. What is in a state of crisis is modernity, that world that began at the end of the eighteenth century.

A crisis of the values of our civilization.

To say that the values of modern society are in a state of crisis is not enough. One must say that the very repository of those values, the place where they are located is in a state of crisis, is tottering. Where are those values installed? In the future. Modern paradises, paradises of work, industry, technique, prosperity, are all in the future. We are witnessing the decline of the future. End of an epoch, end of the future, and beginning of what? I don't know. In any case we are witnessing the invasion of the present. And the present brings with it different values from those of the future. The invasion of the present assumes two forms: rebellions in developed nations and revolts in countries on the periphery, or, as they are now called, underdeveloped countries. Both, as I have already said, refute the forecasts of modern thought concerning the future. Thus, these disturbances and commotions constitute a criticism of lineal time as progress.

In what sense do the "rebellions in the developed world," as you call them, refute progress?

When I speak of rebellions in the developed world I'm not only referring to the rebellion of youth, women, or racial or religious minorities, but also to the rebellion of artists and to all those diffuse and universal manifestations which can be classified as rebellions of sensibility. Rebellions that are not rational but emotional and passionate. They all take the form of negation of the future and its values, which are rational ones; equally, they all take the form of a revaluation of the present, both emotional and corporal. For us the future is a synonym for utopia: the dream of reason, not of passion. The time of the body, the time of pleasure, the time of pain is the present. But the present is also the time of death—a reality which the philosophies of the future conceal from us. The return of the present is the return of the body—a reality which embraces both sides of existence: life and death. The reappearance of the body could open the way to a new eroticism (not a new sexuality). A new *cordiality*.

Why aren't those rebellions revolutionary?

Because they criticize the idea of revolution itself—although their protagonists are seldom aware of the fact. The idea of revolution is inseparable from the ideas of progress and the future. Well, all those rebellions, by affirming present values, corporal and affective values, implicitly postulate the discredit of the future and progress.

Why, in talking about the underdeveloped countries, do you speak of revolts rather than revolutions?

The word "revolution" is philosophical in origin and means the rotation of heavenly bodies. Since the eighteenth century it has meant a violent change of one system for another; also, and above all, it has stopped signifying circular time and instead is used to mean an accelerated progress, by leaps, of lineal time. By using the word "revolt" I'm going back to the origins of language: in the sense of a return to the beginning on one hand, and of an explosion against an authority or unjust situation on the other. The movements of underdeveloped countries are revolts disguised as revolutions. . . . To all revolutionary thinkers, revolution must be the consequence of development, in other words of the changes introduced by industry. Revolution was not a method of achieving industrialization; on the contrary, it was its consequence. Well, whether in Russia, China, or Cuba, "revolution" has been a method of promoting and speeding up development, industrialization . . . Therefore, if we use terms accurately, the revolutions of today have not really been revolutions. I don't mean that they are regressions: they have been and are explosions, revolts. Heroic remedies for the problems of inadequate development, but not for the constitutional ills of our time. Heroic and counterproductive remedies.

In what sense counterproductive?

From Lenin to Nasser and from Mao to Fidel Castro, the problem confronting a revolution in an underdeveloped country is not essentially different from that which confronted the Mexican revolutionaries: in order to carry out the revolution's social and political program the country must be developed, industrialized. Development demands accumulation of capital, whether private or state-owned. To that end the social program of the revolution has to be suspended, even if only provisionally and partially. And that's not all: a bureaucracy of technicians and administrators is also needed, and another political and police bureaucracy to establish social peace, since disturbances would slow up the process of development. The bureaucracy of administrators and technicians guarantees efficiency, but at the same time introduces social inequality, hierarchies, and a regime of privilege. The political bureaucracy suppresses criticism, dissidence, and opposition. Both suppress the revolution. . . .

Bureaucracy is a very old phenomenon

Not in its present form. Leon Trotsky was preoccupied by this subject in his last years. In Trotskyist circles there was much discussion, a little before his assassination, as to the nature of the Soviet Union. None of the Trotskyists of those years considered that the USSR was a socialist state. Trotsky's formula was as follows: the Soviet state is a degenerate workers' state, and its sickness is called bureaucracy. Trotsky thought that Russia's economic and political backwardness explained the bureaucratic usurpation of Stalinism. Faithful to the teachings of Marx, he thought of bureaucracy as a caste not a class. Therefore it was not a constitutional disease of the workers' state, but an accident resulting from well-defined historical causes. Once these historical circumstances disappeared, once the USSR developed, and/or European socialist revolution broke out, Soviet bureaucracy would disappear.

Predictions which have not been fulfilled.

I think we ought to rethink the problem. Firstly, it's debatable whether the Soviet Union was ever a workers' state, degenerate or otherwise. Secondly, there has not been, nor is it probable that there will soon be, a European socialist revolution. Lastly, if the political bureaucracies of the twentieth century aren't a class, what are they? It's difficult to answer that question. However, there is a clue: if the Russian bureaucracy governs in the name of a class—which class is it? Obviously not the proletariat nor the bourgeoisie. So it's probable that the new bureaucracy of the twentieth century is itself a class. Or a new class in embryo.

But there have always been bureaucracies.

Not like those of the twentieth century. There were state or priestly bureaucracies, but not political bureaucracies. That's what's new: officials who are specialists in manipulating the masses, and who enter the party as children just as ancient priests entered the temple. . . . But perhaps you're right: I can think of another example of a historic crisis like ours which was resolved by establishing a bureaucracy. Modern historians, especially Marxists, have accustomed us to think of history as a series of stages: slavery, feudalism, capitalism, etc. Well, in ancient China the crisis of the feudal period (Chou) wasn't resolved by establishing capitalism as in Europe, but by the throne becoming allied to the Mandarins. For two thousand years China was ruled by a bureaucracy of learned specialists in the manipulation of souls and minds. This example shows that there are no ready-made solutions. History is continual improvisation. We are inventing history every day.

And what about the West?

The democratic traditions of the West and its greater development have hitherto hindered bureaucratic dictatorship, dictatorship by a single party. But remember the cases of Germany and Italy. On the other hand, the party system of the West is not exactly a model of democracy, any more than is a model the monopoly of the media of information. As in the last century, England is still an oasis of relative liberty and tolerance, but on the continent the trend toward strong, impersonal states is becoming more marked. In the United States violence has reached shocking proportions: individual violence, group violence, and violence by the police. Apart from oppressing Negroes and *chicanos* the United States is directly or indirectly oppressing whole regions, from Latin America to Vietnam.

They have promised us a "free world."

Freely determined, as Cage says, *by the United States.* . . . The truth is that on both sides of the modern world, East and West, authoritarian tendencies are increasing and nearly always assuming impersonal and bureaucratic forms, from the "military–financial complex" of the United States to the one-party regimes of eastern Europe. So that I find it refreshing to return now and again to libertarian thinking. One must continue the anarchist tradition and reexamine the problem of state and authority. Perhaps anarchist arguments are ingenuous and oversimple, and their violence suicidal, but their moral inspiration is valid and generous. Though the state has been an oppressor from the first, in the twentieth century that oppression is developing horrifying characteristics. It isn't enough to criticize capitalist imperialism and communist bureaucracies: one must analyze the state itself and criticize its function in the modern world. Because in our century the state also means concentration camps, racism, the atomic bomb, and Vietnam.

Would it be correct to describe all that you have been saying as a criticism of progress?

    Of progress, bureaucracies, monopolies, the state, and all the other forces and tendencies that accelerate our disastrous progress toward uniformity among men. Not very systematic criticism and probably overdue. I'm afraid that the evils of progress are irreparable, irrevocable, and irreversible. Think of the case of the underdeveloped countries. An unattractive word which is merely a euphemism used by the "experts" of the United Nations to describe backward countries, and which reveals a linear and progressive view of time. History as a journey toward the future— only *one* future, the same for everyone. On the altars of that unique future the underdeveloped nations have sacrificed their traditions and arts, their ethics and cuisine, their view of nature and their ideas about death. They have disowned their dead and themselves, they have changed their idea of eternity for the image of the future symbolized by New York and Moscow. The strangest —the most obscene thing of all—is that governors of the underdeveloped countries have agreed to this ruinous operation without batting an eyelid. They haven't got rid of poverty, but they have sold their present, past, and future! The only people who were wise enough to set their faces against lethal "modernization" were the "primitives" and, of course, they were exterminated. The way to development is the way to perdition. The way to universal uniformity: to general death.

You think we should preserve differences: isn't that anti-egalitarian?

    Preserving differences isn't the same as preserving hierarchies. Authoritarianism is another thing: a desire for unity and homogeneity, an attempt to impose a single universal model on everyone, whether it is the stone image of a leader or the precepts of a catechism. What sets worlds in motion is the interplay of differences, their attractions and repulsions. Life is plurality, death is uniformity. By suppressing differences and peculiarities, by eliminating different civilizations and cultures, progress weakens life and favors death. The ideal of a single civilization for everyone, implicit in the cult of progress and technique, im-

poverishes and mutilates us. Every view of the world that becomes
extinct, every culture that disappears, diminishes a possibility of
life. In the historical ambit, the action of progress is like that of
entropy in the material ambit: as differences are suppressed,
history grows "cold" and the human species advances with greater
speed toward extinction.

Octavio Paz, one last question: what are your plans for the future?

> To abolish it.

POSTSCRIPT: *New York City,*
January 10, 1972

*After spending a year in Cambridge, England, you returned to
Mexico early in 1971. A few months later, you joined a group of
Mexican intellectuals to found an organization whose aim, so I
have read, is to change the existing system. What made you decide
to take part in politics again?*

> First let me tell you my impressions on returning to
Mexico. When Marie-José and I left England we went by sea from
Southampton, by way of Madeira (a beautiful island), Miami
(a hellish place), the Panama Canal (remarkable for its combination of *fin de siècle* engineering with tropical scenery . . . we
seemed to be passing through an illustration out of a book by
Jules Verne), and finally reached Acapulco, a vast bay surrounded
by buildings that reminded me of Miami. But a dirtier, poorer
Miami. Half-naked children surrounded the ship in canoes and
plunged into the sea for the coins thrown by the tourists. When
night fell, this spectacle was completed by the appearance of a
gigantic lighted cross on one of the highest cliffs of Acapulco. I
was told that it was the tomb of a millionaire. . . . Then we
took a bus along an excellent road through very beautiful yellow
country and arrived at Mexico City. Although it still seems to
me one of the loveliest cities in America, it is a mutilated, disfigured city, and has more smog than New York. It stands fifth
among the cities of the world for contamination of atmosphere,

but not for its libraries, public health, universities, standard of living, etc. We have made great advances, but we have advanced in the wrong way. The negative aspect of our progress has been more marked than the positive. We have the same problems that more developed countries have, but without the resources a developed country has for solving them—and we also have the problems of an underdeveloped country. Mexico City seems to me a mirror reflecting Latin American capitalism, which is capitalism devoid of aesthetic originality. Another feature of the city is the pretentiousness of its government buildings. The Argentine architect Emilio Ambasz told me that they are an affirmation of Mexican *machismo,* but to me they are more like an affirmation of the excessive power of the state. Mexico City is disfigured by the monolithic megalomania of its government buildings and by the speculative delirium of private enterprise. Thus it is the architectonic reflection of the social and political ills that afflict the country: the bureaucratic domination of the PRI (the traditional revolutionary party) as well as domination by the economic monopolies of Mexican financiers and great North American businesses.

Is there any remedy?

Perhaps the only remedy would be political, economic, and urban decentralization. For Mexico City to cease being the sole center of power. For political, economic, and intellectual power to be distributed. For Mexico City to be one of the cities, not *the* city of Mexico. To decentralize Mexico would involve a political struggle against the excessive centralization of the Mexican government and of the political power of the PRI, and of course against the great national monopolies, all more or less connected with North American capitalism. Decentralization implies political democracy and important social reforms. Well, as you see, my thoughts about the ugliness of Mexico City, which is the city I love best, have led me into reflections of a political sort. These ideas coincide, more or less, with those of many Mexicans, among them people who were imprisoned by the regime of President Díaz Ordaz in 1968. Not all of them. Some

of the young maintain falsely extremist positions which I believe
to be unrealistic. Others believe in violence. But violence is the
retroactive shot of the desperate.

Is your party already formed?

Not yet. We are organizing it.

Who is taking part?

One of them is Heberto Castillo, a teacher of mathematics who was imprisoned for two years for sympathizing with
the student movement of 1968. He's one of the most intelligent
and warm-hearted men I've ever known. Another is Cabeza de
Vaca, a student leader who knows the agricultural workers well
and is interested in their problems. Among intellectuals, there
is Carlos Fuentes. We also have a group of students, workers, and
peasants. Someone in great sympathy with us is Vallejo, a rail-
waymen's leader who has been in prison for a long time, an
excellent man with a very clear head, who has directed the working classes. And there are various other small groups which may
perhaps join us. Such as the electricians. Our general aim is to
create a people's alliance of workers, peasants, the middle classes,
intellectuals, students.

Will it be an electoral party?

No. For the present it won't be an electoral party, nor do
we want to be involved in electoral politics. We want to be active
at the level of trades unions, municipal life, and basic social reforms. We are aiming at realism with a minimum of ideology.
In Mexico most parties have been formed by little groups with a
program, who have tried to impose their aims from above down-
ward. Our idea is to proceed in the opposite way.

Why?

Because we believe we are going through a period of
ideological crisis. We believe that socialism of a Caesarist or
bureaucratic type has failed just as badly as bourgeois parlia-

mentary democracy. That's why we want to find new forms of democratic relationship corresponding to the real state of the country. We want to be realistic, and we start from the idea that political programs are meant to serve the people, and not the people to serve political programs. In the Soviet Union the people are at the service of the plan, but we believe that the plan should be at the service of the people. This means that we maintain a critical attitude toward the models of progress offered us by Western neo-capitalism, in particular by the United States and the bureaucratic "socialism" of the Soviet Union. That's my way of thinking, at least, and that of many of my friends.

What are the party activities at present?

We are passing through a period of research. We want to know (1) if the people desire such a party, and (2) what sort of existence they want such a party to have. From this first consultation with the public, from this Mexican reality, a program will develop. I think that this program will operate, at the beginning at least, at the most basic level: that of the workers' trade unions, the peasant organizations and those of the middle classes. All these organizations are at present controlled by the political bureaucracy of the PRI, so that the first point in our program and our activity will concern internal democracy and liberty in the popular unions of workers and peasants. I also believe it to be of fundamental importance to break away from Mexican centralism, whether political or of the economic monopolies.

Who are the opponents of the party?

Firstly, the official party, and the whole of the right, that's to say the PRI. The PRI would like to be able to absorb us but it hasn't succeeded. The traditional parties of the left, and the Communist Party are also against us.

Who are your supporters?

A lot of people who still belong to the PRI: workers, peasants, and bureaucrats, and also a great many from the Communist Party and left-wing groups.

What's the solution to the party's economic situation?

At present we have no money, and I think the Mexican people, who are very poor, will have to support a very poor party. But there's one advantage in this: we shan't have a large administrative apparatus. We want to have a minimum of organization, a minimum of ideology, and a maximum of mobility.

And the government?

As I explained in *The Other Mexico: Critique of the Pyramid*, as a result of the contradictions in the regime, the government has made a move toward democracy, which is healthy even if incomplete, and we must make use of this to organize ourselves.

Is the Mexican situation comparable to that in Chile?

The Chilean situation is quite different. They possess a democratic tradition, which Mexico does not; on the other hand, Mexico has a much more advanced social tradition than Chile.

Do you consider the possibility of becoming president of Mexico?

No, I detest authority.

Your participation in this movement has let you in for some criticism; for example, I hear that García Márquez has accused you of belonging to the establishment.

García Márquez has made himself spokesman for a small group of pseudo-extremists preaching "revolution at once," although they have neither the strength nor the opportunity for creating one! García Márquez is an opportunist of the left, a man without ideas—without ideas, *tout court*.

A famous writer . . .

Yes, famous. What Pound used to call a "diluter," one who spreads and popularizes other people's discoveries. . . . Well, García Márquez came to Mexico last year. He arrived from New York, where he had been awarled a doctorate by Columbia Uni-

versity, started an ultrarevolutionary clamor, received a few
centavos from television (bourgeois), and immediately afterwards
took an airplane to resume his functions as leader of Latin
American guerrillas in the restaurants and bars of Barcelona. . . .

*Since you returned to Mexico, another of your activities has been
editing the review* Plural. *What sort of publication is it?*

I think it is defined by its name. I believe we must
accept the existence of dissension, criticism, and transgression
within Latin American society. So that we need a plural society,
not a monolithic one. *Plural* is fighting from a political and
literary point of view for diversity in critical, political, literary, and
intellectual spheres. On the one hand we want to distinguish
Latin America from Mexico, and on the other we want the pages
of the magazine to act as a link with something more urgent: a
critical evaluation of the true nature of Latin America—of our
Latin American literature, our history and our economy . . . in
fact, a study of the reality of our continent. We also want it to be
a bridge connecting us with the rest of the world—especially
with Europe and the United States. We have therefore published
in our first numbers contributions by Lévi-Strauss, Michaux,
Chomsky, Harold Rosenberg, Galbraith, and Jakobson. We are
also anxious to open our doors to little-known worlds. For instance, in the first number, our friend Kazuya Sakai, who is a
painter but also a scholar, published an anthology of the work of
Kenko, a fourteenth-century Japanese poet and Buddhist monk. In
the second number we published a translation of Lewis Carroll's
Hunting of the Snark, and in the third an anthology of Valéry's
Cahiers.

Would you say Plural *will be the spokesman of the party?*

No, but on a different, cultural level, *Plural* represents
the same thing that the party does on the political level. When
Excelsior offered me the editorship of the magazine it was made
perfectly clear that I wouldn't use it as an organ of political
propaganda, although this doesn't mean that it has no political
opinions. We publish political articles and comments in every
number.

Has it been well received?

The response to this monthly magazine has been extraordinary. At present we print 25,000 copies, and we have 7,000 subscribers in Mexico alone. What we want now is more contributions from Spanish-speaking intellectuals. We would also like more collaboration from Brazilian writers.

What subject have you chosen for your lectures at Harvard?

They will be connected with what I talked to you about in Cambridge (England)—tradition in modern poetry. The first lecture will be called "What Does Being Modern Mean?" and will discuss whether being "modern" in literature means the same as it does in other activities. To me, born in the romantic period, modern literature is a critique of the "modern era." My lectures will constitute a history of the relations between the modern epoch and modern literature . . . incestuous and stormy relations, which have ended in absolute divorce.

Where did you find more knowledge of and interest in Latin American subjects—in Cambridge (England) or Cambridge (Massachusetts)?

Much more at Harvard. The students there are more in touch with contemporary Latin American literature and have a much greater interest in what concerns our continent. Last October they invited me to a round table on Mexican political problems, the other participants being Professor Hirschman, John Womack (author of a splendid biography of Zapata), and Professor Turner, another Mexican specialist. There was an audience of about a thousand. Incredible . . . The Department of Romance Languages at Harvard is first-rate. And I was able to meet and get to know a man there whom I admire: Ramon Jakobson. Also Chomsky and Elizabeth Bishop, one of the best American poets. Women and poetry in both Americas: Sor Juana, Gabriela Mistral, Emily Dickinson, Marianne Moore, Elizabeth Bishop . . . Life in Cambridge (Massachusetts) is vigorous and stimulating. In Cambridge (England) the students have vague notions about Latin American literature, and the values disseminated by

their professors belong to a period before the discovery of
America. An obsolete cult of things Spanish, which no longer
exists even in Spain. . . . But I was happy in Cambridge (England). English social life is still truly civilized. England hasn't
succumbed to North American barbarism like the rest of Europe.

JULIO
CORTÁZAR

JULIO CORTÁZAR

París January 1969

"I was born in Brussels in August 1914. Astrological sign, Virgo; consequently aesthetic with intellectual tendencies; my planet is Mercury and my colour gray (although I actually prefer green)." That's what Julio Cortázar, author of Hopscotch and the story on which Antonioni's Blow-Up is based, wrote in an autobiographical letter from Paris in 1963.* "My birth was a product of tourism and diplomacy. . . . I happened to be born during the days when the Germans occupied Brussels at the beginning of the First World War. I was four years old by the time my family were able to return to Argentina; I spoke mostly French, which left me with a way of pronouncing "r" that I could never get rid of. I grew up in Banfield, a suburb of Buenos Aires, in a house with a big garden full of cats, dogs, tortoises, and parrots: paradise. But I was already the Adam in that paradise in the sense that I haven't got happy memories of my early childhood; too many servants, excessive sensibility, a frequent melancholy, asthma, broken arms, desperate first loves. ("Los venenos" [The Poisons] is mostly autobiographical.) Secondary schooling in Buenos Aires: teacher in 1932. Professor of literature in 1935. First jobs, teaching in villages and country towns; after seven years' teaching in secondary schools I was in Mendoza in 1944–45. Resignation because of the failure of the anti-Peronist movement in which I was involved; return to Buenos Aires. I had already spent ten years writing but publishing nothing or almost nothing (a slim volume of sonnets, perhaps a short story).

---

* Cortázar y el hombre nuevo (Cortázar and the New Man) by Graciela de Sola, Editorial Sudamericana, 1967. Reprinted by permission.

From 1946 to 1951, solitary and independent life in Buenos
Aires; convinced that I was an irredeemable bachelor, a man with
very few friends, music-mad, reading for days on end, cinema
lover, petit bourgeois, blind to everything outside the sphere of
aesthetics. Public national translator. The perfect profession for a
life such as mine was then—egotistically solitary and independent."

Julio Cortázar still works as translator, mainly as a free-lancer
for different UNESCO organizations, but he is far better known
as a novelist, short-story writer, poet, and essayist.

Among the best of his short stories are those from Cronopios
and famas, a collection of short stories that, according to Neil
Millar, are "a dazzle of jeweled nonsense, all set in prose which
is often poetic and often to be felt rather than understood."
Cortázar, to whom "humor is the most serious thing in existence,"
groups people into three categories: (1) cronopios (the artistic,
temperamental, impractical), (2) famas ("the heads of philan-
thropic societies are all famas"), and (3) esperanzas ("they let
things and people slide by them . . . they never take the
trouble"). Cortázar first had the notion of those characters to
be called cronopios while attending a concert given by Louis
Armstrong in Paris in 1952. He then wrote in his review "Louis
enormísimo cronopio" (a revised edition was published in his
book Around the Day in 80 Worlds, 1967): "A world that might
have begun with Picasso instead of ending with him, would be a
world exclusively for cronopios, and in every corner cronopios
would be dancing . . . while Louis, climbed to the lantern of the
street light, would blow for hours on end making fall from the
sky huge pieces of stars made of syrup and strawberries to be
eaten by children and dogs."

If cronopios stand for artistic, temperamental, impractical creatures, then Julio Cortázar is one of them. Therefore, this interview has been conducted in his own personal way. I first met
Cortázar in 1968, in Paris, to get him to agree to do an interview for the Spanish edition of Life. He agreed after I sent him,
at his request, a written questionnaire and then guaranteed that
Life would publish his manuscript exactly as he had written it.
At the beginning the reaction from the New York office, however, wasn't encouraging. So, on a sunny autumn morning, we

met at the Deux Magots. Cortázar, casually dressed, with a gray windbreaker over an open-neck shirt, was waiting, drinking tomato juice and smoking Gauloises. Good-looking, more than six feet tall, slender, with large green eyes, heavy eyebrows, and longish brown hair, in his mid-fifties, he appeared fifteen years younger. Cortázar seems shy—very courteous but reserved. He didn't talk too much about himself and kept to the old formal Argentine custom of addressing people by *usted* instead of the more familiar *tu* or *che*. Our meeting was cordial and we talked about his single visit to New York, where he spent most of the time in the Village; about Cuba, about China . . . about his house in Saignon, his place in the South of France where he retires to write. Finally, I went back to the subject of the interview and was able to convince him to be more flexible: to grant the interview if the editors would agree to send him the galleys for his approval. Since at that particular time, in the offices of the discontinued *Life en español*, the *cronopios* outnumbered the *famas*, the manuscript, which arrived on the promised day, was published verbatim.

Because the interview was politically controversial, the editors were bombarded by letters—unusual enough, since Latin Americans are not particularly known for writing letters. Some of the letters praised the magazine for its democratic approach; others the author for his; and many others accused Cortázar, on false pretenses, of taking money from *Life*.

Since the interview, Cortázar, who has been a defender of the Cuban Revolution from the very first, has been "excommunicated" because he, along with a group of Western intellectuals, sent Fidel Castro a letter of protest over the imprisonment and signed "confession" of the Cuban poet Heberto Padilla. Consequently I asked Cortázar to update his manuscript, but he declined, saying that it still reflects, in general, his current thoughts.

What follows is based on a series of written questions put to me by Rita Guibert on behalf of *Life*, but before answering them it seems to me necessary to explain certain circumstances connected with these pages. It is both morally and practically desirable for a writer to make a habit of expressing his views in publications belonging to his own ideological and intellectual camp; this is not the case here, and both *Life* and I know this and accept it. From our first contact it was understood not only that my consent did not mean "collaboration" with *Life*, but also that it represented exactly the opposite: a raid into enemy territory. *Life* accepted this attitude and gave me the necessary guarantees that my words would be reproduced verbatim. I alone am therefore responsible for them; they have not been adapted to the requirements of a magazine, and it is only fair to say this at once.

My initial mistrust and my request for guarantees surprised the editors of *Life*, just as they will surprise many of its readers. I will begin by enlarging on this, as a practical method of answering some of the ideological and political questions that were put to me. Not only do I distrust North American magazines such as *Life*, in whatever language they appear, and especially those in Spanish, but also I am convinced that all of them, however democratic and advanced they claim to be, have served, are serving, and will continue to serve the cause of North American imperialism, which in turn serves the cause of capitalism by every possible means. I have no doubt that a magazine such as *Life* is internally organized to aim at the utmost objectivity, and that it opens its pages to every shade of opinion; I have no doubt that many of its editors and writers believe that they are thus facilitating what they call a "dialogue" with the ideological adversaries, and so furthering better understanding and perhaps a conciliation. Bitter experience has shown me all too clearly that above and beneath these daydreams (which are often hypocrisy in disguise) an entirely different reality exists. Two years ago, the revelations concerning the activities of the CIA in the sphere of these supposed "dialogues" completely demolished all possible illusions of this sort, and *Life*'s liberal standards are not such as to revive fresh hopes in that field. North American capitalism has realized that the cultural colonization of Latin America— the best possible starting point for economic and political colonization—demands more subtle and intelligent methods than those formerly used; it has now learned how to exploit institutions and individuals who, whether at home or abroad, believe they are fighting it and neutralizing it in the intellectual sphere. There is something diabolical in thus taking advantage of the good will and unconscious complicity of so many people who go on innocently believing that the spread of culture is the best way to peace and progress. In this sense, *Life*'s friendly overtures could be as diabolical as the most aggressive behavior of the State Department, especially in that many of its editorial staff and the great majority of its readers almost certainly believe in the democratic and cultural value of its pages. For my own part, a single glance at any number of *Life* is enough to show me the true face hidden behind the mask. For instance, let my readers look at number 11, for March 1968: the photograph of North Vietnamese soldiers on the cover displays a laudable desire for objective information; inside, Jorge Luis Borges speaks admirably and at length about his life and work; only on the back of the cover does the true face appear: an advertisement for Coca-Cola. There is an amusing variation in the number for June 17 of the same year: Ho Chi Minh on the cover, and Chesterfield cigarettes on the back. Symbolically, psychoanalytically, and capitalistically, *Life* gives us the key to the cipher: the cover is the mask, the back the true face gazing toward Latin America.

Perhaps some reader may ask himself in surprise how such criticisms can be printed in the very magazine that is criticized. He cannot be aware that the devil's dialectics consist precisely in paying a high price in order to attain a far higher prize on another plane: Christopher Marlowe and Goethe illustrated this in their day. If *Life* is true to its apparent aims, it must feel obliged to publish this text, just as I for my part feel obliged to make use of its obligation. When proposing this interview, *Life* insisted that its standards were liberal and democratic, whereas I maintain that Yankee capitalism is making use of *Life*, as it does of so many other things, for its own ends: namely the cultural colonization of Latin America as a means to its economic colonization. We now know that the CIA has given financial support to magazines that have harshly criticized the CIA, in much the same way that the Catholic Church always includes an "advanced" sect, which attacks its encyclicals and councils. The tradition of court jester has not been lost; it is useful and necessary for kings of every epoch, even those of today who smell of gasoline and speak with a Texan accent.

Another of my readers may shrug his shoulders in just as much astonishment when the truth dawns on him: Julio Cortázar is a communist and consequently sees enemies hidden behind every bush. As the time has now come to begin the interview itself, it will be a good idea to explain that I have not reached my brand of socialism by way of Moscow, that it derives from Marx as projected upon the revolutionary situation in Latin America—a situation with its own characteristics, ideologies, and achievements, conditioned by our idiosyncrasies and our needs, and which is expressing itself today historically in such events as the Cuban Revolution and guerrilla warfare in South American countries, and in such figures as Fidel Castro and Che Guevara. As a result of this concept of revolution, my view of Latin American socialism is profoundly critical, as my Cuban friends in particular are well aware, in that I disapprove of all postponement of human fulfillment for the sake of a hypothetical long-term consolidation of revolutionary structures. My humanism is socialistic, which I take to mean that it is humanism in the highest, most universal degree; if I do not accept the deviousness by which capitalism pursues its ends, still less can I accept the deviousness of submitting to the bureaucratic machine of any system, however revolutionary it claims to be. Like Roger Garaudy and Eduard Goldstücker, I believe that the supreme aim of Marxism should only be to provide the human race with means to achieve the liberty and dignity that are of its very essence; this obviously entails an optimistic view of history, entirely opposed to the egoistic pessimism justified and advocated by capitalism, that sad paradise for the few, achieved at the cost of purgatory if not hell for millions and millions of the dispossessed.

At all events, my notion of socialism is not diluted to a tepid humanism tinged with tolerance; although human beings are more important to me than systems, I believe that the socialist system is the only one that may someday carry man forward to his true destiny. To paraphrase Mallarmé's famous lines on Poe (I'm delighted to think of the horror of the purely literary who read this), I believe that socialism, rather than that vague eternity foretold by the poet and the churches, will transform man into his true self. This is why I reject any solution based on capitalist or so-called neo-capitalist systems, just as I also reject the solution of sclerotic or dogmatic forms of communism; I believe that true socialism is threatened by both; I not only believe that they solve nothing, but also that each in its own way and with its differing aims postpones the access of true men to liberty and life.

Thus my solidarity with the Cuban Revolution has from the outset been based on the evidence that its leaders and the great majority of the nation were trying to establish a form of Marxism founded on what for lack of a better name I shall go on calling humanism. I know of no other revolution as enthusiastically supported by intellectuals and artists, naturally moved by this attempt to state and defend human values through economic and social justice. For an intellectual who knows little of economics and politics, this agreement between men like Fidel and Che and the vast majority of Cuban writers (not to mention foreign intellectuals) was the surest sign of their being on the right road; I was therefore always disturbed—as I still am—by any conflicts that might arise in Cuba or wherever socialist revolution takes place, between full expression of the critical revolutionary spirit and other "hard" tendencies (inevitable maybe, but also conquerable, for this is the only true meaning of dialectics) which require intellectuals to give support in their daily work, by instruction rather than by free creation of values. I emphasize this point because it is the best way of answering some of your questions and because I realize that a revolutionary (whether he is intellectual or *guerrilla*, thinker or man of action, or both—it hardly matters in this case) is forced to fight on two fronts, the external and the internal, that is to say against the universal enemy, capitalism, and also against the regressive and ossifying tendencies within the revolution itself, the bureaucratic machinery so often denounced by Fidel Castro, the barrier (already I think mentioned by Marx) which is gradually isolating the leaders of his country and condemning them to view themselves from a distance like someone gazing at an aquarium or enclosed inside one. And because I have referred to Cuba, I want to make it clear (answering one of your questions at the same time) that my support of its revolutionary struggle springs from my belief that it is the first great attempt *in depth* to liberate Latin America from colonialism and underdevelopment. When I am reproached for my lack of political militancy, on behalf of Argentina for instance, I can only reply, first that I am not a militant in politics, and second, that I feel personally and intellectually committed to transcend nationalities and patriotism and serve the Latin American cause wherever I can be most useful. I know too that, living as I do in Europe, it is better to work for the Cuban Revolution than to devote myself to criticizing Onganía and his like in the Southern Tier, and that the best contribution I can make to the future of Argentina is to do my utmost to extend the ambit of the Cuban Revolution on the continent. As I have often said, but must repeat again: patriotism (or why not nationalism, which it so often becomes?) horrifies me when it sets out to subject individuals to an almost astrological destiny governed by their origins and birth. I would ask such patriots as these: Why didn't Che Guevara stay in Argentina? Why didn't Régis Debray stay in France? What the devil were they doing *outside their countries?* I am thinking of the apparent disgust with which Mario Vargas Llosa has been reproached for living in Europe and the indignation against me for attending a cultural congress in Havana instead of giving lectures in Buenos Aires. If political and intellectual quarrels in Argentina ever really brought about a solid revolutionary movement against oligarchies and gorilladom, there would be no justification for my absence; but as I see things today, I am doing what little I can do to further this solid movement in my own way from France, just as I am working for the Cuban Revolution from France. And when I go to Cuba, I go with concrete projects that have no valid equivalents in Argentina today. I am one of a panel that chooses books for a population of which a large percentage have emerged from illiteracy thanks to the revolution, and whose younger generation is eager for education and culture; I work on the collaboration committee for the review of the Casa de las Américas; I attend a congress to discuss the duty of intellectuals of the Third World toward economic and cultural colonialism, a subject that I believe figures infrequently in writers' congresses in our countries. All this, as will be seen, has one main objective: the struggle against imperialism at all levels, both material and mental, a struggle that is spreading from Cuba and through Cuba into the whole continent, not only in the realm of action, leading to martyrdom in the forests of

Bolivia, in Colombia and Venezuela, but also in ideas, in discussions between intellectuals and artists from all our countries, the moral and mental substructure that will one day put an end to Latin American gorilladom and to the backwardness that explains it and gives it its tragic strength.

I find it difficult to speak in a few pages about questions that could be dealt with more effectively by the terminology of passion than that of theory, for not only am I no theorist but also I have never written about such subjects except incidentally, always preferring that my works of fiction and my personal behavior should respectively and in their own ways express my concept of man and the means that tend to facilitate his progress. In an open letter to Roberto Fernández Retamar which has been the subject of some controversy, I clearly said that I would always remain a writer first and foremost, and that this and no other would be my only way of contributing to the revolution; but this statement is not a form of escapism by way of the sublime, and so when you ask me point blank what difference I see between the Soviet intervention in Czechoslovakia and that of the United States in the Dominican Republic and Vietnam, I reply by asking whether any of *Life*'s reporters had seen children burned with napalm in the streets of Prague. And when you ask what is the basis for my anti-Yankee feelings, I answer that as every imperialist system was hateful to me, North American colonialism disguised as help for the Third World, an alliance for progress, decade of development, and other green berets of the same sort is even more hateful to me because it is *false* at every stage, lays claim to a democracy it daily denies to its black citizens, and spends millions on a cultural and artistic policy designed to create a paternal and generous image in the imagination of the underprivileged and simpleminded masses. Here in Paris I have had plenty of opportunities to see with what energy illusions about North American "civilization" are being introduced; this has happened in Moscow also and, too much perhaps, in Czechoslovakia. If this is true of such highly developed countries, what can we hope for from our illiterate populations, our dependent economies, our embryonic cultures? How can we accept gifts, however generous—and some are, no doubt—from our worst enemy? When I am told that the assistance given by the United States to Latin America is less egotistic than it appears, I feel impelled to quote figures. In the last conference of UNCTAD, held in New Delhi at the beginning of 1968, an *official* bulletin (I am not speaking of communiqués from hostile delegations) made the following exact announcement: "In the year 1959, the United States acquired property in Latin America to the value of $775 million, in the form of private investments, of which they reinvested $200 and *kept* $575." These are the facts that so many Latin American intellectuals prefer to ignore when they visit the United States in the cause of cultural cooperation, or on other pretexts. I refuse to ignore them, and this defines my attitude as a Latin American writer. All the same—listen, American—I am proud that my books and those of my colleagues are translated in the United States, where I know we have readers and friends, and I will never deny myself contact with the true values of the country of Lincoln, Poe, and Whitman; I love everything in the United States which will one day contribute to the strength of its revolution, for there will be a revolution in the United States too when the time comes for man to replace flesh-and-blood robots, when the voice of the United States, both inside and beyond its frontiers, will be symbolized by the voice of Bob Dylan rather than that of Robert McNamara.

Although there is much more I could say on this subject, perhaps it is time to talk of literature, because you have asked me a great many questions covering everything from the start of my literary career to the so-called problem of the "exiles." In the chapter devoted to me by Luis Harss in *Into the Mainstream*, I answered many similar questions, and as it is an easily accessible book, it will be best to talk here about different or complementary subjects. The first is that I am always surprised when people speak of my literary career, because for me it has no existence; I mean that it does not exist as a career, an unusual state of things for an Argentine, as my country is crazy about careers of every conceivable sort, as is shown by the immortal figure of Juan Manuel Fangio among others. In Europe, where a writer is often a professional for whom regular appearance in print and the possibility of gaining literary prizes are important, my amateurish attitude usually perplexes publishers and friends alike. The truth is that I don't care a straw for Literature with a capital L; the only thing that interests me is searching for (and sometimes finding) myself in that contest with words which eventually produces a thing called a book. A "career" implies preoccupation with the fate of one's books; in my case, I left Argentina in the very month in which *Bestiario* (Bestiary) appeared, and I abandoned it to its fate without the least remorse. Seven years passed before my second book, *Las armas secretas* (Secret Weapons), rudely disturbed my readers with a story called "El perseguidor" (The Pursuer); what followed was like those police reports in which a man returns home and finds his house turned upside down, the lamp table where the bathtub ought to be, and all his shirts scattered among the geraniums in the patio. I do not know what readers were searching for in my house of paper and ink, but between 1958 and 1960 they stormed the libraries, and my books had to be reprinted so as to refurnish the empty house somewhat; to me in Paris this was unreal and amusing, but it was moving when so many letters began to arrive from young people wanting to discuss things or raise issues; gloomy letters, love letters, letters from people with a text for a thesis, and that sort of thing. The other day I discovered that *Hopscotch* was in its eighth edition; a week earlier I had assured a French critic that the book had only gone into five editions; I am thought rather foolish about this sort of thing here. Of course I do not try to defend my detached attitude; perhaps it is too solitary and in the last analysis conceited or rather perverse; I believe that I am a typical product of our Third World, where a professional writer is nearly always looked at askance and with an ironical smile; I suppose I was conditioned by my time, by the fact that to write was "surplus," a luxury for mothers' darlings or simply an endearing form of insanity; in any case I think distance and the passage of years have intensified my natural love of solitude, which is only interrupted at intervals by the duties I spoke about earlier in these notes. I am told that literature has now become an important career in Argentina, and that in the final straightaway there is more whipping than you would see in *Marat-Sade*; of course that is good insofar as rivalry makes for a better horse-racing breed, and, joking apart, a writer by vocation owes it to himself to be just that, instead of working at odd moments, as I do, and others do whose writing is a sort of luxury that is basically quite bourgeois.

I have spoken elsewhere about the authors who have influenced me, from Jules Verne to Alfred Jarry by way of Macedonio, Borges, Homer, Arlt, Garcilaso, Damon Runyon, Cocteau (who first made me take the plunge into contemporary literature), Virginia Woolf, Keats (but here we are treading on sacred, numinous ground—and I beg the printer not to put luminous), Lautréamont, S. S. Van Dine, Pedro Salinas, Rimbaud, Ricardo E. Molinari, Edgar Allan Poe, Lucio V. Mansilla, Mallarmé, Raymond Roussel, the Hugo Wast of *Alegre* and *Stone Desert*, and the Dickens of *Pickwick Papers*. This list is not exhaustive, it must be understood, and corresponds rather to what UNESCO calls the sample method; at any rate it will be observed that I name no Spanish prose writers, as (with the exception of *La Celestina* and *La Dorotea*) I have recourse to them only to cure my insomnia, nor yet any Italians, although D'Annunzio's novels linger in my memory. I have been asked about the possible influence of Onetti, Felisberto Hernández, and Marechal. I came upon the two first when I was almost grown up, and what took place was tacit agreement rather than influence, no need to get acquainted to realize which were their favorite cafés and tangos; some critics have seen a reflection of Marechal in *Hopscotch*, which does not seem to me hurtful either to Don Leopoldo or to me. Meanwhile I went on writing my books, which followed a course characteristic of all literary development; that is to say they began with poetry, and moved on to the technically more arduous and difficult medium of narrative prose (I hear the grinding of teeth and see the tearing of hair this will arouse), finally producing in that domain the most personal style I could devise, which according to opinions I respect, beginning with my own, makes use of humor to go in search of love—understanding the latter as the most extreme form of anthropological thirst.

Those two last words bring me to another of your questions, as to what part metaphysical speculation has played in my work. I can only reply that such speculation *is* my work; if reality appears to me so fantastic that my stories are quite literally realistic to me, it is obvious that the physical must also seem to me metaphysical, whenever between seeing and the thing seen, or between subject and object, there exists that privileged means of access which we translate into words by calling it, according to circumstances, poetry or madness or mysticism. The truth is that these words are all suspect; metaphysics seems to me to get closer every day to such things as caressing a breast, playing with a child, or fighting for an ideal; but in giving these three examples I am implying a high degree of deliberate concentration, because between caressing a breast and caressing a breast there may be a vertiginous distance or even total opposition. It has always seemed to me—as I explained in *Hopscotch*—that metaphysics is within reach of every hand capable of entering the required dimension, rather as Alice did when she went through the looking glass; and when on some exceptional occasion this hand at last succeeds in caressing the breast that was both very close and completely hidden, can we still go on talking about metaphysics? Did we not invent metaphysics merely out of our poverty, for the same reason that we said the grapes in the fable were sour? They were not so for Plato, whose metaphysics of nostalgia was understood by few except in theory; nor were they for Rimbaud, and his was the fiery metaphysics of the world rooted in the earth, nor again for Che Guevara, and his was the metaphysics of the exact moment when Achilles knows that he will never catch up with the tortoise merely by nostalgia and words, but only if he runs after it and demonstrates that man's life is here below and that the true metaphysics consists in mastering reality and annihilating the phantoms engendered by a misleading fable. I believe that Marx put an end to compensatory metaphysics on the mental plane and showed the way to liquidate them on the *practical plane*; personally I can do without metaphysics, I agree with Sartre that existence precedes essence insofar as existence is like Achilles and essence is like the tortoise; in other words that true existence consists in running to get to the goal and that that goal is here, not in the world of Platonic ideas or in any of the various beautiful paradises of the churches.

Talking of paradise for some reason vividly reminds me of Vanessa Redgrave, and of your question as to what I thought of the changes Michelangelo Antonioni introduced into "Las babas

del diablo" (The Devil's Spittle) to make *Blow-Up*. This subject is not of the slightest intrinsic importance, but it gives me an
opportunity to defend Antonioni from certain unfair accusations,
although the time that has elapsed gives my defense that dismal
air of the rehabilitations often practiced in the USSR. Anyone
who knows us even slightly realizes that both Antonioni and I
tend to be gloomy, which is the reason why our friendly relations
consisted in meeting as seldom as possible, so as not to waste each
other's time, a thoughtfulness which neither he nor I often find
in the people around us. Antonioni began by writing me a letter
that I took to be a joke on the part of some facetious friend, until
I noticed that it was written in a language aspiring to pass as
French—an absolute proof of authenticity. I learned from it that
he had recently happened to buy an Italian translation of my
stories, and had found in "Las babas del diablo" an idea that
had been pursuing him for years; an invitation followed for me
to meet him in Rome. We had a frank conversation there; the
central idea of my story interested Antonioni, but its fantastic
developments left him cold (also he had not fully understood
the end), and he wanted to make his own film, make another invasion of the realm that was natural to him. I realized that the
result would be the work of a great cinematographer but that I
should have very little hand in the adaptation and dialogue, although Antonioni was courteous enough to suggest a collaboration
in the actual filming; so I let him have the story, knowing well
that in his hands it would suffer the fate of the drowned man as
described by Ariel in *The Tempest*.

> *Nothing of him that doth fade*
> *But doth suffer a sea-change*
> *Into something rich and strange.*

That was what happened, but it is only fair to say that I left
Antonioni absolutely free to depart from my story and follow his
own ghosts; in his search for them he met with some of mine,
because my stories are more contagious than they may seem to be;
the first person to realize this and say so was Vargas Llosa, and I
believe that he was right. A long time later I went to the first
performance of the film in Europe; on a wet afternoon in Amster-
dam I bought my ticket like any of the Dutch who had gathered

to see it, and there came a moment, during the rustle of foliage as the camera was raised toward the sky above the park and focused on the trembling leaves, when I had the feeling that Antonioni was winking at me, and that we were meeting above or below our differences; such is the happiness of *cronopios*, and all the rest is of no importance whatever.

You asked me whether *Hopscotch* had influenced the work of younger Latin American novelists, and what sort of influence it had had. The fact is that it is not easy for someone who tries to keep abreast of contemporary writing of different countries, and who also lives in Europe and plays the trumpet, to follow closely the possible development of the genre in his own country; however, I have read enough books by young authors to suspect that *Hopscotch* has meant to many people what one might call an existential shock rather than a literary experience, so that its influence has been extraliterary rather than technical or linguistic, as its author intended when he wrote what has been described as an anti-novel. The noticeable bewilderment the book caused many critics obviously came from the fact that it would not fit into any more or less usual category, and it was significant that they failed to realize that any close comparison of *Hopscotch* to literature involved losing contact completely with the central ideas of the book. Petrus Borel used to say: "I'm a republican because I can't be a cannibal." For my part I should say that I wrote *Hopscotch* because I could not dance it, spit it out, shout it, or project it as any form of spiritual or physical action through any conceivable medium of communication; indeed many readers, especially young ones, felt that it was not strictly a book, or else that it was only a book in the sense that Petrus Borel was a republican, and that it exerted its "influence" in a sphere that was only tangentially connected with literature. By the way, for how long must we go on clinging to libraries? With every day that passes I realize more that those apparently obsolete ivory towers have all their floors right up to the roof occupied by a race of scholars who are horrified by any extraliterary invasion of literature, which they think of as the product of man's conformism, rather than as the free gesture of Prometheus when he stole fire from the gorillas of his day. This brings me back again by analogy to the problem of a writer's "commitment" to his subjects, because

the occupants of ivory towers turn as pale as death at the very
idea of making a novel from situations or figures in contemporary
history, their idea of literature being basically aseptic and
uchronic, stretching out pathetically toward eternity and absolute
and permanent values. *Has* for *h*instance the *Odyssey, h*as for
*h*instance *Madame Bovary,* et cetera. Many writers, painters, and
musicians have stopped believing in such permanence, that books
and art should be made to endure; although they go on writing
or composing as well as they possibly can, they have given up any
superstitious belief in a lasting object, which is really a bourgeois
relic that is being liquidated by the increasingly vertiginous speed
of history. However, the ivory ones say to themselves that subjects
from contemporary history usually become uninteresting or out
of date very quickly, nor do they ever fail to mention in this context some of the poems in Neruda's *Canto general;* they don't
seem to realize that even though he was wrong historically, Neruda
is a poet for all time, and the fact that we find it impossible to
accept his eulogies of Stalin today in no way reflects on his sincerity in writing them. When I published *Todos los fuegos el
fuego* (All the Fires the Fire), I received a good many letters that
praised most of the stories and then complained of my including
the one called "Reunión" (Reunion), whose characters were
transparently intended to be Che and Fidel. In fact, to the ivory
ones, *such subjects are not literary.* As far as I am concerned,
what has ceased to be literary is a book, the idea of a book; we
stand on the dizzy brink of insanity and of the atom bomb, we
are advancing toward the most appalling catastrophes, and books
seem to me among the weapons (aesthetic or political, or both, as
everyone should do what he wants as long as he does it well) that
still might save us from the universal autogenocide in which most
of its future victims are so gaily collaborating. So it appears to me
laughable for some Mexican or Argentine novelist to develop
stomach ulcers because his books are not famous enough and to
organize an elaborate strategy of self-advancement so that publishers and critics cannot forget him. In view of what we see on
the front page of our newspaper when we wake up every morning,
isn't it surely grotesque to think up spasmodic antics aimed at
an increasingly improbable "permanence" when history shows
that tastes and forms of expression will have suffered a vertiginous

change before long? When you ask me my views about the
future of the novel, I answer that I could not care less about it;
the only thing that matters is man's future, with his novels and
television sets and yet-to-be-imagined comic strips and eloquent or
significant perfumes, not to mention that perhaps one of these
days the Martians will arrive on their innumerable little legs and
teach us forms of expression that will make *Don Quixote* look like
a sick pterodactyl. For my part I get stomach ulcers only when I
walk through the outskirts of Calcutta, read a speech by Adolf von
Thaden or Castelo Branco, or discover like Sartre that a child
killed in Vietnam is more important than *La Nausée*. The future
fate of my books or other people's books leaves me perfectly in-
different; such anxious hoarding reminds me of those madmen
who store up clippings of their own nails and hair; in the realm
of literature *also*, feelings for private property must be put to an
end, because the only purpose of literature is to be a common
good, as Lautréamont instinctively felt about poetry, and this no
*h*author can decide, nor can he rule it, from his chryselephantine
tower. A true author is one who stretches his bow to its full extent while writing and afterwards hangs it on a nail and goes to
drink wine with his friends. The arrow speeds through the air
and will hit the target or not, as the case may be; only imbeciles
will try to alter its course or run after it and give it extra shoves
to further their dreams of eternity and foreign editions.

Another of your questions is if I believe in Latin American
literature as such, or only in the sum of regional literatures. It
is obvious that we do make up a sort of literary federation,
differentiated by the economic, cultural, and linguistic color of
each region; it is likewise obvious that no region is greatly interested in what is happening in the others except as readers, and
that a Chilean writer probably owes more to the literature of other
continents than to that of Argentina, Peru, or Paraguay, and vice
versa. And in recent years, when the influence of the best Latin
American novelists has made itself forcibly felt throughout our
literary federation, I do not think that it has exceeded that of
any other important contemporary literature. Despite this (which
may be an excellent thing), analogies in our history, ethnics (with
very variable proportions and constituents), and of course linguistics, subtend, as it were, our very large spinal column, and

ensure Latin American unity on the literary level. But something
I never feel in the least certain about is whether our literature as
a whole is so important and remarkable as many critics, writers,
and readers affirm; a few days ago, when I was in Prague, chatting
with the editors of the review *Listy*, I said that if one of the airplanes taking our best novelists to international congresses and
gatherings were to crash, it would be revealed all of a sudden that
Latin American literature was much more precarious and less rich
than was supposed. Of course this teasing remark was aimed at
García Márquez and Carlos Fuentes, who accompanied me on
their visit to Czech writers and whose well-known horror of losing
contact with the ground made them look noticeably green. But
behind this crack of mine lay a truth, that the so-called boom in
our literature was in no way comparable to the great periods in
the literature of the world, such as the Renaissance in Italy, France,
and England, the Golden Age in Spain, or the second half of
the nineteenth century in Western Europe. We lack a base, a
cultural and spiritual foundation (which depends of course on
economic and social conditions), and although during the last
fifteen years we can congratulate ourselves on a sort of self-
conquest in the sphere of letters (writers who end by writing as
Latin Americans and not as mere adaptors of foreign aesthetics to
regional folklore, and readers who read their own writers and
support them, thanks to a dialectic of challenge and response
that was nonexistent until very recently), it is only necessary to
study a good map, read a good magazine, and take stock of the
precarious situation of our economy, sovereignty, and historical
destiny, to understand that the reality is considerably less important than it is supposed to be by temporary patriots and
foreign critics who glorify and praise us because, among other
reasons, the fashion has changed, because North American novelists have been translated and digested *ad nauseam*, because Italian
neo-realism has come to an end, and because French literature
is in a transitory experimental stage, so that now it is our turn, and
we are marvelous geniuses and King Gustavus of Sweden thinks
the world of us, poor dear. In Cuba, where this need to affirm
Latin American values is likely to lead to exaggerated illusions, I
was asked a few years ago what was the relation of the movement
among Cuban novelists to the general movements in Latin

American prose of today. My answer still seems to me an acceptable one, and I give it in full: "The expression 'general movement' is ambiguous, because a casual reader might imagine it to refer to some collective and coherent effort, whereas in reality the normal characteristics of Latin America in the intellectual sphere—which reflect its other circumstances—are unfortunately still in operation: I am thinking of the frequent solitude and isolation of her intellectuals, and their small number in relation to potential readers. If on the other hand we talk merely of a general tendency, we shall come closer to the truth; it is a fact that in the last two decades, and particularly in the most recent of all, many Latin American short-story writers and novelists have, in spite of geographical barriers and differences of tradition, been united in a vigorous attempt to fulfill their national *and therefore continental and universal* destiny as intellectuals. In that sense the best contemporary Cuban novel-writing is in the same class, and I do not think it differs greatly from kindred literatures, except for the obvious characteristics of subject and language which distinguish our countries. I would like to add that I seem to notice a certain anxiety in the question itself, as if some unjustified timidity lay behind it. Unless of course it conceals the exact opposite of timidity. . . . In either case I regret it, because to speak of Cuban, Peruvian, or Argentine literature is to confine oneself to mentioning a handful of names as against the vast desolation of whole races who have not reached a level whence, any literature can develop full fecundity and significance. No country has done more than revolutionary Cuba to bridge that terrible distance between men and their own literature; but in relation to the hoped-for future, all Latin America is still only at the threshold of its literature, and, above all of the transformation of that literature into spiritual progress and culture for its peoples. Why then try to solve such problems as this question implies, why apply location and qualities to something that in fact hardly exists? We must write more and better, so that someday more and better books will be read. There is plenty of time to talk of movements; for the present, let us get moving without so much talk."

These assertions, which many people will find discouraging (weak people always need to be told they are not), bring me to another of your questions and that is, why Latin American intellectuals have been recognized abroad sooner than in their own countries. If this question had some foundation twenty or twenty-five years ago, it seems to me absurd today. To cite only the most outstanding figures in fiction, neither Borges, nor Juan Rulfo, nor Carpentier, nor Vargas Llosa, nor Fuentes, nor Asturias, nor Lezama Lima, nor García Márquez has depended on foreigners to be understood and for readers to acknowledge his worth; and this is even more true of the poetry of Neruda and Octavio Paz. The fact that I have lived and worked in France for seventeen years might well have had some such effect, yet all my books achieved their success in Spanish, and with Latin American readers. Once again, the problem is one of moral and intellectual underdevelopment; the superstitious belief in an accolade from some great English or German critic, publication by the NRF, or the news that some Argentine novel has been a best-seller in Italy will be cherished for some time to come. One has only to live on this side of the herring pond to be aware how unimportant all these things are, and that good Latin American critics and readers are recognizing their own authentic writers today, without needing some Maurice Nadeau or Susan Sontag to appear at the window, Annunciation-lily in hand. It is more than enough for one of our well-known critics or writers to point out the merits of some new novelist or poet for his books to spread all over Latin America immediately; for instance, I myself recently chanced to help José Lezama Lima and Néstor Sánchez gain the popularity they deserve. In one way or another we have achieved sovereignty in the literary field, thus increasing our responsibilities as creative artists, critics, and readers; the false umbilical cord connecting us with Europe has been cut (the other bonds, those great spiritual arteries, will never be cut—we should only bleed in vain); we are beginning to lead our own life; but the child is still very small, he wets his diapers and falls down all the time; to take him for a mature being would merely be one more illusion, and no less fatal than to continue to be attached to our spiritual mother countries.

This is the chief reason why another of your questions demands a more conclusive answer than critics and writers usu-

ally give. I was asked about the supposed "lost generation" of
Latin Americans exiled in Europe: Fuentes, Vargas Llosa, Sarduy,
and García Márquez among others. In the last few years the
fame of these writers has inevitably intensified a species of conscious or unconscious resentment among those who have stayed
at home (*honi soit qui mal y pense!*), and this has taken the
form of a generally futile search for reasons for their "exile,"
as well as emphatic reaffirmation of determination to remain
in situ on the part of those who work without leaving the corner
where their life began, as the poet says. I have suddenly remembered a tango that Azucena Maizani used to sing: "Don't
leave your suburb, be a good girl, and marry a man of your own
sort," and this whole question seems to me painfully idiotic at
a time when, for one thing, jets and the communication media
have robbed "exile" of that tragic value of eradication it had for
Ovidio, Dante, or Garcilaso, and for another, the "exiles" themselves are surprised every time anyone affixes that label to them
in conversation or an article. Talking of labels José María
Arguedas has given us a whole chemist's shop of them in a
recent article published in the Peruvian magazine *Amaru*. Obviously preferring resentment to intelligence, something always
deplorable in a *cronopio*, neither Arguedas nor anyone else will
get very far by means of these regional complexes, just as none
of the "exiles" would count for much if he renounced his status
as a Latin American in order to attach himself more or less
parasitically to any European literature. Arguedas was annoyed
because I said (in my open letter to Fernández Retamar) that
one sometimes had to go a long way away to see a landscape,
and that supranational vision often led to the essence of nationality being more acutely realized. I regret to say, Don José
María, that I understand that your compatriot Vargas Llosa gave
a picture of Peruvian reality in no way inferior to yours when
he wrote his two novels in Europe. As usual, the mistake is in
applying general conclusions to a problem whose solution is
purely particular; the important thing is that these writers should
not seem like "exiles" to their readers, and that their books
should preserve and extol and perfect the closest possible contact
with their country and its people. When you say that "provincial"

writers, as you call yourself, understand Rimbaud, Poe, and
Quevedo very well, but not *Ulysses,* what on earth do you mean?
Is it thought that living in London or Paris gives the keys to
wisdom? What an inferiority complex that shows! I know a man
who has never left his own district in Buenos Aires, yet he knows
more about André Breton, Man Ray, and Marcel Duchamp
than any European or North American critic. And when I say
know I am not referring to a facile accumulation of index cards
and books, but to that deep *understanding* you seek for in regard
to *Ulysses,* that participation beyond time, whether or not it
finds expression in literary form. You add consolingly: "We are
all provincials, whether nationally or supranationally." I agree;
but there is a slight difference between being a provincial like
Lezama Lima, who definitely knows more about *Ulysses* than
Penelope herself, and one of those provincials devoted to folklore, for whom all the music in the world begins and ends with
the five notes of an Indian flute. Why confuse individual taste
with national and literary obligations? You *do not like* being an
exile, and that is fair enough, but I feel sure that in whatever
part of the world you are you will go on writing like José María
Arguedas; why then should you doubt and suspect those who go
away because that is what *they like?* We "exiles" are neither
martyrs, fugitives, nor traitors; and let our readers stop reiterating
it!

An analysis of the idea of autochthony in Latin American
literature, and one of your questions about living writers, give
me a closing theme for these pages, over which many subscribers
to the magazine must by now be dropping asleep. In Cuba, a
little while ago, they asked me how much importance I attributed to a writer's autochthony and to what extent cultural con-
texts and racial tradition were necessary to me. I replied that
the question seemed to me ambiguous insofar as the notion of
autochthony was also ambiguous. In fact, what exactly does
"cultural context" mean at the present time? If we reduce it to
culture that is exclusively regional, we shall not get very far in
Latin America. And "racial tradition"? I am acquainted with
the use that may be made of these expressions by people who
always tend to think of reality as if it were a guitar. Borges once
asked an intransigent indigenist why instead of getting his books

printed he did not publish them in the form of quipus. * The truth is that the whole problem is unreal. What great writer is not autochthonous, even if his subjects seem to be disconnected from the themes folklorists see as fundamental to their race? The tree of culture is fed by sap from many sources, and what matters is that it should put forth leaves and its fruit be good to eat. The essence of being autochthonous is to write a work that the nation to which the author belongs will recognize, choose, and accept as its own, even if its pages are not always concerned with that nation and its traditions. Autochthony precedes or underlies local and national identities; it is not a prior condition or a measure to which our literature must be adjusted. And I return to all these beliefs when you ask my opinion of a book like García Márquez's *One Hundred Years of Solitude*. It seems to me one of the most admirable of South American novels, because, among other reasons, García Márquez understands better than anyone that feelings of autochthony always act as an outlet and not as a limitation. The setting of his book, Macondo, is incredibly Colombian and Latin American *just because it is much more besides*; it is derived from many other things, born of the multiform and, as it were, dazzling presence of literatures differing widely in time and space. I am not talking of "influences," a horrible professional word clung to desperately by those who cannot find the true keys to genius; I am talking of deep participation, of brotherhood on an essential plane, where *The Thousand and One Nights*, William Faulkner, Conrad, Stevenson, Luis Buñuel, Carlos Fuentes, the *douanier* Rousseau, the novels of chivalry, and many other things contribute to García Márquez's striking originality, that of a novelist who can create a national reality without ceasing to be aware that all the points of the compass surround him. Autochthony? Of course, yes, to choose *his own* reality without rejecting all other realities, to submit them to his creative gift and concentrate all the forces of the earth in this little place, Macondo, which we have now taken to our hearts as an imperishable myth.

In conclusion, I shall return to the beginning of this article, partly from my prevailing awareness of the cyclical nature of

* Peruvian knotted cords.

things, and partly because the ideological or political considerations I began with are the logical and necessary substratum of the literary considerations in the second part. There seems to me to be no use discussing whether our literature is autochthonous if we do not begin by being autochthonous on a national level and therefore on a Latin American one, if we do not achieve a profound revolution in every sphere and project men from our countries into the orbit of a more authentic destiny. We shall only really have our say when our lands and our people are ours. While there are colonists and gorillas in our countries, the battle for a Latin American literature must be—spiritually, linguistically, and aesthetically—*the same battle* that is being fought in so many other lands to put an end to the imperialism that degrades and disunites us.

GABRIEL GARCÍA MÁRQUEZ

GABRIEL GARCÍA MÁRQUEZ

New York City   June 3, 1971

The fact of the matter is that my pursuit of García
Márquez—a special trip from Paris to Barcelona, a two-week wait
in a Catalonian hotel, long-distance calls and cables and letters
from New York to Spain—actually started only after I handed
over to him, during our second and last meeting in the Barcelona
Ritz, the questionnaire I had prepared at his own suggestion. You
see, García Márquez is well known for his resistance to reporters,
and he was at that time only willing to grant a written interview.
Over a cup of tea he promised to have his answers ready in a
couple of days, suggesting that if I wait there I could follow
through my interview with new questions based on his written
statements. But from then on I was unable to reach García
Márquez, although before I left, he did get word to me through
his wife that he would mail me the manuscript—which I never
received.

Six months later, when García Márquez came to New York to
receive the honorary degree given to him by Columbia University,
he answered my telephone call without delay. The following
morning we met at his hotel, the Plaza, where we had an early
breakfast after persuading the maître d' to let us in—not because of
García Márquez's mafioso mustache, but because he was tieless.
Then we borrowed the deserted Persian Room, and this time, with
a whirling tape, we finished in less than three hours the long-
awaited interview.

Gabriel García Márquez (Gabo to his friends) was born in
1928 in Aracataca, a very small Colombian town close to a banana
plantation in a place called Macondo, an even tinier town in the

middle of nowhere, which García Márquez used to explore when he was a child.

Years later, he named the mythical land where some of his stories take place after Macondo, and closed the cycle with One Hundred Years of Solitude, the novel he began when he was eighteen. But as a young writer he had "neither the vital experience nor the literary means" to complete such a work (then called "The House") and decided instead to write Leaf Storm, his first book. Only in 1967, after many years of struggle and frustration in writing it, One Hundred Years of Solitude (his fifth book) was published in Buenos Aires, provoking—as the Peruvian novelist Mario Vargas Llosa wrote—"a literary earthquake throughout Latin America. The critics recognized the book as a masterpiece of the art of fiction and the public endorsed this opinion, systematically exhausting new editions. . . . Overnight, García Márquez became almost as famous as a great soccer player or an eminent singer of boleros." In 1969, the book's translation was selected by the Académie Française as the best foreign book of the year and other translations earned an equally enthusiastic response. But, according to the author, the best reviews he received came from the United States: "They are professional readers . . . some are progressive, others so reactionary, as they are supposed to be; but as readers, they are wonderful."

García Márquez doesn't consider himself an intellectual but "a writer who rushes into the arena like a bull and then attacks." For him, literature is a very simple game and "in a literary panorama dominated by Julio Cortázar's Hopscotch, Lezama Lima's Paradiso, Carlos Fuentes's A Change of Skin, and Guillermo Cabrera Infante's Three Trapped Tigers," writes Emir Rodríguez Monegal, "all experimental works to the limit of experimentation itself; all hard and demanding on their readers," García Márquez, in his One Hundred Years of Solitude, "with an olympian indifference to alien technique, sets himself free to narrate, with an incredible speed and apparent innocence, an absolutely lineal and chronological story . . . with its beginning, middle and end." And, as García Márquez himself says, it is the "least mysterious" of his books because "I tried to lead the reader by the hand so as not to get him lost at any moment."

Similarly, in a way, García Márquez had been led to success by

his friends—because it was his friends who took the manuscript
of Leaf Storm (1955) to the printer when they found it on his
desk after he has gone to Italy in 1954 as a reporter for the
Colombian daily El Espectador. Then in Paris, in 1957, after
the dictator Rojas Pinilla had shut down the newspaper, García
Márquez, who was living on credit in a Latin Quarter hotel,
finished No One Writes to the Colonel; but considering his work
a failure, he buried the manuscript, "tied with a colored ribbon in
the bottom of a suitcase." Subsequently, he returned to Colombia
to marry his fiancée, Mercedes—the same Mercedes of the
"sleepy eyes" engaged to Gabriel in One Hundred Years of
Solitude—and moved for a couple of years to Venezuela where,
while working as a journalist, he wrote Los funerales de Mamá
grande. From Caracas he went to New York as the correspondent
for Prensa Latina—revolutionary Cuba's news agency. Resigning
after several months, and traveling by land through the south
of the United States, he arrived in Mexico in 1961, where he
settled for several years. And there, again, it was García Márquez's
friends who arranged for his two recent books to be published in
1961–2, the same period in which his novel La mala hora, written
in Mexico, was published after winning a Colombian literary contest. His friends had forced him to submit the manuscript to
the competition after persuading him to change the original title,
"Este pueblo de mierda." "The truth is," says Mario Vargas Llosa,
"that without the obstinacy of his friends, García Márquez would
perhaps still today be an unknown writer."

Today García Márquez can allow himself to live as a "professional writer" on the success earned mainly from One Hundred
Years of Solitude—the saga of Macondo and the Buendías, which
starts in a world "so recent many things lacked names and in
order to indicate them it was necessary to point," a world where
carpets fly; the dead are resuscitated; a rain lasts exactly four years,
eleven months, and two days; the first Buendía spends his last
years tied to a chestnut tree in his orchard muttering in Latin;
tiny yellow flowers fall from the sky when he dies; Ursula, his
wife, lives through generations and generations; Aureliano discovers that literature is the best toy ever invented to mock the
public . . . and the chronicle ends when, after more than one
hundred years of the family's struggles to avoid the fulfillment of

an old prophecy, the line of the Buendías comes to an end when out of incestuous union a boy born with a pig's tail is devoured by an army of ants. And with this saga the author confirms what he said some time ago: "Everything is permitted to the writer, as long as he is capable of making it believable."

Postscript: Before leaving New York, García Márquez, who after our interview moved from his previous hotel to an undisclosed address, called to send me "a kiss as a gesture of tenderness." I then asked him how he spent the days in the city. "Great, Mercedes and I spent three delicious days shopping in New York." "Did you visit the museums? Did you go to the country?" "Of course not, and you can add to everything I told you that I don't like either art or nature."

Your resistance to journalists is well known, and in the present case a lot of persuasion and several months of waiting have been necessary to overcome it.

Look, I've got absolutely nothing against journalists. I've done the job myself and I know what it's like. But if at this stage of my life I were to answer all the questions they want to ask me, I shouldn't be able to work. Besides, I should also be left with nothing to say. You see I realize that just because I have a fellow feeling for journalists, interviews have in the end become a form of fiction for me. I want the reporter to go away with something new, so I try to find a different answer to the same old questions. One no longer tells the truth, and the interview becomes a novel instead of journalism. It's literary creation, pure fiction.

I don't object to fiction as a part of reality.

That could make a good interview!

In Relato de un náufrago *(The Story of a Castaway)—a journalistic report written in 1955 for Bogotá's newspaper El Espectador and published as a book in Barcelona in 1970—you narrate the odyssey of a sailor who lived for ten days adrift on a raft. Is there any element of fiction in that story?*

There's not a single invented detail in the whole account. That's what's so astonishing. If I had invented that story I would have said so, and been very proud of it too. I interviewed that boy from the Colombian navy—as I explain in my introduction to the book—and he told me his story in minute detail. As his cultural level was only fair he didn't realize the extreme importance of many of the details he told me spontaneously, and was surprised at my being so struck by them. By carrying out a form of psychoanalysis I helped him remember things—for instance, a seagull he saw flying over his raft—and in that way we succeeded in reconstructing his whole adventure. It went like a bomb! The idea had been to publish the story in five or six installments in *El Espectador* but by about the third there was such enthusiasm among the readers, and the circulation of the paper had increased so enormously, that the editor said to me, "I don't know how you're going to manage, but you must get at least twenty installments out of this." So then I set about enriching every detail.

As good a journalist as a writer . . .

It was my bread and butter for many years, wasn't it? . . . and now as a writer. I've earned my living at both professions.

Do you miss journalism?

Well, I do feel a great nostalgia for my journalist days. As things have turned out I couldn't be a hard-nosed reporter now, which was what I used to prefer . . . going wherever the news was, whether it was a war, a fight, or a beauty contest, landing by parachute if necessary. Although my work as a writer, particularly as I do it now, derives from the same source as my journalism, the elaboration is purely theoretical, whereas the other was done on the spot. Today, when I read some of the things I wrote as a journalist I'm full of admiration, much more than for my work as a novelist, although I can give all my time to that now. Journalism was different; I used to arrive at the newspaper office and the editor would say, "We've got just an hour before this piece of news must be handed in." I think I should be incapable of writing one of those pages nowadays, even in a month.

Why? Have you become more conscious of language?

I think one needs a certain degree of irresponsibility to be a writer. I was about twenty at that time and I was hardly aware what dynamite I held between my hands and in every page I produced. Now, particularly since *One Hundred Years of Solitude,* I've become very conscious of it because of the enormous interest the book has aroused . . . a boom of readers. I no longer think of what I write as if it would only be read by my wife and my friends, I know that a lot of people are waiting for it. Every letter I write weighs me down, you can't imagine how much! Then I nearly die of envy of my old journalist self, and the days when I used to dispatch the business so easily. It was terrific to be able to do that. . . .

How has the success of One Hundred Years of Solitude *affected your life? I remember your saying in Barcelona, "I'm tired of being García Márquez."*

It's changed my whole life. I was once asked, I can't remember where, how my life differed before and after that book, and I said that after it "there are four hundred more people." That's to say before the book I had my friends, but now there are enormous numbers of people who want to see me and talk to me—journalists, academics, readers. It's strange . . . most of my readers aren't interested in asking questions, they only want to talk about the book. That's very flattering if you consider case by case, but added up they begin to be a problem in one's life. I would like to please them all, but as that's impossible I have to act meanly . . . you see? For instance, by saying I'm leaving a town when all I'm really doing is changing my hotel. That's how vedettes behave, something I always hated, and I don't want to play the vedette. There is, besides, a problem of conscience when deceiving people and dodging them. All the same I have to lead my own life, so the m ment comes when I tell lies. Well, that can be boiled down to a cruder phrase than the one you mentioned. I say, "I've had it to the balls with García Márquez!"

Yes, but aren't you afraid that attitude may end by isolating you in an ivory tower, even against your will?

I'm always aware of that danger, and remind myself of it every day. That's why I went to the Caribbean coast of Colombia a few months ago, and from there explored the Lesser Antilles, island by island. I realized that by escaping from those contacts I was reducing myself to the four or five friends I make wherever I live. In Barcelona, for instance, we always mix with about four couples, people with whom we have everything in common. From the point of view of my private life and my character, that's marvelous—that's what I like, but a moment came when I realized that this life was affecting my novel. The culmination of my life—to be a professional writer—had been achieved in Barcelona, and I suddenly became aware that it was a terribly damaging thing to be. I was leading the life of the complete professional writer.

Could you describe what the life of a professional writer is like?

Listen, I'll tell you what a typical day is like. I always wake very early, at about six in the morning. I read the paper in bed, get up, drink my coffee while I listen to music on the radio, and at about nine—after the boys have gone to school —I sit down to write. I write without any sort of interruption until half past two, which is when the boys come home and noise begins in the house. I haven't answered the telephone all morning . . . my wife has been filtering calls. We lunch between half past two and three. If I've been to bed late the night before I have a siesta until four in the afternoon. From that time until six I read and listen to music—I always listen to music, except when I'm writing because I attend to it more than to what I'm writing. Then I go out and have a coffee with someone I have a date with and in the evening friends always come to the house. Well . . . that seems to be an ideal state of things for a professional writer, the culmination of all he's been aiming at. But, as you find out once you get

there, it's sterile. I realized that I'd become involved in a completely sterile existence—absolutely the opposite of the life I
led when I was a reporter, what I wanted to be—and that this
was having an effect on the novel I was writing—a novel based
on cold experience (in the sense that it no longer interested
me much), whereas my novels are usually based on old stories
combined with fresh experiences. That's the reason I went to
Barranquilla, the town where I was brought up and where all
my oldest friends live. But . . . I visit all the islands in the
Caribbean, I take no notes, I do nothing, I spend two days
here and then go on somewhere else . . . I ask myself, "What
did I come for?" I'm not very clear what I'm doing, but I know
I'm trying to oil some machinery that has ground to a halt.
Yes, there's a natural tendency—when you have solved a series
of material problems—to become bourgeois and shut yourself in
an ivory tower, but I have an urge, and also an instinct, to
escape from that situation—a sort of tug-of-war is going on
inside me. Even in Barranquilla—where I may be staying for a
short period of time, which has a lot to do with not being
isolated—I realize that I'm losing sight of a large area that
interests me, out of my tendency to confine myself to a small
group of friends. But this isn't me, it's imposed by the medium,
and I must defend myself. Just another argument, as you see,
which makes me say without dramatization but for the sake
of my work—"I've had it to the balls with García Márquez."

*Your awareness of the problem should make it easier to deal with
this crisis.*

I feel as if the crisis had lasted longer than I thought
it would, much longer than my publisher thought, much longer
than the critics thought. I keep on meeting someone who is
reading my book, someone who has the same reaction that
readers had four years ago. Readers seem to emerge from caves
like ants. It's really phenomenal. . . .

Which doesn't make it any less flattering.

Yes, I do think it's very flattering, but the difficulty is
how to deal with this phenomenon in practice. It's not only

the experience of meeting people who have read the book, and hearing what it meant to them (I've been told amazing things), it's the experience of being popular. Those books have brought me a popularity more like that of a singer or film star than a writer. All this has become quite fantastic, and strange things happen to me: since the time I was on night shift at the newspaper I have been very friendly with the taxi drivers of Barranquilla, because I used to go and drink coffee with those parked at the cab stand across the street. Many of them are still driving, and when I take their taxis today they don't want to be paid; but the other day one who obviously didn't know me took me home, and when I paid him he said to me confidentially: "Did you know that García Márquez lives here?" "How do you know?" I asked him. "Because I've often taken him in my cab," he replied. You notice that the phenomenon is being reversed, and the dog is biting its own tail . . . the myth has caught up with me.

Anecdotes for a novel . . .

It would be a novel about a novel.

The critics have written at length about your work. Which of them do you agree with most?

I don't want my answer to seem unappreciative, but the truth is—and I know it's difficult to believe—that I don't pay much attention to the critics. I don't know why, but I don't compare what I think with what they say. So I don't really know whether I agree with them or not. . . .

Aren't you interested in the critics' opinions?

They used to interest me a lot at first, but now rather less. They seem to have said very little that's new. There was a moment when I stopped reading them because they were conditioning me—in a way they were telling me what my next book ought to be like. As soon as the critics began rationalizing my work I kept on discovering things that were not convenient for me to discover. My work stopped being intuitive.

Melvin Maddocks of Life, said of One Hundred Years of Solitude, "Is Macondo meant to be taken as a sort of surrealistic history of Latin America? Or does García Márquez intend it as a metaphor for all modern men and their ailing communities?"

Nothing of the sort. I merely wanted to tell the story of a family who for a hundred years did everything they could to prevent having a son with a pig's tail, and just because of their very efforts to avoid having one they ended by doing so. Synthetically speaking, that's the plot of the book, but all that about symbolism . . . not at all. Someone who isn't a critic said that the interest the novel had aroused was probably due to the fact that it was the first real description of the private life of a Latin American family . . . we go into the bedroom, the bathroom, the kitchen, into every corner of the house. Of course I never said to myself, "I shall write a book that will be interesting for that reason," but now that it's written, and this has been said about it, I think it may be true. Anyway it's an interesting concept and not all that shit about a man's destiny, etc. . . .

I think the theme of solitude is a predominant one in your work.

It's the only subject I've written about, from my first book until the one I'm working on now, which is an apotheosis of the theme of solitude. Of absolute power, which I consider must be total solitude. I've been writing about that process from the first. The story of Colonel Aureliano Buendía—the wars he fought and his progress to power—is really a progress toward solitude. Not only is every member of his family solitary —as I've repeated often in the book, perhaps more than I ought—but there's also the anti-solidarity, even of people who sleep in the same bed. I think the critics who most nearly hit the mark were those who concluded that the whole disaster of Macondo—which is a telluric disaster as well—comes from this lack of solidarity—the solitude which results when everyone is acting for himself alone. That's then a political concept, and interests me as such—to give solitude the political connotation I believe it should have.

When you were writing it, were you consciously intending to convey a message?

I never think about conveying messages. My mental makeup is ideological and I can't get away from it—nor do I try or want to. Chesterton said that he could explain Catholicism starting from a pumpkin or a tramway. I think one could write *One Hundred Years of Solitude*, or a story about sailors, or the description of a football match, and still keep its ideological content. It's the ideological spectacles I wear that explain—not Catholicism in this case—but something else which I can't define. I have no preconceived intention to say this or the other thing in a book of mine. I'm solely interested in the behavior of the characters, not whether that behavior is exemplary or reprehensible.

Are you interested in your characters from a psychoanalytical point of view?

No, because that would need a scientific training which I don't possess. The opposite happens. I develop my characters and work on them, in the belief that I'm only making use of their poetical aspects. When a character has been assembled, some of the experts tell me that this is a psychoanalytic analysis. And I'm confronted then with a series of scientific assumptions that I don't hold and have never even dreamed of. In Buenos Aires—a city of psychoanalysts, as you know—some of them held a meeting to analyze *One Hundred Years of Solitude*. They came to the conclusion that it represented a well-sublimated Oedipus complex, and goodness knows what else. They discovered that the characters were perfectly coherent from a psychoanalytic point of view, they almost seemed like case histories.

And they talked about incest too.

What interested me was that the aunt should go to bed with her nephew, not the psychoanalytic origins of this event.

It still seems strange that, although machismo is one of the typical features of Latin American society, it's the women in your books who have strong, stable characters—or, as you've said yourself, they are masculine.

This didn't happen consciously, the critics made me see it, and set me a problem by so doing, because I now find it more difficult to work on that material. But there's no doubt that it's the power of women in the home—in society as it's organized, particularly in Latin America—that enables men to launch out into every sort of chimerical and strange adventure, which is what makes our America. This idea came to me from one of the true stories my grandmother used to tell about the civil wars of the last century, which can be more or less equated with Colonel Aureliano Buendía's wars. She told me that a certain man went to the war and said to his wife, "You'll decide what to do with your children." And for a year or more the wife was the one who kept the family going. In terms of litera-ture, I see that if it weren't for the women taking responsibility for the rearguard, the evil wars of the last century, which are so important in the history of our country, would never have taken place.

That shows that you're not antifeminist.

What I most definitely am is anti*machista*. *Machismo* is cowardly, a lack of manliness.

To return to the critics . . . you know that some of them have insinuated that One Hundred Years of Solitude *is a plagiarism of Balzac's* La Recherche de l'absolu. *Günther Lorenz suggested this at a writer's conference in Bonn in 1970. Luis Cova García pub-lished an article called "Coincidence or Plagiarism?" in the Hon-duran review* Ariel, *and in Paris a Balzac specialist, Professor Mar-celle Bargas, made a study of the two novels and drew attention to the fact that the vices of one society and period, as depicted by Balzac, had been transferred to* One Hundred Years of Solitude.

It's strange; someone who had heard these comments sent me Balzac's book, which I had never read. Balzac doesn't

interest me now, although he's sensational enough and I read
what I could of him at one time—however, I glanced through it.
It struck me that to say one book derives from the other is
pretty light and superficial. Also, even if I were prepared to
accept the fact that I had read it before and decided to plagiarize
it, only some five pages of my book could possibly have come
from *La Recherche*, and in the final analysis a single character,
the alchemist. Well . . . I ask you, five pages and one character
against three hundred pages and some two hundred characters
that don't come from Balzac's book. I think the critics ought
to have gone on and searched two hundred other books to see
where the rest of the characters came from. Besides which, I'm
not at all afraid of the idea of plagiarism. If I had to write
Romeo and Juliet tomorrow I would do it, and would feel
it was marvelous to have the chance to write it again. I've
talked a lot about the *Oedipus Rex* of Sophocles, and I believe
it has been the most important book in my life; ever since I
first read it I've been astonished by its absolute perfection. Once,
when I was at a place on the Colombian coast, I came across
a very similar situation to that of the drama of *Oedipus Rex*,
and I thought of writing something to be called *Oedipus the
Mayor*. In this case I wouldn't have been charged with plagiarism
because I should have begun by calling him Oedipus. I think
the idea of plagiarism is already finished. I can myself say where
I find Cervantes or Rabelais in *One Hundred Years of Solitude*
—not as to quality but because of things I've taken from them
and put there. But I can also take the book line by line—and
this is a point the critics will never be able to reach—and say
what event or memory from real life each comes from. It's a
very curious experience to talk to my mother about such things;
she remembers the origin of many of the episodes, and naturally
describes them more faithfully than I do because she hasn't
elaborated them as literature.

When did you start writing?

As far back as I can remember. My earliest recollection
is of drawing "comics" and I realize now that this may have been
because I couldn't yet write. I've always tried to find ways of

telling stories and I've stuck to literature as the most accessible.
But I think my vocation is not so much to be a writer as a
story-teller.

Is that because you prefer the spoken word to writing?

Of course. The splendid thing is to tell a story and
for that story to die there and then. What I should find ideal
would be to tell you the story of the novel I'm now writing,
and I'm sure it would produce the same effect I'm trying to get
by writing it, but without so much effort. At home, at any
time of day, I recount my dreams, what has happened to me
or not happened to me. I don't tell my children make-believe
stories, but about things that have happened, and they like that
very much. Vargas Llosa, in the book he's doing on the literary vocation, *García Márquez, historia de un deicidio*, takes my work as
an example and says I'm a seedbed of anecdotes. To be liked because I've told a good story: that's my true ambition.

I've read that when you finish El otoño del patriarca (The Autumn of the Patriarch) *you're going to write stories instead of
novels.*

I've got a notebook where I'm jotting down the stories
that occur to me and making notes for them. I've already got
about sixty, and I fancy I shall reach a hundred. What is curious
is the process of internal elaboration. The story—which may
arise from a phrase or an incident—either occurs to me complete
in a fraction of a second or not at all. It has no starting point;
a character just arrives or goes away. I'll tell you an anecdote
which may give you some idea how mysteriously I arrive at
a story. One night in Barcelona when we had visitors, the
lights suddenly went out. As the trouble was local we sent for an
electrician. While he was putting the defect right and I was
holding a candle for him to see by, I asked him, "What the
devil's happened to the light?" "Light is like water," he said,
"you turn a tap and out it comes, and the meter registers it as
it comes through." In that fraction of a second, a complete
story came to me:

In a city away from the sea—it might be Paris, Madrid, or

Bogotá—there live on the fifth floor a young couple and their two children of ten and seven. One day the children ask their parents to give them a rowboat. "How can we give you a rowboat?" says the father. "What can you do with it in this town? When we go to the seaside in the summer we can hire one." The children obstinately persist that they want a rowboat, until their father says: "If you get the top places in school I'll give you one." They get the top places, their father buys the boat, and when they take it up to the fifth floor he asks them: "What are you going to do with it?" "Nothing," they reply, "we just wanted to have it. We'll put it in our room." One night when their parents are at the cinema, the children break an electric light bulb and the light begins to flow out—just like water—filling the whole house three feet deep. They take the boat and begin rowing through the bedrooms and the kitchen. When it's time for their parents to return they put it away in their room and pull up the plugs so that the light can drain away, put back the bulb, and . . . nothing has happened. This becomes such a splendid game that they begin to let the light reach a greater depth, put on dark glasses and flippers, and swim under the beds and tables, practicing underwater fishing. . . . One night, passersby in the street notice light streaming out of the windows and flooding the street, and they send for the fire brigade. When the firemen open the door they find that the children had been so absorbed in their game that they had allowed the light to reach the ceiling, and are floating in the light, drowned.

Can you tell me how it was that this complete story, just as I've told you, occurred to me within a fraction of a second? Naturally, as I've told it often, I find a new angle every time —change one thing for another or add a detail—but the idea remains the same. There's nothing deliberate or predictable in all this, nor do I know when it's going to happen to me. I'm at the mercy of my imagination, and that's what says *yes* or *no.*

Have you written that story yet?

I've merely made a note: #7 "Children drowning in light." That's all. But I carry that story in my head, like all the rest, and I revise it from time to time. For instance, I take a taxi and remember story #57. I completely revise it and realize that in an incident that had occurred to me the roses I visualized aren't roses at all but violets. I incorporate this change in my story and make a mental note of it.

What a memory!

No, I only forget what has no literary value for me.

Why don't you write it when you first think of it?

If I'm writing a novel I can't mix other things with it, I must work at that book only, even if it takes me more than ten years.

Don't you unconsciously incorporate these stories in the novel you're writing?

These stories are in completely separate compartments and have nothing to do with the book about the dictator. That happened with *Big Mama's Funeral La mala hora* (Bad Times) and *No One Writes to the Colonel,* because I was working on the lot of them at practically the same time.

Have you never thought of becoming an actor?

I'm terribly inhibited in front of cameras or a microphone. But in any case I would be the author or director.

On one occasion you said, "I've become a writer out of timidity. My real inclination is to be a conjuror, but I get so confused when I try to perform a trick that I've had to take refuge in the solitude of literature. In my case, being a writer is a stupendous task, because I'm a numbskull at writing."

What a good thing to read me! The bit about my real vocation being to be a conjuror corresponds exactly with what I've told you. It would delight me to have success telling stories in salons, like a conjuror pulling rabbits out of a hat.

Is writing a great effort for you?

Terribly hard work, more so all the time. When I say I'm a writer out of timidity, it's because what I ought to do is fill this room, and go out and tell my story, but my timidity prevents me. I couldn't have carried on this conversation of ours if there had been two more people at this table; I should have felt I couldn't control my audience. Therefore when I want to tell a story I do it in writing, sitting alone in my room and working hard. It's agonizing work, but sensational. Conquering the problem of writing is so delightful and so thrilling that it makes up for all the work . . . it's like giving birth.

Since you first made contact in 1954 with the Experimental Cinema in Rome, you've written scripts and directed films. Doesn't this expressive medium interest you any more?

No, because my work in the cinema showed me that what the writer succeeds in putting across is very little. So many interests, so many compromises are involved that in the end very little of the original story remains. Whereas if I shut myself in my room I can write exactly what I want to. I don't have to put up with an editor saying, "Get rid of that character or incident and put in another."

Don't you think the visual impact of the cinema can be greater than that of literature?

I used to think so, but then I realized the limitations of the cinema. That very visual aspect puts it at a disadvantage compared to literature. It's so immediate, so forceful, that it's difficult for the viewer to go beyond it. In literature one can go much further and at the same time create an impact that is visual, auditory, or of any other sort.

Don't you think the novel is a disappearing form?

If it disappears it'll be because those who write it are disappearing. It's difficult to imagine any period in the history of humanity when so many novels have been read as at present. Whole novels are published in all the magazines—both for men and for women—and in the newspapers, while for the almost illiterate there are comic strips which are the apotheosis of the novel. What we could begin to discuss is the quality of the novels that are being read, but that has nothing to do with the reading public, only with the cultural level the state has given them. To return to the phenomenon of *One Hundred Years of Solitude*—and I don't want to know what caused it, nor to analyze it, nor for others to analyze it at present—I know of readers, people without intellectual training, who have passed straight from "comics" to that book and have read it with the same interest as the other things they have been given, because they underestimated it intellectually. It's the publishers, who, underestimating the public, publish books of very low literary value; and the curious thing is that that level also consumes books like *One Hundred Years of Solitude*. That's why I think there's a boom in novel readers. Novels are read everywhere, at all times, all over the world. Story-telling will always be of interest. A man comes home and starts telling his wife what's happened to him . . . or what hasn't happened so that his wife believes it.

In your interview with Luis Harss you say: "I've got fixed political opinions . . . but my literary ideas change with my digestion." What are your literary ideas today at eight o'clock in the morning?

I've said that anyone who doesn't contradict himself is a dogmatist, and every dogmatist is a reactionary. I contradict myself all the time and particularly on the subject of literature. My method of work is such that I would never reach the point of literary creation without constantly contradicting myself, correcting myself, and making mistakes. If I didn't I should be always writing the same book. I have no recipe. . . .

Have you a method for writing a novel?

Not always the same, nor do I have a method for looking for a novel. The act of writing is the least important problem. What's difficult is assembling the novel and solving it according to my view of it.

Do you know whether analysis, experience, or imagination controls that process?

If I were to try and make such an analysis I think I should lose a great deal of spontaneity. When I want to write something it's because I feel that it's worth saying. Still more . . . when I write a story it's because I should enjoy reading it. What happens is that I set about telling myself a story. That's my method of writing, but although I have a hunch which of these—intuition, experience, or analysis—plays the greater part, I avoid inquiring deeply into the question because either my character or my system of writing makes me try to prevent my work becoming mechanical.

What is the starting point of your novels?

A completely visual image. I suppose that some writers begin with a phrase, an idea, or a concept. I always begin with an image. The starting point of *Leaf Storm* is an old man taking his grandson to a funeral, in *No One Writes to the Colonel* it's an old man waiting, and in *One Hundred Years*, an old man taking his grandson to the fair to find out what ice is.

They all begin with an old man. . . .

The guardian angel of my infancy was an old man— my grandfather. My parents didn't bring me up, they left me in my grandparents' house. My grandmother used to tell me stories and my grandfather took me to see things. Those were the circumstances in which my world was constructed. And now I'm aware that I always see the image of my grandfather showing me things.

How does that first image develop?

I leave it to simmer . . . it's not a very conscious process. All my books have been brooded over for a good many years. *One Hundred Years* for fifteen or seventeen, and I began thinking about the one I'm writing now a long while ago.

How long do you take writing them?

That's rather quicker. I wrote *One Hundred Years of Solitude* in less than two years—which I think is pretty good. Before, I always used to write when I was tired, in my free time after my other work. Now that I'm not under economic pressure and I have nothing to do but write, I like indulging in the luxury of doing it when I want to, when I feel the impulse. I'm working differently on the book about the old dictator who lived for 250 years—I'm leaving it alone to see where it goes.

Do you correct your writing much?

As to that, I keep on changing. I wrote my first things straight off without a break, and afterwards made a great many corrections on the manuscript, made copies, and corrected it again. And now I've acquired a habit which I think is a vice. I correct line by line as I work, so that by the time a page is finished it's practically ready for the publisher. If it has a blot or a slip it won't do for me.

I can't believe you're so methodical.

Terribly! You can't imagine how clean those pages are. And I've got an electric typewriter. The only thing I am methodical about is my work, but it's an almost emotional question. The page that I've just finished looks so beautiful, so clean, that it would be a pity to spoil it with a correction. But within a week I don't care about it so much—I only care about what I'm actually working on—and then I can correct it.

And the galley proofs?

In *One Hundred Years* I only changed one word, although Paco Porrúa, literary editor of *Sudamericana*, told me to change as many as I liked. I believe the ideal thing would be to write a book, have it printed, and correct it afterwards. When one sends something to the printers and then reads it in print one seems to have taken a step, whether forward or backward, of extreme importance.

Do you read your books after they are published?

When the first copy arrives I cut everything I have to do, and sit down—at once—and read it straight through. It has already become a different book from the one I know because a distance has been established between author and book. This is the first time I'm reading it as a reader. Those letters before my eyes weren't made by my typewriter, they aren't my words, they are others that have gone out into the world and don't belong to me. After that first reading I've never again read *One Hundred Years of Solitude.*

How and when do you decide on the title?

A book finds its title sooner or later. It's not a thing I consider very important.

Do you talk to your friends about what you're writing?

When I tell them something it's because I'm not quite sure about it, and I generally don't let it remain in the novel. I know from the reaction of my listeners—by means of some strange electric current—whether it's going to work or not. Although they may say sincerely, "Marvelous, terrific," there's something in their eyes that tells me it won't do. When I'm working on a novel I'm more of a nuisance to my friends than you can possibly imagine. They have to put up with it all, and afterwards when they read the book they get a surprise—as happened to those who were with me when I was writing *One Hundred Years*—because they don't find in it any of the incidents I told them about. What I had talked about was rejected material.

Do you think about your readers when you write?

I think of four or five particular people who make up my public when I'm writing. As I consider what would please or displease them, I add or subtract things, and so the book is put together.

Do you generally keep the material that has accumulated while you are working?

I don't keep anything. When the publishers notified me that they had received my first manuscript of *One Hundred Years of Solitude*, Mercedes helped me throw away a drawerful of working notes, diagrams, sketches, and memoranda. I threw it out, not only so that the way the book was constructed shouldn't be known—that's something absolutely private—but in case that material should ever be sold. To sell it would be selling my soul, and I'm not going to let anyone do it, not even my children.

Which of your writings do you like best?

Leaf Storm, the first book I ever wrote. I think a lot of what I've done since then springs from it. It's the most spontaneous, the one I wrote with most difficulty and with fewer technical resources. I knew fewer writers' tricks, fewer nasty tricks at that time. It seems to me a rather awkward, vulnerable book, but completely spontaneous, and it has a raw sincerity not to be found in the others. I know exactly how *Leaf Storm* went straight from my guts onto the paper. The others also came from my guts but I had served my apprenticeship. . . . I worked on them, I cooked them, I added salt and pepper.

What influences have you been conscious of?

The notion of influence is a problem for the critics. I'm not very clear about it, I don't know exactly what they mean by it. I think the fundamental influence on my writing has been Kafka's *Metamorphosis*, although I don't know whether the critics who analyze my work discover any direct influence in the books themselves. I remember the moment when I bought the book, and how as I read it I began to long to write. My first stories date from that time—about 1946, when I had just gotten my baccalaureate. Probably as soon as I say this to the critics—they've got no detector, they have to get certain things from the author himself—they'll discover the influence. But what sort of influence? He made me want to write. A decisive influence, which is perhaps more obvious, is *Oedipus Rex*. It's a perfect structure, wherein the investigator discovers that he is himself the assassin . . . an apotheosis of technical perfection. All the critics have mentioned Faulkner's influence. I accept that, but not in the sense they think when they see me as an author who read Faulkner, assimilated him, was impressed by him and, consciously or unconsciously, tries to write like him. That is more or less, roughly, what I understand by an influence. What I owe to Faulkner is something entirely different. I was born in Aracataca, the banana-growing country where the United Fruit Company was established. It was in this region, where the Fruit Company was building towns and hospitals and draining some zones, that I grew up and received my first impressions. Then, many years later, I read Faulkner and found that his whole world—the world of the southern United States which he writes about—was very like my world, that it was created by the same people. And also, when later I traveled in the southern states, I found evidence—on those hot, dusty roads, with the same vegetation, trees, and great houses—of the similarity between our two worlds. One mustn't forget that Faulkner is in a way a Latin American writer. His world is that of the Gulf of Mexico. What I found in him was affinities between our experiences, which were not as different as might appear at first sight. Well, this sort of influence of course exists, but it's very different from what the critics pointed out.

Others speak of Borges and Carpentier, and think they see the same telluric and mythological approach as that of Rómulo Gallegos, Evaristo Carrera Campos, or Asturias. . . .

Whether I follow the same telluric line or not I really don't know. It's the same world, the same Latin America, isn't it? Borges and Carpentier, no. I read them when I had already written quite a lot. That's to say I would have written what I did anyhow, without Borges and Carpentier, but not without

Faulkner. And I also believe that after a certain moment—by searching for my own language and refining my work—I have taken a course aimed at eliminating Faulkner's influence, which is much in evidence in *Leaf Storm* but not in *One Hundred Years*. But I don't like making this sort of analysis. My position is that of a creator, not of a critic. It's not my job, it's not my vocation, I don't think I'm good at it.

What books do you read nowadays?

I scarcely read at all, it doesn't interest me. I read documentaries and memoirs—the lives of men who have held power, memoirs and revelations by secretaries, even if they aren't true—out of professional interest in the book I'm working on. My problem is that I am and have always been a very poor reader. As soon as a book bores me I give it up. As a boy I began reading *Don Quixote*, got bored and stopped in the middle. I've read it and reread it since, but only because I enjoy it, not because it's obligatory reading. That has been my method of reading and I have the same concept of reading while I'm writing. I'm always in terror lest at some page the reader may get bored and throw down the book. Therefore I try not to bore him, so that he shan't treat me as I treat others. The only novels I read now are those by my friends because I'm curious to know what they're doing, not out of literary interest. For many years I read, or devoured, quantities of novels, particularly adventure stories in which a lot happened. But I was never a methodical reader. Since I didn't have the money to buy books, I used to read what fell into my hands, books lent me by friends who were almost all teachers of literature or concerned with it. What I have always read, almost more than novels, is poetry. In fact I began with poetry, although I've never written poetry in verse, and I'm always trying to find poetical solutions. I think my last novel is really an extremely long poem about the loneliness of a dictator.

Are you interested in concrete poetry?

I've lost sight of poetry altogether. I don't know precisely where poets are going, what they are doing, or even what they want to do. I suppose it's important for them to make experiments of every description and look for new ways of expressing themselves, but it's very difficult to judge something in the experimental stage. They don't interest me. I've solved the problem of my own means of expressing myself, and I can't now be involved in other things.

You mentioned that you are always listening to music. . . .

I enjoy it much more than any other manifestation of art, even than literature. With every day that passes I need it more, and I have the impression that it acts on me like a drug. When I travel I always take along a portable radio with headphones, and I measure the world by the concerts I can hear—from Madrid to San Juan in Puerto Rico one can hear Beethoven's nine symphonies. I remember that when I was traveling by train in Germany with Vargas Llosa—on an extremely hot day when I was in a very bad mood—how I suddenly, perhaps unconsciously, cut myself off and listened to music. Mario said to me afterwards, "It's incredible, your mood has changed, you've calmed down." In Barcelona, where I can have a fully equipped set, in times of great depression I have sometimes listened to music from two in the afternoon until four in the morning, without moving. My passion for music is like a secret vice, and I hardly ever talk about it. It's a part of my most profoundly private life. I'm not at all attached to objects—I don't consider the furniture and other things in my house as mine, but as belonging to my wife and children—and the only objects I'm fond of are my musical apparatuses. My typewriter is a necessity, otherwise I would get rid of it. Nor do I possess a library. When I've read a book I throw it out, or leave it somewhere.

Let's come back to your statement that you "have fixed political opinions." Can you say exactly what they are?

I think the world ought to be socialist, that it will be, and that we should help this to happen as quickly as possible. But I'm greatly disillusioned by the socialism of the Soviet Union. They arrived at their brand of socialism through special experiences and conditions, and are trying to impose in other countries their own bureaucracy, their own authoritarianism, and their own lack of historical vision. That isn't socialism and it's the great problem of the present moment.

When the Cuban poet Heberto Padilla was imprisoned and made a signed "confession," international intellectuals—who have always supported the Cuban Revolution—sent two letters of protest to Castro in the course of a month. After the first letter—which you also signed—Castro said in his May Day speech that the signatories were pseudo-revolutionary intellectuals who "gossip in Paris literary salons" and pass judgment on the Cuban revolution; Cuba, he said, does not need the support of "bourgeois intrigue-mongers." According to international commentaries this showed a rupture between intellectuals and the Cuban regime. What's your own position?

When all this came to light, international and Colombian news agencies naturally began to press me to give my opinion, because in a way I was involved in all this. I didn't want to do so until I had complete information and could read the shorthand reports of the speeches. I couldn't give an opinion on such an important matter merely on the versions put out by the information agencies. Besides, I knew at the time that I was going to receive a Doctorate of Letters at Columbia University. For anyone who didn't know that this decision had been made previously, it might lead them to believe that I was going to the United States because I had broken with Castro. I therefore made a statement to the press, completely clarifying my position toward Castro, my doctorate, and my return to the United States after twelve years, during which time I had been refused a visa:

(Summary of García Márquez's statement to the Colombian press, May 29, 1971):

Columbia University is not the government of the United States, but a stronghold of nonconformism, of intellectual integrity . . . of those who will annihilate the decrepit system of their country. I understand that I am being granted this distinction principally as a writer, but those who grant it are

not unaware that I am infinitely hostile to the prevailing
order in the United States. . . . It is good for you to know
that I only discuss these decisions with my friends, and
especially with the taxi drivers of Barranquilla, who are champions of common sense. . . . The conflict between a group
of Latin American writers and Fidel Castro is an ephemeral
triumph for the news agencies. I have here the documents
relevant to this matter, including the shorthand report of
Fidel Castro's speech, and although it does in fact contain
some very stern passages, none of them lend support to the
sinister interpretations given them by the international news
agencies. Certainly we have to do with a speech in which
Fidel Castro makes fundamental proposals about cultural matters, but the foreign correspondents said nothing about these;
instead they carefully extracted and put together again as
they chose certain loose phrases so as to make it seem that
Fidel Castro had said what in fact he had not said . . . I
didn't sign the letter of protest because I was not in favor
of their sending it. The truth is that I believe such public
messages are valueless as a means to the desired ends, but
very useful for hostile propaganda. . . . However, I will at
no time cast doubt on the intellectual integrity and revolutionary sincerity of those who signed the letter, who include
some of my best friends. . . . When writers wish to take
part in politics they are actually being moral rather than
political, and those two terms aren't always compatible. Politicians, for their part, resist writers meddling in their affairs,
and on the whole accept us when we support them and reject
us when we are against them. But that's hardly a catastrophe.
On the contrary, it's a very useful, very positive dialectic
contradiction, which will continue until the end of mankind,
even if politicians die of rage and writers are skinned
alive. . . . The only pending matter is that of the poet
Heberto Padilla. Personally, I haven't succeeded in convincing
myself that Padilla's self-criticism was spontaneous and sincere.
I don't understand how after so many years of contact with
the Cuban experiment, living daily through the drama of
the revolution, a man like Heberto Padilla could not have
taken before the stand he suddenly took in prison. The tone

of his confession is so exaggerated, so abject, that it seems
to have been obtained by ignominious means. I don't know
whether Heberto Padilla is doing harm to the revolution by
his attitude, but his self-criticism certainly is doing a great
deal of harm. The proof of this is to be found in the way
the text divulged by Prensa Latina was splashed in the hostile
Cuban press. . . . If a germ of Stalinism really exists in Cuba
we shall see it very soon, it will be proclaimed by Fidel
Castro himself. . . . In 1961 there was an attempt to impose
Stalinist methods, and Fidel Castro denounced it in public
and eradicated it in embryo. There is no reason to think that
the same wouldn't happen today, because the vitality, the
good health of the Cuban Revolution cannot have decreased
since that time. . . . Of course I am not breaking with the
Cuban Revolution. Moreover: none of the writers who pro-
tested about the Padilla case has broken with the Cuban
Revolution so far as I know. Mario Vargas Llosa himself
commented on this in a statement subsequent to his famous
letter, but the newspapers relegated it to the corner for invisible news. No: the Cuban Revolution is an event of fundamental importance to Latin America and the whole world,
and our solidarity with it can't be affected by a blunder in
cultural politics, even when the blunder is as large and as
serious as the suspect self-criticism of Heberto Padilla. . . .

*Are the hopes of intellectuals being accomplished by the Cuban
Revolution?*

What I believe to be really grave is that we intellectuals
tend to protest and react only when we are personally affected,
but do nothing when the same thing happens to a fisherman
or a priest. What we ought to do is look at the revolution as
an integral phenomenon, and see how the positive aspects infinitely outweigh the negative ones. Of course, manifestations
such as the Padilla case are extremely dangerous, but they are
obstacles that it shouldn't be hard to surmount. If not it would
indeed be grievous, because everything that has been done—
making people literate, giving them education and economic
independence—is irreversible and will last much longer than

Padilla and Fidel. That is my position and I won't budge from it. I'm not prepared to throw a revolution on the rubbish heap every ten years.

Do you agree with the socialism of the Chilean Popular Front?

My ambition is for all Latin America to become socialist, but nowadays people are seduced by the idea of peaceful and constitutional socialism. This seems to be all very well for electoral purposes, but I believe it to be completely utopian. Chile is heading toward violent and dramatic events. If the Popular Front goes ahead—with intelligence and great tact, with reasonably firm and swift steps—a moment will come when they will encounter a wall of serious opposition. The United States is not interfering at present, but it won't always stand by with folded arms. It won't really accept that Chile is a socialist country. It won't allow that, and don't let's be under any illusions on that point.

Do you see violence as the sole solution?

It's not that I see it as a solution, but I think that a moment will come when that wall of opposition can only be surmounted by violence. Unfortunately, I believe that to be inevitable. I think what is happening in Chile is very good as reform, but not as revolution.

You said of imperialist cultural penetration—in your interview with Jean-Michel Fossey—that the United States was trying to attract intellectuals by giving them awards and creating organizations where a lot of propaganda went on. . . .

I have a profound belief in the power of money to corrupt. If a writer, particularly at the start of his career, is given an award or a grant—whether it comes from the United States, the Soviet Union, or from Mars—he is to some extent compromised. Out of gratitude, or even to show that he hasn't been compromised, this help affects his work. This is much more serious in the socialist countries where a writer is supposed to be working for the state. That in itself is the major compromise of his independence. If he writes what he wants, or what he feels, he runs the risk that some official—almost certainly a failed writer—will decide whether it can be published or not. So that I think that as long as a writer can't live by his books he ought to take on some marginal work. In my case it was journalism and advertising, but no one ever paid me to write.

Neither did you accept the office of Colombian consul in Barcelona.

I always refuse public office, but I rejected that particular post because I don't want to represent any government. I think I said in an interview that one Miguel Angel Asturias was enough for Latin America.

Why did you say that?

His personal behavior sets a bad example. Winner of the Nobel Prize and the Lenin Prize, he goes to Paris as ambassador representing a government as reactionary as Guatemala's. A government fighting against the guerrillas who stand for everything he says he has stood for all his life. Imperialists don't attack him for accepting the embassy of a reactionary government, because it was prudent, nor does the Soviet Union because he's a Lenin Prize winner. I've been asked recently what I thought of Neruda becoming an ambassador. I didn't say that a writer shouldn't be an ambassador—though I never would myself—but representing the government of Guatemala is not the same thing as representing the Chilean Popular Front.

You must often have been asked how you manage to live in a country with such a dictatorship as Spain's.

It seems to me that if you give a writer the choice of living in heaven or hell, he chooses hell . . . there's much more literary material there.

Hell—and dictators—also exist in Latin America.

I'd like to clear this matter up. I'm forty-three years old and I've spent three of them in Spain, one in Rome, two or three in Paris, seven or eight in Mexico, and the rest in Colombia. I've not left one city merely in order to live in another. It's worse than that. I don't live anywhere, which causes some anguish. Also I don't agree with an idea that has arisen —and been much discussed lately—that writers live in Europe so as to live it up. It's not like that. One doesn't go in search of that—anyone who wants to can find it anywhere—and often life is very difficult. But I haven't the smallest doubt that it's very important for a Latin American writer to view Latin America from Europe at some given moment. My ideal solution would be to be able to go back and forth, but (1) it's very expensive, and (2) I'm restricted by the fact that I dislike air travel . . . although I spend my life in airplanes. The truth is that at the moment I don't care where I live. I always find people who interest me, whether in Barranquilla, Rome, Paris, or Barcelona.

Why not New York?

New York was responsible for withdrawing my visa. I lived in this city in 1960 as correspondent for Prensa Latina, and although I did nothing except act as correspondent—collecting news and dispatching it—when I left to go to Mexico they took away my resident's card and entered me in their "black book." Every two or three years I've asked for a visa again, but they went on automatically refusing it. I think it was mainly a bureaucratic matter. I've received one now. As a city, New York is the greatest phenomenon of the twentieth century, and therefore it's a serious restriction of one's life not to be able to come here every year, even for a week. But I doubt if I have strong enough nerves to live in New York. I find it so overwhelming. The United States is an extraordinary country; a nation that creates such a city as New York, or the rest of the country—which has nothing to do with the system or the government—could do anything. I believe they will be the ones to create a great socialist revolution, and a good one too.

What have you to say about the solemn title conferred on you by Columbia University?

I can't believe it. . . . What I find completely puzzling and disconcerting is not the honor nor the recognition—although such things can be true—but that a university like Columbia should decide to choose me out of twelve men from the whole world. The last thing I ever expected in this world was a doctorate of letters. My path has always been anti-academic; I never graduated as doctor of law from the university because I didn't want to be a "doctor"—and suddenly I find myself in the thick of the academic world. But this is something quite foreign to me, it's off my beat. It's as if they gave the Nobel Prize to a bullfighter. My first impulse was not to accept it, but then I took a plebiscite among my friends and none of them could understand what reason I had for refusing. I could have given political reasons, but they wouldn't have been genuine, because we all know, and we have heard declared in university speeches, that imperialism is not their prevailing system. So that to accept the honor wouldn't involve me politically with the United States, and there was no need to mention the subject. It was rather a moral question. I always react against ceremonies —remember that I come from the most ceremonious country in the world—and I asked myself, "What should I be doing in a literary academy in cap and gown?" At my friends' insistence I accepted the title of *doctor honoris causa* and now I'm delighted, not only at having accepted it, but also on behalf of my country and Latin America. All this patriotism one pretends not to care about suddenly does become important. In these last days, and more still during the ceremony, I thought about the strange things that were happening to me. There was a moment when I thought that death must be like that . . . something that happens when one least expects it, something that has nothing to do with me. Also I have been approached to publish an edition of my complete works, but I emphatically refused this in my lifetime, since I have always thought of it as a posthumous honor. During the ceremony I had the same feeling . . . that such things happened to one after death. The type of recognition I have always desired and appreciated is that of people who read me and talk to me about my books, not with admiration or enthusiasm but with affection. What really touched me during the ceremony in the university, and you can't imagine how deeply, was when during the return procession the Latin Americans who had practically taken over the campus came unobtrusively forward saying "Up with Latin America!" "Forward, Latin America!" "Go ahead, Latin America!" At that moment, for the first time, I felt moved and was glad I had accepted.

GUILLERMO CABRERA INFANTE

GUILLERMO CABRERA INFANTE

London   October 5–12, 1970

Basic knowhow for interviewing the Cuban writer Guillermo Cabrera Infante: 1) Diego Offenbach, a British-born Siamese cat, has priority over any reporter. 2) No appointment may interfere with the rerun—on the TV or in a theater—of Cabrera Infante's favorite movies. 3) No interview is granted on weekends when Cabrera Infante's two teenage daughters from his previous marriage come home from their English boarding school. 4) No picture of him, or of his family, may be taken near objects or people Cabrera Infante considers to be under a "diabolic spell."

Then, with time and cassettes, the thing to do is to sit down in the tiger-patterned wallpapered library of Cabrera Infante's London apartment—his castle in exile—and, in the mist of his Cuban cigars and the Cuban cookery of his wife Miriam Gómez, listen to Cabrera Infante's entertaining conversation, which is larded with multilingual puns.

Of medium height, with spectacled, dark eyes, rather long straight black hair and a mustache drooping down to his bearded chin, Cabrera Infante, who was born in 1929, looks Mexican to Octavio Paz, Nepalese to Marie-José Paz, and Chinese to his Cuban friends. In a knee-length red terrycloth robe over bellbottom slacks (as Cabrera Infante dressed for our morning conversations) he looked, to me, like a hippie descended from an ancient Oriental sage.

Like many Cubans, Cabrera Infante talks at breakneck speed, but his talk is a feast of words. With wit, humor, and irony as well as a certain sadness, he talked about his life as journalist, movie critic, movie script writer, and novelist; and, in addition, about his last book, Three Trapped Tigers (referred to mostly as TTT)—a prize-winning novel in Paris, Brussels, and Spain, "a brilliantly loony memoir of life in Havana just before Castro's takeover" in which "even the awful jokes (18,481 of them) are good," about literature in general, about politics, about Cuba's revolution, about its revolutionaries, and about his own participation until his exile in 1965.

Now, Cabrera Infante's only "acts of terrorism" are "against the established Spanish language . . . by means of violent changes and revolutions" done with the typewriter, and graced solely by Offenbach's presence.

On his desk, Cabrera Infante keeps a symbolic twelve-inch-high calamine figure (a fencer without a head) he brought from Cuba. "This fin de siècle athletic figure, so popular in Montparnasse stories," says Cabrera Infante, "dressed with the elegance of a dandy and ready to follow the rules of the game, was probably decapitated by a brutal competitor even before starting to play. I used it as an illustration for my book Un oficio del siglo xx (A Twentieth Century Profession) because to me, at that time, it was the symbol of the hazard that surrounds a writer, particularly in a totalitarian country. Like a sportsman he wants to follow the rules of the game but is decapitated when least expected."

Even though most of his friends are from the movie industry, Cabrera Infante leads a quiet family life in London. He likes to go to the zoo, to ride his bike, and to walk. He has even given up drinking and smoking hash: alcohol, because it used to produce a violent reaction in him; hash, because "it produced in me a physical abulia that fitted my natural disposition but, on the other hand, gave me erroneous and dangerous notions—not only for a writer but for every man—of believing that you are conceiving great ideas, but then when these ideas are submitted to the enlightenment of everyday life you realize they aren't great . . . they aren't ideas at all."

But the ideas and recollections recorded in this interview, although induced only by dark Cuban coffee and cigars in the light of morning hours, were also submitted to a thorough editing by Cabrera Infante, in both the original Spanish and the English translation. Without really changing the original spoken interview, Cabrera Infante inserted new thoughts, enlarged others, treating our interview exactly as he treated Three Trapped Tigers, trying "to fancy what the flame of a candle looks like after the candle is blown out."

Do you belong to the group of expatriate or transplanted Latin American writers?

I don't belong to any group, although I am a writer, formerly from Cuba, who is now living in exile. In the case of the other Latin American writers it is right to say they are transplanted, because they abandoned their cultivated plots—or culture, as it was called by old Vives, the man who invented culture circa 1530, or at any rate invented the word for it—hopscotched to another land and took root in foreign soil as transplants rather than grafts, for no change of skin was involved: they are exotic specimens from the south living in the cultural greenhouse of Europe. Anyway, who are the Latin American writers who live now in other countries than their own? García Márquez, Vargas Llosa, Octavio Paz, Fuentes, Cortá—. . . .

What about Severo Sarduy?

Sarduy has become a naturalized French citizen. (What a verb that one, eh? To *naturalize*—does it mean that he was before an artificial man, or that he didn't have any natural virtues?) Like a good Frenchman, Sarduy lives in Paris. As for the rest—Fuentes is now in Mexico, perhaps for good. Last year García Márquez was offered—and refused—the post of Colombian consul in Barcelona! Vargas was in Peru not so long ago and was invited to the Presidential Palace for an interview with the president-general or colonel or major or whatever rank the man has, who wanted to know the writer's opinion of the military government and whether it was good or bad for Peru. I suppose Cortázar still holds an Argentine passport and can return to Buenos Aires whenever he likes. So that, technically speaking, I am the only exile. Perhaps the other writers feel themselves somewhat exiled in spirit, but the only one who cannot return to his country is also the only one who never so much as dreamed of leaving Havana. In fact, I am the *only* one of them all who would find myself in serious trouble if I ever thought of returning to my country. Or if I returned involuntarily as a result of that hazard of commercial aviation, as frightful as it is frequent—namely, high-jacking.

Would you be put in prison?

I don't know what would happen. Everything is possible under a totalitarian sky. In any case, I don't see my return as being pleasant. On the contrary, it is the stuff my nightmares are made of.

Why did you leave Cuba?

That would be a long story. It would be a very long story. It would be an extraordinarily long story.

We have plenty of time and tapes.

Your tapes, *my* time. It all began with a short 16 mm. film lasting barely twenty-five minutes. This film became, in 1961, the center of a controversy such as has never occurred in Cuba before nor since, up to the present day. As in every totalitarian country, a fierce struggle for power has always existed in Castro's Cuba, and the more totalitarian the country became the more totally it was given over to this most recent form of civil cold wars.

Which were the others?

First came the wars of independence, then those of dependence, then that of dissidence. The last was a war of tendencies. We all know that in capitalist countries an ordinary, everyday struggle for money goes on. In socialist countries— or totalitarian countries as I prefer to call them, since that is their proper name: the rest is labels—there exists an extraordinary struggle for power, because power is much more significant than money, for it involves the whole of life. You might invent a mythical super-millionaire today—a mixture of Onassis, Rockefeller, and the Aga Khan—and this imaginary zillionaire would never have anything remotely approaching the power wielded by Fidel Castro, who is master not only of one island but of a whole archipelago and fleets of merchant vessels and warships, who controls lives and property, is boss of slaves and general of armies, and can unleash a world war—remember October 1962—entirely by himself. When, two hundred years ago, Hegel said of Frederick the Great: "There is only one free man in Prussia!" he was speaking of the prototype of a totalitarian tyrant. There is only one free man in Cuba. In order to govern, this free man creates not only thousands of slaves, but disunion, disputes, and wars between factions. Everyone talks about Castro's Marxism, of how he reads Lenin, and how he had been secretly in league with international communism. These fables conceal the truth, which is that the only book that Fidel Castro has always read, that he used to read in Batista's prison and in the mountains, is *The Prince* by Machiavelli. He was Castro's master. There have been other books—Martí as well as Malaparte's *Technique of the Coup d'Etat*, the *Ides of March* as well as Mao's manual for guerrillas —but his cotside book has always been Machiavelli's encyclopedia of intrigue as a form of government.

We were talking about the struggle for power.

The struggle for power has assumed various forms but it has always been one and the same. For instance, there was a struggle for power in the trade unions between the members of the 26th of July Movement and the Partido Socialista Popular or PSP (the communists). In the army there was a struggle between the factions of the 26th July Movement, with the supporters of Che Guevara and Raúl Castro on one side, and of Fidel Castro on the other, united against and/or allied to, the forces of the Directorio Estudiantil (Students Directory) —who planned and carried out the attack on the President's Palace in 1957, to assassinate Batista (an attempt in which most of the leaders lost their lives)—and the Second Front of Escambray, another guerrilla faction, including old soldiers of the Spanish Civil War and veterans of the Second World War, some of them born in, or citizens of, the United States. In the cultural field the struggle for power was between those who ingenuously believed that socialism was not incompatible with freedom of creation, and the Stalinists who were allied with

cultural reactionaries and openly supported by the PSP and
Che Guevara.

Guevara a Stalinist?

He always was one. The sole difference between him
and the old Cuban communists was that his Stalin was called
Fidel Castro. In spite of his political testament, his first public
action was to hold a meeting for the members of *Nuestro
Tiempo*, a society created by Carlos Franqui and myself among
others in 1950, but controlled, since we left and for several
years, by the PSP, to which it acted as a front organization.
Another early cultural activity of Guevara's—who as an Argentine
was more interested in culture than the rest of the Cuban
guerrillas, for whom if culture meant anything it was the name
of a department of the Ministry of Education—one of the first
cultural events he sponsored was an exhibition of social realism
in the military fortress of La Cabaña, organized and carried out
(luckily) by the worst Cuban academic painters, many of whom
(strange to say) held scholarships from Batista's government!

Why luckily?

Because they were very easily routed on both artistic
and political levels at the same time. If it had been otherwise,
Cuba would have had no modern art to display to ecstatic
political tourists who look upon the works of abstract or pop
art sanctioned by Fidel Castro as triumphs of the revolution,
whereas the first aim of the revolution (or of one of its most
virulently Stalinist factions) was to put an end to freedom of
creation, because totalitarianism cannot allow independence of
any sort—social, sexual, or artistic.

Who are these tourists and what evidence do they provide?

They don't provide evidence, only love songs. The
tourists are innumerable, and range from Susan Sontag and
Graham Greene to the most obscure of interpreters. They are
all doing what the Webbs were accused of by H. G. Wells:

praising a country for what it has ceased to be some time ago. To talk of communist humanism in Cuba is like talking of the politeness of the French in Paris. A little while ago I saw a dithyrambic film made by the national broadcasting station of a country that is in no sense communist—in fact, by the BBC—which consisted of a love song to the freedom of the arts in Cuba, as accompaniment to a film shot by Cuban technicians lent by the Institute of the Cuban Cinema, an organization for state propaganda! But this doesn't happen in England alone. A film about Fidel Castro has been sold to local and national broadcasting stations everywhere in the United States. It was made by a mediocre American cinematographer who spent eight months in Cuba with all expenses paid—by Fidel Castro. When this cinematographer, who has now received the blessing of fashion and myth, first visited Cuba, the only people to welcome him into their houses were those dissident intellectuals whom Castro's government has now put to flight, thanks to a dogmatism described in the film as the liberalism of the left.

Did you meet Graham Greene and the Sontag in Cuba?

Who wants to meet Graham Greene, that Catholic version of Somerset Maugham? Susan Sontag seems to me more interesting. At least her essays and her Swedish film are worth considering, in spite of a certain leftish dilettantism. She was in Cuba in 1960 at a celebration of the 26th July in the "heart of the Sierra Maestra." Among many others present at this fiesta were LeRoi Jones and Françoise Sagan, a fact which shows how much liberal latitude was possible in Cuba at the time. Mademoiselle Sagan played cards the whole time with her little court of friends, all of whom had retired to their air-conditioned train. LeRoi Jones was wearing very different clothes from his present Black (Panther) uniform—a suit of raw silk, cut in the English style, and Italian shoes, and he smoked Gauloises all the time. His only idiosyncracy, in which he differed from the other American Negroes among the guests, was his timidity and shyness, hardly suggesting the image of a nihilist from New Jersey. His gestures, like his clothes, suggested dandyism rather than revolution, and were, of course, decidedly European.

Can we return to the subject of the cultural struggle?

Let us return to it. Digressions are to me, as Laurence Sterne used to say, "the sunshine of conversation." One of the factions in this struggle was represented by *Lunes de Revolución* (the literary supplement of the daily *Revolución*, the organ of the 26th July Movement) which stood for liberalism, tolerance, and ideological and literary experimentations.

Did you once direct the magazine?

Yes, but there's not the slightest complacency nor vanity in what I'm saying. It's only necessary to browse through some numbers of *Lunes* to understand how it was possible for the revolution, culture, and freedom of expression to coexist, even for a short time, in its pages. In opposition to *Lunes* there were a series of organizations, or institutions that were more or less official—or, I should say, more or less obedient, because *disobedience is the capital crime of all totalitarian societies*—and more or less powerful, like the Cuban Film Institute, which was at that time a hangout for the Stalinists. I don't wish to imply that it is not one today, but since Cuban life has become completely Stalinized they have become invisible. But at that time it was truly remarkable how many elements from the old Communist Party, with a perfectly definite ideology and absolutely rigid notions of what culture under the revolution should be like —that's to say they were convinced Zhdanovists—had taken refuge in the Film Institute, which was then beginning to transform itself into the state monopoly it is today, directing the cinema as industry, art and entertainment, owning all cinema theaters, offices of distribution and thousands of pictures, and controlling films of every sort: from virgin film to a spool for a box camera, as well as importing each and every film exhibited in Cuba after 1961! I was one of the founders of the Film Institute early in 1959 and I felt obliged to leave it when Stalinist control made the slightest independent creative effort impossible. I re-

member one of the last discussions I had with Alfredo Guevara
—no relation of the other Guevara: he had never belonged to
the guerrillas in Cuba, Bolivia, or anywhere else—when he decided against letting *Los náufragos de la Calle Providencia* be
made by Luis Buñuel in Cuba because of its "bourgeois ideology."
Buñuel made this film years later in Mexico under the title *El
angel exterminador:* it is impossible to conceive of a more beauti-
fully destructive work of art nor one that had more of the profoundly antibourgeois significance characteristic of the first surrealists. It was therefore inevitable that *Lunes* and the Film
Institute should occupy antipodal political positions. Thus when
my brother, who is now living in New York, and the photographer
Orlando Jiménez, exiled in Puerto Rico, made a brief attempt at
Free Cinema in *P.M.*, which was (ironically) the first and last
attempt at *cine libre* possible in Cuba, the inevitable result was
that the two cultural factions collided violently over the concepts
that deeply affected freedom of creation in a socialist society. Of
course our enemies were right and our battle was doomed to be
lost beforehand: real events in Czechoslovakia and elsewhere have
shown that the concepts of freedom and socialism are mutually
exclusive. But the reason for the controversy would be laughable
if it had not had such a dramatic denouement. The film was made
at the end of 1960 and that same December, at Christmas time,
when orders had been issued for a military mobilization as a result
of rumors of invasion, a lot of people were amusing themselves as
usual in Cuba and ignoring any possible contingency, people who
were still dancing and enjoying themselves under the threat of
atomic war in October 1962. The film showed Cubans leaning
against counters drinking and amusing themselves in various night
haunts and followed their dancing steps as they crossed the bay
to have a ball in Regla, a small town opposite Havana. *P.M.* was
shown on television in the hour sponsored by *Lunes de Revolución* every Monday night, in a program devoted to free cinema
throughout the world, and nothing happened. But problems began to arise when the directors took a copy of the film to the Co-
misión Revisora—in other words the old censorship, apparently
in the hands of revolutionaries but actually of Stalinists—with
a view to showing it in one of the few theaters still remaining in
private hands. To gain this permission it was necessary to leave

the film in the censorship offices, and the Film Institute seized the
opportunity not only to refuse the permission but to confiscate the
copy. This measure has been adopted in other countries, but in
Cuba at that moment, it was not only a cultural provocation but
amounted to a ban on *Lunes,* which had in part financed the
film, and on the television program that had included it: *P.M.*
had in fact been censored as counterrevolutionary! When I heard
this I called a meeting of my colleagues on *Lunes* and we decided
unanimously to draw up a manifesto, protesting against the
censorship and confiscation of the film.

Was this the first manifesto against the revolution?

It was practically the only large-scale demonstration
originating inside the revolution, against any measure enforced
by the revolutionary government in Cuba during Fidel Castro's
long decade of absolute power. It was the first protest and the
last, and I will explain why. We drew up our manifesto, collected
about two hundred signatures of the principal intellectuals and
artists, and presented it to an organization directed by Nicolás
Guillén, an old communist poet, which was the embryo (or
should I say fetus?) of the Union of Writers and Artists of today
—a club, trade union, and *apparat* for censorship and self-
censorship copied from the nefarious Union of Soviet Writers.
At this moment—I am speaking of the days following the invasion
of the Bay of Pigs, in April 1961; I showed the little film on
television at the end of April and the copy was confiscated at the
beginning of May—at this moment Havana was living in some sort
of cultural fever of expectation of some international event
destined as propaganda and publicity for the regime, and similar
to subsequent cultural events like the 1963 International Congress
of Architects, the Tricontinental Conference of Writers of 1967,
and the famous Salon de Mai of European painting and sculpture,
held in Havana in 1968. Four weeks later the First Congress of
Cuban Writers and Artists was announced, to which dozens of
foreign delegates had been invited from both Americas, Western
Europe, and the Eastern and Asiatic countries—the literary lot!
When the government realized that a manifesto–protest bearing

numerous signatures was circulating among the intellectuals, against a measure of one of the state departments and endorsed by the president of the republic—a post-facto endorsement which the Film Institute lost no time in requesting and obtaining from President Dorticós—there was official alarm and agitation lest these discussions and differences, or "disagreements in the bosom of the party" should come to light during the forthcoming congress, which was to be a public, and even international, event —for it is well known that the worst crime against the party is to wash dirty linen in public. A sort of secret movement immediately began to approach Fidel Castro—instigated by Carlos Franqui, director of *Revolución*, with the consent and advice of the PSP's commission for culture—and it was decided to postpone the Congress, due to open at the beginning of June, until the last days of August. Instead of the Congress there would be a series of meetings with Fidel Castro in the National Library. They were very private meetings, confined to well-known and recognized intellectuals: invitations were issued by telephone, and those attending were doubly checked by agents of State Security (still called G2 at this time according to nomenclature inherited from Batista's army, which had copied it from the American army) stationed both at the door of the building and at the door of the library's theater, where the meetings were to take place. Meetings which seem ludicrous today because of the extravagant importance given, so soon after the defeat of the invasion of the Bay of Pigs, to this little film. But the communist world is governed by minorities and keeps a strict watch on the opinions of all groups, however small or ridiculously inoffensive they may seem: no voice is small just because it is innocent and passes unnoticed—above all if it expresses dissent.

Were there many intellectuals in the theater?

It was quite full, not with the ordinary public but with writers, artists, intellectuals, and actors, and on the stage, confronting the auditorium, sat Fidel Castro, President Dorticós, Armando Hart, the Minister of Education (today responsible for ideology), Edith García Buchaca, then communist commissar in the cultural field, later President of the Council of Culture and afterwards a (frustrated) Cuban version of Ekaterina Furtseva, Minister for Soviet Culture.

Why frustrated?

Some time later she fell from grace: she and her husband, Joaquín Ordoqui, a veteran communist leader and vice-minister of the armed forces, were accused of being "imperialist agents" and arrested in 1964. These two have never come to trial but have been living under house arrest ever since Ordoqui suffered a heart attack while being interrogated in the fortress of La Cabaña. Also present were Alfredo Guevara, Alejo Carpentier, Franqui, and revolutionary leaders more or less connected with culture, like Carlos Rafael Rodríguez, and myself as director of *Lunes* and apparent instigator of the protest. (Excuse me while I light a cigar.)

A Cuban one?

Oh yes, although it's called Bolívar. Another very Cuban cigar used to be called a Churchill.

And isn't it still?

Only for export. My sole contact with Cuba, as you see, comes through smoke. I'm privileged in this respect, a privilege I share with Castro, the only man free to smoke as many cigars as he likes in Cuba.

Why is that?

They are strictly rationed.

Cigars?

And cigarettes and sugar and rice and bananas and pineapples and avocados, just as meat and chickens are. Some official reasons given are that they are for export, others that there is too much money in the country and production can't keep up with demand. What is certain is that in Cuba, as in the socialist countries, the only thing that is well run is the Police, Propaganda,

and Paranoia as a system of government. Returning to our encounter with these three Ps . . . Those meetings in the library
were strange in the extreme. By ritual or by chance they took
place on three consecutive Fridays. Everyone spoke, said what
they had to say, more or less, and all at once what had seemed to
be more or less public information about what lay behind the
manifesto and protest and the reason for the prohibition of the
film was converted into a trial, at which the decisive evidence as
to more or less undisciplined, if not counterrevolutionary, behavior, was this innocent experiment in neo-realism and film
texture.

Why was the film held to be counterrevolutionary?

That assumption belongs more to pathology than to
politics. It sprang from the conversion of paranoia into a mechanism for detecting the enemies of the people, of the party, of
man, or whatever that agent of the Great Architect of Utopia is
called. In Cuba, as in all totalitarian countries, there cannot be
a single innocent opinion. It is the reverse of what happens in
England or the United States, where the guilt of an accused man
has to be proved, however overwhelming the evidence at the trial
—videlicet Sirhan Sirhan, Charles Manson, etc. In a totalitarian
country it is just the opposite: all citizens are guilty in some
degree of some offense at some moment of time. All of them,
executioners and victims, are looking for a crime in which they
will meet in its punishment.

It's like Dostoevski.

But it's Kafka, I assure you. It has often been said, it has
been said of the Soviet Union, it has been said of Czechoslovakia
of course, and of the countries of Eastern Europe. What has not
been said is how quickly this Manichaean, medieval, and
Slavonic view of things adapted itself to the tropics and to that
sad island whose natives used to be carefree rather than free. At
the trial, *P.M.* was not so much a prisoner in the dock as Exhibit
A for the prosecution of *Lunes:* it was not the film that was on
trial but the magazine and its liberal concepts of culture—and
also, presumably, the splendidly carefree life of Havana shown by

the film. To religion, everything except fear of God is a sin. To this godless religion, *everything except subjection to terror is anathema.*

What was the actual result of the meetings?

The meetings took place in an atmosphere of uncertainty. Everyone spoke freely, although some of those who spoke freely were freer than others: a few knew what they were talking about, others knew what they had to say. The staff of *Lunes,* the most liberal cultural faction within the revolution, were more than innocent: we were naïve, and like all naïve people we were rash and didn't even notice that machines installed by the Film Institute at the far end of the hall were recording our conversation and that at the end of each day these tapes were taken to the chief of the secret police (who became the Minister of the Interior a few months later) and that dossiers about every one of us were beginning to grow fatter at headquarters. We on the staff of *Lunes,* of course, said pretty clearly what we thought of the confiscation of *P.M.,* and submitted—prophetically, as even our enemies of that time were soon to discover—that a disastrous precedent was being created for Cuban culture under the revolution. On the second day, we who had provoked this trial realized, like Oscar Wilde, that we had invoked disaster. Meanwhile intellectuals who previously seemed eager to speak sat silent, friends rose to declare themselves enemies, and opportunists and people with a grievance profited by the occasion. To take an example: there was an exiled Spanish republican, a mediocre writer who had been literally annihilated by a critic in the pages of *Lunes* two years before, and who united opportunism and bitterness in his person. This vulgar untalented man whose public career was a political slalom and who now lived in internal exile, both intellectual and political, arose from his literary ashes to deliver a diatribe against *Lunes.* His evidence *contra reus* was so decisive that the government immediately rewarded him with the almost lifelong post of ambassador to the Vatican. In the end, as on many former occasions, Fidel Castro reserved for himself the dual function of public prosecutor and judge summing up the case. As always, he had the last word, against which there was no appeal. With a typical gesture, he rose deliberately from his chair, removed his perennial .45 pistol from his hip, laid his gun belt and cartridge case on the table, and walked slowly around it toward the microphone at the front of the stage. The speech he made was benevolently threatening, as if the Jehovah of the Bible had descended among the Cubans, and after showing disdain amounting almost to contempt for the intellectuals gathered there—how many divisions can culture put in the field?—he ended with those unfortunate and now famous words: "With the revolution everything, against the revolution nothing." A phrase which has been glorified everywhere as a sort of oral monument to the intellectual and artistic liberalism of the Castrist regime, whereas it really expresses totalitarian logic disguised by a visibly Orwellian sophism: "Four legs good, two legs bad." One has only to return it to its context to understand the message: those who are with me are good, but those who are against me will be very bad—at the same time I reserve the right to think and to *decide* who and where are my friends and my enemies. It is paranoia turned into a political system! The very end of the meetings in the library, which were all secret, was even more secret. It didn't all end with the publication, without preamble or explanation, of Castro's speech, but it was decided, *in camera*, that *Lunes de Revolución* should disappear. The public excuse was the paper shortage. However *Lunes* was at once supplanted by *three* different publications all strictly controlled by the government and the party! The public congress—pompously called *Primer Congreso de Escritores y Artistas de Cuba*—needless to say, passed without contretemps.

Was it then that you left Cuba?

Oh no, that was much later. It isn't as easy to leave your country as it is to leave a party, even if your country has been transformed into a *single* party. Besides, it's well known that communism, like the Mafia, doesn't allow resignations, it merely enforces expulsions or issues death certificates—and my country had become totally totalitarianly communist. When *Lunes* vanished I was left without a job. They tried to send my salary from the paper to my house, without my working for it, with the tacit agreement that the less often I visited the offices, the better. All

at once those of us responsible for *Lunes* contracted a visible
infection or else an old and hitherto hidden infection suddenly
came to light. No one wanted to touch us even with a ten-foot
pole: we had fallen from grace, and this metaphor can only be
thoroughly understood in a religious society. It was, quite literally,
a fall. We were angels crash-diving into hell or making a forced
landing in the purgatory of silence: we became non-persons. I
refused to receive my salary at home because I knew what use
would be made of this sinecure in the future and I literally sat
down and waited for a new job. Time passed: a month, two,
three, six, eight months and I was still out of work. During this
time I lived on the salary of my wife, Miriam Gómez, who was
an actress in the theater, in films, and on television. I spent my
free time, which was my whole time, writing or meeting my few
possible friends from the magazine, or well-known dissidents—
persecuted homosexuals, drawing-room Trotskyists, visiting foreigners whom no one wanted to see: belated beatniks or early hippies.
While forbidden subjects were being discussed in my house and
we were criticizing the increasingly absurd, feckless, and dangerous state of affairs, I was saying everywhere that I was the first
pimp created by socialism, and making other political jokes closer
to civic suicide than to historic humor. All this created an atmosphere of concern around me, concern on the part of some of
my friends who still held power—and official concern as well.
One of the characteristics of totalitarian states is that the terror
they enforce is less a technique for ruling than a manifestation of
their own fear: they terrorize everyone because they are afraid
of everything. No opinion is innocent, therefore all opinions
must be guilty. Who knows which dissident might create a
heresy or unloose some historical catastrophe—since history is the
providence of materialists? Besides which, many people, both in
Cuba and abroad, were wondering what was happening to me—
someone who had been a member of the Council of Culture,
along with Carpentier and Lezama among others, and had been
elected second or third vice-president of the recently created
Union of Writers, which formed part of the editorial board of
Revolución, yet was now at home without work and politically
plague-stricken. Their concern even reached the president, and
after some more or less private attempts on the part of mediators,

it was decided that I should leave Cuba as a more or less official
exile for a more or less expedient time. I should afterwards return
and be more or less completely rehabilitated. But I should never
recover my lost prestige, nor would redemption ever succeed in
effacing the imprint of my guilt.

So you left Cuba officially?

They offered me a distant post, rather more remote than
if they had sent me to manage a hydroelectric plant in Siberia.
They sent me to Brussels, a city which, viewed from Havana,
seemed to be located on the dark side of the moon. I went to
Belgium as cultural attaché, which in the diplomatic hierarchy of
Cuba is a slightly more important post than a porter's—and there
was no porter at the embassy. I spent my time diplomatically.
Then my first book, a book of short stories called *Así en la paz
como en la guerra* (In Peace as in War), was published in Paris
and Milan and it gained a certain notoriety in Europe. I also
made the most of the little free time left after office hours, re-
ceptions, and the mutterings of protocol in the neighborhood of
the Avenue Vanstong Shoorsheel, not to mention daily *perce-
oreille* interchanges with the Slavonic envoys—"Bang sure,
kamarade!' "Ask à mes yeux l'impasse-a-deur errantré?" "Kamarade, less frais para blame histarique," etc., etc.—and the *dot na*
drinking of everyone's healths except mine, with my tropical liver
averse as it is to viscous vicious vodka, slimy slivowitz, and totalitarian tokay. After surviving these daily ordeals, I used to return
to my house in the Flemish—pronounced Blemished by the
Russians—quarter of Brussels and write *Three Trapped Tigers*,
a book which received the Seix-Barral Prize in Barcelona in 1964.
Thanks to a series of extraordinary coincidences, I ended up
with a lot of business on hand and in sole charge of the embassy
as cherchez-daffy-ears, as my communist colleagues pronounced
the phrase *chargé d'affaires*.

What were these extraordinary coincidences?

One, for instance, happened when the ambassador returned from Cuba on leave and finished up in prison, where he

still is, without coming to trial or being informed what was his crime, although they promised to alleviate his sentence if he confessed!

Incredible!

More incredible still if I tell you that this man, Gustavo Arcos, was one of the surviving heroes of the assault on the Moncada Barracks on July 26, 1953, the putsch which finally carried Castro into power. He was seriously wounded during the attack, having a more than miraculous escape from death, was paraplegic for six months, was taken prisoner, escaped, was exiled in Mexico with the Castros, and as he was unable to accompany them in their invasion of the Sierra Maestra, a brother of his went in his place and was killed in the landing from the *Granma*. But the incredible ceases to be so when it happens daily. What were we talking about?

About the prize, about TTT, and the publication of your other book in Europe.

All this, presumably thanks to the news agency, became known in Cuba, where my friends and enemies alike were beginning to remember me more than I wished. When I went to Cuba for my mother's funeral, they all paid me homage in their own way. But this time my enemies behaved more stupidly or with less concealment and did their best to keep me in Cuba, in silence.

In prison?

It would have come to that sooner or later. They began by obstructing my official return to Belgium, using the services of counterintelligence to cancel the efforts of the Ministry for Foreign Affairs to send me back to Brussels and to paralyze my friends who showed, like Hobbes, that their sole passion was not friendship but fear. Once again I was out of work, as in 1961. Once again my apartment—this time I was living in my father's— was full of dissenters and persecuted people. Once again a vacuum surrounded me—now I was even more alone, since Miriam Gómez had remained in Belgium. But my solitude and my being distant-in-one's-place, my estrangement, gained me the rare privilege of looking at my own country and not recognizing it. Or of getting to know it in its new role. Of seeing that it was not only impoverished but peopled with unhistoric zombies, suffering their new misery in silence: a loquacious race who were being forced to become laconic. Before I first went to Belgium, and perhaps with some precognition of Cuba's future, I used to repeat a phrase from Horace, with more or less parodic variations: "The ruins will find me impavid." On my return I understood that it was easier to parody Horace than to adopt his early existentialism: the ruins of Havana, of Cuba and the Cubans did not find me undaunted, but deeply disturbed. I had thought previously that even if I couldn't write in Cuba, I could at least live there and imitate the vegetable life so prevalent in the island. Now I understood that it wasn't even possible to live in totalitarian Cuba, because liberty is the oxygen of history: when it is present we aren't aware of it and breathe it naturally as if the supply of both would go on forever. Only when they are suppressed do we realize how precious they are! But then it's too late: we are suffocating. As I wasn't interested in reliving the story of my life in the seconds before I asphyxiated, I decided to go out for air. When I informed anyone who would listen that I was determined to leave Cuba *at all costs,* passage money and signed visas immediately appeared. Totalitarian terror is no different from other forms of fear, and as the Spaniards discovered in medieval times, *A enemigo que huye, puente de plata:* all difficulties must be smoothed away for a fleeing enemy even if it means building bridges made of silver. For my part, I remembered the advice of Francesco Guicciardini, that Florentine sage not for nothing a close friend of Machiavelli's: "There are no useful rules for living under a tyrant, except perhaps one, which is the same as for times of plague: fly as far away as you can!"

What part did you play in the revolution?

Fidel Castro decreed that the revolution should be divided historically into the insurrection and the revolution. The insurrection begins with Batista's coup d'etat in 1952 and ends with his flight on New Year's Eve 1958. All the rest, up to the present day, is revolution. This division of the troubled waters of history was based on a very astute political notion: the old members of the PSP, among many others, would be able to bathe in this political Jordan, and a second chance to collaborate would be given to those who had remained apolitical or in a state of cautious expectation before 1959. My work for the insurrection was modest, infinitesimal compared to that of some heroes and martyrs, enormous compared to that of many ministers in the present Castrist regime.

Can you describe it?

I helped edit the clandestine periodical *Revolución*; I was in contact with several revolutionary groups; I transported arms for the directory and explosives for the 26th of July; my house served as a refuge for revolutionaries and terrorists; I attempted to found one or two clandestine organizations, one for young intellectuals and another for journalists—and very little else.

It sounds pretty dangerous.

The only dangerous thing I did was simply to stay the whole time in Havana. Then the revolutionary mythology had not yet suffused the Sierra Maestra and the peasant guerrillas in the same splendid glow that irradiates them today. At that time what was really dangerous was to carry out terrorism or anti-Batista activity in the towns. The "guerrilla" was a place in the Sierra where the revolutionaries took their holidays, a sort of mountain resort. I remember that in 1957 Frank País—a terrorist leader of the 26th of July Movement, assassinated by the police in Santiago—was posthumously praised for having repeatedly refused to leave the city and join up with Castro in the Sierra nearby. Today this story seems to us a fabrication, but perhaps Guevara's failure in Bolivia and the success of the urban guerrillas everywhere may send another revolutionary myth to its source: the city is a place where the guerrillas go to die: a sort of cemetery for white elephants, whereas the good guerrillas go to the mountains when they die: the paradise for believers (in History).

Then you were in favor of the revolution against Batista?

More than that: if the same things happened over again, if we were living in the Platonic year of revolutions, in *l'éternel retour* of history, when 1958 came along I would do the same as I did then. Which does not mean that I am unable to see that the position of the Cuban people is noticeably worse today than it was in Batista's time. Then gangsters were in power, wielding the erratic irresolute power of gangsters, eager for money and violence, but outside the laws of history—historical outlaws. Now the police are in power, with the meticulous organization and implacable method of modern police, who have learned it all from the GPU and the Gestapo: control is complete and all the excesses of power are justified by a blind faith in history, because they are carried out in the name of a better tomorrow. But—*corruptio optimi pessima!*

What do you think is the essential difference between capitalism and communism?

If we transport metaphors from natural history to history and say that capitalism, which is life in Western industrial society, is a rat race, then life in a socialist society—whether industrial, underdeveloped, or "on the road to development"— is a lemming leap, in which huge, maddened hordes surmount every sort of obstacle and hurl themselves unthinking into the sea and to death, in search of an island on the horizon that they will never find: the utopia of irrational man.

Talking of Bolivia and the guerrillas, and those of them who have died, what is your view of Che Guevara? Were you a friend of his?

No. I saw him very seldom, but I learned his methods very early, as early as January or February 1959, and my view of Guevara isn't a fashionable one.

What do you mean?

I mean that when you meet certain historical figures they appear to be surrounded by a somewhat mythical public aura, but in private that extraordinary public atmosphere involving them becomes more tenuous, and as you ascend those historical peaks, the air around them becomes more rarefied and unbreathable. The famous phrase which Malraux quotes at the beginning of his *Antimemoirs*, in which a peasant says that there is no such thing as a great man, seems to me every day more true. I continually feel admiration for the way Gore Vidal deflated the Kennedy myth, simply by reporting the "way it was" in the intimacy of the Kennedy clan, which he called the Holy Family. To write this at the very time when Kennedy had become an American saint was an act of extraordinary courage. My opinion of Che Guevara is so unfashionable and inopportune that my friends consider it a form of madness to make it public. As a revolutionary Guevara is a dubious figure and only after fifty years, when it is possible to judge him impartially, shall we see him as he really is: the avatar of the myth of the warrior, self-created. Or the ready-made guerrilla. Somewhat as we see Lawrence of Arabia today. In other words, a man whose great historical claim is that he has constructed a personal myth through a book and afterwards put his writing into practice: a hero who wrote his own scenario, no more nor less. His importance—as theorist and practician of guerrilla warfare—appears absurd as soon as we discover that when this theorist put his mythical experiences (now exalted as *the* sacred handbook for guerrillas) into practice he was defeated by the sole force that according to those theories could *not* possibly defeat him! Guevara's *Diary*, written in Bolivia, if read impartially as it will doubtless be read one day, is a crushing chronicle of defeat. Crushing defeat not only on a military level, but of each and all of his pretensions (or should I say pretenses?) dictated by a work of fiction that its author offers us as scientific: the chronicles of his activities among the Cuban guerrillas. The theoretical treatise as fiction is perfect and in it everything ends in triumph. The work of fiction as theory is something else. The *Diary*, a captain's log of the carrying out of a fictitious theory, is the testament of a colossal failure, because it is evidence of a disaster that couldn't happen. It is the gospel of a redeemer rejected by those he tried to save. It is the story of a professional guerrilla general who planned the most disastrous campaigns and was routed by amateurs or by professionals with merely amateur knowledge of the science of which he had claimed to be an expert. Finally, it is the program of an active revolutionary more concerned with his *image* as a revolutionary (witness to it are the profuse photographs of the guerrilla chief "in action") than with his revolutionary *activity!*

It was not without significance that Lin Piao, with that common sense that seems to have been invented by the Chinese, when he heard from Guevara's lips this blueprint for red guerrilla warfare, said to him: "All this sounds very good for Comrade Guevara, but very bad for the revolution!" Oriental wisdom.

What about his activities in Cuba then?

An even greater disaster. If the Bolivian campaign was a complete success for Guevara the Martyr, but a disaster from the point of view of the revolution by guerrilla warfare, Cuba was a partial success for Guevara the adventurer, ideologist, and statesman—inside every pirate there is a corsair struggling to get out—but Guevara the Hero was a calamity for Cuba. After he had walked through the Cuban funds and spent some time at the head of Cuban industry, Cuban wealth vanished as if by magic and Cuba's first industry, sugar, is still making desperate efforts to recover from the spells laid on it by this misfired Midas, who converted all the gold he touched into slogans, inefficiency, and blood. The Avatar of Attila as an Argentinian!

And his place in history?

In contemporary history Guevara has ended by figuring in the hagiology of the Loser, along with Jimmy Dean—that's to say, the myth of the young rebel whose useless rebelliousness has failed; and of Jean Harlow—the myth of the beauty that vanishes in death, leaving nothing but her image; and of Humphrey Bogart—the tough guy whose inner tenderness belies his toughness: inside every actor there is an actress struggling to get out. Che Guevara, contradiction of all contradictions, has finally become part of that same decadent mass culture that he himself personally despised so much, that frivolous Western culture governed by fashion: the personality cult reduced to the cult of the image. I wonder whether that profusion of posters, portraits, and shirts printed with the *vera efigies Guevaraensis* would have been possible in the case of a less handsome man, if he had possessed, say, the unpleasant, ferrety face of Raúl Castro. Guevara the Guerrilla finally confirmed the assertion of Wilde the Aesthete: "It is better to be beautiful than good."

But wasn't he an idealist?

To a cruel degree both for others and himself—he treated his own body with the same iron discipline as he did his subordinates and with the same inhuman indifference he showed his enemies—he was preoccupied with his place in history. It is undoubtedly true that this preoccupation was almost unconsciously tinged with an altruism which disguised it, and that his eagerness for historical fame was very different from Fidel Castro's obscene lust for power. It is possible that Guevara was less interested in power as such. He at least knew how to renounce temporal power for a posthumous place in the revolutionary pantheon.

A series of anecdotes about the Sierra Maestra campaign illustrates this difference. Comradeship with his adherents was a much stronger feeling in him than in Fidel Castro. Guevara refused to take advantage of privileges which Castro sought or accepted as his right. For example, if there was only one steak, it would be for Castro, who was uninterested in what his army was eating, and who enjoyed privileges as unknown to his soldiers as those enjoyed by the prime minister are to most Cubans today. Whereas Guevara used always to insist on eating the same as his men. But I wonder whether this stoicism wasn't also part of the warrior myth: the insomniac Napoleon finding a sentinel asleep on the eve of Waterloo and taking his place until the shamefaced soldier awoke; Caesar wearing the same clothes as his legions; Alexander living among the Macedonian rabble, like just another soldier. To these examples we must add those of: Hitler, wearing a uniform without braid or metals; Mao, dressed as a peasant soldier; Caligula, who gained his name from the ordinary legionary's sandals he wore, etc., etc., etc.

*Then how do you explain the fact that Che has become a myth
for youth?*

He's not a myth for "youth," he is a myth for *middle-class*
youth. The Guevara myth has been adopted by the middle-class
young of Western and American countries, especially by students
from more or less comfortably-off families, who express in this
way their need to be in opposition to their parents and get rid
of their adolescent guilt at the same time. Not long ago this was
pointed out by Pier Paolo Pasolini, when he noticed that the sons
of the middle-class parents in Rome were pseudo-revolutionary
students much given to fighting against workmen's sons among
the police force. And there is another half of the world—the
biggest—to whom Guevara says absolutely nothing. I mean
communist China, the Soviet Union, and the countries of eastern
Europe. Guevara is unknown in China and Russia, as a result
of government decrees. But in Czechoslovakia, for example, to
the young people for whom Jan Palach is a martyr and his im-
molation a patriotic act, Guevara represents the very Stalinism
and authoritarianism that they detest and fight against as best
they can. Young people in the West adopt Guevara as another
way of standing up to their parents. Che Guevara and his
symbols represent one form of adolescent protest, but the obverse
of the coin is the connection of these same young people with
drug-taking, a habit which Che not only despised but also attacked, as he was the first who attempted to try summarily to
shoot the peasants of the Sierra who made their living by
growing marijuana.

In the Sierra Maestra in Cuba?

Yes. It was largely inhabited by peasants cultivating
grass, and by outlaws like Crecencio Pérez, who was the first to
give effective help to Castro in the Sierra and who has been
sanctified by the revolution, though he was actually a brigand
who had spent years hiding from justice in the mountains and
lived as a smuggler. Castro made him a comandante of the rebel
army and postponed Guevara's drastic decision to eradicate the
marijuana plantations—until the guerrillas should be stronger.

These young Americans whose protest takes the form of adopting
as their own their parents' nightmares—drugs, with-it fashions,
long hair, causes, heroes—show their inconsistency by protesting
against the Vietnam war and in favor of peace, while at the same
time adopting Che's clothes and image, assuming the poses and
slogans of a man who in no way desired peace in Vietnam or
anywhere else in the world, and whose most elevated dream was
"not one, but two, three, five Vietnams everywhere!" It doesn't
therefore surprise me when I hear many Anglo-Saxons actually
call him *Chic* Guevara.

Chic meaning fashionable?

Chic, meaning to adopt what is in vogue, however far
from our own reality, merely in order to be up-to-date and not
let our opinions grow old. Not long ago, in Los Angeles, I was
introduced to a boy with a pleasant smile, whose conversation had
the eloquent but artificial economy common to hippies, full of
"Too much!" "Outa sight!" "Heavy, man!"—the modern version
of Gary Cooper's "Yep!" He wore a faded denim shirt, patched
Levi's frayed at the bottom, and sandals more venerable than my
gray hairs. When he left me he crossed Sunset Boulevard and got
into a 1970 Ferrari! He was a multimillionaire record producer.
This Californian version of the vow of poverty is chic and nothing
else. (In London he would be dressed in the same way, but he
would be sitting behind opaque windows in the back of a
chauffeur-driven Rolls-Royce.) To support Hanoi from a flat in
Hampstead or declare one's sympathy for the Palestine guerrillas
in the Deux Magots, or failing that, to praise the "struggle of the
urban guerrillas against fascist dictatorship in Uruguay," in the
pages of *The New York Review of Books* is, of course, Chic
Guevara. Chic Guevara is an article singing the praises of World
Revolution in a magazine devoted to fashion or men's clothes, and
insulting the consumer society between pages advertising the most
expensive deodorant for men or a super stereophonic set "for the
man who has everything." Chic Guevara is an actress giving
recitals of revolutionary poems—among others, verses by "the
poet friend of Castro, Joseph Marty," meaning José Martí who
died in 1895!—and accepting, with the same hand that signs

fiery revolutionary manifestos, a scandalously large salary from a
film production company which may well be only Dow Chemicals
branching out. A Jew from San Francisco, London, or Paris who
admits to admiring Yassir Arafat is Chic Guevara. So is a German
poet, escaped from East Berlin, who writes a poem in Munich
dedicated to Castro. Chic Guevara is the famous French revolutionary cinema director of a film financed by an aristocratic
English millionaire on the subject of Black Power, who takes
care that his salary is paid in advance to a numbered account in
Switzerland before he starts work on his "subversive poem."
Early Chic Guevara was an article published in Vogue in 1968,
in which beautiful and elegantly dressed models were shown
taking refuge in smoking ruins, crouching beside armed facsimiles
of Che Guevara and under a title: *"The Guerrilla Line (Revolutionaries by Request)"*! A recent Chic Guevara is Antonioni
making his atrocious *Zabriskie Point*. A senile Chic Guevara was
Lord Russell letting himself be manipulated by a gang of Stalinists
running loose. Chic Guevaras *avant la lettre* were Ralph Ingersoll,
Nancy Cunard, the communist Vanderbilt, the Red Dean of
Canterbury, and Feltrinelli. Jane Fonda is of course Chichi
Guevara. An obscene Chic Guevara is Barney Rosset, tycoon of
pornography, going to cut sugarcane in Cuba, doing willingly
and with a smile the work which thousands of Cubans not far
away are forced to do as slaves for their "sexual deviations" (sic
and sick). Chic Guevara is Omar Shariff studying the "complete
works" of Che Guevara—and the monument to Che Guevara
for all time, his well-deserved epitaph, is of course the film *Che!*

*Then isn't there some profound political thought behind all this
reverence?*

Neither a profound nor shallow one. There's not even
the slightest bit of political information, much less thought or
formulated ideology.

*But do genuine intellectuals in Europe, the United States, and
Latin America also hold these opinions because it is fashionable
to do so?*

Every day I grow more convinced that nothing exists but
fashion, that history is merely a parade of fashions or of the same

fashion repeated, with two or three basic ideas which come and go. In the thirties it became the fashion to support Stalin, and intellectuals like Bernard Shaw and André Gide, to mention only two eminent and contrary examples, unconditionally supported this terrifying tyranny at the time of Stalin's worst repression and brutalities: at the time of the Moscow purges. Many lesser or simply mediocre writers followed Stalin again in his odious persecution of Trotsky: you find the most unexpected names, like Nathanael West's for instance, affixed to Stalinist manifestos. The sole coherent explanation of all this is that at that moment it was the fashion to adopt a mistaken utopian populism which has cropped up again and again in Western political thought for approximately the last two hundred years. Since the French Revolution there have been some periods of reaction and cultivating-your-own-garden, and others of extreme preoccupation with supposedly or actually revolutionary ideologies and movements. What other explanation except fashion can there be when we find Bertrand Russell and Yves Montand fighting in the same movement, marching elbow to elbow with Jean Paul Sartre and Jane Fonda, for the love of Marx! I expect Roger Vadim will someday (and with every justification) make a Schnitzlerian sequel to his *La Ronde*—entitled *La Ronde Rouge*.

You think the intellectuals give their support in an uncritical spirit?

It's possible that even when they possess a critical spirit and can judge the affairs of their countries with full knowledge and objectively, most of the intellectuals who praise Cuba so intemperately are absolutely ignorant of what Cuba was and is. To jump on the vogue-wagon you don't have to listen and stop to meditate—on the contrary, all you need is to take the hint and run after it and pray for it not to leave you behind. All the information most of the neo-Stalinists possess is based on an accumulation of accepted ideas emanating from the professional propagandists of the Cuban Revolution rather than from Cuban realities. How many of these Castro-lovers or Castro-lobbyists are capable of admitting that Castro's triumph in Cuba was not due to its being the backward, isolated island it has become under his government, but rather to the fact that it was one of the most advanced countries of Latin America? Few people are capable of admitting—or understanding—that Castro triumphed over all the other minority parties that were fighting against Batista's tyranny because of his masterly use of a medium so absolutely of the year '60 as television. A much more perfect and finished use, by the way, than that of a Kennedy or a De Gaulle, masters of the medium though they were, and only comparable to the use made of the radio and PA systems that Hitler achieved thanks to Goebbels's genius. How many people know and will admit that the struggle against Batista was by no manner or means a struggle to right economic wrongs, but an attempt to give back to Cuba the political, democratic, and parliamentary flexibility which we had had for more than a decade, which that ambitious tin general had suppressed, and which Castro *solemnly* undertook to restore? How many know, for instance, that 1958 was the year of greatest economic prosperity Cuba had enjoyed since her discovery in 1492? How many young Harvard economists who slip off to Cuba with their wives and all her shoes are capable of understanding that Fidel Castro has created the very poverty he now promises to fight? As Orwell said, "You don't have to live in a totalitarian society to be corrupted by totalitarianism."

What was the position of workers and peasants under Batista's regime?

There wasn't only one, there were several Batista regimes. During the first—which lasted roughly from 1934 to 1944, the last four years ruling constitutionally—Batista created the Confederation of Cuban Workers and put at its head as first secretary-general a leading communist—and a Negro into the bargain—called Lázaro Peña, a man who was going to be used in the same position twenty years later by Castro! This may give some idea of the fantastic political confusion existing in Cuba ever since her independence in 1902. The last secretary-general of the Confederation of Cuban Workers, Eusebio Mujal, was an ex-communist, born in Spain and decidedly anti-Franco, who, before serving Batista, had served President Grau and the Cuban P.C.! To add confusion to political chaos, I can say that there were more Negro ministers in Batista's governments than there are today in the Central Committee of the Cuban Communist Party, and also that 95 percent of Batista's army, including those specially enrolled to combat guerrilla warfare in the Sierra, were Negroes or mulattos! What leader or member of the Black Panthers can possibly understand and discuss this fact, or even admit it? Besides this, the bulk of the Cuban agricultural workers were sugarcane cutters, who were not peasants and didn't even live in the country, many living in villages and towns— I know it well: my grandfather was a cane cutter—others having come temporarily to Cuba for the sugarcane harvesting from Jamaica and Haiti. The rest were large landowners, farmers with average or small holdings, and peasants working on neighboring land. As in the case of workers vis-à-vis the manufacturers, those with small or average-sized farms had the same interests as the great landowners, and their living conditions depended almost exclusively on free trade and the fluctuations produced in the economy by the rise and fall of the price of sugar in the United States and world markets. If Batista had not led the country into a political blind alley, it is obvious that the idea of a revolution would never have entered the heads of most of the workers (who were interested in nothing but salary rises), nor of the peasants, who like most peasants throughout the world are interested only in their vegetable gardens and their harvest and in the almost metaphysical relation between crops and nature. In the late thirties Batista had given Cuba a new constitution, with voting rights for women, and equal opportunities for all races: he had even democratized the extremely racist Cuban navy. He afterwards personally took upon himself the task of suppressing democracy and at the same time promoted himself and his followers from humble sergeants and corporals to colonels and generals from one day to the next. Batista's origins were humbler than those of most of the rulers of Cuba—President Dorticós, the Castro brothers, Carlos Rafael Rodríguez, etc.—almost all of whom, like most of the revolutionary opposition, came from the upper or lower middle classes. In a grotesque historical paradox, Batista went to cut sugarcane on the hacienda of Castro's father, a rich Spanish landowner! (I can vouch for the truth of this because Batista, Castro, and I all come from the same northern district of the

Oriente Province and were born within a radius of a hundred kilometers.) On the other hand, my parents, like all the old communists, remained in sympathy with Batista well into the fifties. As late as 1955 my mother used still to turn out of her house any friends of mine who openly sympathized with Castro. The nature of the political confusion in Cuba—and the inevitable confusion caused by it abroad—can be seen from this curious song which used to be sung in Cuba around 1957:

> Long live Cuba!
> Long live Fidel!
> Down with the black ape
> Now in power!

But who would say that to James Baldwin?

Do you agree with those who put the blame on American colonialism and see socialism as the only solution for Latin America?

There isn't one solution for Latin America, there would have to be twenty solutions because Latin America isn't a country but a continent made up of countries with problems to choose from. I don't know what those solutions are. I'm unfamiliar with Latin American problems because I hardly know those countries and I dislike giving an opinion when I'm ignorant of the subject. The Latin American countries I do know could not seem more different. It would be difficult to find countries more dissimilar and far apart than Argentina and Mexico, two countries differing more completely than Argentina and Bolivia, her next-door neighbor. Not even the deceptive mask of the Spanish language fits either Brazil or Haiti. Is there a continental solution for Latin America? I don't think so. As for colonialism, I have my opinions about colonialism of course, but no solution. It's hard to find a writer able to offer a solution adequate for writing books other than his own, much less useful for putting his country right. People in Latin America talk a lot, shout, argue, gesticulate about the evils of American colonialism, but never about the great responsibilities incumbent on Latin American governments to deal creatively or helpfully with their own local problems, many of which originated long before New England was colonized. All Latin American problems have the same origin in

common: they all come from the wars of independence and their
aftermath of warlords converted into pseudo patricians or patriots,
who were really feudal lords with rights over lives and property
and extraordinary privileges comprising everything from options
to opinions. I've reached the point of repeatedly asking myself
whether in the case of Cuba, whose history I know, the wars
of independence against Spain really represented anything except
the patriotism of its scoundrels and the regionalism of its provincials. I very much doubt whether Cuba is a more independent and democratic country today, a country more concerned
with the desires and needs of her citizens—in a word, with individual and collective happiness—than that still dependent country,
Canada, for instance. I believe that Canada is a much more
independent country today than Cuba ever was. I can't speak
about the other Latin American wars of independence, but I
wonder whether those in Cuba were truly premeditated political
events or rather impromptu operations, movements more literary
than political, more romantic than realistic, suicidal, not life-
giving, unreal and irrational decisions directed by good will perhaps, but essentially messianic and therefore dangerous. Martí
didn't find a solution to his innumerable psychological and historic
contradictions when he made his suicidal dash among Spanish
bullets: he merely left them as a heritage to a nation at the fetal
stage. His death, comprehensible in terms of a *coup de théâtre* in
Hedda Gabler or *Hamlet,* was on the personal level not very
different from the suicide of some late romantic poet (such as
his contemporary the sickly Colombian José Asunción Silva). But
it was transformed by Cuban politicians into an unbearably
messianic and neo-Christian burden to the yet-to-be-born nation.
The words *Martí died for your sins* might well have been engraved on his tombstone. In fact there is a popular song dating
from the beginning of the century which laments:

> *Martí should not have died,*
> *Alas, should not have died!*
> *If Martí had not died*
> *It would have been another story;*
> *This country would have been saved*
> *And Cuba would have been happy.*

One ludicrous detail of the national heritage is that Martí's son was made a colonel of the Cuban army for life—by one of the warlords who survived the war to later become a dictator. What is even more ludicrous is that junior used to lustily sing this song in his bath for the benefit of the neighbors:

> Papa *should not have died,*
> *Alas, should not have died!*
> *If* Papa *had not died, etc.*

The rest of this heritage is horrid. It is represented not only by busts, mausoleums, and veneration for the dead and their whitened sepulchres, but also by a teratology the final denouement of which was to make Fidel Castro—of course!—master of (funeral) ceremonies. In his last 26th of July speech on the occasion of the (*summer!*) Christmas festivities—what other anniversary could be more appropriate?—he displayed the gift given him by yet another Bolivian turncoat, holding it up for all to see: macabre and at the same time unreal, a bluish shape inside a bottle of formol—Che Guevara's hands!

Does that exonerate the United States?

In no way. But General De Gaulle once made a totally cynical remark which is at the same time extraordinarily true: "Nations have nothing besides their own interests." In the whole history of the human race it is impossible to find a nation with an altruistic attitude toward other nations, even toward their neighbors—above all to their neighbors. I don't see why the United States should be more altruistic than England or France, or even Russia, the most notable example of an imperialist country in modern times—viz., Prague, 1968. And China herself, who is entirely in the right in her territorial conflicts with Imperial Russia of today, has committed an act so criminally imperialist as to occupy the small, inoffensive, and religious Tibet. No great nation can escape the epithet of "colonialist"—nor can a good many small ones, like Belgium.

Don't you believe that China is an imperialist power?

Oh yes, certainly. She exercises imperialism in its latest form, a newer type than the economic imperialism of America—

ideological imperialism, which exports political ideas calculated to subvert order in other countries, and of course support the new Chinese order. This sort of political imperialism is also assiduously practiced by Cuba.

By Cuba?

Yes, in accordance with an old geopolitical law which decrees that all islands must become eager to dominate the neighboring continent—e.g., the Greek islands and Sicily in the ancient world, Great Britain and Japan in the modern world. Ever since 1959, Cuba has been trying, and is trying still to dominate the Latin American continent politically, by exporting not only her government's political ideas, but also arms, money, and men trained for the purpose: Venezuela, Bolivia, and Argentina were enclaves of Cuban ideological imperialism in the past, Chile and Uruguay are today. Recent events in Canada and the United States prove that Cuba is trying to exercise her political dominion not only in one neighboring continent but in two!

What is your position among Latin American writers, since your way of thinking is so very different from most of theirs?

One of absolute independence and therefore great isolation. I believe I'm the only one of them all to have the misfortune to have experienced life in a communist country like Cuba, which from an island in a state of revolution became an increasingly bureaucratic, irrational, and totalitarian state. Of course this experience has been invaluable. But if I were not a Cuban it is possible that I should agree with them all completely, as a result of ignorance and the times we live in. But besides being a Cuban, I was in the very heart of the revolution, among those who directed it. I took part in it before many of these partisan writers of today had even heard of Cuba, or even of Marx, or of revolution as a political idea. I know all its leaders, not their names only, but often their nicknames and their private history, besides having a good knowledge of the true political and social state of Cuba for the last thirty years, not only through being brought up in a communist family but also because I lived in extreme poverty for the first twenty-five years of my life. All these accumulated experiences have given me a feeling of deep skepticism toward the political fantasies of Latin American writers, and a hatred for those writers who have revealed themselves as "closet commissars."

"Closet commissars," what does that mean?

You know what a commissar is. According to the dictionary, which follows a Soviet definition, they are officials of a communist government whose duties include political indoctrination and the detection of political deviationists, enemies of the state, etc. In a word, political police. You must have heard in New York, surely, that expression of the homosexual underground which surfaced long ago—"closet queen"? If you combine the two concepts, you'll understand that a "closet commissar" is a *bon bourgeois* who, after years of accepting the capitalist social order, suddenly discovers Marx—or in this case, Fidel Castro—and at the same time the social injustice which has always surrounded him (protected as he was by indifference and political blindness) and decides to "come out" and become an outrageous partisan. There is no worse commissar than the "closet commissar." On the other hand, I don't believe the political opinions of writers should be taken into account, whether they are "closet commissars," fellow-travelers, or old comrades.

Why not?

I don't think writers are any better equipped than other mortals to appreciate political realities. The only thing they can lay claim to is greater familiarity with words and writing, and therefore in expressing their thoughts, and of course the fact that organs for spreading opinions—like books and newspapers—are much more accessible to them than to ordinary people.

Aren't they able to make a better critical analysis?

On the contrary, if one judges the capacity for critical analysis as applied to the politics of writers from Aristotle and Plato, who didn't hesitate to serve the worst tyrants of their day, to the great writers of the thirties, who accepted as gospel the worst lies of Stalinism, one of the most cold-blooded tyrannies known to humanity, and were ready to praise it as the unique hope for the future, one can see just how well qualified writers are to judge the politics of their time and how much their utopian siren songs deserve a hearing. Of course, I don't mean leftist velleities only, for what I say could apply to all right-wing writers from Carlyle to Yeats and Eliot and Pound.

What do you think of the Bolivian coup d'etat? It seems really to have come from the left. Anyhow General Torres has promised to take the road to Lima.

He might as well take the road to Santiago. This coup shows that the military of South America have thoroughly learned Castro's lesson. Peru has applied it very successfully.

What is that lesson?

That the totalitarian wolf can disguise himself as a pink sheep with greater success than as a black one. Which proves that communism is the last refuge of military scoundrels. Thirty years ago it was fascism. At that time all those generals would have taken the road to Ciudad Trujillo, not to Havana.

But they have popular support, particularly that of the Latin American left. It seems that the revolution is now in the hands of the military.

Another turn of the screw of historical materialism. Marx foretold that the workers would make the revolution. Lenin ordained that it was to be an alliance, never completed (I'm thinking of the massacre of Kronstadt and enforced collectivization), between workers, soldiers, and peasants. Mao eliminated the workers and soldiers in favor of the peasants alone. Castro said that it would be the peasant and urban guerrillas. Guevara that it would be the peasant guerrillas alone. Now, Guevara's murderers have discovered a new class of revolutionary—please excuse the rhyme—the military. The support of the organized left doesn't surprise me. Don't forget that I grew up in a communist family which supported a military tyrant like Batista, as all Cuban communists did—and my parents became *Batistianos* right after Batista imprisoned and almost killed them in 1937! It's obvious that had Batista waited until 1970 to carry out his coup d'etat of 1952, he would have had the support of the left who elected him president in 1940. In this sense Batista will one day be seen as a precursor: history will absolve him also.

What do you think of the socialist triumph in Chile?

Curiously enough it's the final defeat of the ideologist who foretold two or three Vietnams in Latin America. That Cid of the guerrillas lost battles even after his death: the communists have gained power through middle-class ballots, not lower-class bullets! I myself am delighted that Allende has won, but for strictly personal reasons. Chile will now supplant Cuba as the Latin American Arcadia on the historical horizon, and the attention Cuba attracted (but has been losing since Castro turned himself into just another pawn in the checkered political games played by the US–USSR) will shift to Chile. Then all the intellectuals who go to Chile as political tourists will stay at the Santiago Hilton, or whatever is the Chilean equivalent of the Habana Libre, still with all expenses paid; they will tour Chile, drink Chilean wines, contemplate the Andes (more majestic now that they are socialist), compare their everlasting starkness to Chilean independence, and go into ecstasies over the propagandist efforts shown them by some Chilean version of Prince Potemkin,*

* Since the recording of this interview, at least two major Chilean contributions to communist ideology have appeared in the newspapers. The first offering was made by President Allende himself: "If every Chilean," he requested in a speech, "did the tiny task of killing ten flies a day, this country in a very short time would be a country without flies." (The International *Herald Tribune*, November 24, 1971.) The second contribution was printed in *Le Monde*, when the French newspaper correspondent in Santiago duly noted a sign painted on a wall: *Los niños nacen para ser felices.* Raved the writer: "The most beautiful slogan the Chileans have produced so far!" But the phrase declaring that children are born only in order to be happy was in fact the title of a *bolero* composed by Zoila Castellanos as early as 1961. Mrs. Castellanos—music-sheet name, "Tania" Castellanos—is a Cuban songwriter—she only writes *boleros*—who is not only a long-time communist but Lázaro Peña's wife. Furthermore, this dictum, a truism disguised as altruism, was conceived by José Martí no later

without noticing that behind the facade life will become increasingly difficult, increasingly poor, and, last but not least,
increasingly sad—as it invariably does in socialist countries, where
(according to a Cuban poet) "All Is Sadness."

Then you don't think Allende will be good for Chile?

I think Chile will be good for Allende. I mean to say,
power will be good for Allende, who has, in the winter of his
political discontent, achieved what he has always wanted, namely,
what politicians and women always desire—and that is power. As
Nietzsche, that philosophical public enemy, said, it is always good
to enjoy a little power before one dies. That is a medicine that
may make the powerful man immortal. In his imagination at
least.

*To take up the allusion to power and women I heard just now—
what do you think of the Women's Liberation Movement?*

There must be some penis-less version of John Knox
among them, because at times their movement sounds like the
first blast of the Fallopian Trumpets against the Monstrous
Regiment of Man!

But are you watching it closely?

I'm scrutinizing it with the greatest interest. After all,
don't forget that I'm practically living in a harem: surrounded
by women—my wife and daughters—and attentively observed by
a eunuch. As you know, Offenbach emits those gentle meows
because he is a *castrato*.

Seriously . . .

I'm perfectly serious. I'm waiting for the moment when
this movement takes over my house and my womenfolk decide

---

than 1895, when he was killed. Ill-conceived by Martí I should have
said, as children are born only to live as they can, then they grow up,
then they grow old and then they die—after having led lives that could
have been happy but most probably were, as Hobbes said, "solitary, poor,
nasty, brutish and short." (G.C.I.)

to pay me back for half the nearly twenty years I've spent supporting them. Thus in my ripe years I will enact the role that Faulkner thought ideal for a writer: the penman as a pimp. Then perhaps I shall write a masterpiece. In this case, a mistresspiece.

I insist . . .

I'm sure you do: you're a woman. Very well, since you insist. As with all American minority movements it sometimes seems that the minorities in search of their own identity lose their wits on the way. An extreme example is a Gay Power pamphlet that a friend has sent me from New York. It contains a picture of a naked Pink Panther exclaiming, *"Soy maricón y me gusta!"* followed by its translation in English: "I'm queer and I like it," and he is described as a Gay Guevara. This militant *maricón* is waving good-bye to his friends and admirers because he's off to do voluntary work cutting sugarcane—in Cuba! Obviously, unlike Barney Rosset, he doesn't know how many thousand Cuban *maricones* (who presumably also "like it") are *unwillingly* cutting sugarcane in Cuba, doing hard labor just because they are queer. As for the women of the lib movement, I'm waiting with interest for one of them to write a new *Contrat Social*, perhaps signing it *La vieille Héloïse:* woman is born free, yet everywhere we find her in chains.

But as a matter of fact, how many female scientists, painters, and writers do you see?

Nor do I see many male scientists, but let me tell you this century might someday be noted for the curse of a scientific discovery made by a woman. I mean radium of course. It's true that Sofonisba Anguisciola is merely a comic name in a picture gallery, but even in this century there have been two or three women painters whom I prefer to more than a dozen men: Mary Cassatt, Georgia O'Keeffe, and Leonor Fini, not to mention the masterly Leonora Carrington. If it is true that many Cuban male painters seem to be women—I say this because of their passive attitude to their environment—the best Cuban painter of all time is a woman, Amelia Pelaez. She was the only artist whom the revolution attempted to efface—from the walls if not from the map. Her superb mural on the facade of the Havana Hilton, made in 1958, was destroyed by the bureaucrat's pickax in 1961. It was a work of fine art that could be considered a murderer, for a chunk of it fell on a woman and killed her! But instead of restoring the mural, they destroyed it entirely—pictorial justice —and it became the first work of art to be condemned for manslaughter—in this case *woman*slaughter. On the other hand, I don't think I need tell you that the first great lyric poet of the West—and possibly the best—was called Sappho. As for literature, although the Random House dictionary describes Jane Austen as an *Engish* novelist, she well deserves her missing *l*—for literature. And Emily Brontë may not be the Victoria Regina of the nineteenth-century novel, but she is something better: its Vagina Rectoria. There's little more to say, except that I wouldn't change *Out of Africa* for the whole of Henry Miller, for the whole of Arthur Miller, for the whole of Warren Miller. Much closer to me, the best Cuban book of all time was written by a woman: *El Monte* by Lydia Cabrera. This book has been totally ignored everywhere, not because its author is a woman but because Lydia Cabrera has been an exile since 1960.

But what do you think of the movement itself?

I've only seen photographs and newsreels, and to judge by those it seems as if many of the demonstrators are bent on proving that Baudelaire was right when he said woman was the reverse of a dandy.

What do you think of all these movements we've been discussing?

Now that the Chinese Cultural Revolution has been paralyzed by its own motor Mao, the United States seems to me to possess the only revolutionary society—or society in violent evolution—that exists in the world.

Would you care to live in the United States?

Yes, certainly. I was in the United States a short while ago, in Los Angeles, San Francisco, Salt Lake City: I traveled all through the Southwest, and found it a fascinating country.

Huxley was right, the Mormon Temple in Salt Lake City is an unforgettably hideous monument. It seemed to me a temple to the devil. Or rather, a temple to the ferocious Jehovah of the Old Testament. The West is the land of westerns: of the epic poetry of today. Los Angeles is indeed the city of the future. As soon as you've taken to the car again and given up one of the few forms of exercise I enjoy, walking, you discover a city made up of urban islands linked together by streams of cars. I found it moving to renew my acquaintance with the country of Chandler and the dear old studios. San Francisco was a disappointment. Like Buenos Aires, São Paulo, and Montevideo, it is a city that is desperately trying to look European. For Americans, both north and south, who are ashamed of being American, these cities appear to be the epitomes of civilization. But to me they are poor pastiches.

And New York?

It was eleven years since I'd seen it. New York revisited seemed to me better than ever. Besides which, the city has become truly democratic. The last time I was there it was still the proud metropolis of an eternal empire. It's more accessible now, and infinitely more democratic.

But violent.

All cities are violent. Man is a violent animal. Where men are most concentrated, in cities, there you find concentrated violence. The only change for the worse I found in New York was in the relation between blacks and whites. There are definitely two cities in Manhattan, one black, the other white. The Negroes undoubtedly have prior rights, which stemmed from an original wrong—slavery—but their tactics are wrong. A black race cannot possibly survive by themselves. It would be a cyst which the great American body of the white—or non-black—majority would finally eliminate, whether by expulsion or assimilation. Assimilation would only amount to that integration for which Negroes have fought so persistently in the past, until the death of Martin Luther King. Expulsion would mean an *apartheid* chosen by the American Negroes, unlike those in South Africa.

Only the temporary refuge of Back-to-Africa remains. But this regressive movement toward Africa through the metaphors of clothes and hair style seems to me as superficial as any other fashion. Within five years it will be one more sartorial memory, like the long jackets of the zoot-suiters of the forties. No American Negro can return to Africa. Not even the blackest Negroes of America, who are the Haitians. American Negroes are more American than Negro, in spite of themselves and of American racists. They are less African than the Negroes of Cuba or Brazil. The moment the Fantis and Ashantis were forced to abandon their drums they cut their umbilical cords with Africa. Richard Wright, who by the way invented the term "Black Power," when speaking of the Negroes of Africa used the phrase: "I was black and they were black, but it didn't help me at all." To the two misfortunes of Franz Fanon, that West Indian writer adopted by extremist American Negroes—"the Negro who wants to whiten his skin is as unhappy as the one who preaches hatred of the whites"—a third must be added: the unhappiness of the mock comeback.

And will Black Power be an effective power in America someday?

I would feel sorry for its members. One of the few everlasting political axioms is that power corrupts and black power would certainly corrupt the blacks. That happy, optimistic, and creative race deserves a better fate. One has only to look at Duvalier—Black Power in the oldest republic in Latin America—to realize that corruption is not confined to special races. The war of extermination against the brave people of Biafra, waged by Negroes, was of a cruelty not seen in Africa since the days of the slave trade.

How do you think Latin American intellectuals will react to these statements of yours?

I won't lie awake trying to imagine. I have never worried about anyone else's reaction, favorable or unfavorable, to what I say. I always say what I think when I'm asked, simply for the sake of peace of mind. I find it calming not to be obliged to keep up one set of political opinions for publication and another at home. The opinion of intellectuals, Latin, Anglo-Saxon, or European, troubles me not at all. I think most of them tend to overestimate the power of the pen, as of the sword, when pen and sword are really no more than inert phallic symbols. In every writer, in every intellectual, in every man who thinks but doesn't act, there lies hidden a pathetic nostalgia for action. Intellectuals feel the same impulse toward action that an impotent man feels toward sex: the same need to be reverent voyeurs. As they aren't capable of taking part in such activity they think it must contain some extraordinary value, the fulfillment of body and spirit, happiness. I don't believe this. I've been closely connected with a lot of men of action, and although I know heroism does exist because I've known heroes, I also know that it is a situation more than a human condition. Men of action never deserve the exaggerated appreciation they get from thinkers. The famous and false dilemma of being either Alexander or Aristotle never arises for anyone who knows that Alexander was a barbarous and brutal drunkard who sometimes, out of mere caprice, condescended to pose as the pupil of a scholar. For this early example of a military bully, Aristotle, science, as well as bisexual practices, were mere amusements to divert a soldier's idle moments between battles. To conclude this incursion into historical simile, I might add that oddly enough Fidel Castro's pseudonym in the Sierra for all communications with the other guerrillas and the towns was—predictably—Alexander. Certainly more than a code name, a key name.

What do you think of the attacks made by Cuban intellectuals on Latin American leftist intellectuals for supporting the Cuban Revolution without participating in any revolutionary activity of their own?

It's that old curse of writers: literary envy, disguised now as political orthodoxy, but seriously aggravated at the present time by the fact that those writers who are attacked—first Fuentes and Neruda, later Nicanor Parra and others—do not have to endure the same paradise to which Cuban writers, whether revolutionaries or not, are condemned for life. Castro, a West Indian version of Jehovah, does not expel them: he forces them to earn

their daily bread by sweating their brows over diatribes written
to order.

What can you tell me about Castro, and his personality?

Without wanting to draw a historical parallel of any
kind, I hold the same opinion that Trotsky had of Stalin, but
with a difference. Trotsky described Stalin as a gangster: in other
words a politician who had been turned into a gangster by the
desire for power. Fidel Castro is a gangster, and worse still, a
gangster who has become a policeman. When I call him a gangster
it's not a mere metaphor but a concrete reference to his past.

Do you know him well?

Better than many of his ministers do. I got to know
Castro in about 1948, when he was fighting in an organization of
gangsters, thinly disguised as revolutionaries, called the UIR.
There was a corner of Havana, in the Calles Prado and Virtudes,
where painters and writers, professional talkers and layabouts
used to meet, along with one or two gangsters who crossed the
avenue to hear what the "artists" were talking about. Castro occasionally used to put in an appearance, always wearing the
aura of a dangerous and persecuted man.

Was he different then from what he is today?

As different, physically, as Hitler the house painter of the
Munich beer houses was to the Fuhrer when in power. At that
time he had no beard to conceal his receding chin, nor the smile
to captivate the unwary. He was very serious and very cautious,
and always wore a double-breasted suit and tie. The loose jacket
was to hide the everlasting .45 pistol at his belt.

What is this UIR?

The initials of the Unión Insurreccional Revolucionaria,
a *Habanero* gang, made up of ex-followers of Guiteras, who was
Minister for the Interior when Grau was revolutionary president
in 1933. His real name was Tony Guiteras Holmes, he was born
in the United States, and was the main character in *We Were
Strangers*, Huston's film based on his life. They were Aprists

(followers of the Peruvian APRA) and anti-*Batistianos* as well as anti-communists. The entire insurrectionary activity of this gang—those were the times of Grau and Prío's constitutional governments, when Batista was an exile on the golden sands of Daytona Beach—was confined to a fight to get public posts in the ministeries and municipalities of the twin cities of Havana and Marianao. The UIR was founded in 1945 by Emilio Tro, a veteran of the American army who, when the World War came to an end, returned to Cuba to organize his own private war. Tro had begun his terrorist activities against Batista in 1934, when only sixteen years old. He was a real psychotic, fascinated by the idea of killing and being killed, like so many other Cuban desperadoes who afterwards became guerrillas in town or country. This *Habanero* gang was organized with a view to exterminating all enemies, private and public, whom Tro had made or would make. Many of his guilty victims—to whom, after machine-gunning them, he fixed a Raffles-like notice saying, "Justice is slow but sure"—were former policemen from Machado and Batista's regimes, others had been members of some group now out of favor, and the rest were innocent victims—a passerby, two unwitting witnesses, and so on. Castro belonged to this gang, and Manolo Castro (no relation but former president of the Federation of University Students and at that time general director of Sport) was a member of a rival group, the MSR, whose ranks included many ex-communists and veterans of the International Brigades in the Spanish Civil War. One night Manolo Castro was talking to someone in the entrance to a cinema, when suddenly another Castro, Fidel, appeared on the battlefield into which the street was all at once transformed. Manolo Castro's death was described in masterly style by Hemingway, in his story "The Shot": ". . . when they killed him he had thirty-five cents in his pocket, no money in the banks and he was unarmed." He was assassinated according to an old and infallible blueprint for murder, originating in the gang wars of Chicago and copied and perfected by the UIR, with that Japanese-like talent Cubans have for adapting and improving foreign models. A car arrives and opens fire on the place where the enemy is supposed to be. When the attacking car moves on, the enemy comes out to investigate and perhaps fires impotently at his disappearing assailant. At this moment a second car appears at full throttle and riddles the opposition from behind. In this case the second car was represented by two men on foot, who shot Manolo Castro in the back. One of these men was Fidel Castro. This is why the Trotskyist epithet of gangsters is more applicable to Castro than to Stalin.

Was he prosecuted?

No, he was accused. But for what murder was Capone ever indicted?

What sort of person really is Castro?

Psychologically? A paranoic who has been turned into a schizophrenic by absolute power. One of the rebel leaders told me a story about him which gives a perfect portrait of the tyrant as a young man. One day, about thirty years ago, he met Fidel Castro in a street in Santiago de Cuba and noticed that he was behaving strangely, hiding between two pillars and looking to right and to left as if expecting to be attacked. This old friend of his asked, "Is anything the matter, Fidel?" and Castro replied: "No, nothing. I was waiting for the bus." "Then why do you hide as if someone was after you?" his friend asked. Castro's answer was: "One never knows."

But for a man who has led such a violent life this must be normal behavior.

But Castro wasn't yet fifteen at the time! Of course no one was chasing him and his days as leader of a gang were yet to come, and in Havana.

Now let's flash forward to twenty-five years later: 1959, Castro is prime minister, his popularity is unparalleled in Cuban history; his fame as a soldier and man of action is comparable only to the legendary lives of certain heroes of the wars of independence. He arrives at the offices of *Revolución*—half of whose staff would have gladly given their lives for him—to look at some photographs which he wants to censor before publication. The photos aren't ready. They are drying in the darkroom. The darkroom is at the far end of the office on a mezzanine floor reached by a spiral staircase. The sub-editor of the paper, a hero-worshipper of Castro, offers to accompany him there. They go upstairs to the dark empty room and Castro looks at the photos one by one. As they leave, Castro starts down the spiral staircase in front, but after two steps he turns and asks his companion some irrelevant question. After another two steps he turns again and asks another question. His companion notices that with each question Castro's hand goes to his hip and rests on his pistol. After the third question the sub-editor says: "Let me go first, Fidel. I know the way." End of questions and halts on the staircase. These reactions are signs of paranoia. The fact that a doctor is always at his side—two of his personal doctors have already died: the first, Dr. Fajardo, attacked in error by his escort, and the second doctor, Dr. Vallejo, died of heart failure before he was fifty—and his acute Hitlerian headaches are signs of paranoia that has become hypochondria. There is a terribly revealing anecdote illustrating this paranoia converted into schizophrenia. When Fidel Castro heard that his supposed friend Ben Bella had been dismissed by Boumédienne, after the usual accusations of a coup prepared by the CIA, agents of imperialism, etc., he exclaimed very characteristically: "I knew he was a dangerous type," meaning Boumédienne. "Hell! When he spent a whole day fishing with Raúl and me, from four in the morning till dusk, the only thing he said was 'Good morning' when he arrived, and 'Good night' when he went away! He didn't say a single word the *whole* day long! People who don't speak are always very fishy!" You notice how schizophrenic it was to reach such a conclusion simply from a man's taciturnity, which was after all understandable in a visiting Moslem who spoke very little Spanish and had come to Cuba more or less under compulsion. It's not very far from the famous phrase Shakespeare gives to Julius Caesar, in his advice to Mark Antony while keeping an eye on Cassius: "Such men are dangerous!" It must also be remembered that Stalin judged possible traitors—and many came to trial for this in Moscow—by the way that they avoided or met his gaze. Communism, considered as a science, owes as much to Mesmer as to Marx!

Have these anecdotes been published before?

I don't think so. There are many characteristic stories about Fidel Castro that have never been published. Those who took part, or told them, are either very close to Castro or are still members of his government, or if they are not in Cuba they are afraid of the long arm of a tyrant. In my case, I haven't told these stories before, nor others of the same sort, some of which I witnessed or was co-protagonist in, because of a certain personal aversion to narrative literature. There's a typical anecdote involving your compatriot Guevara and Castro in a sort of fable for future revolutionaries. It was told me by a friend, Major Duque, a veteran of the Sierra and of the Bay of Pigs, who later fled from Cuba in a rowboat. I'm not sure if you know that Che had become a first-rate marksman in the Sierra, although before he came to Cuba he hadn't used a weapon except in his precarious guerrilla training in Mexico. One day in the Sierra Maestra—one of those terrible days of guerrilla warfare when boredom had been crushingly severe—Fidel Castro invited Guevara to a shooting match as a distraction after the siesta. Others were amusing themselves throwing stones at the vultures. The rest were still asleep or looking for berries. But Duque wasn't asleep and Castro chose him to act as arbiter. Of course Castro hit the bull's eye every time, whereas Che failed to come anywhere near his usual standard. Much pleased with himself, Castro went on to other activities typical of those field days in the Sierra, and Duque stayed talking to Guevara. "Che," Duque wanted to know, "why did you shoot so badly today? You can shoot much better than that." Che looked at him slyly, smiled his ironic Argentine smile, and said: "And would you have liked me to outdo Fidel?" This was the beginning of Guevara's way of the Cross, one of the stations on the road to Bolivia.

What other anecdotes of this kind do you remember?

It's rather like "what the guerrilla butler saw!"

I was thinking of some interchange you may have actually taken part in.

I had a few direct contacts, naturally enough, with Fidel Castro. The Chinese have a saying that it's easier to contradict a dragon than the emperor. And besides, this future exile has never had a natural gift for sycophancy. The final parting of the ways between us was, of course, the "conversations in the library," where mine was one of the few authoritative voices to dissent. But before he issued his definitive *Words to Intellectuals,* I remember an occasion when the surrealist poet Baragaño and I were eating supper at dawn in a restaurant in El Vedado, aptly named the Peking, after having put the magazine to bed at four in the morning. Suddenly Castro appeared at the door, unexpected as ever, noctambulist as ever, as surrounded by his formidably armed escort as ever. He recognized us and came and sat at our table. Baragaño and I were in agreement not only about the magazine, but about a certain secondhand Trotskyism.

Why secondhand?

Because Baragaño is now as dead physically as my Trotskyism was politically at that time. Baragaño had lived in Paris, known Breton personally, had his work published in surrealist magazines—in a word: he shared all the surrealist superstitions in both art and politics. Trotsky was for me at that time some sort of revolutionary beacon, whereas now he is a revolutionary Bacon: his theory of permanent revolution is a political Laputa: every revolution, as the Mexican said, inevitably degenerates into government and ends by being a new order that is even more oppressive than the old order that was being fought against yesterday. After flirting with one or two *revolutionary groupies* who accosted him and telling the leader of his retinue in an undertone to make a note of the address of the more audacious of these camp-followers, we left. It was already morning but we went on talking in the street. Baragaño and I tacitly decided to share our worries with Castro. At that time, early in 1960, a certain individual was making a secret stop in Cuba on his way to Czechoslovakia as compulsory but submissive guest of the revolutionary government: this was Trotsky's assassin, the man known as Jacob Mornard or Ramón Mercader, who (as few people are aware) is undoubtedly a Cuban. He was born in Santiago de Cuba and his mother was, at that time at least, called Caridad Mercader. The parodies of Trotsky in *TTT* were derived from this fact. As a political curiosity of the time when the new revolutionaries coincided in history with the Stalinist dinosaurs and to disabuse those who want to see fresh hope in neo-totalitarianism, I can tell that it was still possible in 1965 to go to the Cuban Embassy in Paris and be admitted to that elegant Art Nouveau apartment on the Avenue Foch by a stunning receptionist. Not a dark Cuban beauty but a lady of about sixty-five, very thin, with deep-set shifty eyes and very nervous gestures. Her real name was Caridad Mercader, although I never found out what alias she used with visitors. I wonder what the innumerable Trotskyist visitors would have said if they had known that they were welcomed at the Cuban Embassy by the mother of Trotsky's assassin! As every reader of Deutscher or Gorkín knows, Caridad Mercader was a ferocious Stalinist at the time of the Spanish Civil War and exercised a powerful influence over her assassin son.

How did she come to be receptionist at the Cuban Embassy?

     She was a second or third cousin of the ambassador's wife, both from Santiago. Since this ambassador, Harold Gramatges, besides being a mediocre composer, had been a former cultural tool of the Stalinists in the Cuban PSP and was posted to the embassy in Paris through the combined efforts of Che Guevara and Raúl Castro, it doesn't seem to me a coincidence that Caridad Mercader was also to be found taking refuge on Cuban territory in France.

    But to return to that Havana dawn when Baragaño and I were talking to Castro in the entrance to the Peking, we asked him how it had been possible for the revolutionary government to agree to let Ramón Mercader stay in Cuba after his recent liberation from the Mexican prison of Lecumberri. We knew through cables and the direct contacts of *Revolución* with the government that Mexico wanted to get rid of Mercader and that Castro had given his personal permission for him to spend a week in Havana before getting lost for good in that totalitarian labyrinth behind the Iron Curtain. Fidel Castro answered our question with a characteristic formula combining mystery and revelation: "Well, we really did it because we were asked to by a government to which we owe a lot, a *great deal*. We owe much to these people and their government, which has done us a great favor." Baragaño and I understood that he was referring to Novotny's government. Czechoslovakia had just sent Cuba a large shipment of arms, in the greatest possible secrecy and apparently on lengthy credit. Then he added: "Besides, we"—ever since he became dictator of Cuba Castro had used the royal plural when talking, like Queen Victoria—"we didn't order Trotsky to be killed!" (This mixture of political expediency and historical self-justification is typical of Castro, a lawyer educated by Jesuits.) This explanation was followed by an incident which in time was to become doubly ironic. From Trotsky and his assassin, he moved on to Trotskyism, our leftish infantilism, meaning *Lunes* and its first issues, in which we had published every sort of revolutionary literature because we were fatally ahead of the times and fending with both official right and official left: with the right wing of the 26th July Movement which influenced the magazine and with the periodical *Hoy*, organ of the PSP, as well as with the Catholic and conservative daily papers, now no more. The printing in *Lunes* (*de Revolución*) of Trotsky's writings, the communist manifesto, Saint-Just's speeches, and essays by Breton, Orwell, Malraux, and Koestler caused a sensation in Havana, where it was some time since an important paper had published anything of the sort. Referring to these issues of *Lunes*, Fidel Castro said: "All this premature extreme left activity of yours strikes me as very bad, very ill-timed. Not because I'm afraid of it," he added turning to point to the name of the street on a sign, "because if you like I'll give orders this moment for this street to be called Karl Marx Avenue! But one must bide one's time."

But surely it was extraordinary that Castro should have felt obliged to discuss secret affairs of state, and explain them to people who weren't members of the government, after all?

Of course those explanations were made in private. If we had asked those same questions in public, in front of television cameras for instance, we would have received an angry diatribe in reply. His image as a leader ready to enter into discussion is completely false. He is one of the political figures who least likes to be contradicted, even over trivialities, quite apart from fundamental differences or effective forms of opposition. Castro won't even allow minorities to exist within his own group. One can't talk of parties because the existence of the Communist Party of Cuba is a fiction. Every day that passes makes it clearer that in Cuba even such fictitious parliamentary forms as the Supreme Soviet won't ever exist. In Cuba there is not even a constitution to regulate public life! Cuban life is ruled by the most appalling illegalities: there every action, public or private, is potentially criminal in intent.

And how about those who supported the revolution at the beginning, what did they make of Castro's personality?

I used to think myself that he had changed, that the bullying gang-leader had been left behind in some pigeonhole of history. His journey through the United States, Canada, and Latin America, during which I was among his suite, convinced me of the opposite. When I got home I said so to my friends who thought I was exaggerating. At that time I was obsessed by the idea that Castro would become a Cuban version of Nasser. Time has shown that Castro and Nasser are merely avatars of the tyrant. On his *camaradas* and close collaborators Castro exercised—and still does —the same influence that Hitler exercised on his followers. One of the architects of Nazism—both in a literal and figurative sense—Albert Speer, in his recent book described Hitler's personal magnetism and also mentioned his susceptibility to any adverse criticism. Castro's minions, like those of Hitler or Stalin, used to react to his personal foibles as sub-products of power and showed their pleasure or displeasure according to the degree of favor or disfavor they were enjoying.

What is your present position—political, ideological, and philosophical?

One, I'm anti-utopian: I believe that Arcadia, Paradise, or whatever that horizon is called, lies behind us, always in the remote past and never in the future. Two, I believe that all ideologies are reactionary: power corrupts ideas as well as men: *communism is merely the poor man's fascism.* Three, philosophically speaking I am a complete skeptic: not a single corpus of irrefutable ideas exists. Like all skeptics I feel drawn to stoicism. A system of superstitions helps one to dominate the feelings of solitude imposed by one's own agnosticism—but—but—the operative word is doubt.

At the risk of seeming gossip-loving, can I ask you to comment on Castro's private life?

I would rather not, and if your question seems gossipy, it's because it is. But after all, history is only a sequence of two or three decisive pieces of gossip, stitched together by theories which are discredited sooner or later. The theory of history changes but the practice of gossip remains. Historical gossip is the *sole* possible relation between Tacitus and Plutarch and Gibbon and Toynbee and Schlesinger.

Are you never afraid of reprisals for what you say?

I'm less afraid of external attacks by *sbirri*—intellectual and physical: there are all sorts—than of internal attacks from my conscience. But I ought to recognize this fear runs in the family. It is much in evidence in my wife, Miriam Gómez. As my brother wrote from New York, when advising every sort of caution after my public statements in 1968: "Do remember that although you aren't Trotsky, Fidel Castro is *not* Stalin either."

Then can I ask you some more political questions before passing on to literary ones?

I would have preferred all the questions to be literary, but it's obvious this century has become a religious one: one can't get away from politics.

What do you think of the present Soviet leadership?

I saw a picture of Podgorny, Brezhnev, and Kosygin welcoming Pompidou to the Soviet Union, in the paper this very morning. I thought these three were the gray men with the flannel, suite.

What's your view of China?

Although many of my friends in Cuba called me the Chinaman and Octavio Paz's wife, whenever Paz says I look Mexican, insists that I come from Nepal, the Chinese continent has always seemed to me as inscrutable as its content. China is an enigma contained in a riddle, enveloped in mystery, shrouded by the unknown, and placed at the center of a maze. I can never be sorry enough that I didn't accept the invitation I received to visit China in 1960, which I refused for trivial reasons. Although perhaps my visit would have increased my ignorance.

What do you think of Mao?

One of those Chinese emperors who always knew that books lasted longer than men and of course much longer than the ideas contained in them.

Do you believe ideas are perishable?

Everything is perishable, even books: books too will die. The ideas contained in some books die before the books do. For instance, the Hellenic ideal has been dead for centuries. However, books like the *Odyssey* and the *Iliad* which preceded the Hellenic ideal by several centuries, those books are still alive today and will continue to live for some time to come. Sappho's works are still alive, although in fragments, and refuse to die: they are immortal. I don't know how long Mao's little book will live, but there is no doubt that the cultural revolution, which seems to be a translation of Bismarck's *Kulturkampf* into Mandarin, is really the opposite: the subordination of the state to the church, practically equivalent to the false burial of the living king at Yuste: the emperor undergoes a living death so that his ideals shall live in his death. What really destroyed Charles V's empire was the absence of a book. Mao has insured himself against similar disregard, and when this materialist in a country without gods or heaven for the believer does actually die, he will leave his book as a proof of eternal life: the vehicle, as it were, of his revolutionary soul—*the little red riding book!*

How does the new attitude of the Church in Latin America strike you?

It's the same old line but reversed: the Church is capable of going to Canossa in search of power.

How do you explain this?

What can one say about the different ways a drowning man can clutch at safety? The Church is a declining power that has managed to survive in hostile historical waters: it isn't strange that it should attempt the impossible to keep afloat. Blessing spaceships and establishing relations with Tito are also the gestures of shipwrecked priests. If the last century proved that secular science—in other words modern technology—was incompatible with the Church, this century of ours has shown that it is possible to have religion without churches: true communists, the neo-Buddhists, and the hippies are just as religious as many *padres.* However, to a man who belongs to no church, the agony of Christianity becomes more repugnant as its efforts at self-absolution *in extremis* become more humble and sincere. The Anglican Church may give money to the South African rebels, but this generosity *in articulo mortis* will never efface the criminality implicit in Cecil Rhodes's famous phrase that it was the duty of every good Christian in Africa to evangelize and at the same time make a profit. As for the Catholic Church, no progressive Pope —a contradiction in terms—can make people forget the agreement with Hitler, Pius XII's indifference to the extermination of the Jews, and the concordat between the Vatican and Mussolini's Rome—to confine ourselves to the present century alone. Can the Catholic Church in Spain possibly efface its complicity with fascism which exterminated the republic by performing some Basque gestures? As for Latin America the contradiction is nowhere more obvious than in Cuba, where the papal nuncio

behaves with all possible courtesy to the Castrist regime in an
endeavor to efface the Church's collaboration with Batista's
regime—and to draw a veil over the fact that this same Fidel
Castro they are praising today was excommunicated by Pope
John XXIII in 1961! How can such adulation coexist under the
same soutane with the recollection of all those unhappy believers
who were shot between 1959 and 1965 and who went to the wall
in the fortress of La Cabaña, exactly opposite the archbishop's
palace, crying *Viva Cristo Rey?* The sole coherent explanation was
offered by an intellectual belonging to the literary Catholic group
Orígenes, when he confessed in 1965: "We must be very grateful
to Fidel Castro. After all, thanks to him, we have achieved
something never achieved before in the old republic: we have
eliminated competition." This Catholic intellectual was alluding
to the campaign of extermination that was being carried out by
the Castrist regime at that time against Jehovah's Witnesses, Ad-
ventists, and other Protestant sects, grouped together under the
official nickname of *batiblancos* (white robes) and mercilessly
persecuted. Perhaps this cynical communicant was right when he
said: "After all, we mustn't forget that Fidel was educated by
us." He was presumably referring to the Society of Jesus.

And what about the Catholic Church in Latin America today?

    It has been Cubanized.

*Then we must accept the fact that Cuban influence in Latin
America may not be total, but is at least enormous, don't you
think so?*

    Not only in Latin America but in both Americas and
Europe as well. This charming, long unhappy island, as Hemingway so well described it, has been a too frequent Pandora's box:
it has presented humanity with three plagues in less than half a
millennium. The first was the venereal cancer of syphilis, when
the island was discovered and put on the map by Columbus.
Afterwards, when its geography was a projection of Spain's
history, the vegetable cancer of tobacco spread the vice of smoking throughout the world. And since Cuba took possession of her
own history in 1959, the third plague, the geopolitical cancer of

Castroism, has flooded and befouled the world, invading it with second-rate religion and Marx toy guns.

Aren't you afraid for your family in Cuba?

No, because my closest relations have long been communists. My father, for instance, is an obviously inoffensive man, and an addict, rather than an adherent, of the dictates of the party, of which he was a founder. My mother died some years ago, and the rest of the family have very little contact with me. I realize that my solitude, like my being so far away, is a luxury. Other Cuban writers can't say the same. That is why they are unable to speak so freely.

Do you feel a real need to return to Cuba?

I feel a physical need for the tropics but not for Cuban soil. When someone needs soil he only needs about six feet of it. Certain hot climates give me a sense of physical well-being. That is sun-worship rather than patriotism. For instance, when I was in California I felt at home. I like sunshine and heat and detest cold, rain, darkness, mist, and snow: everything that goes to make up the English climate.

Then why did you choose to live in London rather than Paris or Spain or the United States?

It was actually London that chose me. I've chosen very few things in my life—even my departure from Cuba was a product of disillusionment rather than choice. Of course my disillusionment had a lot to do with the lack of choice, a characteristic common to totalitarianism everywhere. I lived in Madrid for nine months, and I've never felt so alien to my surroundings as I did in Spain. Our common language was like an abyss between us. I couldn't get into the United States unless I declared myself a political refugee. I've never enjoyed Paris for more than a weekend, with all the superficiality involved in a weekend holiday. The City of Light has never been a lighthouse for me. I've never found the verbal candy of the French language pleasant to the ear. On the other hand, I've always had a passion for English. Ever since I first found English hidden behind a screen as a child, its mystery fascinated me. Chance and screen-writing took me to London, but the choice was mutual. I like living here. I like the English character. Living so close to the English, as one does in London, I've learned to distinguish their good characteristics from the bad ones. Parochialism is one of the bad things, but that's an islander's failing: perhaps it is one aspect of the charm of islands. Cuba was also a parochial society, but parochialism has drowned in her imperialist wishful-sinking. There's another defect of the English soul: hypocrisy. But hypocrisy allows room for a certain urbanity. The most hypocritical Latin American race, the Mexicans, are also the politest, the most urbane. But I prefer hypocritical urbanity to the brutal frankness of Spaniards, or rather Castilians, and to the downright rudeness which now replaces the once proverbial courtesy of the French. And England is the country that invented modern justice, with her institutions—taken for granted here, but seen to be priceless where they have been lost—such as habeas corpus, the search warrant, and the inviolability of the home. In England it is absolutely true that a man's house is his castle and that this is not only the privilege of feudal or modern lords. Besides, symmetry is one way of fighting against the omnipotent god we superstitious atheists worship—Chance. I am pleased by the equilibrium of my having been born and spent half my life—I left Cuba when I was exactly thirty-three—in an island close to the mainland at the southern extremity of the northern hemisphere in the Atlantic Ocean, only to land up in another island, close to the mainland at the northern extremity of the northern hemisphere in the Atlantic Ocean! Such parallel coincidences give one the same certainty of being alive that a mirror provides. You see your reflection, therefore you exist. That's what we call symmetry.

So you like the English?

I like Englishwomen even more. But, like the Chinese and the Jews, they are one of the few altogether admirable nations. I don't believe in the existence of superior races, but if there are any superior nations this is one of them. Somewhat given to Indian abulia: as so often happens in history, the conquered race ended by conquering their conquerors. But it's a pity that, like the Indians, the English have no sense of humor.

Might this lack of sense of humor drive you to leave England some day?

No, but that practical joke, the income tax, might.

Could you live in the United States?

But they've invented that teasing taxation there too!

Did you discover anything new in America?

You sound as if you were talking to Columbus.

Well, did you come across anything new in the United States?

Possibly in New York. It was ten years since I had visited that megalopolis. I find that it's a much more democratic city today, that by losing its superiority as the metropolis of an empire it has gained in humanity. Before it was a vertical version of Rome under the Caesars. Now everything looks rundown. I like this decaying that is actually a decadence. Grandeur is just a form of folly.

Perhaps that's because you don't come now from one of the colonies.

It's possible. But the last time I was there I didn't exactly arrive as an immigrant. As a matter of fact I was with Fidel Castro's *corps de guerrilla*. Although, to complete your allusion, it was perhaps a case of the scribe sneaking into the metropolis among the legions returning wreathed in laurels—the wreaths made of clippings, naturally.

What did you find in California?

That Hollywood had vanished and Los Angeles is there instead.

Were you disappointed?

As much as a faithful Moslem who goes to Mecca and finds the Ka'ba stone reduced to gravel. But there are still some gods in that Olympus—to mix the myths together with my metaphors.

Who for instance?

Mae West. That Artemis–Aphrodite even now receives tributes with an archaic but still warm smile.

Did you get to know her personally?

Certainly I did.

What is she like?

As before, better than before. She's the triumph of sex over death, or in this case senility. Nothing but a symbol remains of the former paradigm, yet it is a living sign. Mae West conquered Hollywood and she survives as a star in its heaven.

Do you think the American film is in a decline?

I think the movies in general, now that they have become film, are in a decline. But the American film is no more in a decline than the French, which has always been decadent. Because Hollywood is dead, the movies, the spectacle, are moribund. The *cinema de camera* doesn't interest me, it never has. The symphonic film from Hollywood has been the only one for me. Others have always been exceptions: marginal notes on the history of the cinema, which is the history of the century. But the true history of film, the course of its history is to be found in the making and development of Hollywood. The Golden Age of Film began in 1929 with the start of the talkies (that was the year of *Broadway Melody,* of the birth of Mickey in *Steamboat Willie,* of *All Quiet on the Western Front,* of *Morocco,* including Dietrich and her myth, the year when Garbo spoke for the first time, and of course of *Little Caesar:* all made or screened during that year of my birth) and went on until 1949, the year when *Letter from an Unknown Woman, A Double Life, On the*

Town, An American in Paris, The Set-Up, were made or shown,
all for me films belonging to my private mythology, and of
course *The Asphalt Jungle*, when the greatest myth of all,
Marilyn Monroe, made her appearance. The rest is Hollywood's
death-agony, the decline of a great popular art and the industry
which made it possible, both at the same time. But in those two
glorious decades the gods of that Olympus were alive and kick-
ing the collective consciousness. Now they have disappeared, are
dead—or murdered by those deicides of the cinema, the critics.

Et tu Brute? You were a cinema critic yourself.

That was when I was earning my living by writing about
films. But my love, my passion for the movies goes much further
back. The first time I went to the movies I was twenty-nine *days*
old, taken by my mother who was crazy about the movies and
whose motto (when I was a boy) was "Cinema or Sardines." It
meant that we either ate or saved money to go to the movies. Of
course I can't remember anything about the first film I ever saw,
which was a revival of *The Four Horsemen of the Apocalypse*,
with the immortal Rudolph Valentino among the ghosts. But my
first memories are connected with pictures on a screen, on a wall:
the lights and shadows of motion pictures. I remember films I saw
when I could not have been more than three years old: so that I
was looking at films before I learned to read at the age of four—
in other words I could read in the movies before I could in books.
To me, the cinema has actually been more than a school, it has
been an education. I've also seen it as a serious substitute for religion for a primitive pagan such as myself. One of the proofs of
Hollywood's decadence is that it has been trying to de-mythify the
movies ever since the early fifties and reducing that amazing
catalogue of minor gods and goddesses, the film stars—all of them
still alive on the screen and many of them in real life as well—to
the status of ordinary mortals. Of course the movies have been
supplanted by television, which converts daily life into a collection of dynamic images: and now where once there were gods
and goddesses there is nothing but confusion and primeval chaos.
We have killed the gods of film too, without knowing how to fill
their place. Naturally there are still some good films being made

and seen, but it is now too late for the myth and too early for the essentials. That was what I felt on my arrival in Hollywood.

Did you go there to write a scenario?

No, I went to adapt the script I had written in London to its locations in mid- and southwest America. As usual I found life copying literature and instead of my having to adapt the screenplay to reality, reality followed my script, even down to some proper names, chosen haphazard which afterwards turned up in my path just as if they had been planted there. Nor was it a question of names only. In my script there was a blind DJ. When the director of my film and I were looking for a suitable locale in Denver, we found that a blind DJ had been there before!

Is it true, as I was told in New York, that Fox Films thought that script the best they had read for a long time and Darryl Zanuck insisted on collaborating with you?

That is the legend derived from the truth and the truth is that Richard Zanuck sent a telegram saying that my script was the best he had read since *Butch Cassidy and the Sundance Kid.* Old Darryl Zanuck was carried away by the plot and thought up a short scene for the beginning which was entirely in the right spirit of the film. Of course it was incorporated. Not only as a buttress to that modern cathedral, the film, but in homage to that old creator of myths, Zanuck.

What is the name of the film?

The same as the script's, *Vanishing Point.*

What is it about?

A myth, of course. It's a version of the western epic, in the form of an epic of the car. It's the old theme of the western— one man all alone, fighting against adversity—translated into modern terms. It deals with a journey beset with dangers and adventures until the very end. As you see, it's one of the many variations on the voyages of Ulysses, except that this time it doesn't end in Ithaca but in death.

Did you write it in English?

All my scripts are written in English. To avoid the professional paranoia of those who write for the cinema, I have not only written these scripts in a different language from my books, I have also signed them with a pseudonym. Paranoia overcome by schizophrenia, as you see.

What is your pseudonym?

Cain.

But you use the same for your film criticisms, don't you?

No. My film criticisms are signed G. Caín, pronounced Cah-ín. The scripts by Guillermo Cain, as in Kane.

Why do you use such a cruel pseudonym?

It's an old story and harks back to words as usual. It comes from the first syllable of my first name and the first syllable of my surname. Of course, I've benefitted from the three thousand years of publicity attached to the name of the first of wicked men.

Will Vanishing Point be one of those films that are good to make and also to see?

How can I tell? A film can never be better than its director. There's a saying that a good director can always make a good film out of any book—and that includes the phone book. Its counterpart is another saying. A bad director can make a bad film out of the best script in the world—and that includes the Scriptures. Everything depends on the talent of that little Little Caesar, the film director. If the talent of directors is judged by their megalomania there can be no doubt that the director of *Vanishing Point* has enormous talent.

Why did you suddenly stop writing film criticism in 1961?

More and more films from Soviet Russia and other communist countries began to be shown in Cuba. Obviously these films didn't need to be criticized. That is the sole point where art and propaganda coincide: true works of art and the products of propagandists need no criticism. They are, of their very nature, imperishable or essentially temporary, acritical—they require excessive praise. Following Count Keyserling's example, I believed that when you cannot tell the truth it's better not to talk at all. So I decided to be silent. As this political state of things became permanent, I shut up for good.

In the prologue to Un oficio del siglo xx (A Twentieth-Century Profession) *the book of your collected cinema criticisms, Cabrera Infante, writer of the prologue, says of G. Caín the critic: "Caín did irreparable harm to the spectator: he believed he had invented the movies." Why?*

That's a game between the writer and his double. Trying to divest myself utterly of my critical side, my profession, I decided to give the professional a personality and separate him completely from myself. It was obviously impossible: we turned into Siamese twins. By attributing all my faults as a critic to my alter ego I was merely objectifying myself, but since the critic was now an individual this objectification became a new game, with mirrors this time. That sentence, taken out of context, doesn't reveal the fact that what separates me from Caín is the same as what unites us: the umbilical cord of our love for the movies, which is a brotherly union not between the two of us but of each with the same mother.

You also say: "It was this form of intellectual democracy which made him always refuse to think of the reader as an animal of another species, a member of an inferior race." Do you think this is the normal attitude of a critic to his reader?

It's in fact the attitude of all didacticism, whether artistic, philosophic, or political. Every writer who sets out to enlighten his reader methodically, like a schoolmaster, profoundly despises him. That's why I've never tried to avoid difficulties in my writing. If the reader understands what I'm saying, fine. If he doesn't understand, it still seems to me fine. I'm not offering him anything but possible communication under conditions of equal-

ity. My ideal is absolute identity between reader and writer. If
that is not entirely possible, I will accept gradation, but never
degradation, of one or the other.

*To judge by the quality of many television programs, some plays,
and some films, don't you think they underestimate the public
they are intended for?*

Not necessarily, if you are referring to various sorts of
entertainment. Playwrights, showmen, and impresarios—I include
Shakespeare and Lope de Vega among the first, since the Swan
of Avon talked of the public as "groundlings" and the Phoenix
among Authors made it plain that to please the public one must
speak "like a fool"—all entertainers in fact, have always shown
that their prime concern was to vulgarize a spectacle so as to put
it within reach of most of their patrons. Every show is a vulgar-
ization because you can't have a spectacle without spectators. If
the theater seems to have become respectable about mid-cen-
tury it is because the movies had taken over responsibility for
vulgarity when it stole the public away from the stage to the
screen. Nowadays the big screen seems more reputable and it is
the small screen that has to wear the sanbenito for vulgarity. But
there's a paradox here. The area of television programs that needs
the largest audience, and therefore had to be vulgarized, is the
one that is becoming most refined and carrying furthest the aim
of transforming television from a medium of communication
into an art. I'm referring, of course, to the commercials. Some
television advertisements are really minor works of art, whereas
most of the programs themselves consist of mere information or
mediocre illustrations of novels, or miniaturizations of films. The
language of some of the advertisements, their syntax, texture,
and elliptical manner of transmitting a given message seem to me
exemplary. Since the language is the message and vice versa,
it can be all form. In other words, all art.

Who do you think are the best cinema directors of the present day?

For some time now I've believed *la politique des
auteurs* to be as false as the *nouvelle vague* which inspired it. I
prefer *la politique des étoiles*. Thus any film of Edward G. Robin-

son's will leave me in ecstasies over his power to stir the feelings. There is no more tragic line in all modern tragedy than his exclamation at the end of *Little Caesar*. "Mother of Mercy, is this the end of Rico?" this Chicagonistes asks incredulously before he expires. Humphrey Bogart, in spite of the recent vogue for his charming—how many people realize that this word is more apt than "charismatic," though they come from the same Greek root?—and charmed face, is another extraordinary presence, even in his most mediocre moments. I always smile when I remember his toughness in metaphors least connected with his profession as tough guy, even when asking a pal to turn off the wireless: "Lefty, kill that radio," he says in *High Sierra*, immortalizing the Hemingwayized Huston who wrote the dialogue. James Cagney combines the tragic sense of life and the poetical toughness of both Bogart and Robinson but outdoes them in his graceful gait, like a dancer who has taken a false step. How can one credit any writer or director—even though we have to do with Ben Hecht and Howard Hawks*—with the comically sinister repetition of the word "Expensive" in the mouth of Muni–Scarface? Or, in this same masterpiece, the coin which the ever-indifferent George Raft flips into the air with his thumb and catches on the palm of his right hand? These two film stars—gods incarnate—transcend all socio-economic theories about the relation between money and power. Of course they are more accurate than some vulgarly partisan—that is to say apoetic, that is to say didactic, that is to say Marxian—play by Bertolt Brecht.

Then in your view there are no great cinema directors?

Yes, of course there are. There's Hitchcock, there's John Ford, there's Howard Hawks, there's Vincente Minnelli, there's Raoul Walsh on occasion. These filmmakers appear incapable of committing any gross error. Yet they are not infallible—though Hitchcock and Ford often seem so.

---

* On second thought I'm probably being unfair here to W. R. Burnett who wrote not only *Little Caesar* and *High Sierra*, the novels, but also originated *Scarface* and *Nobody Lives Forever*, besides writing all of *The Asphalt Jungle*. Most probably he and not John Huston wrote the Bogart line, as he certainly wrote Edward G. Robinson's famous last phrase.

And which would you include from the European cinema?

Certainly not Godard, though I would have once. Nor Bergman: I have sworn never to see another of his taciturn Scandinavian sagas-of-the-mind. Nor would I include Antonioni, whose last film, *Zabriskie Point*, throws serious doubts on all his previous work and suddenly reveals him as a false and extremely frivolous opportunist: three grave flaws that I had not even suspected in Antonioni's so-called art.

Is this so very serious in the world of entertainment?

It wouldn't be in Busby Berkeley with his animated dollies and his complicated optical choreography, but it is serious in someone who comes forward as an interpreter of modern life, a sort of contemporary soothsayer, and is suddenly revealed as an expedient camp-follower.

Isn't the same true of Fellini?

On the contrary. Fellini is an illusionist. His *Satyricon* is a supreme act of temporal magic, a journey in the top-hat of time. Everyone knows the veneration I feel for the book itself, which is the earliest modern novel. And I've always wanted to translate it into Cuban, not into Spanish, but into terms of the decadence and creation of Batista's last years and the first years of the revolution in Havana, when a wholly pagan, nocturnal, and amoral *mundo* was happily whirling to its end. My novel *TTT* was an imperfect attempt to approach that ancient, masterly model. Now we have such a translation: Fellini's *Satyricon* illuminates and goes beyond its prototype. There's a moment in the film, during Trimalchio's banquet, when the camera moves among the dense ranks of Roman diners and suddenly stops, so that we see at the far end the face of a girl looking straight at the camera: recognizing the spectator as an uninvited but welcome *voyeur* of this pre-Christian last supper. This mutual recognition gave me a mental thrill that I have seldom received from that space-time machine, the film.

What does literary creation mean to you?

Words, words, words.

Don't you think the writer's mission is to describe the world he has happened to live in?

I don't believe writers are missionaries, nor that a writer has any duty as such. The writer's sole duty, if he has one, is to write as well as he can. Of course I'm not talking of fine writing or of the polished prose of a master, I'm speaking of carrying one's possibilities as a writer as far as they will go, at all costs—the possibilities of literary creation as such, the possibilities of writing and the possibilities of language.

Are you only writing novels at present?

I never think in concrete terms of novels, stories, memoirs, essays, articles, or anything of the sort. I never think in terms of literary forms, I think in terms of literature. Like Wilde, I find a veil of words between me and reality. I always think in terms of the blank page and the words I shall write on it, one after another, and the interconnection of those words, their interplay, their replay, their play.

Play as in interaction?

Play as in play. For me, literature is a game, a complicated game, abstract and concrete at the same time, taking place on a physical plane—the page—and on the various mental planes of memory, imagination, and thought. A game not very different from chess but without the connotation of science-game which many people insist on conferring on chess, as a form of amusement and self-absorption at the same time. I always write for my own amusement and if afterwards there are readers who can read what I write and be amused with me, beside me, I rejoice that we can share this diversion a posteriori.

Then you don't suffer when you write, like many writers?

Like everyone else, I'm troubled by the loneliness of the writer, be it a long-distance or a short-story writer. It's much more amusing to engage in collective activities, like making films or politics, for example. Writing is a solitary activity, not only because one has to be alone to work—particularly for me, who worked as a journalist on a newspaper, where there is a continual hubbub of people coming and going—but also because of the double solitude of the blank page. On the other hand it's a constant torment to know that it doesn't matter how well you write, it doesn't matter how well you have linked one word with another, it doesn't matter how well certain expressions fit into the general design of the page: none of this matters when you know that it could all be done better—that is everlasting torture. First there is the immediate torture of the Melvillean whiteness of the page, its terrible blankness of possibilities, and afterwards the mediate torture of the page covered with signs which may mean everything or nothing, but are always subject to innumerable, infinite variations.

Is the page you write on so important to you?

I conceive of literature in relation to the page, even though I often can't see the plan of a page, its appointed plan, until it has been typed. And even after it has been typed I'm not fully aware of the play between its components until the page is in print, when it already seems too late. Naturally, sometimes I can't see the writing for the words, but I always conceive of reading in relation to printing in any of its forms: typewriter, newspaper, or book.

Do you correct much?

Eternally. In my case, the task of correction doesn't end even when the book is printed. I don't understand those writers who talk of a book being finished, meaning written, copied, or printed, and then decide to forget about it. It's yet another fiction originated in the nineteenth century, a century in which all forms of public utterance were disastrous because they were tinged with so much mystification presented as science. For me, a book is always susceptible to correction and improvement, because perfection is not a state but a goal. As I don't believe in improvisation I believe in improvement. The translation of *TTT*, a

book that was published in Spanish many years ago, has been
more of a refurbishing than a removal.

It must have been very difficult to translate TTT.

One can never translate the voices and my book started
from the concept of oral literature, of writing derived from speech
and the voice. In this case the narrative took shape in Cuban
speech and voice. Narrative in the traditional sense was not vital
to this book, wasn't even important. It seemed as if a great many
stories were being told, whereas in reality there were only two or
three basic stories, repeated and altered by the voices, and since
the only things that can be translated are texts, never voices, the
work of translation was very laborious. But I kept reflecting
that in spite of the closeness of French to Spanish—their gram-
matical complexities and many roots being identical—a translation
into French would be the hardest, not to do, but to succeed in—
and so in fact it turned out.

Shouldn't it have been just the opposite?

Yes, if I had been interested in linguistic structures or
even in certain textural elements in *TTT*. But I was more interested in the tempo, the beat and rhythms of writing and speech
than in finding equivalent versions in words. Besides, French is a
very restricted language, pigeonholed as it is by its Academy,
depending always on correctness, on what should or should not be
said. The commonest phrase I heard from the lips of my translator when we were working together for a month in my house
here, was "Ça, ce n'est pas français!" I had a hard job convincing
him at the outset that my text was not Spanish either and that
the licenses I allowed myself were not allowed by the Royal
Academy of the Language nor by the most liberal of Spanish dictionaries, and often did not even belong to everyday Cuban
speech. My acts of terrorism against the established Spanish
language would not be allowed anywhere because my book
proceeded by destructions meant as constructions, and re-created
daily language by means of violent changes and revolutions
within the sentence, in the phrase and even in the heart of language, which is the word.

But didn't you come across the same difficulties with English?

With the English version—one can't call it a translation
—a creative accident occurred. The first translator of the book was
an English poet who knew very little Spanish and no Cuban, who
had brought off some miraculous translations of Latin American
poets, and although he did the best he could, he could do very
little with *TTT*. Even though I adopted many of his rhythms,
which were sometimes excellent, I took advantage of his disadvantage plus the fact that my collaborator had housebroken the
book, at the same time producing a collection of good rhythms,
English turns of phrase, appalling malapropisms, flagrant mis-
understandings, and errors which, once accepted, became
trouvailles and were transformed by me from defects to effects,
thus ignoring the story and the general plan, and rewriting the
book as an English work. Later on, an American girl called
Suzanne Jill Levine, a pupil of the Toledan translator Gregory
Rabassa, collaborated in this version, and brought to it that sense
of humor characteristic of New York Jews, which is based on play
upon words and confronts reality with strict verbal logic. Nothing
was closer to my purpose in *TTT* than the philosophy of life expressed by the Marx Brothers, and in Jill Levine my three Marx-
istigers had met their Margaret Dumont! While by day Jill Levine-
Dumont was busy destroying with alice aforethought the remains
of the stiff-upper-and-underlips, the sometimes metaphrastic construction of the English version of *TTT*, by night I went on building my constructions on the destruction of a phrase, of a word, of
a phoneme—and even went so far as to treat proper names as
subjects for linguistic experiments, as I did in Spanish. At this
moment the book has been typed and I'm still working on the
fair copy, which is not the first nor will it be the last, since I often
get up in the middle of the night to add a parody here, a pun
there and one more inversion over there—which is exactly the
way the book was written originally.

Why didn't you write it in English straightaway?

The written page has a curious fixity, like photographs:
it can be shortened, cropped up, retouched, enlarged, framed
and/or printed, but its essence will remain unchangeable. Once a

work has been fixed in one language it is practically impossible
for its author to write it anew in another. He can translate it,
para- or metaphrase it, but never write it *again* in another language. A translation will always be a transplant, and rewriting—
as the word indicates—is something added to the original text.
Translations can take one of two courses according to the limitations imposed by the impenetrability of language: they can only
be literal or explanatory. That's the reason why translations are
always longer or more awkward than the original, however diffuse or botched it may be. The translator is a hesitant writer. But
true writers rush in where translators fear to tread. The translator
is in blind despair where the writer wasn't worried by darkness
but amusing himself among the shadows. The translator is always
coming across passages he *must* explain or expand. Or else he
achieves the uppermost obscurity of literalism. As an author, I
acted as jury, prosecution, and defense of my text, and the
translation was the true culprit. Thus I sentenced parts of the
book to disappear or reappear at my summons, or condemned
them to oblivion according to a judgment that always seemed
to the translator obscure, strange, inexplicable—or in the worst
cases arbitrary when I was merely being just. This form of poetic
justice can never betray the original book. And in any case, even
if it did it would prove that the subject of the book, treason, was
its hypothesis and that (dialectically speaking) its antithesis
would end by becoming its thesis: it takes a translator to catch a
traitor.

*In an interview with the critic Monegal, published in Paris in
1968, you said you didn't want to call your book a novel. Why
not?*

The generic subtitle of novel was attached to it by
my first publisher, not by me. I have always called the book by its
tongue-twisting name—or by its initials out of kindness to
strangers. *TTT* isn't a novel in the traditional sense—why does it
then have to have a label attached to it? Would anyone think of
calling the *Alice* books novels? But in view of the fact that some
publishers, some publicists, and many critics insist on calling

Tristram Shandy, Ulysses and *Finnegans Wake* novels, perhaps I can let them call *Tres tristes tigres* one.

What does the title Tres tristes tigres *mean?*

That's not the title, that's the name of the book. What's in a name? Merely the three first words of a tongue-twister I believed Cuban but actually belongs to Spanish American folklore. I used it because I wanted the book to have the fewest possible literary—which are always the most *extra*-literary—connotations. Starting with the cover, I wanted the book to suggest practically nothing about its content, and this was the nearest thing to an abstract title, since the number *"tres,"* the adjective *"triste,"* and the common noun *"tigres"* are united by nothing but the difficulty of pronouncing them, and because it is a made-up phrase. Namely, a phrase that has not been made but has lost its meaning by senseless repetition like jingles or swear words: language used either as publicity or in a moral sense, usage I have always found fascinating. I was also pleased by the doubtless poetic justice of a once formal tongue-twister ending as a mere meaningless game, and also by the inevitable metaphysical connotations—after Blake—of this wild beast among wild beasts (an animal which, like that epitome of wildness the exotic liana, inhabits other tropics, other jungles) and that diffuse feeling of uneasiness called sadness (the most "literary" of metaphysical ills and the most "human" of animal feelings) expressed by a Latin word. Besides, I have all my life felt perturbed by the frightful asymmetry of the three, glowing obscurely in the jungle of the mind.

Someone said that your book was a book for men rather than women. What do you think about that?

It's possible. Everything is possible on the other side of the looking glass of the page, where readers live. No one has expressed that view from Poppaea's head to me before, but—a curiouser thing—when translating the book into English I found that there was an intimate relation between the male characters, that comradely love that doesn't exist between women. Moreover, in *Three Trapped Tigers* one of the protagonists becomes a terrifying or terrified mysogynist, more offensive in English than in Spanish and infinitely more significant, perhaps because this expression of *machismo* is much more common in the Spanish-written literature and among Spanish-speaking races than in the Anglo-Saxon culture. This is why I think it may be true that the ideal reader of my book should be a man and not a woman, without pressing the subject of the ideal reader. In any case my wife hasn't read the whole of this book, although it's dedicated to her and she's also very much present in it. That at times avid reader Miriam Gómez prefers *One Hundred Years of Solitude*, which she has read several times.

Are the characters in TTT real?

There are not, there cannot be, real people in a book of fiction. I'm inclined to think that even in biographies there's a distance between the person written about, the writing of a life and the subsequent reading of it, which charges the most authentic documents with irreality. There are no people in *TTT*, only characters. Though in the manner of Edgar Allan Poe— who inaugurated this form of fiction in Western literature, just as he created the detective story and science fiction—several real people are mentioned by name in the book. Poe put himself into some of his stories under his own name but in fictitious circumstances. Likewise I have included some old friends from Havana, with their own Christian names, surnames, and addresses, but in the book their last names figure as false names and their addresses as landmarks in the urban labyrinth of Havana. All these names do not conceal character but a voice, a different texture among the different voices that make up the book, and, at times, as protagonists in a play which may or may not be their own game. As I've said many times, the book is a gallery of voices.

Is that why you advise one to read many of the pages aloud?

It seems to me that certain difficulties are solved and certain obscure passages become clear and totally comprehensible when they are read aloud, and of course it would be best if I read them myself. When my secretary and I were checking the English typescript she had made, and I had to read some sections of the book aloud while she rested her voice, she was surprised to find that many passages that she had had difficulty over became clear at once, and only then did she understand them. But of course every book, and mine in particular, requires more attentive reading than it gets from ordinary reading aloud.

Sense of humor predominates in your book, and that's rather uncommon in Latin American literature.

Many people have been astonished when I said that I would like the book to be taken as a huge written joke. Some try to find strange symbols in the characters and take some of the situations as symbolic or prophetic. This postscriptum symbology is at the reader's expense. I would prefer everyone to consider the book solely as a joke lasting for about five hundred pages. Latin American literature errs on the side of excessive seriousness, sometimes solemnity. It is like a mask of solemn words, which writers and readers put up by mutual consent. *TTT* is intended to deflate many of these pretensions—I only hope it succeeds and *TTT* becomes TNT to them.

What is your chief concern when you're writing?

I don't have any concern, either large or small, when I'm writing. I write with a great feeling of enjoyment, with the object of playing first and then observing the casual or causal play that establishes itself between the words, while selecting the possibilities of play which they provide me with among themselves, and the play of relations we all establish while waiting for the reader to stop being a shy spectator and join in the game. This playful activity is more apparent in *TTT* than in any of my other books. What is less obvious is my plan of frequently allowing chance to change and establish the rules of the game. This intrusion of the aleatory into the sphere of play leads to my preserving unexpected mistakes caused by my clumsy typing or errors I may make in my first draft. In *TTT* I have retained printers' errors because I believe they contributed to the web of the book —web, not in the sense of plot but of texture. I have also allowed the censor's scissors to collaborate in *TTT*.

The censor? What censor?

The Spanish censor, of course, not that of my own country. In Franco's Spain *TTT* was, like every book, submitted to censorship, but after all published, sold, and criticized. However, in Fidel's Cuba my book is not merely banned, it is considered anathema.

Why? It's obvious that TTT isn't a political book.

There isn't a more apolitical book in the whole history of Latin American literature. Neither is there a more independent one. Perhaps that's the reason and the unreason of this prohibition: all freedom is subversive. Totalitarian regimes are more afraid of individual liberty than vampires are of the cross.

How did the book come to be censored in Spain?

The first version of my book, which was then called *Vista del amanecer en el trópico* (View of the Dawn in the Tropics) was banned. The second version, *TTT*, which represented a return to my first plan for the book, was passed by the censor on condition I accepted the recommended cuts, which were twenty-two in number.

There are twenty-two cuts in your book?

Yes, but they are small cuts and some of them really amusing. For instance every time the word *teta* (tit) appears it is either cut or replaced by *seno* (breasts). If I talk of a *"military academy"* it is turned into a Platonic academy. My Catalan publisher advised me to accept the cuts so as to make it easier for the book to be published in Spain and sold in Latin America. But there's one part of the book where the censor didn't add to its obscurity, but contributed by elimination a final master touch. As you know, the epilogue is a monologue spoken by a mad woman sitting on a seat in the park beside the Malecón in Havana. This crazy speech is literally taken from real life, since it is virtually a shorthand record of the senselessly repetitive speech of a mad woman actually sitting in that park on a sunny day many years ago. Almost at the end of her echolalic monologue she mentioned God, among a lot of things I don't remember, because she was obsessed by religion and the Catholics and her monomaniac monologue included strange references to both. The censor thought this tirade sounded heretical and cut two or three of its final sentences. The book now ends where his censorial scissors decided we had had enough, and the last phrase aptly says: "Can't take it any longer." The French translator, who reinstated all the censored passages, wanted to include these final phrases. But I advised against it, because it seemed better for the book to stop abruptly in that curiously effective way as a result of the creative censor's intervention—and it's true. Curiouser and curiouser, it was here also, in this ending, where the English translator contributed most to the book. That last phrase, *Ya no se puede más*, was mistranslated by him as "Can't go no further" and instead of redressing it into "Can't take it any longer," I kept it as it was—and that's how *Three Trapped Tigers* fittingly ends. *Per errata ad ars!*

Do you believe literature can create a language?

Language is a convention, a use and a usage, a necessity. It's impossible to conceive that by means of literature—which is in itself an extraordinary use of the convention of language—*another* language can be created. Ever since the written word has existed—another convention, following thousands of years after the first conventional use of language—writers have tried in vain to escape from that mesh of conventions. Literature is not music or mathematics, which are alternate—or rather alternating—languages, different from the daily communication of speech and writing. Therefore it is impossible to create an autonomous literary language, without committing the aesthetic errors of writing belles lettres, or of excessive preoccupation with style, the writer being drawn *à la rigueur* into that post-Flaubertian flood of fine writing, full of rounded and beautiful phrases: the well-written novel and the worries of *le mot juste* which appears to me the most idiotic of pursuits.

Why?

Because the beauty of a phrase, of writing, what is called style—a confusion of the part with the whole: style and pen are derived from the same etymological root—has less to do with literature than with oratory, as understood by the ancients and until the modern age. On the other hand, the creation of a unique and therefore hermetic language, full of multiple and secret associations exclusive to the writer and elaborated in a work of literature, as is the case in *Finnegans Wake*, exhibits language as it is *not*, for this literary neo-language is badly in need of explanations, scholia or skeleton keys to explain not the whole book, which would be an aesthetic or rhetorical achievement, but to clarify a single sentence. This has nothing to do with language communication but with its absolute opposite—cryptology, the disguise of language through cipher. In other words: the contrary of communication: that failure of language which represents any writing that is deliberately hieroglyphic.

Your book is written entirely in the first person—does this mean that it is autobiographical?

          Not in the least. I've often felt sorry that the book was written in the first person. Too many of my readers will be bound to identify this or that character with the author, but with many characters other than the customary first-person narrator the reader would have to look further afield (among more living people to be considered as personae) than in the case of the writer who systematically uses the first person singular—for example, Somerset Maugham in his narrative "I" in *The Moon and Sixpence*. Like other writers before me, I have fought against the association of a grammatical *devoice* with the person of the writer, ever since parts of the book began appearing in magazines. But it was impossible to write my book in any other way. I've insisted that *TTT* is a gallery of voices and there is no other way of exactingly expressing these individual voices than by the first person singular. When I write a really autobiographical book I shall take care to fictionalize myself, as I have already fictionalized my critical alter ego, and write it in the third person singular —or perhaps plural.

Why do you suppose that your book, which is written in Cuban as you say, has had such a success in Spain and Latin America?

That has always astonished me. I always thought the book would be incomprehensible except to a very small number of persons living specifically in Havana at a given period and in my own surroundings. In other words, to my most intimate friends and enemies. But with the passage of time I've tended to explain it by reflecting that the humor and eroticism with which the book is filled have made it considerably easier to read, not by gilding the variegated alien corn, but by sugaring it. There is, also, a certain specific behavior at night in a city—the so-called night life—which is common to most men of a certain age living in certain towns in the twentieth century, since living by night has that wicked appeal always connected with sex—and sin. I said in the twentieth century and I was wrong. I would have been wrong even if I had said the nineteenth, eighteenth, or fifteenth centuries. This communion with deadly night sin could well have happened in pre-Christian eras. If I identify myself so much with the literature of the decline of Rome—I'm thinking specifically of the works of Petronius and Sextus Propertius—it is because they were the first writers to celebrate night, not night as part of nature but the opposite: night as history. A time for erotic adventures, of *correrías* as we say in Spanish, or "nights on the tiles," and of possible relations between certain women who inhabit that dark night world and certain young men with sufficient leisure to frequent it. That sort of night is common, I believe, to all mortals, after Caesar, who have had the good fortune to live in a big city when they were young, and have felt the curiosity to travel to the center of antinatural life and get to know the inhabitants of that nether world, which to the working man who goes to bed early or to the peasant, or anyone living in the country, is as remote and hidden as the other side of the moon.

Your book has been extraordinarily well received by critics wherever it has been published, but where has that criticism been most intelligent and fair, in your opinion?

In the two capitals of France—Paris and Buenos Aires.

Seriously.

Seriously I'm talking seriously. The most intelligent critics of my book have published criticisms in your capital and in

Paris, where for instance, in one of the justest and most felicitous
phrases, in my view, the critic of *Le Monde* said that *TTT*
marked a meeting between the detective story and semiology.
The only thing I disapprove of in the rest of this intelligent appreciation is its comparison of my work to French literary fashions
that have never interested me.

What do you think of structuralism as a method?

I don't know anything about it. When I first read the
term, about three years ago, I thought it was some new method
of building, something like reinforced concrete.

But of course you know the people of Tel Quel *Review?*

Yes, I know Sollers and Ricardou personally. I met them
in 1963 at a festival of experimental cinema held at Knokke-le-
Zoute, to which I had to go for diplomatic reasons: I was Cuban
cultural attaché in Belgium at the time. I was driving along the
road, in my little Fiat 600, looking for the arcane address of my
hedonic hostess, when I came across two white figures lost in
the dark Flemish night. I stopped the car and invited them to get
in and drove them to their destination—which turned out to be
the same as my own. They were Sollers and Ricardou, casual
guests at the same party for intellectuals—which ended, like all
Flemish feasts, in a kermesse. Later, in the wee hours, Sollers and
I drove off in my car, much as Rine and Silvestre do at the end of
TTT, taking two Belgian girls to a secluded club in Zeebrugge,
both of us swathed in the doubly mental mists of alcohol and
memory and of course in the everlasting real fog of Flanders.
Phillip kept behaving like Peter Sollers: a noisy accompanist repeating again and again in the Spanish he had learned in Madrid, "But I don't know what the hell this girl wants!" while re-
sisting her sexual assaults. All this magnified by the smallness of
my car and the *telquellian* insistence of the Belgian girl—whose
name, curiously enough, was Ondine Flamand! Earlier in the
evening, I remember the late Lucien Goldmann, the sociologist
of the novel, and Ricardou, the semiologist of the novel, having
an ardent argument at table, presumably about aesthetics. I can't
help thinking that both were trying in vain to capture the at-

tention of our hostess. I say in vain because, intrigued by my silent but exotic Caribbean charisma, she was less interested in disentangling the entwined arguments of the young French-man and the old Hungarian, than in sinmortally coiling her shapely legs around one of mine—evidently in search of anthro-pological knowledge.

What have you to say about modern anthropology?

The same as I would tell you about that of the past. Anthropologists of the past declared that man was descended from the ape. So I suppose that, just for a change, modern anthropologists have discovered that man descended from an ape. If they are revolutionaries they will say that apes are de-scended from man, if they are evolutionists, that man is going ape.

Can you say something about the works of Lévi-Strauss?

They seem to me excellent. Very durable. I've had two for several years, although I wear them almost every day.

Two? Two what?

Pairs of trousers, of *Levi's,* made by Levi-Strauss and Co. of San Francisco, Cal.

Do you think literary forms are tending to combine poetry and the novel?

The novel obviously springs from epic poetry—that is to say, not from one form but from a poetical ambit which sur-rounded the ancient world with an oral and mythical aura, begin-ning with the first known examples of the epic and inspired by those absolute masterpieces the *Iliad* and the *Odyssey,* continuing with the medieval epics, which degenerated into the romances of chivalry and led to the great caricature of them all, *Don Quixote* —indubitably the first truly modern novel because it is the first novel self-consciously written as such. It is a parody and satire of an ambit degenerated into a genre, a psychological study of charac-ter, a great meeting point between epic and lyric, a play upon the themes of reality and literature, and a self-commentary that is also an essay on the novel. Like *Hamlet, Don Quixote* is so many things at the same time to so many that it would be useless to make a list of them. To find its true counterpart we have to wait until well into the twentieth century for a novel which is everything that *Don Quixote* was, and once again represents a meeting between the form and its fountainhead. I am referring, of course, to *Ulysses*. It was not by chance that Joyce found a title and a model for his book in that first epic novel in verse, the *Odyssey*. Cervantes takes epics as his models for the novel form. Joyce repeats the motion in order to destroy that false generic distinction and allow the novel to create for us a poetic, mythical ambit. Ever since Joyce, poetry and the novel have approached each other so closely that there are books like Nabokov's *Pale Fire* in which it is impossible to separate them. Although while fusing poetry and the novel inseparably together Nabokov respectfully preserves their limits, like the weird water discovered by Gordon Pym. But when *Pnym's* dividing knife fails to cut in, the novel, our novel, is poetry and prose at one and the same time. This is what makes the modern novel untranslatable: it's all voice and no text.

Can one talk of a Mexican, Argentine, or Cuban novel?

No, but you can talk of novels written by Cubans, Argentines, Mexicans, Colombians, etc., all of whom make use of the same written language—although of course they don't speak it in the same way.

Then the Latin American novel does exist?

The Hispano-American novel exists.

What is the difference?

Latin America *must* of necessity include Brazil and Haiti today, and perhaps in the future French Canada—nations so different that they even talk different languages. Hispano-America is joined together by the same tenuous umbilical cord that binds us to that infinitely far-off country Spain. That tether is Spanish. The Spanish language is the sole thing we have in common, not as to our origins but because it is the verbal structure on which our thought is precariously erected. There is no one more different from an Argentine than a Mexican. . . .

And we are a long way off too.

Certainly, but what has a Uruguayan in common with a Bolivian, except language? Those plateau-dwellers who only speak Quechua seem like men from different planets when seen from Montevideo.

But you Caribbeans are all very much alike.

If the Colombians from the coast, the Venezuelans, Dominicans, Puerto Ricans, and Cubans look like one another it is because for the last four centuries Cuban culture has dominated the Caribbean when its shores were outside the Indian orbit, because Havana was a great city when Barranquilla, Caracas, and San Juan were mere hamlets, and because culture has always been made, in the west of the Graeco-Latin tradition, in cities. The only urban exception was Santo Domingo, whose metropolitan possibilities were annihilated by the historical cataclysms which have periodically scourged that tiny, divided, unhappy island. The Spanish language alone has proved itself imperishable throughout the colonial changes Latin Amerca has suffered. It is not surprising that our novel, more than any other of its previous avatars, is ruled by language.

But what do you think is the cause of the present boom in the novel? Our common language has united us for nearly five centuries and it is only now that there are readable novels in Latin America.

Not true. There is no more "readable" novel in Latin America than those written by Machado de Assis in Brazil, almost a century ago.

I'm sorry; in Spanish America then.

That's another matter. The novel is evidently a bourgeois form. I detest that adjective because its connotations reach beyond literature and coincide with those of sociology—a detest-

able, or at least negligible science—and it also occurs in the Marxist
analysis of literature, and both the sociological and Marxist ap-
proaches to literature seem to me the worst possible ways. But
the novel is obviously the literary form in which the middle class
recognizes itself and, when it is not produced by middle class inhabitants of the cities, is consumed by them. Stendhal said that
the novel was a mirror moving along a road, and he would have
done better still to say that it was a mirror moving through the
streets and revealing, whether well or badly, delineated or deformed, the bourgeois population: in other words citizens, city
dwellers. The fact that the novel exists in Spanish America at the
present time is due to the rise to power—to wealth, which is a
form of power—of the Latin American middle classes in big cities
such as Mexico City, Buenos Aires, Caracas, Lima, Bogotá,
Montevideo, and San Juan. These are the great buyers of novels
—although buyers and readers do not always coincide. Many
buyers only read the titles or perhaps the author's name of the
books they buy, as has undoubtedly happened to Cortázar's last
novel and the first by Lezama Lima. Such works have the glamour of what is unknown but possessed: an esoteric object on top
of a table. But it is only right that these bourgeois want to look
at themselves in their own mirror, not an alien one, and are as
tired of seeing other cities depicted in novels as of looking at the
photos of amiable unknowns. The latter function is more than
adequately carried out by magazines, newsreels, and television.
This explains why, for the first time, there has appeared in Latin
America that epitome of literary success inaugurated by Cervantes,
which American gigantism has converted into our own version of
instant posterity: *el* best-seller. The combination of the Spanish
article and the English compound noun shows how recently it has
appeared: today, with Mario Vargas Llosa, García Márquez and
Manuel Puig, we have Latin American writers whose works easily
sell more than a hundred thousand copies. For the first time in
the history of Latin American literature there are writers who
can live on their writings—and live well.

*How do you explain the success of Cuban writers like yourself and
Lezama Lima in other parts of Latin America, in terms of your
theory about the "bourgeois mirror"?*

I think I've made it clear that this mirror is a linguistic one. At the same time the first and only Cuban edition of Lezama's book was sold out in a few days. I'm sure that the same would have happened to *TTT* and *De donde son los cantantes* (Where Do Singers Come From?), the novel by Sarduy, if these books had been allowed in Cuba.

And the success of other Latin American writers, such as Borges, who don't write novels—how do you explain that?

The success of the Latin American novel has attracted the attention of a large public in and outside America to the existence of Latin American literature. What is new is the massive nature of this success, the fact that people recognize and get to know this literature, not that it exists. The Argentinian is not the first American Spanish-speaking author to receive worldwide recognition in his lifetime. Somewhat before Borges, the Mexican, Juan Ruiz de Alarcón, was drawing level with Lope, Calderón, Tirso, Cervantes, and Quevedo in the seventeenth century, gaining not only fame and a place among those giants of the Spanish Golden Age, but also that wry homage *inter pares*—literary jealousy. Rubén Darío, two and a half centuries later, is another eminent example who, as well as triumphing in Europe—and who wants to have a literary success in Australia?—changed the whole course of literature in the Spanish language, in this case poetry, which was never the same again. There are other cases that appear in every history of Spanish literature, though they are minor classics: the Inca Garcilaso, Sor Juana Inés, Martí, Lugones, Reyes. As things always go by threes, Borges, the third of our great classics, has succeeded in sufficiently irritating the oyster of the language for it to produce the baroque pearl of the "new novel."

You think he has contributed a great deal?

Like every classic, Borges has crystallized and reunited the separate elements of our reality—the essential American reality, not the regional—and made them evident dramatic models. The same thing has happened to the Latin American novel today as happened to the Russian novel in the last century. Pushkin and

Gogol were the poetic and prose propellants that drove Russian
literature out of its regional inertia and set it in universal motion.
Borges, who is the most important writer in Spanish since the
death of Quevedo, has by raising reading from a state of passivity
to an active one, and by uniting certain epic elements which he
himself calls "South American" with certain intimate experiences,
and placing them on a level where they receive the greatest possible attention because of their literary value, has given those of
us who follow him a model to imitate—and there is not a single
Hispano-American writing today who can set aside the influence
of Borges and his work—a model that is not imposed from abroad
by fashion, but has arisen amongst us and in our own manner.
Borges is our Gogol and our Pushkin rolled in one.

*Looking back, it looks to me as though your bête noire is literary
regionalism.*

                It has never interested me. Regionalism always tends
to produce a literature as narrow as its own frontiers. The only
possible pleasure it gives comes from that exotic flavor called
local color. Even the work of a writer as remarkable as Faulkner
is weighed down by this parochial ballast. This is why I've always
been more interested in Hemingway than in Faulkner. While
Faulkner is certainly a poet, Hemingway was much more of an
artist. Literature which doesn't aspire to the condition of art is in
my opinion condemned to failure beforehand. It was the return
to regionalism that wrecked the Spanish novel after it had been
practically the begetter of the genre in the modern age.

Which Spanish authors are your favorites?

                None. As I'm not a palmist I don't read authors but
books. Among my favorite books I would place *El libro de los
ejemplos*, *El libro del buen amor*, *La lozana andaluza*, *La
Celestina*, *Guzmán de Alfarache*, *El lazarillo*, *El buscón*, *Don
Quixote*, and very little else. Then, after a leap over three
centuries of noisy silence, Sender's *El rey y la reina*, Santos's
Tiempo de silencio, and Goytisolo's *Don Julián*, which is the
only truly baroque book written in Spain in the last three centuries. Of course among great Spanish novels of this century that

I have read, I ought to have put almost first *Niebla* by Unamuno, who is the only great writer produced by the so-called Generation of '98. Everything Unamuno touched—essay, poetry, fiction—he converted into a moving metaphysical adventure, if not a work of art.

And Ortega y Gasset?

Ortega has once more shown that literature is made with words, not ideas. It is not uncommon for a thinker to express himself so outrageously badly—and not in the sense of bad writing but of *el bello estilo* and the prose style of *littérateurs*.

Doesn't Baroja interest you at all?

No one who writes so badly can be altogether bad, but as a novelist Baroja is a major disaster. His best novels are sub-sub-Flaubert . . . half a century later. As for his personal philosophy, it proves that one can be an anarchist and a reactionary at the same time.

Why do none of the new Latin American writers seem to be in the least interested in contemporary Spanish literature?

Nor do the older writers. Look at Borges. The explanation is that for some time Spanish literature has merely been an impressive catalogue of mediocrities.

A result of the Civil War perhaps?

It began before the Civil War of 1936–39. About five centuries before, to be precise. Spanish decadence began with the expulsion of the Moors and the Jews, that unjust diaspora of Semites, it was consolidated by the Counter-Reformation and culminated in 1588, in the hecatomb of the Invincible Armada. The civil war, like the American Wars of Independence—external civil wars—or the year of disgrace 1898 in Cuba, were merely an anticlimax. Decadence was already present when Cervantes, Quevedo, Góngora, Lope, and Calderón gave the Edad de Oro the rich reputation it owes solely to these few writers of genius. The cruel fun that some of them made of the Mexican, Alarcón, proves that none of them could see that hunchback visitor from outer Spain as the shape of things to come: the baroque pearl. Darío, at the end of the last century, and García Márquez today have been latter-day avengers of that early *cena delle beffe* played on Alarcón: they have lived—one still lives—in Spain under constant assault from the climbing sycophancy that must endure all mountain peaks of talent in a vast plain of talentless-ness.

How do you see your own contribution to the novel in Spanish?

I wish it could be seen, not by me but by others, as the unstable foundation for some future leaning tower of disre-spect. Enough of sacred cows! In literature, life, politics, history, and language let nothing human be considered divine.

Do you think technology will put an end to books?

I don't believe in any form of immortality: only eternity is eternal. I don't understand why among all human creations a book has to be everlasting and live longer than its creator: man himself is bound to vanish. But it seems to me that certain mod-ern technologies considered as narrators do no more than illustrate books. Besides, a book is itself a technology: there are no *natural* books.

Do you express your humor better in writing than in speech?

Absolutely. I don't think I'm someone who is thought *simpático*, though I belong to that professionally *simpático* race, the Cubans. You have to be with me for some time to get to know my special brand of humor—long enough to find the key to it. In my books—viz., *TTT*—I begin by providing the reader with those keys. At home, only Miriam Gómez and my daughters can appreciate my sense of humor, simply because during our associa-tion I've provided them with a skeleton key—not only to its meaning but also to its sense.

What influence has the cinema had on your writing?

None on my writing, which is an excrescence: but on me, as its receptacle, enormous. I was born with a silver screen in my mouth. But it's not my sole passion.

There have been others then?

There are others: sex, dreams, fear. When I was a boy I had a passion for comic strips—the funnies—as well as films. I learned to read because my parents hadn't time to read me all the funnies I needed in order to grow up. So that when anyone talks about Burroughs nowadays I always think of Edgar Rice, not William. Just as Hogarth doesn't call to my mind the mediocre English painter but the stupendous illustrator of Tarzan every Sunday.

Aren't you interested in music?

Very much. Its influence is as evident in my books as the movies.

What sort of music do you prefer?

All sorts, including pop which specially interests me by the way it takes music back to its origins. That is to say, if music is thought of as organized sound, rock music has taken sound back to noise, to rocks—to the musical stone age. In canned rock, music meets with *la música Cubana*. I've always lived inside music: to me, music is melted architecture.

What is your favorite reading?

Fragments, any sort of fragments.

Have you wanted to be a writer ever since you were a boy?

I never indulged in that form of infantile paralipsis of being a writer when I was grown up. When I was a boy, the activities that interested me were sport and shooting—not to mention others which are miles away from me now. However, when I was a youth my daydreams were first to be a great baseball player and if I couldn't get into the American Big Leagues, at least that I would be a professional *pelota* player in Cuba. I was shaken out of these fantasies by a rude blow between the legs from, of all things, a ball, which threw me to the ground. When I woke up minutes later that dream was gone for good. Afterwards I longed to play the bongo or be a drummer. All of them pure adolescent fantasies as you see, especially as my sense of rhythm is as poor as my muscular coordination.

How did you become interested in literature?

It happened, like so many things, during my *bachille-rato*. I was a fairly good student, although I paid very little attention in class. I never worked hard, but I got fairly good marks and, moreover, never cut classes. But one day I listened —perhaps too attentively—to my teacher of ancient and classical literature. He was giving a talk on the *Odyssey* and was telling us about Ulysses' return to Ithaca incognito: how no one recognized him except his dog Argos, who afterwards died of happiness. I don't know whether it was the pathos the professor infused into his lesson or my love for dogs, but the fact is that I began to be interested in this particular lesson, then in his classes, then they became the only ones that interested me, and finally I left the schoolroom for the school library, where I spent the hours I should have been in class, reading.

Did you begin to write then?

I began to read everything I could lay hands on, in Spanish and English. But I still didn't think seriously of writing at that time. At that time I wanted—just fancy!—to be a painter. I had been good at drawing since a boy, for a child that is, but I became a really poor painter. My brother began to paint when he was barely fourteen years old and in an almost masterly way, and as a young man he had already become one of the most interesting new Cuban painters, just when I realized my own mediocrity. At this time I was collaborating on the student magazine of the *Instituto* where I was studying, and making linguistic jokes in my usual fashion, jokes out of everyday remarks, alliterations, inversions, Carrollisms *avant la lettre* and Joyceisms *avant* the pun, and a friend of mine—a sort of mathematical genius who went mad later on—either in a moment of late lucidity or of dementia praecox suggested my becoming a writer. At the time the idea seemed to me so preposterous that I rejected it, because it connected literature—or at least a possible kind of literature —with my sophomoric jokes. It was obviously an act of pure recognition: everything I write is sophomoric, according to some critics.

When did you publish your first writings?

Years later, when I was eighteen. Before this came a definite crisis in my studies and my choice of a career. My father wanted me to study medicine and I too was convinced that medicine was my vocation until the day when, purely as a pun, I visited the dissecting room in the medical school and was suddenly confronted by shelves full of corpses in readiness for the anatomy lesson. It was the first recognized crisis in my life and it practically put an end to my studies and to family harmony. During those days I wrote a story for fun and took it for fun to the magazine *Bohemia,* which was—for Cuba—a combination of *Life, Time,* and *Reader's Digest.* Also in fun (as it were) they published it at once and my fun was transformed ipso facto into a vice, then into a neurosis, then into a profession, until now it is a combination of neurotic game, vice, and profession. Two or three years later, when I was studying to be a journalist, writing became a dangerous game. At the beginning of Batista's dictatorship I published a story, in *Bohemia* to be exact, which contained *English* profanities. I went to prison and was suspended from studying journalism for two years.

Is this story in your first published book?

Yes, along with other evidence of my unliterary but vital apprenticeship.

What are you doing at present?

I'm working on another book of stories, which was also the author's first work: I'm translating *Dubliners* somewhat as a task imposed by my publisher and myself. I wanted to read this book closely and a translation always begins with an attentive reading.

Aren't you writing another book?

Yes, in my head, every night. On paper I'll do it when the translation is finished. This novel has been financed by a

Guggenheim grant, which will allow me to write it without worrying about how to pay that close collaborator of every writer, the milkman.

When you think of a new book, do you first give it a title?

First of all I think of the form of the book. It's impossible to dissociate literature from its form. Anyone who thinks of content as something foreign to and separate from form is no artist, as Nietzsche said.

Do you make a plan before you begin to write?

I always have a definite plan when I write. Before I set down the first word I have to know where the last will go. Then perhaps I fill the vacuums in the form—that imagined diagram or puzzling crossword—with sections of writing at the beginning or end of the book. I may also take chunks from the end and place them in the middle or at the beginning, but they will always be related to the design, which is greater than the sum of its parts. Writing is for me the creation of a concentric chaos. Sometimes I make this chaos with my pen and find its center armed with scissors and a bottle of glue.

You don't believe in inspiration?

I believe quite as much in inspiration as I do in the method of sitting down to write every day. Any method is good. Even anti-method is good, if used methodically. But I don't care for the method inherited from Balzac of sitting down to write every day, whether one wants to or not. I know that the writer who sits meekly down to his typewriter, according to clock and calendar, will have to wait, just as I do, for certain moments of enthusiasm to crystallize his verbal (or mental) associations on the page. Whether you call it inspiration, either at the time or later, it amounts to what I call desire to write, or creative enthusiasm. The same condition corresponds to all these names and it doesn't occur every day nor at the same time every day. The legend of the writer as super-professional or as a workman of literature has no appeal for me. But although I don't keep office hours nor hours for writing, I write all the time: in my mind, at the typewriter, in bed, sometimes awake and often when I'm asleep.

And from what I've been able to observe, you are very much a family man.

Thanks to exile rather than to my profession. Exile breaks up and reunites families to an extraordinary extent. There's really no middle course to take with the eternal insecurity caused by emigration. Now I have only two interests: literature and my family. Not necessarily in that order.

Do you mean your immediate family, your wife and daughters?

And Offenbach too.

Your Siamese cat with lilac points?

Exactly. Although the fact is that before Miriam insisted that we must have a cat living with us, I had an enormous prejudice against cats, animals I couldn't understand. Not only has Offenbach won me over and helped me understand him (and cats in general, and through cats wild beasts and the animal world), he has also made ours an Egyptian household: we worship a cat in here. *Cave Catta!* The more I know dogs, the better I love cats. Offenbach is called Offenbach because of his voice, which often offends Bach.

How have you and Miriam gained your reputation in South America as a swinging couple?

Where do South American reputations come from? I don't know. Perhaps it has something to do with some articles I wrote to earn my living when I came to live in London around 1967–68. In those I spoke of the death of Swinging London, like someone who has watched a myth die. Maybe those who refuse to admit its demise have decided to associate us—who are still among the living here—with it so as to keep it alive. After all, a person who was drowned in the *Titanic* can never describe the wreck of that human leviathan.

Are you religious?

No, but I'm extremely superstitious. As the theory of superstition embraces every aspect of daily and nightly life, superstition is a sort of religion for me.

Does that include the cross you have behind your door?

That's to keep off vampires. Actually it was put there by Miriam Gómez, who is an extremely religious person. My superstitions rarely coincide with the organized ones people call Christianity or Catholicism. I'm a primitive, therefore my religion must be called superstition.

What do you most detest and never wish to set eyes on again?

Cruelty, especially cruelty to animals. But above all torture and murder, which are the extreme manifestations of cruelty. A bully. A bully as a pure entity and a bully as a symbol: every swaggering tough guy is my personal enemy. The platonic bully, especially the political bully. Injustice, but even more, injustice carried out in the name of justice. Slavery, prison, fear, poverty, and of course death. The latter are my abstract *bêtes noires*. Among the concrete and abstract *bêtes noires* is history. Among the concrete ones are—politics, illnesses whether of body or soul, reptiles, a telephone call late at night or early in the morning, the ballet and social realism. Although many of these things fascinate me as much as I detest them. Among the things I never want to experience again are Godard and Bergman's films, an execution, a speech by Fidel Castro, and being inside a tropical storm.

What are your predilections?

Living, living in a democracy, islands, a tropical storm seen from afar, my house, literature, the movies and television—or better still an old film on television. Above all, certain moments peculiar to the movies: seeing rain in a film, tropical rain, but not when disaster is involved—more like in *Slattery's Hurricane* than in *The Rains Came*. Or the unexpected revelations of a film. For instance, Bogart's hands trembling with combined fear and rage in *The Maltese Falcon;* the mastery of Bubbles's solo in *Cabin in the Sky;* Henry Fonda coming out of the barber's and sitting on the porch in *My Darling Clementine;* Marlene Dietrich incarnating Catherine the Great, tongue in cheek but winking at Von Sternberg, in *The Scarlet Empress;* the stark sexuality of Angie Dickinson in *The Killers,* that latent danger in her golden thighs; the culmination of Cary Grant and Hitchcock's art in any scene from *North by Northwest;* James Cagney starting up to dance in *Yankee Doodle Dandy,* and the artful dodges of Buster Keaton. The prairies and deserts of westerns and the real desert of the American Southwest. The films of John Ford. Dreams and cinema dreams like *King Kong* or *Dark Passage.* The conversations between Sancho and Don Quixote, English poetry in Shakespeare and Yeats, the epigrammatical and apparently immoral but truly moral elegance of Wilde in some of his pages, Conrad's rancid prose, Hemingway's hurried prose, the prussic acid prose of Nabokov, the prudish prose of Borges, the combination of prose and pranks in Twain, Carroll's dream-language, Joyce's multi-paronomasia, the absurd sense of humor of Ring Lardner, and of Perelman, derived from Lardner, from Joyce, and from those Blooming Brothers—Harpo, Chico, and Groucho. The radiance of the city in some pages written by Fitzgerald, possibly the most civilized writer of the century. The charm of modern life as represented in some American films of the thirties or by Vincente Minnelli. The image as a form of rhetoric in Orson Welles and the rhetorical imagery of Raymond Chandler. The fine art of Dashiell Hammett as a murderer. The music of Bach, the music of Bach according to John Carlos, the music of Vivaldi according to Bach. Certain symphonic passages of Beethoven, Brahms, and Mahler; many more of Wagner; great chunks of Tchaikovsky; all Mozart's music, especially all his operas; *Verklärte Nacht,* and all the decadent German or French music that preceded and followed it and is possible to hear. Gaudi's architecture; many Art Nouveau facades (and the Art Deco typefaces and all the Art Nouveau and Art Deco objects I've seen). A few villages in the south of Spain, London, and of course my memories of Havana. Armstrong's eternal gaiety and the enormous summons to happiness of his music and the jazz of his period; the exact moment when Charlie Parker begins to play a solo. Coltrane's eternal melody; Negro irreverence—so evident in Cuba and the United States; the way Cubans talk and many Americans, like Gary Cooper, Jack Benny, or Bill Cosby. The triumph of vocation even beyond death, as in the case of Lampedusa and his *Leopard*, or of the Cuban singer Fredy. The company of my daughters and the company and lovemaking of/with Miriam Gómez. Offenbach's careless-yet-conscious grace in some of his natural poses. My memories of first masturbating, of the first time I made love, of first learning to read from the funnies, and the dynamic but static images of Chester Gould, Milton Caniff, Hogarth, Alex Raymond, Will Eisner, et al. But above all, the privilege of memory, without which none of the things mentioned above would have any meaning—or importance.

Finally, I would like to say that to end a conversation with the things I like best goes against the grain of my usual pessimism. I only allow it because I respect order and because the interviewee must always be the host of the interviewer. But also because, as Jack Buchanan said to Jeanette MacDonald before getting into the train that goes beyond the rainbow: "I like happy endings."

A Note About the Interviewer

Rita Guibert was born in Buenos Aires and studied at the University of Buenos Aires, from which she received a B.S. in chemistry. In New York, where she has lived for fifteen years, she has worked extensively in the magazine field. Her articles have appeared in the *Paris Review, Intellectual Digest, Review 72, Revista Iberoamericana,* published at the University of Pittsburgh, and the Spanish edition of *Life,* for which she was a reporter for five years.

A Note on the Type

The text of this book is set in Electra, a typeface designed by W. A. Dwiggins for the Mergenthaler Linotype Company and first made available in 1935. Electra cannot be classified as either "modern" or "old style." It is not based on any historical model, and hence does not echo any particular period or style of type design. It avoids the extreme contrast between "thick" and "thin" elements that marks most modern faces, and is without eccentricities which catch the eye and interfere with reading. In general, Electra is a simple, readable typeface which attempts to give a feeling of fluidity, power, and speed.

Composed, printed, and bound by
Kingsport Press,
Kingsport, Tennessee

Typography and binding design by Virginia Tan